The Food Service Manager's Guide to Creative Cost Cutting:

Over 2,001 Innovative and Simple Ways to Save Your Food Service Operation Thousands by Reducing Expenses

Published By:
ATLANTIC PUBLISHING GROUP, INC.

THE FOOD SERVICE MANAGER'S GUIDE TO CREATIVE COST CUTTING: OVER 2,001 INNOVATIVE AND SIMPLE WAYS TO SAVE YOUR FOOD SERVICE OPERATION THOUSANDS BY REDUCING EXPENSES

BY DOUGLAS ROBERT BROWN

Published by **ATLANTIC PUBLISHING GROUP, INC.**

ATLANTIC PUBLISHING GROUP, INC • 1210 S.W. 23rd Place • Ocala, FL 34474-7014

800-814-1132 • www.atlantic-pub.com • sales@atlantic-pub.com

SAN Number :268-1250

Member American Library Association

Printed in the United States of America.

ISBN 0-910627-61-4

ISBN 978-0910627-61-0

Brown, Douglas Robert, 1960-

  The food service manager's guide to creative cost cutting : over 2,001 innovative and simple ways to save your food service operation thousands by reducing expenses / Douglas Robert Brown.

     p. cm.

  Includes index.

  ISBN 0-910627-61-4 (alk. paper)

  1. Food service--Cost control. 2. Food service management. I. Title.

TX911.3.C65B78 2005

647.95'068'1--dc22

                    2005008954

        10 9 8 7 6 5 4 3 2 1

WARNING DISCLAIMER

This book is designed to provide information in regard to the subject matter covered. It is sold with the understanding that the publisher and author are not engaged in rendering legal, accounting or other professional services. If legal or other expert assistance is required, the services of a competent professional should be sought.

It is not the purpose of this manual to reprint all the information that is otherwise available to the author and/or publisher but to complement, amplify and supplement other texts.

Every effort has been made to make this manual as complete and as accurate as possible. However, there may be mistakes, both typographical and in content. Therefore, this text should be used only as a general guide and not as the ultimate source of information.

The purpose of this manual is to educate and entertain. The author and the publisher shall have neither liability nor responsibility to any person or entity with respect to any loss or damage caused or alleged to be caused directly or indirectly by the information contained in this book.

ART DIRECTION, COVER DESIGN & INTERIOR DESIGN: Meg Buchner • e-mail megadesn@mchsi.com

BOOK PRODUCTION DESIGN: Laura Siitari of Siitari by Design • www.siitaribydesign.com

Foreward

by Beth Dugan, MS • *Owner, Food Write*

Whether you own a small family café or a fine dining establishment, *The Food Service Manager's Guide to Creative Cost Cutting* is a book that will help you save money in running your restaurant. Chock full of ideas touching on every area, this book is designed to save you money and help you spend your cash wisely. With each chapter focusing on a specific area, you can immediately jump to your problem area or browse to get a feel for the main issues.

The best part of this book is that each chapter, while fully integrated, is a stand-alone unit on a specific topic. This means that if you have a specific area that you would like to address, then just go to that chapter and begin saving money. Some specific groupings are listed below.

If your establishment is still in the planning stages, this book will help by showing what to focus on before you open. *Chapter 1 – Analyzing the Numbers* goes through the fundamentals of creating a business plan, which will help you focus your efforts where they are needed most. Look at *Chapter 2 – Profit Planning and Cost Control* for some issues to decide on before opening. *Chapter 5 – Set the Tone—Your Restaurant Interior* will help you to create a great front-of-the-house area, while *Chapter 20 – Productive Buildings* shows you where to spend the money now, during construction, to reap the cash rewards later when you are open. *Chapter 6 – Find Your Niche—Set Yourself Apart* will address ways to create a unique establishment. *Chapter 14 – Building Your Team—The Foundation of Success* will show you some tips for determining and minimizing labor before you open.

If you are up and running, this book can be used as a reference guide for specific topics. If you know or think that your problems are related to food costs and pricing, then check out *Chapter 3 – Profitable Pricing* and *Chapter 22 – Essentials of Controlling Food Costs*. Look at *Chapter 23 – Reducing Food Costs* and *Chapter 26 – Purchasing, Receiving and Storage* for a quick overview on the subject.

If your issues revolve mainly around employees, then look at *Chapter 4 – Pleasing Customers* for why employees are so important. *Section III – Controlling Labor Costs* goes into detail how to attract, retain, promote and train great employees. If you suspect fraud or theft, look at *Chapter 12 – Security and Theft Prevention*.

Instead of cutting costs, why not increase revenue? If you are looking for good marketing ideas, read *Chapter 3 – Profitable Pricing*, *Chapter 4 – Pleasing Customers* and *Chapter 5 – Set the Tone—Your Restaurant Interior*. *Chapter 7 – Marketing for Profitability* and *Chapter 25 – The Menu, Standardized Recipes and Menu Pricing* are also filled with great ideas.

If you have a liquor license, whether a freestanding bar or part of a restaurant, check out *Section V – Controlling Liquor, Wine and Beverage Costs*. Even if your bar is not part of a separate restaurant, check out *Chapter 4 – Pleasing Your Customers*, *Chapter 6 – Find Your Niche—Set Yourself Apart* and *Chapter 7 – Marketing for Profitability* for more ideas to use.

For some truly unique cost-cutting ideas, usually not found in other books, look at *Chapter 8 – The Bottom Line*, *Chapter 10 – Trimming Operational Costs and Chapter 11 – Reducing Maintenance and Repair Costs*. Since a dollar saved is a dollar earned, this section is a treasure trove of unique nuggets to help you save money.

Serve good food well and watch your dollars in and out. We hope you enjoy this book, and check out more titles from Atlantic Publishing at **www.atlantic-pub .com**.

Table of Contents

SECTION I—MAXIMIZE PROFITS: STRATEGIES AND TIPS

Chapter 1   Analyzing the Numbers

Write a Great Business Plan—If You Haven't Already! 25

Financial Analysis...27

The Present Financial Status of the Food Service Industry.....................27

Chapter 2   Profit Planning and Cost Control

Cost-Control Records—Get It Right..30

Get Computerized 30

Chart of Accounts 31

Point-of-Sale Systems 32

    POS Enhancements...34

Crucial Elements of Cost Control—Profit Planning 35

Accurate Day-to-Day Cost Control 37

Standards Are Key to Any Cost-Control Program 37

Cost Ratios 38

    Food-Cost Percentage...38

    Calculating Inventory 40

Essential Sales and Turnover Calculations 40

Profitability Ratios 42
The Balance Sheet 43
    Why Is the Balance Sheet Important to You?........................43
The Statement of Cash Flows...45
Simple Tips to Help You Compile Your Financial Reports Faster 46

Chapter 3   Profitable Pricing

Pricing 47
Determining Prices...48
Other Factors That Will Help You Determine Prices 48
Internal Controls 49
    Control Systems...50
Purchasing and Ordering...51
Inventory, Storage and Accounts Payable.................................51
Labor Productivity..52
Pricing Beverages 53
Beverage Inventory Control 54
Tricks of the Trade..56

Chapter 4   Pleasing Customers

Service Guarantees 57
Meeting Expectations—First Impressions 58
Customer Response—Actively Seek Feedback 59
Better Service, More Tips—15 Top Tips!....................................60
Provide Taste Samples 62
Healthy Food Preparation and Cooking—Without Sacrificing Taste
    and Flavor! 62

Chapter 5   Set the Tone—Your Restaurant Interior

A Place to Impress 65
Create a More Inviting Ambiance 66
    Attention to Detail...67
    Drowning Out Operation Noises 67
    Keep Temperatures Comfortable..68
    Inviting Furniture..69
    Buying Carpet..70

Other Environmental Considerations 71

    Cleanliness, Tidiness and Comfort—A Few Basics You Can't Ignore 71

    Clean, Presentable Restrooms 72

Tricks of the Trade...74

Chapter 6   Find Your Niche—Set Yourself Apart!

Food and Entertainment 75

Expand Your Services 76

Handling Customer Complaints 77

Turn Negatives into Positives 78

Offer a Fast Lunch..79

Provide "Add-Ons" and Specialty Items 79

Provide Consistently Excellent Service 80

Tricks of the Trade...82

Chapter 7   Marketing for Profitability

The Real Value of Marketing—Spend Your Money Where It Counts! 83

Develop a Unique Selling Position 84

Build a Web Site 84

    Sample Restaurant Web Sites....................................85

    Other Online Marketing Opportunities 86

Traditional Marketing Techniques..87

Other Innovative Marketing Techniques 88

    Get to Know Your Customers 88

    Actions That Grab Attention......................................89

SECTION II—CONTROLLING OPERATING COSTS: STRATEGIES AND TIPS

Chapter 8   The Bottom Line

Basic Cost-Control Skills 95

Developing a Food Service Operational Budget—The Basics.................96

    Key Operating Budget Costs......................................97

    Sales Reports and Forecasting 98

    Cash Flow—The Essentials.......................................98

Renting and Leasing..99
Insurance Costs 100
Equations for Your Business 101
Getting Organized 102

Chapter 9   Look at Your Restaurant Objectively

Surveys..104
Market Research 105
Tricks of the Trade...106

Chapter 10 Trimming Operational Costs

Office Expenses 107
Trim Phone Expenses...109
Energy Expenses 111
Extra Energy-Saving Tips...113
Range-Top Operation—General Energy-Saving Tips 115
Range-Top Operation—The Specifics 116
Dishwashing—Reduce Operating Costs...118
Functioning at Optimum Efficiency...119
Get the Most from Your Icemakers 121
Waste Management 121
Other Great Opportunities to Reduce Costs 123
Tricks of the Trade...125

Chapter 11 Reducing Maintenance and Repair Costs

Linen, Utensils and Equipment..127
On-Premises Laundry 128
Employee Uniforms..129
Janitorial Services...129
Repair Expenses 130
Preventative Maintenance 131
Painting Expenses 133
Liability Expenses 134
Furnishing Maintenance 135

Chapter 12 Security and Theft Prevention

Explore the Underlying "Excuses" for Theft 137

Reducing Employee Theft 138

Giveaways 139

Guest Checks 139

Register Practices 140

Bank Deposits/Accounts Payable 141

Identify and Prevent Bookkeeper Theft 142

Manager Theft—The Danger Areas 143

Reducing Customer Fraud 144

Keeping Your Own House in Check 145

Security 146

Electronic Security 147

Chapter 13 Breakage, Spoilage and Storage

Breakage Prevention 149

Spoilage Prevention 151

Storage 152

    Hygiene 153

    Rodent and Bug Prevention 154

SECTION III CONTROLLING LABOR COSTS: STRATEGIES AND TIPS

Chapter 14 Building Your Team—The Foundation of Success

Service Is Paramount 159

Profits Are Everyone's Business 160

People Are Assets 161

High Turnover Rates 161

Reducing Your People Costs 162

Management Commitment 163

Hiring Team Members 164

Your Challenge 164

Restaurant Employee Classifications 164

The Right Person for the Job 165

Clarifying Your Needs 165
Tasks 165
Skills and Responsibilities 166
Skill and Experience Training Expectations 167
Your Budget 168
Writing Job Descriptions 168
Job Description Tips and Resources 168
Your Employee Package 169
Wages 169
Gratuities 170
Employee Benefits 170
Costly but Valuable Benefits 171
Where to Find Your Next Employees 172
Advertising for People 173
Tips for Writing Powerful Ads 174
More Places to Find Help 174
Trainees for Hire 175
Outsourcing, Temps and Leasing 176
A Diverse Workforce 176
Employee Search Resources 178
Selecting the Right Candidate 179
Getting Ready to Interview 180
The Interview Process 181
Ask Probing Questions 182
Listen Intently 183
Judging Attitudes and Appearances 183
Pre-Employment Reviews 184
Hiring the Best Person for the Job 184

Chapter 15 Saving Payroll Dollars

Saving Payroll Dollars 187
Offer the Right Benefit Package..188
Tax Deductions and Credits...189
Take Advantage of Benefit Discounts and Subsidies 190
Government Employment Programs 191
Disabled Worker Programs 192
Other Helpful Tax-Savers 193
Hidden Payroll Expense Savings 194

Other Payroll Resources 195
Tricks of the Trade 196

Chapter 16 Training Employees

Teaching Success 197
Invest in Training 198
    Reasons for Training 198
Train the Trainer 198
Your Training Needs 199
Specific Training Areas 199
Setting Goals and Expectations 200
Establishing Quality, Productivity and Performance Standards ... 201
    Productivity Standards 201
Training Plans 203
Starting Off Right 203
Meetings 205
Culinary and Hospitality Programs 205
In-House Training Programs 206
Adult Education 206
Tricks of the Trade 208

Chapter 17 Employee Supervision

Leadership 209
Lead by Example 210
Empowering People 210
Employee Motivation 211
Employee Attitudes 212
Challenge Your Employees 213
Leadership Tips 213
Employee Policies 214
Gone but Not Forgotten 215
Drug and Alcohol Problems 216
Employee Problems 216
    Disciplinary Action 217
    Terminate Wisely 218
Employee Turnover 219
    Why They Leave 219

The Cost of Turnover...220

Chapter 18 Scheduling Your Staff

The Eight Basic Scheduling Steps....................................221
Scheduling Truisms...222
Schedule Types and Patterns..223
Other Possible Scheduling Methods 224
The Negative Impacts of Understaffing............................225
The Negative Impact of Overstaffing.................................226
Scheduling Tips and Hints...227
Computerized Scheduling 227

Chapter 19 The Productive Workplace

Productivity 229
Productivity Is Also a Quality Goal....................................230
Productive People..230
Streamlined Tasks 232
Work Smarter, Not Harder..233
Adopt Technology..234
Other Ways to Save Labor Costs 235

Chapter 20 Productive Buildings

Building in Efficiency...237
    Site Selection 237
    Select Materials That Do the Work 238
Healthy Environments 239
Ergonomics..239
The Air We Breathe 240
Productive Environments 241
    Beautiful and Carefree...242
    Traffic and Workflow..242
    Front-of-the-House Support Stations 244
    Back-of-the-House—Your "Factory" 244
Employee Energy Boosters 245
Kitchen Design..245
Laborsaving Equipment 246
    Front-of-the-House Labor-Savers 247

Communication Systems...247

POS Systems...248

Front-of-the-House Tools..248

Back-of-the-House Equipment 249

Purchasing Inventory-Control and Kitchen Equipment.....................249

Prep Equipment 250

Cleaning Equipment...250

Waste and Recycling Equipment...251

Storage Fixtures...251

Cooking Equipment..251

More Cooking-Equipment Tips...252

Beverage Tips 253

Other Cooking Innovations 253

Laborsaving Equipment Resources..254

Manufacturer Lists, Articles, Reviews and Other Resources 254

SECTION IV—CONTROLLING FOOD COSTS: STRATEGIES AND TIPS

Chapter 21 The Basics

Getting Organized 259

Food Sales and Costs Survey 260

What Does Your Food-Cost Percentage Really Mean? 260

The Key to Controlling Food Cost Is Reconciliation...........................261

Practical Examples 261

Chapter 22 Essentials of Controlling Food Costs

Yield Costs...275

Menu Sales Mix 276

The Menu 276

Menu "Do Nots" 278

Chapter 23 Reducing Food Costs

Setting Menu Prices 279

Menu Costs...280

Calculating Food and Drink Costs...281

Standardized Recipes 281
How to Economize Without Reducing Quality 282
Portion Control 283
Manage Costs—Increase Sales 285
Other Cost-Saving Tips 286

Chapter 24 Food-Cost Problem Areas

Math and Cost Ratios 289
Beginning Inventory 289
Ending Inventory 290
Food-Cost Percentage 291
Cost Calculations—The Basics 291
Daily Food-Cost Analysis 293
Weighted Food-Cost Percentage 293
Raising Prices 294

Chapter 25 The Menu, Standardized Recipes and Menu Pricing

Menu Sales 297
Food-Cost Tracking 297
Recipe Information 300
Menu Pricing 301
How Indirect Factors Can Help Increase Profits 302
Calculating Entrée and Meal Food Cost 303
Math and Costing Software 305
Food-Cost Percentage Pricing 305
Factor Pricing 306
Actual-Cost Pricing 307
Gross-Profit Pricing 307
Prime-Cost Pricing 308
Menu Sales Analysis 309
Analysis Simplified 310
Analyze and Classify Your Menu Sales Mix 312

Chapter 26 Purchasing, Receiving and Storage

Food Purchasing 313
Dealing with Suppliers 315

Inventory Levels 316
Purchasing and Ordering...318
Purchasing Specifications 319
Purchasing and Inventory Software.......................................320
Inventory, Storage and Accounts Payable..............................322
Purchasing Kickbacks and Gifts 324
Purchasing Ideas 324
Receiving Goals..325
    Receiving Policy..325
    Receiving Tips 326
Getting What You Paid For 328
Purchasing and Storage Policies...328
FIFO and Labeling 329
Storage 330
    Dry Storage..330
    Refrigerated Storage 331
    Deep Chilling 332
    Frozen Storage 332
    Organize Your Storage Areas 332
    Storage Spoilage Prevention 333
Issuing...335

Chapter 27 Production and Service

Involve the Crew 337
Kitchen Space...338
Kitchen Design..339
Cooking Procedure Tips 341
Thermometers and Cooking Temperatures.............................343
    Calibrating a Thermometer...343
Preparation for Service...344
    Portioning 345
    Compute Yield Percentages 347
    Yield Tests...348
Presentation...349
    Plate Arrangement 349
Guest Tickets and the Cashier 350
    Cashier's Report Form..352
Tricks of the Trade...354

Chapter 28 Kitchen and Food Safety

Basic Knife Safety 357

Tips for a Burn-Free Kitchen 358

Other Avoidable Kitchen Hazards... 359

Food-Borne Illness.. 359

    What Makes Food Unsafe? 360

    Weighing the Risks... 360

    Common Food-Handling Problems 361

    What You and Your Staff Can Do to Prevent Food-Borne Illnesses 361

    Hand-Washing Exercise... 362

    Thawing and Marinating 363

    Cautions for Cold Foods.. 363

    Web Site References 364

Food Irradiation 365

HACCP.. 365

Chapter 29 Technology

Electronic Ordering Systems... 367

POS Systems 368

Hospitality Equipment 369

Technology Maintenance 370

Tricks of the Trade... 372

SECTION V—CONTROLLING LIQUOR, WINE AND BEVERAGE COSTS: STRATEGIES AND TIPS

Chapter 30 Budgeting and Forecasting

Grasp the Basics About Budgeting.. 377

    Choose the Right Budget Plan for Your Business 378

    Adapt Your Chosen Budget Plan to Suit Your Establishment............ 378

Budget Control—Introduce Cost-Effective Initiatives 379

Develop a Forecasting Strategy That Is Relevant and Realistic 380

Make Forecasting Work for Your Establishment 381

Budgeting and Beyond—Look to the Future............................. 381

    Computerized Budgeting and Forecasting 382

Cost-Volume-Profit (CVP) Analysis—The Key to Budgetary Success 383
Monitoring Your Budget Plan 384

Chapter 31 Cash Control, Costing and Margins

The Basic Mathematics of Profitability 385
Measuring Bottle Yield 386
Drink Pricing for Optimum Profits 387
Take a Fresh Look at How You Apply Your Pricing Strategy 387
Markups—Where to Pitch Them 388
Bar Cash-Control Procedures...389
Tighten Up Daily Cash Procedures..390
Take the Hassle out of Cash Reconciliation...391
Gross Profits—The Lowdown 392
Common Cash-Control Problems—Troubleshooting 392
Tricks of the Trade..394

Chapter 32 Beverage Purchasing Strategies That Work

Customize a Buying Strategy That Reduces Costs...................................395
Tighten Up Your Purchasing Procedures 396
Buy Quality 397
A Good Purchasing Security System Can Save You Big Bucks 398
Keep Purchasing Procedures Simple 399
Define Your Purchasing Duties 400
Streamline Your Receiving Procedures 400
Define Your Purchase Specifications—Define Your Standards 401
Reduce Purchasing Costs...402
Legal and Ethical Issues—Avoid Expensive Mistakes 403
Tricks of the Trade..405

Chapter 33 Beverage Inventory Control

General Inventory Procedures 407
Make the Most of Your Storage Areas...408
Track Inventory—Track Costs...409
Monthly and Annual Inventory Control 410
Inventory Levels Affect Cash Flow 410
Manage Your Stock Wisely and Maximize Profits....................................411

Reduce Inventory Pilferage 412
Reduce Costs—Streamline Issuing Procedures 413
Inventory Valuation Made Easy 414
Bar Inventory...415

Chapter 34 Portion Control Behind the Bar

Portion Standardization—Putting It into Practice 417
Precision Portioning Boosts Profits.......................................418
Control Portions and Meet Customer Expectations 419
Monitor Portions Effectively 420
Improve Portion Control in the Restaurant............................421
Reduce Waste, Reduce Portion Costs 422
Mixed Drinks—Get the Proportions Right 422
Serve Drinks in the Correct Glassware 423
Pouring Beers and Ales in the Correct Portions.....................424
Alcoholic Beverages and the Law—Strict Portion Control 424

Chapter 35 Beverage Theft

Insider Theft 427
Bartender Theft—Top Ten Common Ploys 428
Common Employee Theft Techniques....................................429
Introduce Theft-Reduction Procedures That Are Easy to Enforce............431
Minimize Inventory Theft 432

Chapter 36 Drink Selection

Develop a Successful Beer Program 433
Make the Right Choice of Wines..434
Nonalcoholic Beverages—An Area of Opportunity...................436
Cocktails—Reduce Costs While Increasing Customer Satisfaction 437
Trim Liquor Costs..438
Choose Drink Mixes Carefully—Make an Impact on Cost Reductions......439
Choosing the Right Suppliers for Your Beverage Requirements 440
Boost Profits by Choosing the Right Drink Recipes 441
Identify Loss Leaders and Turn Them into Profit....................442
Choose Well Liquors Wisely—Mistakes Can Bankrupt Your Business......443

Chapter 37 Bar Staff Recruitment, Management and Training

Good Staff Is a Business's Greatest Asset—Hire the Best 445

Tips for Reducing Labor Costs 446

How You Train New Employees Can Have a Major Impact on Your

Business.. 447

Front-of-the-House Management Tips 448

Ongoing Training Is One of the Most Effective Ways of Retaining Staff ... 449

Winning Personal Serving Techniques—Set High Standards.................... 450

Practical Tips for Training Bartenders.. 451

Employee Mismanagement Can Bankrupt Your Business 452

Bartender Recruitment and Selection Tips 452

Keep Staff Happy—Keep Labor Costs Down 453

Chapter 38 Other Opportunities to Control Costs in the Beverage Industry

The Working Environment—Cunning Cost-Reducing Tips 455

Extra Cost-Reducing Serving Tips.. 456

Extra Cost-Reducing Staffing Tips 457

Dispensing Draft Beer—Cost-Reducing Tips 457

Shop the Opposition 458

Banquet Beverages—Tips for Reducing Costs but Not Quality 459

Market Your New Bar—Profit-Boosting Tips 460

Tips for Streamlining Your Bar Par Procedures 461

Encourage Bartenders to Do More Than Serve 462

Surprise Your Customers with New Ideas on a Regular Basis 462

Streamline Bar Layout 464

Sales Are Slumping, Trade Is Dwindling—What Do You Do Next? 466

Top Ten Tips for Increasing Tips.. 467

Additional Bar Equipment That Will Help Reduce Costs........................ 469

Chapter 39 Essential Cost-Cutting and Time-Saving Forms

Forms Table of Contents... 471

Glossary of Terms

State Restaurant Associations

Trade Publications and Journals

Index

Remembering A Friend

We recently lost our beloved pet "Bear," who was not only our best and dearest friend but also the "Vice President of Sunshine" here at Atlantic Publishing. He did not receive a salary but worked tirelessly 24 hours a day to please his parents. Bear was a rescue dog that turned around and showered myself, my wife Sherri, his grandparents Jean, Bob and Nancy and every person and animal he met (maybe not rabbits) with friendship and love. He made a lot of people smile every day.

We wanted you to know that a portion of the profits of this book will be donated to The Humane Society of the United States.

–Douglas & Sherri Brown

THE HUMANE SOCIETY
OF THE UNITED STATES ©

The human-animal bond is as old as human history. We cherish our animal companions for their unconditional affection and acceptance. We feel a thrill when we glimpse wild creatures in their natural habitat or in our own backyard.

Unfortunately, the human-animal bond has at times been weakened. Humans have exploited some animal species to the point of extinction.

The Humane Society of the United States makes a difference in the lives of animals here at home and worldwide. The HSUS is dedicated to creating a world where our relationship with animals is guided by compassion. We seek a truly humane society in which animals are respected for their intrinsic value, and where the human-animal bond is strong.

Want to help animals? We have plenty of suggestions. Adopt a pet from a local shelter, join The Humane Society and be a part of our work to help companion animals and wildlife. You will be funding our educational, legislative, investigative and outreach projects in the U.S. and across the globe.

Or perhaps you'd like to make a memorial donation in honor of a pet, friend or relative? You can through our Kindred Spirits program. And if you'd like to contribute in a more structured way, our Planned Giving Office has suggestions about estate planning, annuities, and even gifts of stock that avoid capital gains taxes.

Maybe you have land that you would like to preserve as a lasting habitat for wildlife. Our Wildlife Land Trust can help you. Perhaps the land you want to share is a backyard—that's enough. Our Urban Wildlife Sanctuary Program will show you how to create a habitat for your wild neighbors.

So you see, it's easy to help animals. And The HSUS is here to help.

The Humane Society of the United States
2100 L Street NW
Washington, DC 20037
202-452-1100
www.hsus.org

SECTION I

Maximize Profits:
Strategies and Tips

SECTION I

Table of Contents

Chapter 1
Analyzing the Numbers.................................. 25

Chapter 2
Profit Planning and Cost Control 29

Chapter 3
Profitable Pricing 47

Chapter 4
Pleasing Customers 57

Chapter 5
Set the Tone—Your Restaurant Interior 65

Chapter 6
Find Your Niche—Set Yourself Apart!............. 75

Chapter 7
Marketing for Profitability............................. 83

Chapter 1

Analyzing the Numbers

Write a Great Business Plan—If You Haven't Already!

Don't skimp on the business plan. If you are operating now, it's not too late to write that plan. Don't just be in business, have a financial plan; your business plan is the road map. If possible, take your time at the planning stage of your business and write a well-constructed, detailed business plan. Failure to do so is one of the commonest causes of business failure. Make sure that your plan covers the following basic information:

- Projected startup costs

- Personnel

- Insurance

- Rent

- Depreciation

- Loan payments

- Advertising/Promotions

- Legal/Accounting

- Miscellaneous expenses

- Supplies

- Payroll expenses

- Salaries/Wages

- Utilities

- Marketing costs

- Inventory costs

- Training costs

- Projected Profit and Loss Statements

- Projected Balance Sheets

- Any other known facets of running your restaurant business

- Additional costs:

    - Outsourcing labor costs for construction

    - Maintenance

    - Web site creation

    - Additional online marketing expenses

Business profile. Include a business profile explaining the business, the history, economic and industry trends, target audience, marketing concepts, and operational procedures.

Financial section. The financial section of your business plan should include:

- Loan applications you've filed

- Capital equipment and supply list

- Balance sheet

- Break-even analysis

- Pro-forma income projections (profit and loss statement)

- Pro-forma cash flow

The income statement and cash-flow projections should include:

- A three-year summary

    - Detail by month for the first year

    - Detail by quarter for the second and third years

Check out Quick Plan Restaurant Plans online at **www.atlantic-pub.com** for more information. Several books are available to assist you in writing a comprehensive business plan—two recommendations are *How to Write a Great Business Plan for Your Small Business in 60 Minutes or Less* and *Opening a Restaurant or Other Food Service Business Starter Kit: How to Prepare a Restaurant Business Plan and Feasibility Study*—both available at **www.atlantic-pub.com**.

Financial Analysis

In order to make profits, you need to plan for profits. Many restaurants offering great food, great atmosphere and great service still go out of business. The reason for this is that they fail to manage the financial aspects of the business. This means that poor cost-control management will be fatal to your business. Furthermore, good financial management is about interpreting financial statements and reports, not simply preparing them. A few distinctions need to be made in order to understand the language we are now using:

Financial accounting. These figures are primarily for external groups to assess taxes, the status of your establishment, etc.

Managerial accounting. These figures provide information to internal users that become the basis for managing day-to-day operations. This data is very specific, emphasizes departmental operations, and uses non-financial data like customer counts, menu sales mix and labor hours. These internal reports break down revenues and expenses by department, day and meal period so they can be easily interpreted, and areas that need attention are apparent. Daily and weekly reports must be made and analyzed in order to determine emerging trends.

The Present Financial Status of the Food Service Industry

Presently throughout the entire food service industry, operating expenses are up and income is down. After taxes and expenses, restaurants that make money, according to the National Restaurant Association, have bottom lines at 0.5–3 percent of sales. This tiny percentage is the difference between being profitable and going under. This drives home the importance of controlling your costs and understanding the numbers. A lot can be done to control costs and it begins with planning. Here are the basics:

Cost control is about numbers. It is about collecting, organizing, interpreting and comparing the numbers that impact your bottom line. This is not a job that can be delegated. These numbers are your controls; they are what tell you the real story of what's going on in your restaurant.

Understanding the bottom line. Understanding this story and its implications on your bottom line comes only with constant review and the resulting familiarity with the relationships between these numbers and the workings of the business. This may seem like drudgery, but it is, in fact, your key to understanding the meaning behind your numbers. Once you have mastered the numbers, they'll tell you the story behind your labor productivity, portion control, purchase prices, marketing promotions, new menu items and competitive strategy. This knowledge will free you to run the best, most profitable operation you can.

Chances of getting your money back. According to government statistics, a restaurant investor has a 1-in-20 chance of getting his or her money back in five years. Furthermore, the consensus of many successful restaurateurs is that 80 percent of the success of a restaurant is determined before it opens. This means you must prepare. And part of that preparation is integrating an ongoing profit-planning and cost-control program into your business.

Cost controls. This can be doubly important if you are fortunate enough to start out doing great business. This is because high profits can hide much inefficiency that will surely expose itself during times of low sales. Too many people become cost-control converts only after suffering losses; this is shortsighted. The primary purpose of cost controls is to maximize profits, not minimize losses. Controlling costs works because it focuses on getting the most value from the least cost in every aspect of your operation. By keeping costs under control, you can charge less than the competition or make more money from charging the same price.

Spending controls. These are huge operating freedoms and opportunities that are not afforded you if you don't know what you're spending and, therefore, can't control that spending. Furthermore, most of the waste that occurs in restaurants can't be detected by the naked eye. It takes records and reports, whose meanings you've mastered interpreting, to tell you the size of the inefficiencies that are taking place.

Chapter 2

Profit Planning and Cost Control

This is not accounting or bookkeeping. Profit planning and cost control are the information-gathering tools. Profit planning and cost control can be defined by explaining their purposes:

- To provide management with information needed for making day-to-day operations decisions.

- To monitor department and individual efficiency.

- To inform management of expenses being incurred and incomes received and whether they fall within standards and budgets.

- To prevent fraud and theft.

- To provide the groundwork for the business's goals (not for discovering where it has been).

- To emphasize prevention, not correction.

- To maximize profits, not minimize losses.

The idea of prevention versus correction is fundamental. Prevention occurs through advanced planning. Your primary job is not to put out fires, it's to prevent them—and to maximize profits in the process.

Cost-Control Records—Get It Right

The larger the distance between an owner or manager and the actual restaurant, the greater the need for effective cost-control records. This is how franchisers of restaurant chains keep their eyes on thousands of units across the world. Many managers of individual operations assume that since they're on the premises during operating hours, a detailed system of cost control is unnecessary. Tiny family operations often see controls the same way and view any device for theft prevention as a sign of distrust towards their staff. This is shortsighted, because the main purpose of cost control is to provide information to management about daily operations. Prevention of theft is a secondary function. Cost controls are about knowing where you are going. Furthermore, most waste and inefficiencies cannot be seen; they need to be understood through the numbers.

Understanding those numbers means interpreting them. To do this effectively you need to understand the difference between control and reduction:

- Control is achieved through the assembly and interpretation of data and ratios on your revenue and expenses.

- Reduction is the actual action taken to bring costs within your predetermined standards. Effective cost control starts at the top of an organization. Management must establish, support and enforce its standards and procedures.

Get Computerized

Our advice is no matter what type or size of your food service operation, get your operation computerized. It's extremely difficult to compete successfully without utilizing technology, at least to some degree. Today the investment for a basic computer and accounting software is less than $2,000 and could be as little as $1,000. The investment will deliver immediately in savings in accounting fees and your ability to get true insight into your business.

QuickBooks®. Our favorite restaurant accounting package is the veteran QuickBooks by Intuit. The 2005 version of QuickBooks is rich in features,

including built-in remote-access capabilities and Web interfaces. Reports are generated in a few seconds that would take hours to calculate manually. The reports are also flawless, eliminating the human-error factor. This program now has a point-of-sale option that was the only limiting factor prior to this new release. The 2005 version of QuickBooks is available at **www.quickbooks.com**. Another popular accounting package is Peachtree®, available at **www .peachtree.com**.

The main purpose of cost control is to provide information to management about daily operations. Cost controls are about knowing where you are going. Furthermore, most waste and inefficiencies cannot be seen; they need to be understood through the numbers.

Tasty Profits® **software.** If you are just setting up your accounting program and decide to use QuickBooks, we recommend an add-on product called "The Tasty Profits Guide to QuickBooks Software for Restaurants." This helpful guide to QuickBooks enables you to save thousands of dollars doing your own accounting with its proven, easy-to-use system. Simply install the disc that is included with the "Tasty Profits Guide" directly into your computer. Download the pre-configured restaurant accounts, and you are ready to go. You will have instant access to all your financial data, accurately calculate food and bar costs with ease, reconcile bank and credit card statements, track and pay tips that are charged to credit cards, and calculate sales tax automatically. The program currently costs about $70 and is available at **www.atlantic-pub.com** or call 800-814-1132, Item # TP-01.

Chart of Accounts

Restaurant accounting requires specific procedures; concentrate on the essentials. The following suggestions will point you in the right direction:

The Uniform System of Accounts for Restaurants (USAR). The National

Restaurant Association publishes a simple, easy-to-use accounting classification system for restaurants. This valuable book, prepared by CPAs, includes examples of balance sheets, wage-control reports and an expense-classification system. If you take only one idea from this book, we recommend you use this system. You can order online at **www.restaurant.org** or by calling 800- 424-5156. USAR is an essential guide for restaurant accounting. It establishes a common industry language that allows you to compare ratios and percentages across industry lines. The goal of this comparison is to create financial statements that are management tools, not just IRS reports.

The Operations Report. The National Restaurant Association also publishes a report entitled *The Operations Report*, based on an annual survey of operator income statements. Conducted jointly by the association and the accounting firm of Deloitte and Touché, the report provides detailed data on where the restaurant dollar comes from and where it goes for four categories of restaurants: three types of full-service operations (with per-person check sizes under $10; between $10 and $25; and $25 and more) plus limited-service operations (fast-food).

Utilize the same chart of accounts to compare your operation with others. Ratios enable you to compare the operating data of a specific hotel or restaurant to the average for a group of similar establishments. You may, for example, compare the assets of your restaurant with the average assets of restaurants of a similar size in order to determine if yours is as financially healthy as it should be. You can easily compare food costs and other cost figures for comparisons.

Point-of-Sale Systems

The most widely used technology in the food service industry is the touch-screen point-of-sale (POS) system. The POS system is basically an offshoot of the electronic cash register. Touch-screen POS systems were introduced to the food service industry in the mid-1980s and have penetrated 90 percent of restaurants nationwide. From fine-dining establishments to fast food, the touch-screen is effortless. Such systems will pay for themselves. According to information published by the National Restaurant Association, a restaurant averaging $1,000,000 in food-and-beverage sales can expect to see an estimated savings of $30,000 per year. Understanding the numbers collected by a POS system will give the operator more control over inventory, bar revenues, labor scheduling, overtime, customer traffic and service. Understanding POS data ultimately clarifies the bottom line, knocking guesswork out of the equation.

Point-of-sale systems are crucial for reducing loss. If your servers simply can't obtain any food or beverage without a hard-copy check or without entering the sale electronically, you have eliminated most of their opportunity to steal. Many electronic systems are available in the industry, and once initial training and intimidation are overcome, they can seriously reduce the amount of theft and shrinkage in your restaurant. These systems also allow you to instantly see which items are selling best at different times of the day. This enables you to order more efficiently and keep inventory to a minimum. They also allow you to automatically subtract from inventory all the ingredients used in the items you sold. These can be invaluable tools for tracking employee productivity, initiating promotions and contests, and generating weekly, daily, by meal or hourly sales reports. Point-of-sale systems collect invaluable data for you to interpret.

Here is the lowdown:

A POS system comprises two parts: the hardware, or equipment, and the software, the computer program that runs the system. This system allows waitstaff to key in their orders as soon as the customers give them. Additional keys are available for particular options and specifications, such as "rare," "medium-rare" and "well-done." Some systems prompt the waitstaff to ask additional questions when the item is ordered, such as, "Would you like butter, sour cream or chives with the baked potato?" Some will suggest a side dish or a compatible wine.

Processing the order. The order is sent through a cable to printers located throughout the restaurant: at the bar and in the kitchen and office. All orders must be printed before they are prepared, thus ensuring good control.

Payment. When a server has completed the ordering, a guest check can be printed and later presented. Most POS systems allow certain discounts and require manager control over others. Credit cards, cash and checks can be processed separately and then reports can be generated by payment type.

Some benefits of using a POS system include:

- Increases sales and accounting information.
- Customer tracking.
- Reports waitstaff's sales and performance.
- Reports menu-item performance.
- Reports inventory usage.
- Processes credit card purchases.

- Ensures accurate addition on guest checks.

- Prevents incorrect items from being ordered.

- Prevents confusion in the kitchen.

- Reports possible theft of money and inventory.

- Records employee time-keeping.

- Reports menu-sales breakdown for preparation and menu forecasting.

- Reduces time spent walking to the kitchen and bar.

POS Enhancements

Many POS systems have been greatly enhanced to include comprehensive home delivery; guest books; online reservations; frequent-diner modules; fully integrated systems with real-time inventory; integrated caller ID; accounting; labor scheduling; payroll; menu analysis; purchasing and receiving; cash management; and reports. Up-and-coming enhancements and add-ons include improved functionality across the Internet, centralized functionality enabling "alerts" to be issued to managers, and voice-recognition POS technology.

To improve efficiency, the Visual-Pager System® by Microframe is a smart choice for staff paging. The Visual-Pager display can be hung near the food pickup window or in the kitchen. When an order is ready for the server, the chef or food expeditor then enters either the server's number or the POS number in the keypad, and that number is shown on the Visual-Pager display. The display can be programmed to blink slowly if the food has been waiting for a short period of time or blink fast if it has been waiting too long. This ensures faster service for the guests and helps prevent hot food from getting cold. The Visual-Pager System is available in both wired and wireless versions.

Visual-Pager System® by Microframe
www.restaurantpager.com • 800-635-3811

Crucial Elements of Cost Control—Profit Planning

There are ten primary areas that are central to any food and beverage operation and, therefore, are crucial elements of profit planning.

Purchasing. Your inventory system is the critical component of purchasing. Before placing an order with a supplier, you need to know what you have on hand and how much will be used. Allow for a cushion of inventory so you won't run out between deliveries. Once purchasing has been standardized, the manager simply orders from your suppliers. Records show supplier, prices, unit of purchase, product specifications, etc. This information needs to be kept on paper and preferably computerized. Purchase food items according to usage. For example, if you plan to use tomatoes by blending and mixing them with other ingredients to make a sauce, then purchase broken tomatoes as opposed to whole tomatoes. However, if you intend to use tomatoes to decorate a dinner plate or as a topping, then opt for high-quality produce, such as baby plum vine-grown tomatoes.

Receiving. This is how you verify that everything you ordered has arrived. Check for correct brands, grades, varieties, quantities, correct prices, etc. Incorrect receivables need to be noted and either returned or credited to your account. Products purchased by weight or count need to be checked.

Storage. All food is stored until it's used. Doing so in an orderly fashion ensures easy inventory. Doing so properly, with regard to temperature, ventilation and freedom from contamination, ensures food products remain in optimum condition until being used. Expensive items need to be guarded from theft.

Issuing. Procedures for removing inventory from storage are part of the cost-control process. Head chefs and bartenders have authority to take or "issue" stock from storage to the appropriate place. This is a much more important aspect of cost control than it seems, because in order to know your food and beverage costs, you need to know your beginning inventory, how much was sold, and your ending inventory. Without this data, you can't determine accurate cost figures.

Rough preparation. Roughly prepared ingredients are finished off prior to plating. The quality and care with which this is done determines the amount of waste generated in preparation of standard recipes.

Preparation for service. How your staff minimizes waste during preliminary preparation is critical.

Portioning/transfer. Food can be lost through over-portioning. Final preparation should be monitored regularly to ensure quality and quantity standards are being adhered to. This is such a crucial element to cost control that many managers are assigned to monitor order times, portions, presentation and food quality with an eagle eye.

Order taking/guest check. Every item sold or issued from the kitchen needs to be recorded. This can be done by paper check or computer. Basically, it needs to be impossible for anyone to get food or drinks without the items being entered into the system. No verbal orders for food or beverages should be accepted by or from anybody—including management and owners.

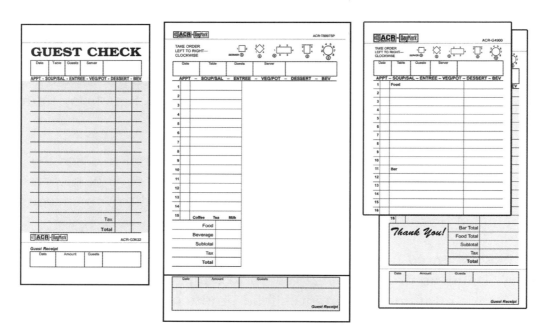

Sample Guest Checks from ACR by DayMark. From left to right: single-sheet guest check; 2-part carbonless guest check; duplicate carbon-backed guest check. For more information or to order, contact DayMark at 1-800-847-0101 or visit www.daymark.biz.

There are a wide variety of guest checks available. DayMark Food Safety Systems offers a complete line of guest checks including single sheets, carbon-backed and carbonless.

Cash receipts. Monitoring sales is crucial to cost controls. Under/overcharging, falsification of tips and lost checks must be investigated after every shift. Sales information from each meal period must be compiled to build a historical financial record. This record helps you forecast the future.

Bank deposits/accounts payable. Proper auditing of bank deposits and charge slips must be conducted.

Accurate Day-to-Day Cost Control

Cost control is an ongoing process that must be part of the basic moment-to-moment breathing of your business. A continuous appraisal of this process is equally as integral to the functioning of your restaurant.

There are five key elements to an effective cost-control strategy:

1. Planning in advance.

2. Procedures and devices that aid the control process.

3. Implementation of your profit-planning program.

4. Employee compliance.

5. Management's ongoing enforcement and reassessment.

Furthermore, your program should be assessed with the following questions:

- Do your cost controls provide relevant information?

- Is the information timely?

- Is it easily assembled, organized and interpreted?

- Are the benefits and savings greater than the cost of the controls?

This last point is especially important. When the expense of the controls exceeds the savings, that's waste, not control. Spending $30,000 on an automated liquor dispensing system that will save you $5,000 in waste is ineffective.

Standards Are Key to Any Cost-Control Program

Predetermined points of comparison must be set, against which you will measure your actual results. The difference between planned resources and resources actually used are the variance. Management can then monitor for negative or positive variances between standards and actual performance and will know where specifically to make corrections.

These five guidelines illustrate the uses of standards:

1. Performance standards should be established for all individuals and departments.

2. Individuals must see it as the responsibility of each to prevent waste and inefficiency.

3. Adherence—or lack of adherence—to standards must be monitored.

4. Actual performance must be compared against established standards.

5. When deviations from standards are discovered, appropriate action must be taken.

Your job is to make sure standards are adhered to. Is your staff using measuring scoops, ladles, sized bowls, glasses and cups; weighing portions individually; portioning by count; and pre-portioning? These are all useful tools to make sure standards are met and your cost-control program is implemented effectively.

Cost Ratios

Owners and managers need to be on the same page in terms of the meaning and calculation of the many ratios used to analyze food, beverage and labor costs. It's important to understand how your ratios are being calculated so you can get a true indication of the cost or profit activity in your restaurant. Cost control is not just the calculation of these numbers; it's the interpretation of them and the appropriate (re)actions taken to bring your numbers within set standards. Consider the following:

Food-Cost Percentage

This basic ratio is often misinterpreted because it is often calculated in so many different ways. Basically, it is food cost divided by food sales. However, whether your food cost is determined by food sold or consumed is a crucial difference. Also, for your food-cost percentage to be accurate, a month-end inventory must be taken. Without this figure, your food-cost statement is inaccurate and, therefore, basically useless. This is because your inventory will vary month to month, even in the most stable environment (which yours probably won't be initially), because months end on different days of the week.

Distinguishing between food sold and consumed is important because all food consumed is not sold. Food consumed includes all food used, sold, wasted, stolen or given away to customers and employees. Food sold is determined by subtracting all food bought at full price from the total food consumed.

Maximum allowable food cost (MFC) is the most food can cost and still return your profit goal. If at the end of the month your food-cost percentage is over your maximum allowable percentage, you won't meet your profit expectations. This is how you calculate it:

1. Write your dollar amounts of labor costs and overhead expenses and exclude food costs.

2. Refer to past accounting periods and yearly averages to get realistic cost estimates.

3. Add your monthly profit goal as either a dollar amount or a percentage of sales.

4. Convert dollar values of expenses to percentages by dividing by food sales for the periods used for expenses. Generally, don't use your highest or lowest sales figures for calculating your operating expenses.

5. Subtract the total of the percentages from 100 percent.

6. The remainder is your maximum allowable food-cost percentage (MFC).

100 – {monthly expenses (– food costs) + profit goal (monthly)}
= % MFC food sales

Actual food-cost percentage (AFC) is the percentage you're actually operating at. It's calculated by dividing food cost by food sales. If you are deducting employee meals from your income statement, then you are calculating cost of food sold. If there is no deduction of employee meals—which is true for most operations— then the food cost you're reading is food consumed. This is always a higher cost than food sold, and if inventory is not being taken, the food cost on your income statement is just an estimate based on purchases and isn't accurate.

Potential food-cost percentage (PFC) is also called your theoretical food cost. This is the lowest your food cost can be because it assumes that all food consumed is sold, and that there is no waste whatsoever. It is found by multiplying the number sold of each menu item by the ideal recipe cost.

Standard food-cost percentage (SFC) is how you adjust for the unrealistically low PFC. This percentage includes unavoidable waste, employee meals, etc. This food-cost percentage is compared to the AFC and is the standard management must meet.

Prime food cost includes with the food cost the cost of direct labor. This is labor incurred because the item is made from scratch; for example, baking pies and bread, trimming steaks, etc. When the food cost is determined for these items, the cost of the labor needed to prepare them is added. So prime cost is food cost plus necessary direct labor. This costing method is applied to every menu item needing extensive direct labor before it is served to the customer. Indirect labor cannot be attributed to any particular menu item and is therefore overhead. Prime cost is the total cost of food and beverage sold, payroll and employee benefits costs.

Beverage cost ratio is calculated when alcoholic beverages are sold. It is determined by dividing costs by sales—calculated the same way as food consumed. A single beverage ratio can't be standardized because the percentage will vary depending on the mix of hard alcohol, wine and beer. Spirits run a lower cost percentage than wine and beer, and as such, it is recommended that alcoholic beverages be split into their three categories.

Beverage sales do not include coffee, tea, milk or juice, which are usually considered food. Wherever you include soft drinks, know that it will reduce the food cost, since the ratio of cost to selling price is so low.

Calculating Inventory

When conducting the ending or physical inventory, use scales for food and special scales for liquor for the most accurate determination. Place inventory sheets in the same order as the room is stocked. Use a separate sheet for each area. Include on the form your inventory unit, units per case, pack or size, par and vendor code. Use two people: one to count (a manager) and one to record the figures (preferably an employee from a different area). For example, have the bar manager assist in the food inventory and the kitchen manager help in recording the liquor.

Essential Sales and Turnover Calculations

In order to keep tight control of the financial side of your operation, you'll need to understand and use the following calculations:

Check average. This calculation is not just total food and beverage sales divided by customers served. Of course, this is one way to determine your check average, but it is important to see how this figure compares to the check average you need to meet your daily sales goals. If you are coming in under what you need, you should look at your prices. Check average should be determined by each meal period, especially when different menus are served for each meal. Standards need to be set on how customers who order only a drink and no food are counted.

Seat turnover. This refers to how many times you can fill a chair during a meal period with another customer. Restaurants with low check averages need high seat turnover.

Inventory turnover. Inventory turnover is calculated by dividing cost of food consumed by your average inventory (this is simply your beginning inventory plus ending inventory, divided by two).

Ratio of food-to-beverage sales. This is simply the ratio of their percentages of your total sales. In restaurants with a higher percentage of beverages than food sales, profits are generally higher because there is a greater profit margin on beverages.

Sales mix is the number of each menu item sold. This is crucial to cost analysis because each item impacts food cost differently. If your restaurant does a huge breakfast business and the one down the street does a big lunch, your food costs are going to be different than theirs.

Break-even point (BEP) is simply when sales equal expenses. Businesses can operate forever at break-even if there are no investors looking for a return on their money. To determine a break-even analysis, you need to break the costs into two categories: fixed costs and variable costs. Fixed costs remain constant regardless of sales volume and include items such as rent, insurance, property taxes, management payroll, etc. Variable costs will increase or decrease in relation to sales changes and includes such items as food and beverage costs.

Contribution margin is your gross profit. It is what remains after all expenses have been subtracted from 100 percent net.

Closing point. Closing point is when the cost of being open for a given time period is more expensive than revenue earned. This means that if it cost you $2,000 to open today and you only made $1,800, your closing point expense will be $200.

Sales per square foot. This refers to the total annual sales for the establishment divided by the total square footage for a given period. For example, the sales for the year are $1,000,000, the total square footage is 7,500; thus the sales per square foot is $133.33.

Income statement (often called profit and loss statement or P&L). This is the scorecard for a business. Part of a company's financial statements, it summarizes revenues and expenses during a specific period of time. It shows the revenue, expenses and profit or loss. It shows these things for some period of time, usually a month or a year. For example, an income statement is usually titled: "Income Statement for X Business for the period ending December 31, 2004."

Profitability Ratios

Profitability is often measured in percentage terms in order to facilitate making comparisons of a company's financial performance against past years' performance and against the performance of other companies. When profitability is expressed as a percentage (or ratio), the new figures are called profit margins. The most common profit margins are all expressed as percentages of net sales. Let's look at a few of the most commonly used profit margins that you can easily learn to use to help you measure and compare firms:

Gross margin percentage is the resulting percentage when gross profit is divided by net sales. Gross profit equals net sales less cost of goods sold (gross profit ÷ net sales = gross margin). Therefore, gross margin percentage represents the percentage of revenue remaining after cost of goods sold is deducted. Let us take a look at a simple example: Net sales = $1,000; cost of goods sold = $400; gross profit = $600. In this example the gross margin = 600 ÷ 1,000 = 0.60 or 60%. Since this ratio only takes into account sales and variable costs (costs of goods sold), this ratio is a good indicator of a restaurant's efficiency in producing and distributing its products. The higher the ratio, the higher the efficiency of the production process.

Operating margin. As the name implies, operating margin is the resulting ratio when operating income is divided by net sales (operating income ÷ net sales = operating margin). This ratio measures the quality of a restaurant's operations. A restaurant with a high operating margin in relation to the industry average has operations that are more efficient. Typically, to achieve this result, the company must have lower fixed costs, a better gross margin, or a combination of the two. At any rate, companies that are more efficient than their competitors in their core operations have a distinct advantage. Efficiency is good. Advantages are even better.

Net margin. As the name implies, net margin is a measure of profitability for the sum of a restaurant's operations. It is equal to net profit divided by net sales (net profit ÷ net sales = net margin). As with the other ratios, you will want to compare net margin with other restaurants in the area and in the industry overall. This is one reason that using the standard chart of accounts is so highly recommended. You can also track year-to-year changes in net margin to see if a company's competitive position is improving or getting worse.

The higher the net margin relative to the industry (or relative to past years), the better. Often a high net margin indicates that the company you are examining is an efficient producer. However, as with all the previous profit margin measurements, you always need to check past years of performance. Strong profit margins that are sustainable indicate that a company has been able to outperform their competitors consistently.

The Balance Sheet

Often referred to as the basic business financial statement, the balance sheet shows three things about a business: assets, liabilities and owner's equity. It is important to know the rules used in recording assets and liabilities and in constructing a balance sheet. It is also important to understand the proper and improper uses of this statement. If you don't know these things, either learn them or hire someone (a CPA) who can advise you. You'll need to understand the basic terminology:

Assets. Assets are things that are owned by the business.

Liabilities. Liabilities are things that are owed to others.

Owner's equity. Owner's equity is the difference between assets and liabilities. Owner's equity can be thought of in this way: If the business were to liquidate all the assets and pay off all the liabilities, what is left would be owner's equity. The owner would have a right to keep this equity. The listing of assets on the balance sheet is customarily done at cost or adjusted cost. Inventory, a common asset, would be recorded at cost value even though it may be sold for more or less than cost in a liquidation situation. A building, another common asset, might have appreciated in value, but this added value would not be recognized on the balance sheet.

Why Is the Balance Sheet Important to You?

Many restaurant operators often fail to look at the balance sheet. The balance sheet is the fundamental report of a company's possessions, debts and capital invested. The balance sheet is the first financial document your banker or investor will look at.

You can use the balance sheet to examine the following:

- Can the company meet its financial obligations?
- How much money has already been invested in this company?
- Is the company overly indebted?
- What kind of assets has the company purchased with its financing?

Liquidity ratios. The following liquidity ratios are all designed to measure a company's ability to cover its short-term obligations. Companies will generally pay their interest payments and other short-term debts with current assets. Therefore, it is essential that a company have an adequate surplus of current assets in order to meet their current liabilities. If a company has only liquid assets, it may not be able to make payments on their debts. To measure a company's ability to meet such short-term obligations, various ratios have been developed.

You will need to study the following balance sheet ratios:

- Current ratio
- Acid test (or quick ratio)
- Working capital
- Leverage

Current ratio. The current ratio measures a company's ability to pay their current obligations. The greater extent to which current assets exceed current liabilities, the easier a company can meet its short-term obligations (current assets ÷ current liabilities = current ratio). After calculating the current ratio, you should compare it with other restaurants. A ratio lower than that of the industry average suggests that the company may have liquidity problems. However, a significantly higher ratio may suggest that the company is not efficiently using its funds. A satisfactory current ratio for a company will be within close range of the industry average, which for most restaurants is between 0.5 and 1.25. This is much lower than most other industries, but keep in mind that the restaurant business is mostly a cash business and can operate quite well with a lower ratio.

Acid test or quick ratio. The acid test ratio or quick ratio is very similar to the current ratio except for the fact that it excludes inventory. For this reason, it's also a more conservative ratio (current assets – inventory ÷ current liabilities = acid test). Inventory is excluded in this ratio because inventory cannot always be quickly converted to cash.

Working capital. Working capital is simply the amount that current assets exceed current liabilities (current assets – current liabilities = working capital). The working capital formula is very similar to the current ratio. The only difference is that it gives you a dollar amount rather than a ratio. It, too, is calculated to determine a firm's ability to pay its short-term obligations. Working capital can be viewed as somewhat of a security blanket. The greater the amount of working capital, the more security an investor has and assurance that they'll be able to meet their financial obligations.

Debt. Many times a company does not have enough liquidity—cash available to pay current debts owed. Being over-leveraged (debt higher than current assets) is a common cause of business failure.

The Statement of Cash Flows

The simplest form of a statement of cash flows is a listing of cash coming into the business and cash going out. Think of a checkbook register: You record cash that you deposit into your bank account and you record each check that you write. You don't record anything else—just cash you get and cash you pay out. You need to know the following facts about cash flow statements:

The rules. With business cash flow, the same simple rule applies. If it is either cash received or cash paid, it is listed. If it is not cash, it is not listed. If something is purchased but no cash is paid, it is not recorded on the statement of cash flows until the cash is actually paid out. Of course, one of the great aspects of the restaurant business is that it is primarily, if not exclusively, a cash business.

A statement of cash flows is different from an income statement (profit and loss statement). The latter is kept on the accrual basis of accounting. Accrual accounting, which is used with most businesses and all businesses with inventory, recognizes sales when they are made, even if the cash is collected at a later time. It also recognizes expenses when incurred even if paid 30 or 60 days later.

Other expenditures. There is spending in business that is not immediately reflected on the income statement. When inventory is purchased, there is no entry on the income statement even if cash is paid for the purchase. When equipment is bought with cash, only a part of that purchase is usually reflected in the current income statement. The rest is shown on future statements by way of depreciation expense. These types of transactions would show up on a statement of cash flows but not on an income statement.

Four-week accounting period. Companies typically close their books and prepare financial statements at the end of each month. The problem for a retail business, such as a restaurant, is that there are uneven number of days and uneven number of the type of days in a month. For example, you may have an extra Saturday, which would skew numbers upwards. Consider using a four-week accounting period so you can compare apples to apples.

EBITDA. This refers to earnings before interest, tax, depreciation and amortization (profit before any interest, taxes, depreciation or amortization) have been deducted.

Simple Tips to Help You Compile Your Financial Reports Faster

- Get a computer—the best you can afford.

- Get a great software package, such as QuickBooks, and a POS system.

- Order Tasty Profits or use the National Restaurant Association's chart of accounts in conjunction with your accounting software.

- Close the accounting period internally, using a four-week accounting period; don't wait for your accountant. Use your CPA to assist in quarterly reports, end-of-year and tax planning.

- Utilize online banking services—including bank account reconciliation.

- Have missing documents faxed or e-mailed to you. If necessary, estimate; you can adjust later.

- Do your bookkeeping daily, so it doesn't get away from you.

- POS systems should be linked to your accounting software.

- Time clocks should be linked to your accounting software and possibly to your POS system.

Chapter 3

Profitable Pricing

Pricing

Pricing is an important aspect of your revenues and customer counts. Prices that are too high will drive customers away, and prices that are too low will kill your profits. But pricing is not the simple matter of an appropriate markup over cost; it combines other factors as well. Price can either be market-driven or demand-driven:

- **Market-driven prices** must be responsive to your competitors' prices. Common dishes that both you and the place down the road sell need to be priced competitively. This is also true when you're introducing new items for which a demand has not been developed.

- **Demand-driven items.** These are items which customers ask for and where demand exceeds your supply. You have a short-term monopoly on these items and, therefore, price is driven up until demand slows or competitors begin to sell similar items.

Markup. A combination of pricing methods is usually a good idea since each menu item is usually different. Two basic theories are charge as much as you can, and charge as little as you can. Each has its pluses and minuses. Obviously, if you charge as much as you can, you increase the chance of greater profits. You do, however, run the risk of needing to offer a product that customers feel is worth the price; otherwise you will lose them because they won't think you're a good value. Charging the lowest price you can gives customers a great sense of value but lowers your profit margin per item.

Determining Prices

Prices are generally determined by competition and demand. Your prices must be in line with the category in which customers place you. Fast-food burrito joints don't price like a five-star restaurant, and vice versa. Both would lose their customer base if they did. While this is an exaggeration, the point is still the same: You want your customers to know that your image and your prices fit into that picture. Here are four ways to determine prices:

Competitive pricing. Simply based on meeting or beating your competition's prices. This is an ineffective method, since it assumes diners are making their choice on price alone and not food quality, ambiance, service, etc.

Intuitive pricing. This means you don't want to take the time to find out what your competition is charging, so you are charging based on what you feel guests are willing to pay. If your sense of the value of your product is good, then it works. Otherwise, it can be problematic.

Psychological pricing. Price is more of a factor to lower-income customers who go to lower-priced restaurants. If they don't know an item is good, they assume it is if it's expensive. If you change your prices, the order in which buyers see them also affects their perceptions. If an item was initially more expensive, it will be viewed as a bargain, and vice versa.

Trial-and-error pricing. This is based on customer reactions to prices. It is not practical in terms of determining your overall prices, but it can be effective with individual items to bring them closer to the price a customer is willing to pay or to distinguish them from similar menu items with a higher or lower food cost.

Other Factors That Will Help You Determine Prices

Whether customers view you as a leader or a follower can make a big difference regarding how they view your prices. If people think of you as the best seafood restaurant in the area, they'll be willing to pay a little more. Here are some other considerations:

Service determines people's sense of value. This is even truer when the difference in actual food quality between you and the competition is negligible. If your customers order at a counter and bus their own tables, this lack of service cost needs to be reflected in your prices. Also, in a competitive market, providing great service can be a factor that puts you in a leadership position and allows you to charge a higher price.

Location, ambiance, customer base, product presentation and desired check average all factor into what you feel you can charge and what you need to charge to make a profit.

Internal Controls

It is estimated that about five cents of every dollar spent in U.S. restaurants is lost to theft. Clearly established and followed controls can lessen this percentage. Begin by separating duties and recording every transaction. If these basic systems are in place, then workers know at each step of the way that they will be held responsible for shrinkage. Management Information Systems (MIS) are common tools for accumulating, analyzing and reporting data. They help establish proper rules for consistent and prompt reporting and set up efficient flows of paperwork and data collection. In short, their goal is to prevent fraud on all levels. While no system is perfect, a good MIS will show where fraud or loss is occurring, allowing you to remedy the situation.

In most restaurants, the majority of internal theft occurs in and around the bar. In tightly run establishments, cash is more likely to be taken by management than hourly workers because managers have access to it and know the system well. Hourly workers tend to steal items, not cash, because that's what they can get their hands on. Keeping food away from the back door and notifying your employees when you are aware of theft and are investigating can have a deterring effect.

The key to statistical control is entering transactions into the system. This can be done electronically or by hand. Either way, if food or beverages can be consumed without being entered into the system, your system is flawed and control is compromised.

Five other cost-control concepts are crucial to your control system:

1. **Documentation** of tasks, activities and transactions must be required.

2. **Supervision and review of employees** by management intimately familiar with set performance standards.

3. **Splitting of duties** so no single person is involved in all parts of the task cycle.

4. **Timeliness.** All tasks must be done within set time guidelines; comparisons then made at established control points. Reports must be made at scheduled times to detect problems.

5. **Cost-benefit relationships.** The cost of procedures used versus benefits gained must exceed the cost of implementing the controls.

The basic control procedure is an independent verification at a control point during and after the completion of a task. This is often done through written or electronic reports. Verification determines if the person performing the task has authority to do so and if the quantity and quality available and performance results meet set standards.

Control Systems

There are a variety of systems designed to help with controls. COMMLOG, **www.commlog .com** offers a comprehensive line of unique, fully customizable logs including a manager communication log, reservation log, switch shift log, request off log, banquet log, kitchen log and bar logs. Created by hospitality professionals, COMMLOG's unique structure guides users through all parts of leaving a great note, improving communication and follow-up. COMMLOG utilizes a plastic coil binding so the log lays flat when open. COMMLOG is available in either letter (8.5" x 11")

COMMLOG's Manager Communication Log available at www.commlog.com or by calling 1-800-962-6564

or legal size (8.5" x 14") and can be customized at no extra charge for specific restaurant use.

Purchasing and Ordering

What exactly is the difference? Purchasing is setting the policy on which suppliers, brands, grades and varieties of products will be ordered. These are your standardized purchase specifications; the specifics negotiated between management and distributors how items are delivered, paid for, returned, etc. Basically, purchasing is what you order and from whom. Ordering, then, is simply the act of contacting the suppliers and notifying them of the quantity you require. This is a simpler, lower-level task. Here are the basics:

Develop a purchasing program. Once menus have been created that meet your customers' satisfaction and your profit needs, develop a purchasing program that assures your profit margins.

Be efficient. An efficient purchasing program incorporates standard purchase specifications based on standardized recipes and yields that, with portion control, allow for accurate costs based on portions actually served.

Ordering. To order the necessary supplies, your operator needs to be able to predict how much will be needed to maintain purchase specifications, follow standard recipes, and enforce portioning standards. When these are done well, optimum quantities can be kept on hand.

Buying also has its own distinctions. Open or informal buying is face-to-face or over-the-phone contact and uses largely oral negotiations and purchase specifications. In formal buying, terms are put in writing and payment invoices are stated as conditions for price quotes and customer service commitments. Its customer service is possibly the most important aspect of the supplier you choose, because good sales representatives know their products, have an understanding of your needs, and offer helpful suggestions.

Inventory, Storage and Accounts Payable

Ordering effectively is impossible unless you know your inventory. Before an order is placed, counts of stock should be made. Many software programs are able to determine order quantities directly from sales reports, but without this kind of system, you must inventory what you have on hand before ordering. The taking of inventory must be streamlined because it must be done as frequently as you order. It mustn't be an unpleasant late-night debacle that is done only rarely and only when it has to be. Whether your inventory system is by hand or computer, its purpose is to accomplish the following:

- Provide records of what you need.

- Provide records of product specifications.

- Provide records of suppliers.

- Provide records of prices and unit of purchase.

- Provide a record of product use levels.

- Facilitate efficient ordering.

- Increase the accuracy of inventory.

- Facilitate the inventory process.

- Make it easy to detect variance levels in inventory.

Records and reports. With such a system, the records generated and kept are extensive and valuable. You will have records of what you purchased, product specifications, your primary and alternative suppliers, price, and unit of purchase. Equally important, reports will indicate the par usage level between deliveries. These statistics allow for month-to-month comparisons to be made between units in a multi-unit operation.

Labor Productivity

Labor costs and turnover are serious concerns in today's restaurant market. Increasing labor costs cannot be offset by continuously higher prices. Maximizing worker productivity so few can do more, has become a key challenge to the restaurateur. This is especially true since the food service industry continues to be an entry-level arena for the unskilled and often uneducated. Qualified applicants are still few in the restaurant industry. A few of the causes of high labor costs and low productivity are poor layout and design of your operation, lack of labor-saving equipment, poor scheduling and no regular detailed system to collect and analyze payroll data. The following are some suggested ways management could improve these areas for greater efficiency:

Scheduling. The key to controlling labor costs is not a low average-hourly wage, but proper scheduling of productive employees. Place your best servers, cooks, etc., where you need them most. This requires knowing the strengths and weaknesses of your employees. Staggering the arrival and departure of employees is a good way to follow the volume of expected customers and to minimize labor costs during slow times. Use scheduling software such as Employee Schedule Partner, available at **www.atlantic-pub.com**. Some POS systems have scheduling software built into them.

On-call scheduling. When your forecasted customer counts are inaccurate, scheduled labor must be adjusted up or down to meet productivity standards. Employees simply wait at home to be called if they are needed for work. If they don't receive a call by a certain time, they know they're not needed. Employees prefer this greatly to coming in only to be sent home and by tipped staff that don't want to work when business is slow.

On-break schedules. When you can't send employees home, put them on a 30-minute break. Include a meal. Deduct the 30 minutes from their time cards and take a credit for the cost of the meal against the minimum wage obligation.

Pricing Beverages

Pricing beverages is not just a cost-markup exercise. The markup of alcohol in restaurants is often lower than in bars where liquor makes up the majority of sales. Prices reflect the uniqueness of an operation and the overhead operating costs. Section V covers beverages extensively, but below are some general tips to monitor your liquor costs accurately:

Record the sales of each type of beverage separately. Use separate keys for wine, beer and spirits on your register or point-of-sale system. Unless an electronic system is used, however, a detailed sales mix is difficult to obtain.

Responsibility. Make your alcoholic beverage purchaser or buyer responsible for ensuring that adequate amounts of required spirits are on hand.

Unlike food and supplies, purchasers are not required to shop around for the best deal for the following reasons:

- Specific dealers only sell specific brands.

- Wholesaling of alcohol is state regulated and controlled.

- Prices are published in monthly journals, and there is little change from month to month.

- Only quantity discounts are available.

- Purchase is done by brand name.

Beverage Inventory Control

Although purchasing and ordering alcohol is much simpler than purchasing and ordering food, the need to inventory correctly is no less crucial. In fact, alcohol needs to be guarded and inventoried more rigorously because of its cost, ease of theft, and possible abuses. Liquor inventory should be kept locked in different storerooms, cages or walk-ins than other inventory. Only authorized individuals should have access to these areas, and requisitions must be filled out to record withdrawals.

Replenish your stock from "stamped" or marked empty bottles. These prevent bartenders from bringing their own bottles in and selling them. If this does occur, it's virtually impossible to detect without marked bottles because there will be no inventory shortages. If you have drops in sales levels of $50–$100 in one night, these are signs of phantom bottles in your inventory.

Auditing. Inventories need to be audited to ensure your liquor is actually in the storeroom, and deliveries need to be checked for accuracy. It is recommended that a purchase order, not the driver's invoice, should be used to verify deliveries.

Controls for determining dispensing costs, recording sales and accounting for consumed beverages can be done three different ways:

1. **Automated systems that dispense and count.** Systems range from mechanical dispensers attached to each bottle to magnetic pourers that can only be activated by the register. These systems are exact, reduce spillage, and cannot give free drinks. Basically, liquor can't be dispensed without being put into the system.

2. **Ounce or drink controls.** This requires establishing standard glassware and recipes, recording each drink sold, determining costs of each drink, comparing actual use levels to potential consumption levels and comparing actual drink cost percentage to potential cost percentage.

3. **Par stock or bottle control.** This is a matter of keeping the maximum amount of each type of liquor behind the bar, then turning in all empty bottles for full ones. No full bottles are given without an empty one coming in. A standard sales value per bottle is determined based on the drinks it makes. A sales value is determined from consumption and compared to actual sales for variances. If less was sold than consumed, investigate.

Standards at the bar are as important as in the kitchen. Dispensers, jiggers or other measuring devices should be mandated to ensure portion controls. Regular inventory also needs to be done to watch for fraud and theft. Management needs to be expected to meet set standards. Whenever managers change shifts, you must verify inventory to make sure that numbers reported are "actual" and haven't been adjusted to meet costs.

Atlantic Publishing offers an inexpensive Liquor Bottle Control Program which provides consecutively numbered stickers and a log book. Management applies the non-removable stickers to the bottles when the bottles are received and placed in inventory. Next, log the inventory numbers in the log sheet and record the dates when issued to the bar and returned empty for exchange. This is a very effective yet inexpensive method of tracking the bottles from being stolen or a bartender bringing in their own bottles as each bottle is marked. The kit includes 1,000 labels, copies of the log book and CD-ROM with log book in Microsoft Excel format. For more information, contact Atlantic Publishing at 1-800-814-1132 or visit **www.atlantic-pub.com**.

The Depot Bar and Restaurant in Missoula, Montana, has been in business for 31 years. A recurring problem with all restaurants is what to do with leftover food. Longtime owner Mike Muncey describes how he turned one such problem into a plus.

We started out as a kind of chophouse serving steak and seafood. Then we added rooms for banquets as well as a place where customers could dine and socialize in a more casual atmosphere. Because we are known for our prime rib, we always need to have plenty on hand. If a group of customers walks into the restaurant at 9:30, you can't say to them, "We're out of prime rib." On the other hand, you can't keep leftover prime rib for very long and sell it at the same price. The quality would noticeably suffer.

Our solution is fairly simple. The next day we slice the meat really thin and then sell prime rib sandwiches in our casual area. We also put prime rib meat on our pizzas. Customers are willing to pay $10 for a sandwich and a little extra for a pizza because the quality is far beyond what you'd expect in a typical pub fare. This way, everybody wins.

Chapter 4

Pleasing Customers

There are some areas of a food service establishment where you can focus on the flip side of cutting costs: increasing profits. Customer service is one of those areas. After all, the old adage says, "One satisfied customer will tell another person; a dissatisfied customer will tell twelve people."

Service Guarantees

You've got to guarantee specific services to build up trust and loyalty among your customers. Service guarantees require you to:

- Focus on results

- Set standards

- Generate feedback

- Acknowledge failures

Use your guarantee as a yardstick. By setting a standard, you have quantifiable standards by which to measure your service. For example, if you guarantee customers their order within 15 minutes of placing it, then you now have a result to achieve and a standard to live up to. One minute over those first 15 minutes forces you to acknowledge failure.

Learn from your failures. A service guarantee gives you something that can actually be measured and results that are easy to see. It also helps refine and improve upon your existing service and procedures.

Meeting Expectations—First Impressions

Identify customer needs and expectations. Set yourself apart—from day one. Here are some simple tips:

Identify demand. Recognize that your guests have expectations of your service and make preparations based on three main criteria:

- Price

- Quality of food and presentation

- Location

Identify expectations. Make sure that price reflects service. If your check average is $6.25, customers probably expect fast food, paper napkins or even plastic utensils—they may even expect to pour their own ice and drinks. At that price, self-service is quite acceptable. However, if customers spend $25, expectations are rather different. Diners paying higher prices don't expect to pour their own drinks. In fact, they'd expect to have their glasses refilled by the time they were half empty!

Exceed expectations. Include a complimentary appetizer, a free glass of wine, free valet parking, or umbrellas when it rains.

Insist on exceptional behavior and manners from your waitstaff. This applies particularly to the front-of-the-house. Courtesy costs nothing.

Timely arrival of food. Make sure that all food is served promptly and at the correct temperature.

Ambiance. Offer an ambiance that meets guest expectations. A pleasant welcome, comfort and cleanliness are the main factors by which your establishment is judged. But, of course, small, individual touches can set your restaurant apart.

Directions. When people call for directions to your restaurant, ask them if they have a fax machine or e-mail. It's much easier to send written instructions. Have some pre-printed direction sheets or a standard e-mail text ready. If, however, you have to explain over the phone, be sure to give them landmarks to look for in addition to street names. Have the directions on your Web site. Link to Web sites that provide directions for your customers.

Customer Response—Actively Seek Feedback

Feedback is very important. Take the initiative to talk to your guests:

Feedback surveys. These have their place, but a lot of people don't bother to fill them out, as they've developed the impression that they aren't taken seriously. Be seen to respond. Go and speak with your customers—you will learn.

Manager presence. Guests always enjoy talking to the manager or owner. If they aren't happy about something, they will not always tell the waitstaff, and if they are told, the waitstaff may not tell you. Walk around and ask customers if they are enjoying their meal and the service they're receiving.

Attentive waitstaff. Don't tolerate the quick throw-away line, "Everything okay?" as staff whisk past the table, with no intention of waiting for a response. Be different: train staff to stop, listen and respond.

Hire a well-known chef to design your menu. Hiring a well-known chef to design your menu will gain attention from the media, the restaurant industry, and especially local customers within the area. Use the example from the golf courses designed by Arnold Palmer or Jack Nicklaus. In other words, the chef can design the menu, but not actually be there to cook it.

Send a thank-you note. For customers who fill out surveys, guest cards, and other personal information, send them a simple thank-you note for their efforts. If you have their personal contact information, you could also send out thank-you notes to people just because they chose to dine at your restaurant.

Better Service, More Tips—15 Top Tips!

Go beyond service expectations; your staff will see more tips and you will see more revenue. Good service is the difference between receiving 10 percent and 30 percent. Here are 15 top tips for increasing gratuities:

1. **Be competent and confident.** Familiarize yourself with the menu. Prove that you're capable of describing every single dish in a way that makes your customers crave the food from your description. Also, show that you can juggle multiple tasks and requests, without faltering or slowing down.

2. **Greet customers immediately.** No matter how busy you might be, take a moment to greet your guests within the first two minutes of them being seated. This lets them know you are aware of their existence and that they have been acknowledged. Let them know that you will be right with them in a few moments. Don't ignore them just because you can't take their order at that precise minute. You can still greet them and put them at ease.

3. **Direct eye contact.** Whenever you're addressing multiple guests at a table, look into the eyes of the individual to whom you are speaking. If you are addressing the entire table, be sure to shift your gaze to everyone present so that they all feel they are being included in the discussion. Don't talk or greet them as you are moving away or walking by. Stop and give them your undivided attention, even if only for a few seconds.

4. **Remember names and use them.** If a guest gives you their name, use it. Whenever it feels appropriate, address a customer by their name, especially if they're a regular. If a customer leaves a personal information card or even if they happen to be wearing a business name tag during their lunch break, show them that you've noticed. It makes them feel more comfortable with you as their server.

5. **Remember preferences.** When a customer returns, greet them as if you know them well and try to recall their likes and dislikes. Remember, for instance, how they prefer their food prepared.

6. **Give a recommendation.** Offer a recommendation on the menu that you like the best. Encourage them to tell you what kinds of foods they like. Make another recommendation based on what they've just told you.

7. **Introduce yourself creatively.** First, introduce the food and the specials. Start by telling them about your favorites on the menu. Once you've

engaged their attention and sparked their interest, then introduce yourself. When you first approach a table and start with the standard, "Good evening, my name is Jack and I'll be your waiter tonight," they aren't paying attention to who you are and they don't really care. Five minutes later most of them probably still won't know your name.

8. **Offer special comforts to single diners.** Offer them the newspaper. If they already have reading material or paperwork, try seating them in a well-lit area. If they seem inclined to talk, linger a little longer than you normally would and chat with them.

9. **Leave extra napkins.** Always leave three to four napkins per person at a table. One or two napkins are never enough. Finger foods require getting messy, children are bound to make lots of messes, and some people simply don't like wiping their hands and fingers or mouth on the same napkin more than once.

10. **Replace used silverware.** Whenever you clear the table of appetizers, a salad or soup before the main course, ensure that you also remove the dirty silverware. Bring clean silverware to the table, immediately. Don't expect your guests to use the same silverware for dessert or the main course.

11. **Recognize left-handed patrons.** If you notice a customer re-setting their glass and silverware on the opposite side from where you have placed them, then follow their example for anything else you bring them. Most likely, they are left-handed and will appreciate your attentiveness.

12. **Place coffee cups in a ready-to-grasp position.** While this is only a small gesture, the extra effort will be noticed and rewarded at the end of the meal.

13. **Ask permission before pouring refills.** This shows attentiveness without hassling the guests. Always use a fresh cup for coffee and tea refills.

14. **Settle the check promptly.** When guests indicate that they are ready to go, try to settle the check as promptly as possible. Don't make them wait.

15. **Provide calculators at check time.** Provide a credit card-sized calculator inside the folder of the bill or attach it to the tray with the bill. People come to your restaurant to relax and for enjoyment. The last thing they want to do is to calculate math in their heads. Groups sometimes need to split costs of appetizers, desserts and drinks in addition to their meal.

Provide Taste Samples

Nothing beats the experience. Allow your guests to taste samples before they actually order. This can be done for actual meals, desserts and especially wine. The following suggestions should give you ideas on how to develop this system within your own restaurant.

Appoint an employee. Choose one employee to handle the sampling for each shift. For improved guest interaction, try to pick a member of staff with an outgoing personality and an easy smile. Offer this person a bonus or percentage of each additional sale they make as a result of the samples they display and urge customers to try.

Use unique serving platters. Use serving platters that are decorative and reflect the image of your restaurant or the sample items on display. Be bold! You want them to attract attention as your server goes from table to table. Be creative and use coordinated colors that blend well together.

Create small portions. Cut all samples into tiny portions. Provide each guest with a small plate or napkin. The idea is to whet appetites and convince guests to try something new.

Provide samplers with a unique uniform or a few different accessories. Make them visually appealing. Complement the restaurant theme or ambiance. For example, if the sampler has a platter full of seafood, then a nifty sailor outfit would be perfect.

Practice the selling script. Before samplers go out on the floor, have them practice their script, how they should approach customers, and the best way to phrase answers to potential questions. Descriptions should be credible and sound natural, not rehearsed. Ensure that your samplers are in the business of show selling—that means that their presentation should be as good as the food itself.

Healthy Food Preparation and Cooking—Without Sacrificing Taste and Flavor!

The way food is prepared is very important to many people. Your restaurant and your staff must adapt to the demands of change. Consider the following:

Cooking methods mean healthier choices. More people are becoming health conscious but at the same time don't want to give up the luxury of great taste! Instead of deep-frying, bake items such as French fries in the oven. Offer steamed vegetables. Use healthier cooking oils and ingredients.

Cut out the fat in beef. Order lean cuts of beef such as top round, tenderloin or sirloin. Have your kitchen staff trim all visible fat before cooking. Use extra lean ground sirloin for casseroles, chili, tacos, spaghetti sauces and skillet dishes. If you have cooked ground beef, throw it in a strainer and rinse it well with hot water. Substitute ground beef with ground turkey. These simple tips can lower the fat intake by as much as 50 percent! Tell your customers what you are doing.

Use nonstick pans. You need to invest in some nonstick pans. If necessary, use cooking sprays that are less fattening and healthier.

Drip the fat away. Place a rack inside the pan when cooking or baking beef. This allows most of the fat to drip away from the meat.

Use stock or broth. Try basting or searing beef with stock or broth instead of oil. Also, create great-tasting sauces for beef roasts by adding stock or broth into the pan juice. Bring it to a quick boil for thickness and then add your seasoning and herbs or a touch of wine.

Substitute oils. Whenever a recipe calls for oil, substitute with a combination of flavored oils, herbs or stock. Fresh garlic, hot and sweet peppers as well as fresh ginger are great for adding flavor without the fat. Create some great unique recipes by experimenting with a variety of combinations.

Use more marinades. To add ethnic flavor, use more marinades, which also tenderize and enhance the flavor of food. You can cook healthily without involving a great deal of extra time and effort. Cater to guests' needs and wants.

Cook with low-fat cheese. Try using low-fat or reduced-fat cheese in some recipes that call for cheese. To enhance flavor, sprinkle fresh-grated Romano or Parmesan cheese. Make sure your guests are not faced with sacrificing taste for a healthier meal.

Reducing fat content. If you must use oil, use it sparingly. Put the oil in a spray bottle and spray just a little on a slice of bread before toasting. Instead of using shortening, use vegetable oil and reduce the amount called for in the recipe by at least a fourth. These are simple steps that you can take for your low-fat menus. For baking, check with the American Diabetes Association, as cutting the fat in baked goods may result in an unusable product.

Lowering cholesterol. If guests are ordering from a low-fat menu, they could also have high-cholesterol problems. Therefore, prepare the food with that in mind. For recipes with eggs, substitute two egg whites for each egg.

Lighter desserts. Serve cake with pudding or fruit topping instead of frosting. Use fruits for moistness rather than glaze. When possible, use vanilla extract as a sweetener instead of sugar.

Chapter 5

Set the Tone— Your Restaurant Interior

A Place to Impress

The way that your restaurant is designed and the layout of your dining room floor can make or break your business. Consider the following type of arrangements when opening a new restaurant or instigating renovations. You may be surprised at the difference a few alterations and additions can make.

Environment does make a difference. Position the doorway entrance directly in front of the pedestrian sidewalk traffic. Most doorways are located perpendicular to a sidewalk, but if you redesign your entrance at an angle, it creates a more welcoming first impression.

Energy-flowing arrangements. Have a curve-based bar design. A bar with a straight design gives the impression of rigidity and inflexibility, while a curve-based design exhibits a feeling of harmony and symmetry. It projects a community atmosphere and builds more welcoming warmth.

Best Restaurant Equipment and Design, www.bestrestaurant.com, 800-837-2378, has a history of designing such restaurants as Applebee's, Bennigan's, T.G.I. Friday's and Ponderosa Steakhouse.

Milton Architects, www.miltonarchitects.com, 713-522-4171, specializes in commercial designs for restaurants and retail buildings.

Coe Construction, Inc., www.coeconstruction.com, 970-663-7336, specializes in new construction and remodeling of restaurants.

Create a More Inviting Ambiance

Have you ever sat in an empty room where you could hear your conversation literally bouncing off the walls? An empty restaurant might persuade your guests that people aren't eating there for a reason. Try enhancing your bare dining area by creating an impression of a cozy, full dining room.

Use moveable room dividers. Install moveable walls or room dividers. This gives you flexibility, with the option to remove the dividers when your restaurant is at full capacity. Create a "smaller" dining room at slower hours of business. Your guests will hardly notice the difference as long as the transition is quietly and smoothly executed.

Visual elements. Introduce visual elements such as plants, trees, mirrors, curtains and other artistic objects. It helps to break up the room into smaller, interesting sections.

Background music. Soft background music can help to eliminate the echo effect of voices, laughter and other noises. Loud music can be just as distracting as the absence of noise. Try adjusting the volume so that it meshes with the background noise without completely drowning out the conversation of those sitting at a table together.

Adjust lighting levels. Ever noticed how many elegant restaurants have dim lighting? This is done for a reason. It not only produces a romantic atmosphere, but it also diverts attention away from empty seats. Adjust the lighting so that the occupied seats are highlighted to attract attention away from the unoccupied seats.

Custom design. Consider having several small dining rooms located off of the main dining room. These rooms could also be used for private dining parties, celebrations or other events. The convenient thing about them is that when the restaurant is half empty, these rooms are easily closed without having to post unfriendly signs that read, "This Section Closed."

Presettings. Always have the table prepared and preset before guests even see their table. It provides a nice welcoming gesture. Have the candles lit, flowers in place, and wine glasses gleaming.

Light a candle for dessert. If you display a dessert tray to guests, place a lit candle in the center of the tray. This provides an elegant glow around the selected desserts and sets the mood.

Attention to Detail

Never underestimate the importance of attention to detail. Let your guests know that you'll go those extra steps to make a special occasion of their dining experience. Try the following suggestions:

Provide purse hooks. Mount small hooks under the bar and the tables for women to hang their purses. Sometimes there isn't a great deal of space for a woman's purse, especially at a bar.

Check for personal items immediately. As soon as your guests leave the table, look in seats and under the table and chairs for possible items that may have been forgotten. You may find a simple toy, a purse or a sweater, but your customers will be very appreciative if you save them a trip before they leave the parking lot.

Install appropriate lighting. Make sure that the blinds are lowered to block out overly bright sunlight or car headlights at night. Try contacting the following companies for decorative lighting effects:

- Complete Restaurant Design and Installation, **www.werkheiserelectric.com**, 610-938-3960.

- Habitat, **www.habitatweb.com**, 303-443-5402, specializes in restaurant and lighting design with nationally licensed architects and interior graphic and lighting designers.

Drowning Out Operation Noises

Are guests at tables near the back being disrupted by loud noises such as banging pans and cookware, cooking, the dishwasher, etc.? In some restaurants, this type of clatter adds to the ambiance, but in most instances, a calmer, more relaxed dining environment is preferable. Try the following:

Background music. Have background music playing to drown out some of the kitchen noise. Make sure that the music is appropriate to the theme of the restaurant.

Plants. Place large plants toward the back of the dining room. Objects can block some of the noise.

Door shields. If the sound continues to be overbearing, consider replacing your current doors with a thicker substance to block out some of the noise. Or consider placing inexpensive carpet over the doors and possibly walls. Check with your fire code enforcement office first, however; you may have to treat the material with a fire-retardant substance.

Keep Temperatures Comfortable

A combination of a hot kitchen and a room full of warm bodies within the same building calls for careful temperature control. Keep in mind the following basics:

Thermostat control. As the temperature in a restaurant tends to be a bit warmer than the average building, keep the thermostat between 67°–69°F. Adjust the temperature accordingly, until it feels right.

Summer-time adjustments. In the summer when the temperature outside is hotter, you might need to lower the thermostat to 65°F to keep the air-conditioning pumping at the right level.

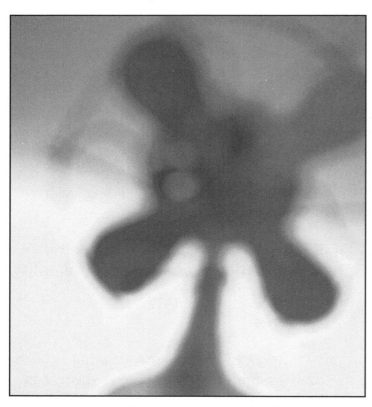

A combination of a hot kitchen and a room full of warm bodies calls for careful temperature control.

Invest in the best. If you can afford it, the best temperature-control systems have a dual operating function where you can adjust the temperature settings as needed for each area of the restaurant. You can contact any heating and cooling company from your local telephone directory and order a programmable thermostat. These new systems are known for being easy to install.

Programmable thermostats. Install programmable thermostats that will automatically adjust the temperature, including the heating and air-conditioning systems. Also, consider installing separate controls so that unused areas can be adjusted as needed. This will not only save on your utility bill, but also make your employees and guests feel more comfortable. Two nationwide heating and cooling companies that service restaurants are Comfort Systems USA, **www.comfortsystemsusa.com**, 800-723-8431; and Sunray Heating Inc., **www.sunrayheating.com**, 800-734-4600.

Inviting Furniture

Take an objective look at your restaurant furniture. How comfortable and inviting does it look to customers? You want guests to linger, so give them a reason to do so—in comfort. Consider the following:

Hard chairs. If you have hardback wooden chairs, consider adding color-coordinated cushions to the seat and back. This will not only add color and decoration to your dining room, but it will also give the room a cozier look.

Basic ergonomics. Ensure that the seat height is appropriate to the table height. While this may vary according to the individual size of each person, try to go with the size of the average male.

A few places where you can order restaurant furniture include:

- American Chair and Seating, **www.chair.com**, 800-FURNITURE

- AMI, Inc., **www.arionmfg.com**, 800-942-7466

- Barstools-Inc., **www.barstools-inc.com**, 706-235-1670

- Delta Furniture, **www.deltafurniture.com**, 514-329-1889

- Iron Furniture, **www.ironfurniture.com**, 800-738-4894

- Wood Seating Inc. **www.restaurant-chairs-manufacturers.com**, 718-755-6216

Table wobbling? Nothing is worse than sitting at a wobbly table; it is hard to eat, distracting to talk, and beverages get spilled. There are two solutions: wobble wedges and super levels. Wobble wedges are small, clear, angled leveling devices that basically take the place of all those sugar packets you see on the floor. Super levels screw into and replace the existing table feet. Both systems work great and are available at **www.atlantic-pub.com**, 800-814-1132, wobble wedges Item # WW-01; and super levels Item # SL-12.

A welcoming host desk. Keep it as subtle as possible. An oversized host desk can appear somewhat intimidating. Whether remodeling or making your first selection, keep it simple. Try Tableworks, Inc., **www.tableworksinc.com**, 800-214-7745.

Buying Carpet

Don't buy the most expensive carpet, as it will receive a lot of abuse and traffic. What good is a durable carpet four years down the road if you can't remove the stains? The reality is you'll be replacing carpet in a few years, whether or not you want to. Here are a few tips when purchasing carpet for your restaurant:

Solution-dyed carpet. Be sure to buy solution-dyed carpet. This type of carpet is ideally suited to a restaurant environment.

Short pile. Don't purchase thick carpet that can harbor more dirt, dust and grime. Buy the thinner carpet that is easier to clean and vacuum on a regular basis.

The following companies provide carpeting:

- Antron, **www.dupont.com**, 800-4DUPONT

- Carpet Fair Commercial Division, **www.carpetfaircd.com**, 800-296-3247

- Carpet One, **www.allfloors.com**, 305-234-3000

- Carpet Solutions, Inc., **www.millijack.com**, 941-574-5394

Nationwide carpet cleaning and restoration companies include:

- ChemDry, **www.chemdry.com**, 800-243-6379

- Milliken and Company, **www.milliken.com**, 800-257-3987

- Rainbow International, **www.rainbowintl.com**, 800-583-9100

- ServPro, **www.servpro.com**, 800-SERVPRO

Other Environmental Considerations

Once you've taken a fresh look at your interior from the customer's point of view, turn your attention to the finer details. It can make a world of difference to the overall effect. Don't forget the following:

Fresh flowers and plants. Have fresh flowers and plants in the lobby area and in the dining room. If flowers and petals start to droop, remove them. Being around a dying plant can be depressing. Using artificial plants might be an even better idea.

Keep roaches away. When building or remodeling your restaurant, roach-proof your walls or put boric acid into the walls while they are open. This prevents cockroaches and saves on your exterminator bill in the long run. Where there is food, there are bugs. Contact the National Pest Management Association to find a reputable pest-control company in your area. Their Web site is **www.pestworld .org**, or call their main office at 703-573-8330.

Get rid of flying pests. A cheap, economical and safe way to get rid of flying pests is to put red cider vinegar into a cup and mix it with a little detergent. It attracts the pesky little flies and they die. Plus, you don't have to spray your kitchen or restaurant with foul-smelling bug spray.

Sheetrock in moisture areas. Install sheetrock in the kitchen and bathroom areas where water and moisture are most prevalent. All sheetrock should be at least 1/2-inch thick or more, off the floor. This prevents the moisture from soaking into the bottom of the sheetrock and ruining the wall. Apply a 6-inch concrete board along the border where the floor and wall meet. This is the best method of preventing possible water damage to sheetrock walls.

Cleanliness, Tidiness and Comfort—A Few Basics You Can't Ignore

When it comes to cleanliness and tidiness, standards must never, never slip. There's nothing like cleanliness and tidiness for creating a welcoming atmosphere and a good impression. But, on a more practical note, it only takes one less-than-impressed customer to shatter your fine reputation! Consider the following basic but important issues:

Stick to a strict routine.

Clean spills immediately. Avoid the possibility of slips and falls!

Place chairs at empty tables where they belong—under the table. Keep aisles clear.

Clear and clean all tables as soon as customers have vacated them. This applies even if no one is currently waiting for a table.

Create an impression of orderliness. Ensure that wrapped silverware and table fixtures are in place.

Aromas and odors. Keep trash away from the dining area.

Spills on carpets. Avoid the possibility of lingering ugly odors. Clean and shampoo any spills immediately, before the stain and smell become too difficult to remove.

Scented candles. Try making the atmosphere more pleasant by burning scented candles at each table. Make sure, however, you choose a scent that won't overpower or conflict with the customers' food. Another option you could try is to use the Smelleze Restaurant/Bar Deodorizer pouch. Order it from **www.no-odor .com**. It cleanses the air by absorbing and neutralizing unpleasant odors and works in an area of up to 400 square feet.

Ventilation. Install a ventilation system that is powerful enough to cope with the demands of your restaurant. Don't forget that the aroma of a grilled steak can make a customer's mouth water, but the smell of a burnt steak can have the opposite affect!

Provide a cleaning checklist. Create a cleaning checklist for each shift. Include the date, time and specific personnel and their duties. Some people know they should do certain duties, but they won't put the extra effort in without you spelling it out for them. Make sure each individual knows the tasks they are to perform and the standards required of them.

Clean, Presentable Restrooms

Don't become so obsessed with the dining room area that you forget the restrooms. Nothing is worse than walking into a foul-smelling bathroom with toilet paper and paper towels everywhere! Apart from the obvious, insist on the following:

Assign the bathrooms to two employees every shift. Stick to a strict rotation from one employee to the next. Ensure that the toilets are clean and wiped down properly, during and after every shift.

Clean up splashed water on the sink counters and from the floor. Wipe off soap drippings. Again, this procedure should be performed during and after every shift.

Keep a can of air freshener for customers in each stall. Place some potpourri and/or scented candles on the counters.

Clean the mirrors as needed.

Never, ever run out. Ensure a proper supply of toilet paper, soap and paper towels.

The Twisted Chicken is a small restaurant in McGregor, Iowa, that has gotten consistently positive reviews from customers and critics. Owner Kim Hayes discusses some of the reasons she's been successful.

We have no menu in print, save the one we do nightly. Since we are so small, we have very little storage, so it's in and out with the food weekly. That also makes it fresh and always in season. Not having a menu to be tied to is a fortune-saver for us.

One mistake I made at my coffee bar early on was that I purchased top-end chocolate and caramel to go into the mochas—Guittard chocolate flown in from Seattle. I now know that Hershey's chocolate in a mocha works just fine, as does a lesser caramel.

One small suggestion I have regarding controlling costs is not to allow waitstaff to blot up spills with bar and lunch napkins. It's usually the first thing they reach for. Use bar towels instead, as they are laundered.

Finally, my advice on keeping employees happy and productive is to laugh with them and treat them with respect, yet also make sure they reciprocate with respect as you must also be an authority figure. Create projects for them to keep them productive, since they would really rather be busy than standing around. Phrase things as if they were the customer and they will gladly do as you ask; for example: "All customers deserve a clean chair and table, don't you agree? If you were a customer, wouldn't you like to sit at a clean table and on a clean chair?" They can only say yes!

Chapter 6

Find Your Niche— Set Yourself Apart!

Food and Entertainment

People usually dine out for more than just the food. Reward guests for choosing you rather than your competitors. Give them a reason for wanting to come back. That means you need to exceed their expectations. Here's how it's done:

Help guests' party. When a group is dining out to celebrate a birthday or an anniversary, get the staff together and sing "Happy Birthday" to them. Offer a free complimentary dessert for the birthday person or couple having the anniversary. For an anniversary, you could have someone from the restaurant, maybe a manager or yourself, dedicate a toast to their long years of marriage and many more years of happiness to come.

Take pictures. If you notice a guest with a camera, offer to take pictures for them. That way everyone there can be in the photo. Be sure to find out exactly how to operate the camera. Most likely, they will appreciate the extra effort you have taken to help them preserve a special memory.

Keep cameras on hand. Keep a Polaroid camera at each station to help guests preserve those special memories. Old friends are always getting together and dining out—and often they forget to bring a camera along. Imagine their surprise when you pull out your Polaroid. Or, invest in a digital camera and offer to e-mail patrons their photos. This is a great opportunity to collect addresses for later e-mail promotions!

Expand Your Services

One of the best ways to attract customers, new and old, is to expand your range of current services. You can do this by offering new menu items as well as more of a selection of the types of menu items already offered. Here are a few ideas:

More alcohol-free alternatives. Offer more than simple coffee with sugar and cream. Invest in an espresso machine and offer customers a wide selection of high-quality beans. Grind the beans freshly each time.

Tea can be more than just tea. Offer decaf, herbal and hot tea as well as iced tea. Provide both unsweetened and sweetened tea.

Different juice options. Have a variety of juices to choose from so that you can increase sales from those customers that would normally opt for water as opposed to sodas, coffee, tea or wine beverages. Many parents don't want their children drinking sodas and tea.

Vegetarian meals. More and more people are turning away from meat. Ensure that you grasp this segment of the market by offering a good selection of meat-free meals.

Banquet and private parties. If you have the space available, begin by catering wedding banquets on Saturdays between the hours of 10 a.m. and 4 p.m. You'll be exchanging a Saturday of uncertain business at various rates for a Saturday of guaranteed business at a fixed price and menu.

Menus in Braille. Have a few menus translated and produced in Braille. This is a simple service that most restaurants don't think about. Impress your customers by being equipped for everyone who visits your restaurant. See **www .quikscrybe.com** or **www.access2020.com**.

Bilingual menu. Go the extra mile and have a few menus translated and produced in other languages. Start by translating the most common spoken non-English language in your geographic region.

Handling Customer Complaints

Despite all our efforts to the contrary, things do sometimes go wrong. We have to handle it as best as we can. If you are realistic enough to acknowledge this fact, then you have the ability to be one step ahead of your competitors—simply by being prepared. There are, however, certain "damage limitation" measures that you can take to preserve your untarnished reputation.

Don't keep a customer waiting. The instant you hear a customer complaining, drop what you're doing. Go immediately to the customer who is making the complaint. Don't keep an already agitated individual waiting a moment longer than is necessary. They want their issue resolved—now! Your goal is to keep matters from escalating and getting out of hand.

Stay calm and objective. Approach the customer with a warm smile and a genuine openness. Politely ask them to explain the issue and listen to them as intently as possible. Don't try to argue with them or to explain the other person's viewpoint. When a customer is already angry and upset, they don't care. Likewise, they care less about your policies and procedures. If they want something that goes against your regular policy, say something like, "Normally that isn't our policy, but I will make an exception." That may be all they want to hear.

Apologize no matter what. Even if you believe the customer is being irate and ridiculous, apologize. It doesn't matter who is really wrong. At this point, it is your job to make this customer happy, once again. You've got to appease them. Tell them you're sorry, because that is what they want to hear. Then ask them how they would prefer you to resolve the problem. Simply ask them what they want you do to, but be sure to phrase the question in a way that won't sound condescending or sarcastic. For instance, don't say, "Well, what would you have me do?" Instead, say something like, "I'm really sorry. How best could I make it up to you?"

Take immediate action. If possible, immediately remove whoever or whatever caused the problem. Exceed their expectations by not only fixing the problem, but also offering them something more. Don't stop until they seem satisfied and overwhelmed by your efforts.

Thank them for bringing the issue to your attention. Let them know that it helps you to be more efficient when you are aware of issues that need attention. After they leave your restaurant, be sure to follow up with a personal phone call or a handwritten note the next day.

Turn Negatives into Positives

There will always be situations that happen beyond your control, but they don't have to turn into disasters. Turn a negative issue into a positive alternative. Here's how:

Suggest other options. When items sell out, offer other alternatives to your guests so they aren't sitting there wondering what to choose next.

Smile, accidents happen. When spills and messy accidents happen, smile and clean it up as quickly as possible. Show more concern for the customer experiencing the embarrassment than the mess. Reassure them that it's okay and that it isn't a problem. Offer to replace drink and food if necessary.

Resolve problems quickly. If a guest expresses any kind of displeasure, immediately focus on how to make them happy again.

Open lines of communication. Establish a toll-free number for customers to call and leave feedback. This allows customers to make a formal complaint to someone other than the person that they perceive to have caused the problem.

Freebies for waiting. When guests have to wait to be seated, offer them something to entice them to stay. Offer them a free beverage, peanuts, bread sticks or something else that's simple and easy to serve.

Guests who arrive at closing. Politely inform them that the restaurant is closing, but you will do everything in your power to see that they have an enjoyable meal. Serve them promptly, but not in obvious haste. Concentrate on the closing tasks you can do without interrupting your late guests; ignore the ones you cannot do while they're still there. In other words, don't dim the lights on them, cut off the background music, vacuum, or stack up empty chairs around them. Remember, closing time is when you stop seating guests, it is not the time you actually stop serving guests.

Offer a Fast Lunch

A fast lunch is one of the best ways to maximize profits.

Guarantee a fast lunch in fifteen minutes—or it's free.

Stopwatches. Buy cheap stopwatches at a local discount store. Place them at each table. Prove that you mean what you say! Have the waiter or waitress set the timer as soon as orders are taken.

Be selective. Make sure you limit the program to certain menu items that can be prepared in the time frame you've set.

Restrict offers to small parties under a specific number of individuals.

Provisos about add-ons. For example, make it quite clear that you may need to adjust the time when appetizers are ordered.

Make sure that you have extra staff to cover lunch hours. Lunch hours are critical, as employees must get back to work by a certain time. But remember, if you do it well, your program will definitely gain attention and increase your lunch sales enough to offset a few free lunches.

Provide "Add-Ons" and Specialty Items

Add-on options, where a customer might receive an additional side item for a small additional price, greatly increase your overall sales volume. Branded items, likewise, offer great opportunities for maximizing profits. Bear in mind the following:

Promote add-ons. Encourage servers to offer them to customers when they are placing their orders. For example, some dishes are served with a side salad or bread sticks, but others are not. Offer a side salad for $1.99 extra when a customer is ordering a dish that has no additional side orders with it. If you sell a total of 100 side salads a day, that's an additional gross sale of $199 or

$72,635 per year.

Develop a signature item. Choosing a signature item from your menu takes planning and preparation.

Brand your menu items. Promoting brand-named ingredients in items can increase your profits by as much as 20 percent! Often a brand name is synonymous with quality. Doesn't "a layer of Grey Poupon™ Dijon Mustard" sound much more enticing than simply stating "a layer of mustard"?

Provide feature items every day. It keeps your regulars from getting bored with your menu, while keeping you and your staff innovative and constantly creating new and exciting meals. It also gives you a chance to promote low-cost menu items and increase sales of those particular items.

Create a signature dessert. Every dessert menu needs a signature dessert. The idea is to have people craving one of your desserts just at the thought of it. Display the unique aspects of each dessert item through photos or on a dessert tray that you display right at the table. It's hard for people to ignore dessert if it's right in front of them.

Create signature icons. Place a miniature "icon" beside the signature item you want to promote on your menu. This is an immediate indication to your guests that this item is special and receives extra attention in preparation, as your establishment takes pride in its success and popularity.

Provide Consistently Excellent Service

It's no secret that if a guest returns twice in a month as opposed to their once-a-month visit, then you've just doubled your sales. This is the best way to increase sales. All you have to do is provide consistent excellent service in every facet of your restaurant. Customers need to know that they can rely on your service. Review all aspects of your restaurant, from external appearance to employee attentiveness to the quality of the food you serve to your guests. Take an overview:

Consistency is the key. Ensure that standards of service never slip. If customers visit one day and everything is perfect, but the next visit provides a disastrous experience, your credibility is undermined.

Be flexible. While it is necessary to have a measure of control, you also need to be flexible. Changes are always taking place in the food and beverage business and organizational goals continue to evolve. As new technology develops, new ways of doing things will affect how procedures are used in your restaurant. Adapt to these changes without interrupting the quality of the flow and service to the guests.

Bernie Bellin owns **RED CUMMMBERBUND CATERING**, *a private catering business based in Franklin, Wisconsin. An acknowledged expert on the use of edible flowers, he has been involved with food service for more than 20 years. Here are his top 10 tips for a successful food service operation.*

1 Be flexible in menu planning. This allows you to take advantage of seasonally reduced items. Everything has a season, and food purchased in season will almost always cost less.

2 Use the seasonal items you buy in a variety of ways—vegetables can be the entrée, soup, or in some cases, even dessert. Don't be stuck looking at a tomato and only think of a salad.

3 It can pay to be aware of seasons in different parts of the world. Our food comes from numerous countries and is reasonable at different times of the years in different continents.

4 Prep food yourself when the cost savings justifies the time or you know that you will have staff to be kept occupied.

5 When staff are not prepping food, make sure they are cleaning work surfaces again and again—including edges where food may "hang." Don't forget to wipe down appliances often and counters all the time.

6 Take a good, long look at your food prep space and location. Set it up so there is the least handling/carrying of items from raw to cooked. Moving things around causes wet floors, increases chances of dropping containers, and consumes valuable time.

7 Plan each process step by step, and don't be hesitant to re-think it from time to time. Take a few minutes to watch your staff and how they work with your planning process. Ask them if it is working or if are they moving things around too often and having to revisit a process with the same food item.

8 As much as is possible, try to use every food item before it spoils. Be creative. Add as a garnish, an extra item, or use in stock. All are a little more work, but when it spoils, it is totally wasted.

9 Point out to your staff, again and again, safety and health tips. Add a funny story to the instruction. Washing of hands is so crucial, yet many staff will look at it as a waste of time and want to just wipe them off on a towel or apron.

10 Remember: People eat with their eyes and nose before their mouth. Create something they will want to try.

Chapter 7

Marketing for Profitability

The Real Value of Marketing— Spend Your Money Where It Counts!

Marketing isn't a one-time campaign to get your business up and running. What many companies fail to realize is that marketing is an on-going process.

Forward planning. As soon as one marketing expedition is over, have a plan and a strategy in place for the next marketing venture. It's the surest way of gaining new customers.

Use your marketing budget to target areas in the same vicinity as your restaurant. People are more likely to drive 3–5 miles to a convenient, familiar area to try a new restaurant than 8–10 miles out of their way to an unfamiliar environment.

Take advantage of cross-promotion. Often you can team up with retailers, entertainment companies, clubs and organizations to promote an event or a special offer that may directly or indirectly promote your restaurant. For instance, you could offer all skaters at a local skating rink a free dessert during a particular weekend.

Promote through community events. Community events such as fundraisers, parades, carnivals and festivals provide excellent opportunities to promote your restaurant. Become involved and participate where possible. You'll be surprised at how well such simple techniques like these can enhance your business and name recognition.

Be a community role model. Whenever disaster strikes in your neighborhood, be available to assist in whatever way possible: food, ice, fresh water. People will remember that more than any whole-page ad you could take out in a local newspaper.

Develop a Unique Selling Position

Every business needs a unique selling position. Sell the part of your business that is different from everyone else's. It can be the fact that you have exceptional desserts, an outstanding signature item, are the only seafood restaurant on your side of town, or offer free appetizers. Choose the points you want to sell and use them as a slogan with your logo. Also, try the following suggestions:

Use "niche" marketing tactics. Decide on a factor or aspect of your business that is better than all the rest. Promote that idea at every opportunity that you get. It could be that you are known for the best Southern food or that you're the only family entertainment restaurant with fun and activities for the whole family. Other ideas are that you could provide the best "home-style" meals in your region or become the health spot for people wanting a broad selection without sacrificing good taste.

Initiate "four-walls" marketing. Begin your marketing campaign by marketing your business right inside the walls of your restaurant. Set up easel posters, suggestion boxes and decals in the lobby area. Include noticeable register toppers and brochures at the checkout counter. Hang posters of signature drinks in the bar area. The dining room is your best marketing area, as customers spend most of their time here. Post special boards and provide tabletop displays and specialty menus such as water, beer, desserts and, of course, a wine list.

Build a Web Site

Today, every restaurant needs a Web site. You want them to find you, not your competitors. The following tips offer a few important "musts" when creating a

Web site:

Photos. Upload mouth-watering pictures of your signature items and other great-tasting dishes.

Be sure to have a contact page with your phone number and e-mail address. Provide a map with directions on how to find your restaurant. Provide a link where customers can type in their address and receive printed directions to your establishment.

Gizmo Graphics Web Design, **www.gizwebs.com**. A professional Web design company utilizing the latest technology, Gizmo Graphics offers low-cost, high-quality Web design services catering to the food service industry.

Monitor your Web site traffic. Monitor your Web site traffic through such services as **www.sitemeter.com**. This way you can tell from where the majority of your traffic is coming, whether by search engines or through other links and affiliates. Most importantly, you'll know which affiliate links are worth paying for and which ones aren't.

Online reservations. There are many Web-based services available such as **www.open-table.com**, a computerized reservation and guest-management system. Designed with input from hundreds of restaurants, Open Table is a complete solution. All hardware is provided, including a sturdy touch-screen monitor placed at your host stand. Also check out **www.iseatz.com** and **www .dinnerbroker.com.**

Sample Restaurant Web Sites

At right is an example of a successful and well-designed restaurant Web site, **www.anthemboston .com**. The site features online reservations, a photo tour, a downloadable menu and chef's biography. Anthem is located in Boston at 138 Portland Street and is well-known for its American cuisine.

Another good example is **www.wildfirerestaurant .com**. Wildfire transports you to the aura of a 1940s dinner club. From the décor to the jazz music, Wildfire has style, warmth and atmosphere that is carried through the Web site with use of colors, photos and music.

Other Online Marketing Opportunities

Build on the power of your Web site. Create an interactive Web site where you can communicate with your customers and they can communicate with you. Allow them to e-mail questions and you post the answers. Post a recipe of the day. Create trivia questions and offer rewards and surprises. Encourage your visitors to participate.

Affiliate links. Try to establish affiliate links to other operations similar to yours, as well as your vendors and local cinema and entertainment sites. Also consider linking with other food service organizations, nutrition sites and food and beverage-related industry businesses. Join other online restaurant communities and post your expert advice. People will appreciate your help, as well as come to know your name and your restaurant. It's free self-promotion and an excellent avenue by which to spread the word about your business.

A few online restaurant communities you could check out include:

- **www.atlantic-pub.com**

- **www.chefnet.com**

- **www.food.com**

- **www.nmrestaurants.com**

- **www.webfoodpros.com**

Create an online community. Invite your chef to participate in sharing his or her culinary expertise. Provide a forum where other restaurant businesspeople can discuss the industry, post questions, and exchange advice.

Create an online newsletter. It's hard to find a Web site that doesn't have its own newsletter. Increase your reputation and awareness of your own business. The best part is it costs nothing to send 10 or 10,000,000 e-mail newsletters. Include quality and interesting content but, of course, promote the restaurant. For example, you could produce a newsletter on the new arrival of the Beaujolais Villages wines from France, its history, etc., and promote the "Beaujolais Villages Night on Wednesday" at your restaurant.

Send online press releases. Share culinary news-breaking information with the rest of the world. Send a press release through online services as opposed to the traditional methods of postal mail. This way you have a better chance of reaching more people at a significantly lower cost.

Traditional Marketing Techniques

In your search for innovative advertising methods, don't overlook the more traditional approach. It is, after all, "tried and tested" in the restaurant promotion market. Consider the following techniques:

Billboards. If you are located just off of a major highway, you will definitely want to consider investing in a billboard sign along the highway. This will attract the traveling public passing by.

Use radio broadcast advertising. Radio advertising has several advantages: It costs less to reach a higher percentage of potential guests over newspaper advertising. The lower costs allow for more frequent broadcasts. Radio is also one of the most effective media at instantly getting people to recognize and maintain a slogan message.

Newspaper advertising. When choosing a newspaper in which to advertise, you must consider the circulation size, locality, ad size and rates.

Advertise at movie theaters. Most cinemas now feature revolving screen adver-tisements before the actual movie previews begin. These are great for local adver-tisements, as they're shown several times in rotation.

TV advertising. Don't forget about special TV advertising. Select a local cable TV station or advertise on an appropriate cooking channel.

Other Innovative Marketing Techniques

Apart from the tried-and-tested marketing techniques, you may wish to branch out and try the following:

Donate edible leftovers. Restaurants often have edible leftover food at the end of each day. Several food banks in your local area could pick up the food and transport it to where it's needed the most.

Outdoor display. Invest in an eye-catching outdoor display. Locate it above your restaurant for maximum impact. Place a classic car, airplane, inflatable giant monster or hot air balloon.

Include surprises in carry-out orders. For every carry-out order, include a surprise gift such as a piece of candy, a thank-you note, a discount coupon, or some other nice goodie. People will appreciate the thoughtfulness.

Write free articles. Consider writing free articles for restaurant and food industry-related e-zines and printed magazines. Many of the editors would love to receive an article from someone with experience in the field. Often the editor will include a short bio about the author at the end of the article.

Offer a bed-and-breakfast combo. While you may not be a bed and breakfast, if there is a hotel near you, try to team up together. Whenever they have special conferences that might bring in a thousand or more guests, offer some free breakfast incentives to the hotel's conference-goers. In addition, you can promote an affiliate program with hotels in your area. The idea is that you provide something for them in return for them distributing your brochures, providing a slot for your restaurant in their informational channel, etc.

Press kits. Put together a press kit containing sales letters, brochures, a menu sample, news clippings, business cards, etc. Send it to your local chamber of commerce.

Share your knowledge. Share your knowledge with others and earn respect and recognition for your business. Achieve this through part-time classes at a local college, trade school or cooking classes in the restaurant.

Get to Know Your Customers

Spend a couple of weeks gathering information from customers at each meal. Try to choose a time that doesn't involve a holiday or a local community event that might bring in a lot of non-locals. Try the following tips:

Use a guest book. Ask your patrons to fill out a guest book. Collect such information as birth dates and anniversaries. Have an employee transfer the information into a computer database system to use as a mailing list to send promotional material to customers.

Use note cards. Keep small note cards on regular guests so that everyone in the restaurant is familiar with their likes and dislikes, table preferences, and any other pertinent information that will enable you to treat them like royalty. Try rewarding your staff for increasing the note card collection and for reaching a specific number each month.

Create club memberships. Extend extra privileges and restaurant paraphernalia that is exclusive to members. For example, introduce unique items such as mugs or glasses. Make them different in either color or design. Engrave customer names on them. Or, maybe, provide free T-shirts, hats or other items that they can wear and advertise your restaurant. Consider offering these items based on how many specific items they might have ordered over a period of time, such as oysters, barbecue ribs or some other specialty item.

Follow-up contact. Thank customers for choosing your restaurant. A personal handwritten postcard makes an even better impression.

Fax a thank-you note. After a large business group dines at your restaurant, send them a thank-you fax at the office. Tell them you enjoyed serving them and hope to see them again soon.

Send celebration cards. Once you've acquired a list of personal information, you're in a position to send customers anniversary and birthday cards.

Actions That Grab Attention

There are several small actions you can take that will grab the attention of potential guests passing by your restaurant. Don't ignore simple free marketing techniques that have worked for decades. Here are some tips:

Use window displays. A sign in the window works well, but a moving object in the window is so much more effective. For instance, The Rainforest Café is built and decorated around a nature theme/amusement park design. How about a dancing gorilla in the window?

Use chimes. Signs have to be seen to be recognized. Use chimes at the entrance of your building. They sing to customers who aren't paying attention in a way that signs do not.

Use large, distinctive glassware. For special drinks use large, distinctive glassware. Make guests turn their heads and take notice as your staff passes by carrying those unique beverages.

Menu highlighting. Simple, but effective. Use boldface, italic or a different color. You could also use callout words such as "special," "new," "traditional" or "tasty" beside the item.

SECTION II

Controlling Operating Costs:
Strategies and Tips

SECTION II

Table of Contents

Chapter 8
The Bottom Line 95

Chapter 9
Look at Your Restaurant Objectively 103

Chapter 10
Trimming Operational Costs 107

Chapter 11
Reducing Maintenance and Repair Costs 127

Chapter 12
Security and Theft Prevention 137

Chapter 13
Breakage, Spoilage and Storage 149

Introduction

Controlling Operating Costs: Strategies and Tips

Controlling the operating costs of a restaurant is a constant management task. Indeed, it sometimes takes a little lateral thinking to understand that cost savings can be accomplished in a variety of places and in a variety of ways—some of which may be less than obvious!

Thankfully, improvements in technology and management techniques allow smart restaurant operators to keep operating costs within the boundaries needed to generate a profit while still providing their customers with the level of service that they need to generate repeat business. The food service industry is in a state of constant change, particularly due to the nature of pricing fluctuations and rising labor costs. A restaurant manager must be prepared to develop and monitor costs in all controllable areas to maintain profitability.

Some costs you just cannot change. These are the fixed or semi-fixed operating costs, which include such items as union agreements;

minimum wage rates; tax rates; rent; permits; and fees, such as franchise fees; licensing fees; etc.; insurance; and real estate taxes. Fortunately, many costs can be reduced considerably, without reducing quality or efficiency. Some of the controllable and flexible operating costs include purchasing, receiving, storing, food handling, outside services, food preparation, repair and maintenance, advertising, cooking, merchandising, serving methods, staff training, food and beverage cost controls, accounting and legal services, staff productivity, cash handling, housekeeping, and sanitation.

As a restaurant operator, you will often find that your bottom line is manipulated by outside circumstances, including competition, weather, quality of your services, food selection, local conventions and events, promotions, discounts, pricing, and more. Armed with the information in this book, you will find actual tips that produce profitable results, without consuming all of your time in unnecessary research or experiencing painful trial, risk and error.

Chapter 8

The Bottom Line

Basic Cost-Control Skills

The first skill you need when running a restaurant does not involve whipping up a hollandaise sauce or steaming broccoli. The first skill you need is to have a grip on accounting and cost control. When you understand the financial side of the food service business, you can then make small tweaks on an almost-daily basis to increase your bottom line. Neglect to pay attention to the numbers and you may not even realize how much money you are losing. The decision to succeed in the food service industry will require serious planning, structured thought and hard work.

Establish your control systems by using the following straightforward steps:

Overview. Define your business goals and objectives.

Business plan. If you haven't already done so, develop a business plan that spells out, in detail, how your goals and objectives are to be achieved.

Organizational plan. Develop an organizational structure that can achieve the desired objectives and goals.

Put it in writing. Set up policies and procedures to be followed by the staff.

Hire and train management and operating personnel.

Implement the plan. Make regular corrections and adjustments to meet goals.

Operational controls. A restaurant needs to exercise control in a number of operating areas. Budgetary control is used to help achieve these objectives. The main operational areas include:

- The quality of food and beverages.

- Employee costs and performance.

- The control of equipment, utilities and other physical assets.

- Control over sales and cash.

- Operating expenses.

Developing a Food Service Operational Budget—The Basics

Put financial control implements into action by first making a budget. QuickBooks and other software programs can assist you with this. The great advantage of using one of these software programs is you can easily compare your budget to your actual figures any time you like in a matter of seconds. Here are the basics:

Gather the essential information. Management needs to collect the following types of information:

- Actual operating statements and budget figures from the previous year.

- The restaurant's financial goals.

- Sales statistics broken down for each category from the past.

- Any change in restaurant operating policies; for example, eliminating lunch service or adding a catering service.

- Regional, local and national economic conditions.

- Sales and expense trends in all categories.

- Menu prices, customer preference, portion size and food costs.

- Payroll information.

Follow these basic steps to prepare a budget:

Estimate sales revenue. This is often the most difficult part of the budget due to its volatility.

Estimate expenses that are related to sales such as food, liquor, wine and operating supplies.

Use industry resources and your sales history to help you come up with an operating budget. You can find restaurant business information and publications that give guidance with setting up budgets at the National Restaurant Association's Web site at **www.restaurant.org**.

Key Operating Budget Costs

Your operating budget will reflect your priorities in terms of how you spend your money, the expenses you will incur, and how you will meet those expenses (income).

If you're a start-up operation, your operating budget should also include money to cover the first three to six months of operation. It should allow for the following expenses:

- Personnel

- Food costs

- Liquor costs

- Operating expenses

- Insurance

- Rent

- Depreciation

- Loan payments

- Advertising/Promotions

- Legal/Accounting

- Supplies

- Payroll expenses

- Salaries/Wages

- Utilities

- Dues/Subscriptions/Fees

- Taxes

- Repairs/Maintenance

- Miscellaneous expenses

Sales Reports and Forecasting

A simple tool to assist you in the budgeting process is a Sales History Form. Financial statements are great, but this will help you remember specifics from a year ago. Use sales and expense forecasting and market research to track how many customers you are currently serving, what they eat, and how often they visit your restaurant. Compare this information with how many customers you want to be serving, what they want to eat, and how often they might return. Basically, a sales history tells you what you have done in sales in the past and helps you forecast what to expect in the future. This form should record customer counts, daily sales and daily costs. Remember, the more information you track, the more information you have at your disposal to help with cost-cutting decision making. See *Chapter 2 – Profit Planning and Cost Control* for additional tools and tips to help with reports and forecasting.

Cash Flow—The Essentials

Consultants who specialize in restaurant businesses say that owners/managers don't pay enough attention to cash flow, which, in simple terms, is the measure of how much money you really have in the business. You'll need to familiarize yourself with the following basics:

Statement of cash flows. This most important report tells you if your business is on or off target. Use your own computer program to generate this report or get your accountant to run a report. A statement of cash flows starts with the bottom of your profit and loss statement—the line that shows your net income. Several adjustments are then made to that number, including reducing the income by invoices recorded as income that have not yet been paid, adding back depreciation, adjusting for bills that your business has not paid, and several other adjustments.

Funds. Your organization can accomplish very little without adequate funds. Ensure your cash reserves are adequate to cover slow months, make emergency repairs and improvements, and implement marketing projects.

Set realistic targets and goals for growth for your business. For example, aim to acquire 100 new repeat customers every month. Lower operating expenses next month by 2 percent. By letting your staff know that they can do their part, you will be able to meet your goals and build your business accordingly.

Renting and Leasing

The following tips can make a big difference in reducing your restaurant operating costs.

Plan early for lease re-negotiations. At least a year before your lease expires, evaluate and analyze other rental options and costs. This will leave you about six months to negotiate with the owner.

Consider taking on a longer lease. Request a break in the monthly lease payments and ask for an annual inflator clause in return for signing a longer lease. Also request a few more months of free rent than you need when renewing your lease since this is often the easiest negotiating point for landlords to offer as an incentive.

Place caps on escalator clauses. Make sure that your rent doesn't rise dramatically if inflation increases. Since operating-expense clauses are broadly defined, they tend to favor the landlord.

Place a maximum cap on your share of yearly operating costs increases. This is called common area management (CAM) in shopping centers. If your share of operating costs seems excessive, use a "lease auditor" to analyze the terms. They should determine if all the operating costs being charged back to you are allowable under the terms of the lease. Check the Yellow Pages to locate a lease auditor in your city. Try to get options to renew your lease and lock in low rates for several years.

Space. Verify the accuracy of the square footage specified as the "rentable space" upon which your payments are calculated. Measure your space carefully and compare it with the square footage stated in your lease.

Try using a third party to do the preliminary negotiations.

Research the lease terms of other tenants in the building. Find out what concessions they are receiving and about their plans for moving.

Question the Common Area Management. Compare your CAM charges with national averages that are available from the Urban Land Institute at 1025 Thomas Jefferson St. NW, Suite 500 West, Washington, D.C. 20007, 800-321-5011; **www.uli.org** or **www.icsc.org**. Insert an amendment giving you the right to include audit costs in the CAM. Look for clauses that say "CAM charges include but are not limited to." Detail CAM expenses that are excluded such as structural repairs or depreciation.

Watch for commonly used landlord clauses. Examples include:

- Requiring a tenant to pay for unlimited future increases in operating expenses.

- Obligating you to pay for costs of other tenants who ring up high utility charges.

- Allowing eviction if you do not maintain a certain sales volume.

- Making you comply with new mall operating hours that would be unprofitable.

- Requiring you to pay for capital expenditures that may be referred to as "reserves and replacements."

Analyze the details in your lease billing. Pinpoint miscalculations, wrong rates, inaccurate square footage and overcharges for pass-throughs and items not authorized by the lease contract. Lease analysis experts estimate approximately 30 percent of commercial lease arrangements result in over-billing.

Request the ability to sublease your space.

Insurance Costs

All of your insurance products should be reviewed every year. Take a closer look at the following issues:

Liability insurance. If you have liability insurance, you may need a higher amount of coverage. You may want to adjust your deductibles based on past experience, and you may be due a better rate because of your claim history.

Compensation. With workers' compensation insurance, you need to make sure that your employees are properly classified. Consider removing the owner from workers' compensation if covered elsewhere.

Premiums. Your premium is based on a rate assigned to each classification of employee and the amount of gross wages paid. Certain job descriptions put an employee at greater risk than others, such as a chef versus an office bookkeeper.

Health insurance. You also should review your health insurance coverage and shop the market for group programs that may be more suited to your employee base. Look closely at the invoices you receive from your health insurance carrier; you will be amazed at what you may find—employees who have not worked for you in months, family premiums for single individuals, etc. Put someone in charge of reviewing this invoice every month to ensure that you are paying the correct amount for eligible employees only.

Equations for Your Business

Figuring your costs, income or expenses is fairly simple once you know the formulas for doing so. Simply use these basic formulas to decipher these simple business issues:

Calculating the controllable operating-, food- and beverage-cost percentages. Take your cost of all food sold, divide by the food revenue, and then multiply by 100 to find your food-cost percentage:

(Total Food Cost ÷ Total Food Revenue) x 100 = Actual Food-Cost Percentage

For example, your total monthly food cost is $40,000. Your total food sales for that same year is $100,000.

(40,000 ÷ 100,000) x 100 = 40%

Calculating target food costs. In order to make this figure useful to you in finding ways to cut expenses, you'll also need to determine your target food cost. Let's say your target food cost is 35 percent. Now, what actions can you take to decrease your actual food cost? We'll talk about this in more detail in Section IV.

Number of guests required to be served to break even. Take your average of the guest checks, subtract the variable costs per guest, and then divide that into the total fixed costs to find the number of guests.

Number of guests required to be served to meet rising variable costs.

1. Add your old variable costs and the additional variable costs that you now have.

2. Take that number and subtract it from the guest check average (this will be B).

3. Next, take the total fixed costs and add the desired net income you require (this will be A).

4. Then, take "A" and divide by "B" to find how many more guests you will need to serve to meet your expenses.

Number of guests required to serve to meet income goals.

1. Take the total fixed costs and add your desired income (A).

2. Then use your customer check average less the variable cost per guest (B).

3. "A" divided by "B" will give you how many customers you must serve in order to meet your income goals.

Finding your guest check average. The total annual revenues divided by the total number of guests gives you this average.

Figuring the labor needed per guest. Take your total labor costs for a period of time, divide by the number of guests for the set period of time, and the answer will be how much labor is involved.

Calculating the yield percentage involved in your recipe. Take the product loss divided by the weight required for portioning.

Getting Organized

Being organized is probably the easiest way to save money, as making sure your sales and usage taxes are paid when they are due allows you to avoid costly penalties and interest fees, which results in large savings to your bottom line. Similarly, many communities and states offer discounts for paying your property and sales taxes early.

Are you utilizing all the discounts available to you? Many bills offer discounts for advance or prompt payment, especially when it comes to utility bills. Also, your suppliers will often run specials on end-of-line items, slow movers, new products, or things that they've managed to acquire at a better-than-normal rate.

Debt. If at all possible, pay off all business debt. Debt is one of the major causes of failure among small businesses today. Interest on loans can quickly eat away at your profits.

Chapter 9

Look at Your Restaurant Objectively

I t's often easy, when you get distracted by day-to-day tasks, to fail to see your establishment in the same way as others see it. There could be a lot going on that you wouldn't agree with right under your nose, but how do you step back and get an outsider's perspective? Here are some suggestions:

Online information about the competition. A good resource to check on the competition is at **www.restaurantnews.com** and click on the "financials" link. This page gives you financial information for over 50 restaurant chains throughout the United States.

Customer surveys. Use customer surveys to find out what your customers want from your restaurant, what makes them happy, and what they don't like. Try to meet their demands. Have your servers give customers the survey and a pen with their check and allow them time to sit after their meal so they can fill out the form. You may want to consider giving your customers a thank-you token, such as a coupon for a free appetizer for their help. Surveying customers will not only tell you how to make your patrons happier, it may also uncover ways to cut costs. For example, your survey results show that the majority of your customers don't eat the packaged crackers you serve with salads.

You may want to consider getting rid of these crackers (and their expense) or replacing them with a less expensive alternative.

Hire a mystery shopper to go undercover and check out your business. A mystery shopper plays the role of a "regular customer." They compile the information on their customer experience into a report to you. They'll tell you how helpful the servers were, how well the food was presented, how it tasted, how clean the restaurant was, how long they had to wait for their table and meal, and what improvements need to be made. Find them online at **www .secretshopnet.com** (Secret Shopper), **www.mysteryshopperjobs.com** (Mystery Shopper), and **www.mysteryshop.com** (Mystery Shop).

Consider being the mystery shopper yourself. Or send a couple of employees to do research. The cost would only be that of a meal! You can find a complete Restaurant Shopper's Report in Chapter 39 of this book.

Surveys

Surveys and market research are a great way to find out what's really going on in the minds of customers, potential customers and employees. Try the following:

Web sites. For ideas on how to create surveys for your customers, locals and staff, visit these Web sites:

- www.custominsight.com

- www.surveysite.com

- www.formsite.com

- www.hostedsurvey.com

Survey cards. Monitor customers to find out which advertising they remember. Hand out survey cards for each customer, asking them where they heard or read about your establishment. Remember to reward customers for filling out surveys and let them know the information is appreciated. Send thank-you notes or coupons to participants.

Market Research

Market research is an important way to find out what type of customer you should be targeting, what these customers spend on eating out and what they want. Here are some Web sites that offer market research information:

MarketReasearch.com. This Web site has market research for the restaurant industry available for downloading. Costs run anywhere from two hundred dollars to several thousand dollars for reports that include titles such as *Fast Food in the USA; Dining Out Market Review;* and *Top Market Share Sandwich, Pizza and Chicken Chain Restaurants Survey.*

American FactFinder. This Web site, **http://factfinder.census.gov/servlet /BasicFactsServlet**, lets you search, browse and map U.S. Census' data, including economic, population, geographical and housing statistics.

CACI Information Decision Systems. This site allows you to order demographic information by zip code. Pricing is by subscription or information can be priced per requested report. Log on to **www.esribis.com** for a free sample of reports and a free zip code search.

Service Annual Survey. This part of the U.S. Census' Web site offers annual estimates of receipts for some service industries. This information can be found at **www.census.gov/svsd/www/sas.html**.

U.S. Bureau of Economic Analysis. This Department of Commerce agency hosts a Web site at **www.bea.gov**, which provides publications and data on businesses by industry.

Manero's, *a successful restaurant in Palm City, Florida, has been in business for over 30 years and has a second location, J. Arthur's Restaurant, in Maggie Valley, North Carolina. Co-owner/restaurant manager John Mahoney is a big fan of buying in bulk whenever it makes sense.*

In general, buying in bulk will save you 15 to 20 percent, so if we know for sure that we're going to use a product within a certain amount of time, we purchase it in bulk. We buy frying oil pumped off a tanker into our oil storage tank, 200 to 300 gallons at a time. That's a substantial savings. We buy every liquor deal that comes along, but only on products we normally carry—not what the liquor company wants to move. Another tremendous savings for us is in cutting our own meat. We are primarily a steakhouse, so purchasing whole loins and cutting them ourselves is much less expensive than buying precut. We have customized our menu to utilize the beef trimmings that would otherwise hit the soup pot or the trash. We have a Black & Bleu Salad on our menu as an outlet for small pieces of tenderloin leftover from cutting filets. We blacken them and put them atop a heaping bleu cheese salad. We do similar things with small pieces of fresh fish and striploin ends.

Also, we've started a loyalty program that has shown great potential. Only about 20 percent of our customers dine with us more frequently than once a month (an industry average for our segment). Increasing that percentage is huge. We have been able to administer the program via e-mail so the costs are minimal. Customers get food and beverage points. When they reach 500 points, they can redeem $25 worth of food or drink. The customer gets an effective 5 percent discount on their purchase, but our actual costs are about 2 percent. We send out a newsletter each month and congratulatory cards on special occasions. All of the correspondence contains Manero's coupons. It has been a real driver of business.

Chapter 10

Trimming Operational Costs

Office Expenses

As much as you'd like to avoid office, electricity, gas, phone, food, labor and beverage expenses, they're a fact of life. But you don't have to let these expenses run out of control. With a few simple rules and an eye on the bottom line, you can keep those expenses down to a minimum. Here's how:

Use part-time employees. You may find that part-time personnel with a confirmed list of duties will be less inclined to "fill time." Additionally, depending on the length of the shift, a part-time employee might not need a meal break, which is another expense. You also can save money on benefits, such as health insurance, retirement plans, etc., by using part-time employees.

Outsourcing. If some office tasks are too important to leave in the hands of inexperienced, busy or part-time employees, consider outsourcing the task to an expert in the field. Outsourcing your bookkeeping to a professional who comes in one day a week is far more cost effective. To compare rates for human resources outsourcing services, log on to **www.BuyerZone.com**.

Compare prices online. Comparison-shopping sites compare prices from a number of online shops. Comparison sites cover virtually everything available for purchase. Try **www.google.com**, **www.dmoz.org** or **www.crosssearch.com**.

Buy printing online. You can secure bids from and deal directly with a range of domestic and international printing companies by posting your job specs on the Printing Industry Exchange™ Web site at **www.printindustry.com**. Printers will then send their bids straight to you—and you'll deal directly with them throughout the job. On the other hand, why use a printing company at all when you can create your own office stationery? With a PC or Mac, some nice card stock, a laser printer, and some graphic software (such as Quark and/or Photoshop), it is possible to create your own business cards, flyers and menus without going out-of-house. If you have the time and talent, get to it!

Menu design and printing software. Quality menu printing can cost you a lot of money, so do yourself a favor and laminate your menus so that they're waterproof and easy to clean. With the advent of the personal computer, there have been a few menu design software programs developed in recent years. The software is generally very easy to use, with built-in templates, artwork, etc. Your finalized menu can be printed out on a laser printer. Color, clipart, photos, artwork and graphics may be added. One such software program is Menu Pro™. An extensive demonstration of the software may be found at **www.atlantic-pub .com** or call 800-814-1132.

Payroll. Try QuickBooks. Get a quote from online payroll service firms to see if outsourcing this task will save you money. If payroll recordkeeping is a significant part of a full-time bookkeeper's job, then outsourcing it may enable you to realize savings by going to part-time help. Outsourcing may also be a solution to problems with costly payroll accounting staff turnover and training costs. Online payroll Web sites include Payroll Online, EasyPayNet, PayMaxx, Paychex and Oracle Small Business Suite's Payroll.

Consider using an electronic bill-paying service to save time on mailing and paperwork. It works especially well for recurring monthly bills. By timing your bill payments electronically, you can wait until the last due date and stretch your working capital. QuickBooks has an electronic bill-paying service built in to the program. Companies like CheckFree license their bill payment engine to financial institutions, so ask your bank if they offer this service at a reasonable cost. Before signing up for this service, compare the cost of paying your bills online with your current process. Web sites that connect you to the convenience of electronic bill payment include eBillPay (free for six-month trial), Oracle Small Business Suite, Checkfree.com, StatusFactory, Yahoo BillPay, Paytrust.com and PayMyBills.com.

Consider bulk mail. If you advertise by sending out circulars, you should look into using bulk mail rates. Log on to the United States Post Office Web site at **www.usps.com/directmail** for more information on using bulk and direct mail for marketing.

Is postage use monitored in your office? Is postage only used for business needs or do employees sometimes throw their phone bill check in with your invoice payments? Who has access to the postage meter or stamps?

Watch for telephone solicitations. Be skeptical of unsolicited calls, particularly for office supplies and toner for office machines. These scammers will often act as if they know you and then ask for the model of your printer of copy machine. They will then ship and bill you for replacement parts, toner, etc., that you didn't order. Designate certain employees as buyers with authority to issue purchase orders for supplies. Check documentation, such as purchase orders, before paying bills or accepting shipments. If the vendor ships items that are different from the brand, quantity or quality you ordered, you can legally treat it as unordered merchandise. To find information about common scams and report fraud, go to the Federal Trade Commission's Web site on office supply scams at **www.ftc.gov**.

Use postcards. Use creative, attention-grabbing postcards instead of always producing a more elaborate, costly mailing piece. Since they are not heavily used for direct mailing, individual postcards stand out. With large savings in postage, production and lead times, postcards can be a cost-effective way to build traffic with a captivating photo or illustration on one side and compelling copy on the other. Even plain postcards with a personal note to customers or prospects can get powerful results for about 30 cents each.

Trim Phone Expenses

Many business operators don't even look at their utility bills, but those that do can often find ways to reduce their monthly outlays on phone calls with a little smart thinking and forward planning. Consider the following:

Do you know who is using your business telephone and where they are calling?

How long do your employees spend on the phone? Do they use it while on a break, at lunch, before work, after work, or during time that they should be spending on customers? Make it a blanket rule that employees should not have access to restaurant phones unless they are engaging in specifically outlined business activities, such as taking orders and reservation calls.

Make a pay phone available in the restaurant for your employees' needs. This will not only save you money, but can actually make you money as most pay phone operators work on a profit-share basis with the establishment they're in. Visit G-Tel at **www.payphone.com**, 800-884-4835.

Keep an employee phone log. If employees must use your office phone, consider keeping a log of all employee phone use and to where the call was made so that any toll charges can be paid by the employee, not your business.

Do you need unlimited calling set up for your fax line? If your fax always seems to be in use, this may save you additional fees and taxes.

Flexibility. You may want to consider having a cell phone or cordless telephone handy so you can address business calls while you're moving about your establishment. If you don't have a cordless telephone, you will find yourself constantly being called back into the office to answer the phone. Not only will it cost you time in your daily activities, but also money!

Cut the cord. Get cellular phones equipped with nationwide calling. Use the cell phones for all long-distance calls.

Use "800" numbers. When calling a vendor, don't use their direct number if it will be a long-distance call. Instead, use their toll-free number.

Compare long-distance rates and carriers available in your area at least once every three months. Are you getting the best deal? Consider changing your telephone carrier if you can get a better deal, and always ask for a rate better than advertised. You'll be surprised how often you can get what you ask for!

Long distance. To compare long-distance phone rates between multiple suppliers, try using the following sites: Lower My Bills at **www.lowermybills.com** or Telecommunication Research at **www.trac.org**.

Check your phone contracts and bills. Ensure that you are on the right plan and are paying for the right plan. Also, check that you are receiving the appropriate discounts and that all phone lines are covered by the discounts.

Fax it. Faxing is less expensive than mailing, and using a computer/fax modem is the least expensive and saves the most time, paper and ink. One analysis shows that labor cost per page will run about 15 cents for mailing compared with

2 cents for faxing.

Fax lines. Do you have too many phone lines? Can some be cancelled? Consider eliminating your dial-up account line and a fax line by switching to a cable modem or DSL and then using e-mail as a fax such as E-Fax, **www.efax.com**, or MaxEmail, **www.maxemail.com**.

Use a low-tariff telecoms provider for long-distance or international calls. Use selective call blocking, for example, on international calls, and call log recording to highlight any misuse.

Energy Expenses

According to the National Restaurant Association, an average restaurant spends 2 percent of its revenue on energy and only 0.05–4 percent of its gross revenue becomes profit. If a restaurant owner reduces energy consumption by 25 percent, profit will increase from 4 to 4.5 percent of revenue, the same as a 12.5 percent increase in sales. Even the smallest cost-saving procedure can save you thousands of dollars a year if you stick with it. EPA research breaks down energy use by a typical restaurant as follows: cooking, 23 percent; water and space heating, 19 percent each; lighting, 11 percent; cooling, 8 percent; refrigeration, 6 percent; ventilation, 5 percent; and office equipment, 1 percent, to name the big ones. Tightening just one practice can lead to long-term savings. Consider the following possibilities:

Most electric companies have departments devoted to helping you reduce power costs. Call your local electricity supplier and ask them to send someone out to help you keep costs and wastage to a minimum, and they will, in all likelihood, do so for free.

Use timers on everything. Use timers for all of your lights in case employees forget to shut them off at the end of the day. The use of timers will ultimately create savings in your electrical costs and can also be used as a break-in deterrent to give the impression someone is in the building late at night. In addition, install timers to turn water heaters off when the restaurant is closing and to turn them on two hours before opening in order to reach the desired temperature. Consider installing a solar water heating device.

Timers and motion detectors. Often employees will carelessly leave a light on in walk-in coolers. Consider using a timer or motion detector on these lights so that a few minutes after an employee forgets to shut off the lights, they turn off automatically. Also be sure that employees shut walk-in and reach-in doors completely. This can be a huge energy drain!

Air-conditioning. Many air-conditioning systems are designed to work at a low rate, even when the temperature is perfect, just to keep air flow moving. If you have windows and doors that can be opened during a nice breezy day, have the air conditioner turned off altogether.

Consider adding a heat pipe system. This can dramatically improve the moisture removal capabilities of many air-conditioning systems, yet actually lower power bills at the same time. Air can be pre-cooled by simply transferring heat from the warm incoming air to the cool supply air. This "bypassing" can be accomplished by placing the low end of a heat pipe in the return air and the high end in the supply air. Heat is removed from the warm upstream air and rerouted to the cool downstream air. This heat, in effect, bypasses the evaporator, although the air that contained the heat does indeed pass through the A/C coil. The total amount of cooling required is slightly reduced and some of the air conditioner's sensible capacity is therefore exchanged for additional latent capacity. Now the unit can cope with high-moisture air more efficiently. See **www.heatpipe.com/heatpipes.htm** or **www.lanl.gov/orgs/pa/science21 /HeatPipes.html** for more information.

Cleanliness and efficiency. The coils on the back of your refrigerators and coolers work far less effectively when they're clogged with dust, ice and grease. Ensure that at least every two month, a staff member turns off the refrigerators for ten minutes and cleans the coils thoroughly. Also, drain and flush hot water heaters every six months to remove minerals that have settled on the bottom of the tank.

Check rates. In many areas, gas and electric companies have become deregulated. If your business is in one of these areas, do some research to see if your current carrier is giving you the best possible rates.

Use lower-wattage light bulbs. Look for longer-lasting light bulbs that don't require as much energy. Halogen lights are another good alternative. They're more expensive to purchase, but they last a good deal longer than fluorescent lights. Retrofit with energy-efficient lighting; specifically, re-lamp to lower-wattage bulbs. Switch from incandescent to high-efficiency fluorescent. Install dimmers, motion sensors and photocells to control lighting automatically. Dimmable ballasts are available for T-8s as well as a new generation of compact fluorescents. Consider high-pressure sodium or low-wattage metal halide lamps for outdoor lighting. Install compact fluorescents in the kitchen exhaust hoods. According to the EPA's Energy Star Small Business Advisors, converting fluorescent fixtures to T-8 fluorescent bulbs with electronic ballasts can save 20–50 percent a year.

Have a contractor look at your property to calculate your building's heat

loss. All buildings lose heat through windows, doors, the roof, etc. Have someone look at your building to pinpoint areas that may need your attention. Perhaps your windows need weather-stripping or you may need to add additional insulation in spots.

Turn off equipment. Turn off personal computers and copiers at night if not in use. If left running all night long, one office's PC may waste more power than the lights used all day. Also, turn kitchen appliances off when not in use. Remember, most kitchen equipment takes less than 20 minutes to pre-heat.

Extra Energy-Saving Tips

Here are some more tips for making big savings on energy costs:

Implement an equipment startup/shutdown schedule. Draw up a step-by-step startup/shutdown checklist. Have all employees follow this routine.

Mirrors. The use of mirrors throughout your establishment will maximize the effect of your lighting as well as give your room the illusion of increased space.

Turn off exhaust hoods when the appliances are not in use.

Infrared fryers. Replacing a conventional gas fryer with an infrared gas fryer can boost profits by as much as $600 a year.

Turn parking lot lighting off automatically with a photocell.

Walk-in freezers or coolers. Installing a plastic strip curtain over the entrance can save up to $200 a year per refrigerator. See **www.rackandshelf.com** or **www .koroklear.com**.

Coffee warming. Bunn-O-Matic, **www.bunnomatic.com**, has designed special lids for its coffeemakers to keep steam and heat from leaving the coffee—a move that not only saves coffee-warming energy, but also the extra energy required to condition the air. Always store coffee in insulated containers instead of on the holding coils of the machine. This will ensure quality and reduce energy loss.

Make sure you replace furnace filters on a regular basis. Clogged filters can cause a furnace to overheat and shut down.

Sensors. Install sensors or timed switches in nonessential lighting areas, such as storerooms. Also, install low-temperature occupancy sensors or timed switches in walk-in coolers and freezers to control lighting.

Ensure that dishwashers and garbage disposal units are running only as needed. Install low-flow pre-rinse spray nozzles on dishwashers to conserve water.

Monitor temperatures. Every degree of cooling increases energy use by 4–5 percent. Stick with 78°F for occupied cool, or 68°F for occupied heat.

Skylights. Install skylights to provide natural sunlight to illuminate a building's interior.

Heat water for hand washing to 110°F instead of 140°F. Don't reduce the temperature of water serving the dishwasher, though. Use antibacterial soaps to ensure food safety. Or you can check with your local health department for the lowest temperature allowed for a hand-washing station.

Install flow restrictors or aerators in piping and on faucets. These can reduce water flow by about 50 percent.

Insulate new piping. Insulate and/or repair existing hot water piping and tanks. In a system with about 200 feet of piping, good insulation will save approximately $50 to $75 per year. Also install drain covers on all sink and floor drains (available at **www.atlantic-pub.com**).

Install magnetic disposer-saving products. For attractive flatware, staples, bottle caps and more, see **www.atlantic-pub.com**.

Repair leaky faucets. A hot-water faucet dripping at the rate of 1 gallon an hour consumes 9,000 gallons per year and wastes $50 to $120 in energy. Use faucet-control devices available at **www.atlantic-pub.com**.

Use a motion-controlled water system in the kitchen. This means that your basin taps automatically turn on when something is placed in front of them. Overuse of water in the prep of food and washing of dishes is unnecessary and costly. A system like this allows you to use water only when it's needed and automatically turns off when it's not.

Insulate the water heater tank. Insulation kits cost very little and will pay for themselves in energy savings in 12 months or less. Follow manufacturer's directions.

Use lock covers on thermostats to ensure tamper-proof temperature settings.

Preheat cooking equipment no longer than manufacturer's recommendations. Turn down cooking equipment when order activity is slow.

Solar coatings. Apply solar "clear" coatings to reduce solar heat from large southern- and western-facing windows.

Make sure HVAC economizers are working.

Change all air filters regularly.

Replace worn door gaskets on walk-in coolers and freezers. Make sure automatic door closers are working. Lubricate refrigerator and freezer hinges and latches. Tighten loose hinges to prevent air leaks.

Keep the evaporator fans free of debris.

Ensure that evaporative coolers on air units are well-maintained and functioning properly.

Schedule food preparation wisely. Cook some items during off-peak periods. Consider whether some items can be cooked by the ovens, fryers or steamers rather than by less energy-efficient range tops, griddles or broilers.

Preheating. Do not preheat steam tables, grills, broilers, etc. If you must preheat, 10–30 minutes is generally adequate.

Microwave ovens. They use significantly less energy than other equipment and can be used for thawing, partially cooking and reheating food. Also, be sure you are using a commercial-grade microwave oven that is tailored for food service operations. See **www.amanacommercial.com** for a complete list of commercial products by Amana.

Avoid carbon and grease buildup. This can make your cooking equipment work harder and use more energy. Purchase Sokof, an approved carbon remover available at **www.atlantic-pub.com**.

Range-Top Operation—General Energy-Saving Tips

Whenever possible, do not use the range top. Instead, use other equipment, such as steamers and ovens, that use less energy and add less heat to the kitchen. Also:

Use the proper-sized pots and pans for individual burners. Placing a ten-gallon pot on the smallest burner on your stove will consume far too much energy in cooking, while placing a tiny pan on a huge burner will see most of the energy being used completely wasted. Electric burners or heating elements should be at least one inch less in diameter than the pot.

Place pots close together. Placing pots as close as possible on the range top will reduce heat loss and perhaps allow you to turn off a section.

Cover all pots. Covering pots reduces heat loss and causes the food to cook faster. If possible, use glass or clear lids.

Turn heat off a few minutes early. Residual heat in the burner and pot will continue to cook the food.

Range-Top Operation—The Specifics

Make a major impact on reducing range top operating costs. Adopt some (or all) of the following procedures:

GRIDDLE OPERATION:

Preheat the griddle approximately six minutes. Six minutes is sufficient preheating time for a 350°F temperature requirement.

Heat only a portion of the griddle. If the griddle can be heated in sections, heat only the sections needed.

Cover griddled products. This reduces cooking times. It also allows some items to be cooked on one side only.

Use griddle weights. Placing weight on bacon and sausage or other griddled products will shorten cooking time, but may alter the food appearance.

OVEN OPERATION:

Keep oven doors closed. Every second the oven door is open, the temperature drops 3–10 degrees.

Don't use two ovens when one will do. Bake products requiring the same temperature in one oven.

Don't preheat unless necessary. Preheating is usually necessary only for baking products.

Don't set the thermostat higher than needed. The oven will not heat up any faster.

Don't use aluminum foil. Wrapping potatoes or other products in aluminum foil retards baking because the foil reflects the oven's heat. If you want to use aluminum foil, wrap the potatoes after cooking.

FRYER OPERATION:

Fry from 300°–350°F. Higher temperatures are inefficient. (For older fryers, the temperature may have to be set to 375°F—check your manual.)

Idle the fryers at 200°F. This conserves up to 50 percent of energy use.

Melt fat and oil before frying. First, bring it to the proper temperature in a steam-jacketed kettle. This is more energy efficient than using the fryer's coils to melt it.

Keep fat above coils or elements. Be sure the fat level is kept above the coils or elements. If they are even partially exposed, 25 percent of the heat entering the fryer can be wasted.

Have foods as dry as possible when frying. A large amount of energy is needed to change water drops or ice on frozen products to steam. Food such as potatoes and chicken can be partially cooked by steam and then finished and browned in a fryer.

STEAM COOKING:

Begin cooking procedures in a steamer. Partially cook your product in a steamer and finish it with your usual cooking method. Remember, steam is the most efficient form of cooking because it cooks moderately, transfers heat rapidly, requires little preheating, and shortens cooking time.

Cover steam-jacketed kettles. Clouds of steam indicate unnecessarily high temperatures and put a further load on your ventilating system.

Steam tables are energy wasters. Do not preheat them longer than necessary, and turn them off when not in use.

Dishwashing—Reduce Operating Costs

Here are some tips that can significantly trim your dishwasher operating expenses:

Air-dry dishes. Do you really need your dishes to be power-dried at the end of the dishwasher cycle at all times through the day? During slow periods, or at the end of the night, leave the dishes to air-dry, thereby saving energy and reducing your operating expenses.

Fully load the dishwasher. Be smart about the use of the hot-water pre-rinse hose. Heat water only to the temperature required for specific uses within the facility, such as a 140°F supply to a dishwasher.

Keep the dishwasher temperature at the correct level. Dishwasher water temperature should be set at the lowest point allowed by local health department guidelines to conserve the energy needed to heat your water. Standard temperatures are 140°F, wash; 160°F, power rinse; 180°F, final rinse. Using hotter water than necessary wastes energy. DayMark Food Safety Systems offers removable dishwasher labels that change from white to black when the dishwasher's calibrated temperature is reached.

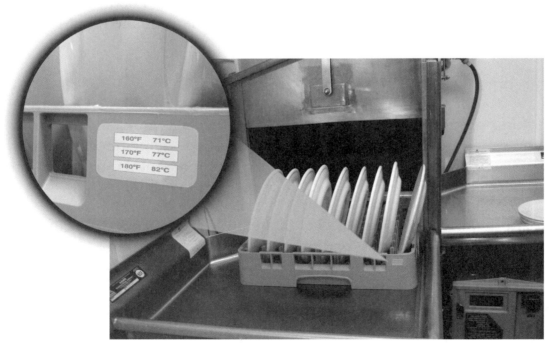

Three-Temperature Dishwasher Labels available from www.daymark.biz or call 1-800-847-0101 for more information.

Save even more electricity by actually turning the dishwasher off when not in use. Just leaving an appliance switched on for hours at a time costs your business money.

Consider substituting chemical rinses for hot-water rinses if codes allow. A chemical solution such as a bleach-type product could be used instead of 180-degree water for the final rinse.

Turn off booster heaters. Turn dishwasher water heaters off when the machine is not in use and at closing.

Check power rinse. Make sure that the power rinse on the dishwasher is turned off automatically when the tray has gone through the machine.

Clean the dishwasher regularly. Check wash and rinse jets after each use. Empty the scrap trays frequently. Use a de-liming solution regularly. Lime buildup clogs the wash and rinse jets.

Functioning at Optimum Efficiency

If you want to reduce your kitchen operating costs, getting the most from your equipment is not an option—it is a necessity! Bear in mind the following:

Check all thermostats. Have the thermostats on your ovens checked at least bi-monthly. If your thermostats are off-kilter, you could be using more (or less) gas than you need to, with potentially disastrous results concerning the quality of your meals and your expenses. Check thermostats with a thermometer and adjust them if necessary. Thermometers for all types of kitchen use may be found at **www.atlantic-pub.com**.

Keep gas flames adjusted. Properly adjusted gas flames should be all blue with a firm center cone. A yellow-orange tip means that some gas is not being burned. There should be no visible smoke.

Inspect pipes regularly for leaks. Hot water and steam leaks are great energy wasters. Replace all valves or gaskets that show leakage. Replace washers in dripping water faucets.

Check overheating ovens. Ovens that become excessively hot on the exterior surface have insufficient or deteriorated insulation, which should be replaced. Also check oven door gaskets for a tight fit.

Separate food items into several categories. This is more energy efficient than storing them all in one large freezer. Items should be separated according to the frequency they are needed. Store infrequently used items away from frequently used items; for example, beef patties and French fries can be stored together in one freezer; other items used less frequently can be stored in another freezer. Label items to avoid searching with the door open.

Don't set the thermostat below the required temperature. Though doing this fractionally decreases the freezing or cooling time, it uses significantly more energy.

Don't store food in a way that blocks circulation within the refrigerator. Use several trays so that cold air can circulate around all the products.

Kitchen layout. Locate the refrigeration equipment away from sources of heat, such as ovens and grills. Also, ensure that your stoves, hot plates, microwaves and ovens are located far away from coolers and air-conditioning vents. If your hot plate is being "cooled" by an air conditioner, you'll be spending more than you need to on gas just to keep it at a level temperature.

Are there leaks developing in the seals of your cooking equipment? Have your staff on the lookout for steam leaks when you have your pots and pans covered. Of course, steam will escape naturally if a lid isn't fastened, but if it's coming from one spot only and a little too easily, then your lid might be out of shape and allowing energy to be wasted.

Keep foil burner trays under the burners. This saves time in cleaning and keeps your energy focused where it should be: on the food.

Place thermometers in refrigerated units and ovens. Monitor them on a regular basis to make sure all of your units are functioning properly and that food is being stored at the correct temperatures. Thermometers for all food service applications may be found at **www.atlantic-pub.com**.

Outlet pipes. The pipes from your hot water outlet to your dishwasher should be a maximum of 48 inches, from one outlet to the other. If your pipes are running the length of an entire wall, your water will lose heat over the course of that trip and will be far less effective in the wash.

Protect your equipment. Purchase any available protective rails, guards and bumpers for all of your equipment. These are generally offered as accessories. They need to be provided both on the mobile equipment and fixed equipment that you own.

Get your hot water back. Heavy hot water usage warrants consideration of a heat exchanger or needs to be reclaimed to recapture and reuse "waste" heat before it has been truly lost. In a commercial restaurant, heat in the to-be-discarded washing or rinsing water may be recaptured before the water goes down the drain and used to preheat cold water via a heat exchanger. Whether the investment in the reclamation device is cost effective depends on the amount of water being used, its "discard temperature," and the cost of installation. Hot gas heat exchangers, installed in the hot gas line (between compressor and condenser), recover heat from refrigeration systems. Water circulates through the heat exchanger, transferring heat directly to where it is used or to a hot water tank.

Rooftop spills and grease. Contamination generated from exhaust ducts and ventilators cost food service operators thousands of dollars each year. Rooftop grease spills are also a major health and safety hazard. Such grease spills also pose a safety hazard, particularly in relation to slip and fall accidents that, in return, cost thousands of dollars in workers' compensation and personal injury claims each year. See the following Web sites for more information: **www.greasetrapworld.com**, **www.darlingii.com/restaurant/restaurant.htm**, **www.worldstoneinc.com** or **www.environmentalbiotech.com**.

Get the Most from Your Icemakers

A waste chill recovery (WCR) heat exchanger could be applied to any icemaker in order to improve its energy efficiency. The WCR device is basically a type of "shell and tube" heat exchanger that pre-cools water being charged to the icemaker with cold wastewater being discharged from the icemaker. This results in significant energy savings. Contact Maximicer, 13740 Research Blvd., Suite K-5, Austin, Texas 78750, 512-258-8801, fax 512-258-8804 or toll-free at 800-289-9098. To reach Maximicer on the Web, go to **www.maximicer.com** or e-mail ice@onr.com. Another good source is Fast Ice Products: Environmental Industries International, Inc., 4731 Highway A1A, Suite 216, Vero Beach, Florida 32963, phone 561-231-9772, fax 561-231-9773 or toll-free at 800-373-3423.

Pre-chill the water in your icemakers. Run the water lines for your icemakers through your walk-in cooler to pre-cool the water prior to use.

Waste Management

Effective waste management is one of the best ways to reduce restaurant operating costs. Here are some simple tips:

- Reduce the volume of waste that goes into the waste disposal unit.

- Order items in reusable tubs.

- Purchase condiments in bulk, and refill dispensers.

- Switch to soda and beer dispensers rather than offering bottles and cans.

- Use concentrated cleaning agents.

Bulk buy. This refers particularly to dry foods that can be stored in ingredient bins.

Bale and recycle cardboard. Also recycle plastic bottles and aluminum cans. Recycling isn't only about being environmentally conscious, it also helps you reduce garbage collection expenses and even make a little money on your waste, rather than forking out money to have it hauled away. If you sell bottled beer, put any returned recycling deposits towards the price of your next order.

Crush and recycle all aluminum cans. Crushing the cans allows you to place a lot more into a smaller space, greatly reducing the space needed to keep them. You wouldn't throw away the pennies from your cash drawer, so why throw away the pennies each aluminum can will bring?

Use pulpers. Rather than sending all the chopped-up waste down the drain by using the disposer, pulpers draw waste down into cutters that mince it into tiny bits. The resulting slurry, which is 95 percent water and 5 percent waste, is then forced through a press or extractor. The remaining pulp is discharged down a chute into bags to be placed in a dumpster. See **www.insinkerator.com**.

"Gun" dispensers. Rather than using costly bottles and cans of soda in your drinks, install a gun dispenser that runs from a post mix system. The cost of soda dispensed from these systems is barely a few cents per drink compared with the cost of bottled products, saving you not only a great deal in cost, but also in waste management, spoilage, storage space and delivery.

Are your linens, cutlery and glassware walking out with the trash? Often kitchen staff can take a very cavalier attitude towards what goes into the trash. If only a few pieces of silverware are lost per shift, that quickly amounts to a significant cost to your business. Surveys demonstrate that flatware is the leading item purchased by operators industry-wide. Why? Because so much flatware goes into the trash! Perform occasional inspections of the kitchen trash to ensure you're not letting inventory be thrown away. Use tray savers and magnetic retrievers to keep your trays and silver in service and out of the trash. See **www.atlantic-pub.com**.

Sewage disposal. Some cities offer markedly lower sewage charges if a restaurant uses a pre-treatment wastewater system. Contact your local city officials and check if you qualify for any discounts.

Other Great Opportunities to Reduce Costs

The phone, electricity and gas aren't the only utilities where you can make big savings if you're a smart manager. Consider the following opportunities:

Renegotiate your credit card discount rates. This could result in huge savings. A 1 percent discount for a restaurant grossing $1,000,000 per year could result in a $10,000 savings. It pays to shop around when looking for a merchant account provider. Some banks charge high setup fees, whereas others charge no application fees. All merchant account companies charge some type of usage fee. Typically they offer a "discount rate," which ranges from 1–4 percent. There may also be an additional fee for each transaction. In addition, you may also be charged a monthly statement fee of about $10–$20. Negotiate with your bank and contact your state restaurant association; they may have negotiated a lower rate for members. Use comparison services such as **www.searchmerchants.com** or **www.merchantexpress.com**.

Group and organization dues and discounts. Review the organizations that your business belongs to and make a list of what discounts, specials and/or promotions you receive in return. If the local chamber of commerce is charging you a membership fee, you should expect a return on that investment that goes far beyond the tea and cookies they put out at the monthly meeting. Ask for promotions to increase local business, discounts from suppliers, community events—anything that will bring you a tangible return. If you don't get what you want, cancel your membership and save the cash for your own marketing.

Sell as many gift certificates as possible. A gift certificate sale is like an interest-free loan from your customer. They give you cash in exchange for a piece of paper that may or may not be redeemed at some future date. In effect, you have free use of their money. Use a computer program such as Giftworks, which may be found at **www.atlantic-pub.com**.

Table decorations. Centerpieces don't always have to include fresh flowers, candles and other items that will require ongoing maintenance. Consider using a bowl of water with colored stones and small floating tealights. These are very inexpensive, and the effect can be extremely ambient.

Landscaping. For your exterior landscaping, have perennial flowers planted rather than plain shrubs. Perennials will flower year after year, they don't need trimming, and you will not have the expense of replanting flowers every year.

Donations. When asked to donate to a local charity, offer instead to provide a gift certificate or host the group's meeting in a separate room for no charge. This way, you will preserve cash and bring people into the establishment.

See if your bank will accept quarterly financial statements from you instead of requiring monthly numbers as a condition of your loan.

Control spending. As an alternative to departmental budgets, ask people to justify everything they spend.

Push for cash discounts. Many suppliers offer free freight once you hit a certain volume. See if you can bundle orders together to take advantage of the savings. Also, to generate cost-cutting ideas, invite your vendors to a cost-cutting party.

Lease equipment. Consider selling off equipment you currently own and leasing it back. Leasing companies will lease back your existing facility or capital equipment. You would receive cash up front and make periodic lease payments plus interest. There are buy-out options at the end of the lease.

Reduce music licensing fees from BMI and ASCAP. There is a way to receive one low-cost license from these organizations. The National Licensed Beverage Association (NLBA) recently negotiated a group license agreement covering most of its members, costing $30 per participating store per year. You automatically become a member of NLBA by joining your state licensed beverage association. See **www.nlba.org** for more information.

Conserve cash and join a barter club. Barter allows you to buy what you need and pay for it with otherwise unsold products—food and beverages or even catering services—without the use of cash. Almost anything and everything can be purchased with barter services. Nationally, over 250,000 businesses are involved in barter. Check out these Web sites: **www.barterwww.com** or **www.barterbrokers.com**.

Free consulting. Get the professional advice you need for free. The Service Corps of Retired Executives (SCORE), **www.score.org**, 202-205-6762, is a network of retired businesspeople who volunteer management assistance. U.S. Business Advisor (**www.business.gov**) is a government Web site that provides one-stop access to federal information and services.

Mike Stoner and Duffy O'Neil are co-owners of **North Star American Bistro***, a restaurant in Shorewood, Wisconsin, that's gotten rave reviews during its short existence. Mike Stoner recalled one of the early challenges they faced.*

We opened our bistro in October 2004. When spring and summer rolled around, we decided that we wanted to offer seating outside on the sidewalk in front of the restaurant, but we needed additional tables and chairs. We got some price quotes for the patio furniture we liked and in the amount we would need and found it would cost us $3,500. We decided that was too big of an expenditure in the first year, so we opted instead to purchase used table bases from a new/used restaurant supply store. Then we had a local hardware store cut pressed wood to fit the table bases and we simply screwed the wood onto the bases. All of this cost only $500. We cover the wood tops with white linen tablecloths and white butcher paper. We think they ended up looking nicer than the much more pricey patio tables would have been.

We had been renting folding chairs to supply a party room with a 50-person capacity. On average, we'd rent 30 chairs a week at $3.25 a chair. We wanted to get rid of that pesky rental fee and we needed to get chairs for the outside tables. So, we got a deal from one of our food purveyors to purchase a line of discontinued chairs that were originally $90 each for $53 each.

We put those new chairs in the main dining room and put the older chairs formerly in the dining room in the party room. We ended up having enough chairs left over to supply the patio. What we're saving on chair rental will cover the cost of the new chairs in eight months.

Many business operators don't even look at their utility bills, but those that do can often find ways to reduce their monthly outlays on phone calls with a little smart thinking and forward planning.

Chapter 11

Reducing Maintenance and Repair Costs

Linen, Utensils and Equipment

Do you keep inventory of your cutlery, crockery, serving equipment, glassware, napkins, tablecloths, silverware and prep equipment? If not, why? All of this equipment costs you money. If these items are accidentally thrown out or if every staff member takes a few glasses, a tablecloth, a few plates and some silverware home, you're looking at a huge dollar loss. Also consider the following:

How do you take inventory of large quantities of silverware and tableware? Weigh one spoon, then a bus pan containing all the spoons. Subtract the weight of the bus pan itself and then divide the total weight of the spoons by the weight of one spoon. The number you get will be very close to the number of spoons or other silver items you have on hand.

Use heat-resistant rubber spatulas and spoons. New technology has recently brought us flexible scrapers, spatulas and spoons that can take the heat, up to 400°F without staining, melting or fraying! All items are dishwasher-safe and available at **www.atlantic-pub.com**.

Use recycled products. If you use paper napkins in your restaurant, consider purchasing recycled paper-based products as a cost-effective, environmentally sound alternative.

Are tablecloths really necessary? Perhaps you'd be better off, financially and aesthetically, in doing without tablecloths altogether. Why not try some elegant reusable placemats instead? Cover the tables in glass and use interesting items such as maps, decorative dried flowers and local memorabilia. Be creative! For example, a sports-themed restaurant might use pennants, baseball cards, etc.

Use napkin rings and bands. Napkin bands or rings save time and money. Put a napkin band around each place setting and set them aside when there is spare time, thus saving labor. It speeds table setting and employee productivity. Napkin bands help you keep the silverware clean and they also help you conform to the rules set forward by the FDA and in developing a HACCP system. Most companies can also customize or print your logo on the band. For a great source, see **www.colorkraft.com**, 866-382-4730; or **www.daymark.biz**, 800-847-0101.

On-Premises Laundry

If you currently use a linen service to have napkins and tablecloths cleaned, it might be worth investigating whether it would be more cost effective to set up your own laundry area on the premises. You would need to consider:

- Capital investment dollars.

- Operating costs.

- Savings and projected payback of the investment.

- Daily and weekly laundry volume in pounds.

- Equipment capacity requirements.

- Number of operators required to meet expected laundry capacity.

- Total daily, weekly and monthly operating costs.

- Unit cost per pound of laundry.

- Utility consumption information for all machines used.

Employee Uniforms

Your employees' uniforms can cost you a great deal of money. Consider basic black shirts, pants and skirts, for example, that are provided by your employees. Here are some other cost-saving ideas.

Aprons aren't only for kitchen staff. An apron doesn't just keep you're staff from staining their clothes, it also provides a uniform look to your employees and makes them far more noticeable as staff. If you're providing uniforms for your employees, supplying an apron to preserve their clothing could save you a bundle in wear and tear.

Do you even need to worry about uniforms? Often a general look can be just as effective as having a uniform; for example, requiring all your staff to wear blue shirts with black pants, golf shirts with your logo, or even just matching caps.

Janitorial Services

When you're considering your janitorial options, is it better to go with your own cleaning staff or would it pay to have a professional service come in after hours and give everything the industrial scrub-down?

Compare contractors. The hiring of contract companies to meet your cleaning needs must come only after studying the price and quality of various contractors. Ask yourself how often do you feel that this particular cleaning need must be met in your restaurant. Does this service company have references? Ideally, your expenses for this type of service should not exceed 0.2 percent of your overall sales. If you can find a service that will handle the job at less than your employees' hourly wage rate, grab it!

Keep the restrooms clean. Making sure the restroom has toilet paper and paper towels and that the floors are swept will considerably reduce your janitorial costs. If you can incorporate these jobs into your employees' "general duties" job descriptions, the extra expenses will be minimal.

Parking lot. Keeping your parking lot clean is not as big of a chore as it may sound. At the beginning of a shift, have one of your bussing staff take a broom to collect stray cigarette butts and papers. Having one person do this every day for even just ten minutes will save you money in your daily operating expenses. Perhaps this will enable you to reduce the use of parking lot janitorial services to once a week.

Carpet cleaning. Consider getting your carpet stain-guarded. Keep area rugs or runners in the entrance of your dining area so as to pick up water, mud and even snow from ruining your carpet.

Cleaning supplies. To save money on cleaning supply expenses, try using rags instead of paper towels to clean surfaces throughout the restaurant. Paper towels can be very expensive over the course of an entire day's cleaning, while washable rags cost little and can be used again and again. See **www.chixtowels.com**.

When redecorating, pick drapes and curtains that can be machine washed. This way, waitstaff or management can easily take the window treatments down, have them cleaned overnight and have them re-hung by morning.

Repair Expenses

Always prepare for problems. Repairs are always going to be needed from time to time. Even when you do your utmost to look after your equipment, things break, accidents happen, and they can be very costly. So how can you reduce these unavoidable expenses?

Maintenance management software. Use a software program to assist you to schedule maintenance and record the maintenance history and procedures. On the Web, visit **www.faciliworks.com**, **www.expresstechnology.com** or **www .softwarecorp.com**.

Downtime. When a vitally important piece of equipment isn't functioning, it is important to factor into repair expenses the cost of downtime as well as replacing broken equipment.

Keep a listing of every piece of equipment you own. Note the model numbers, brand names, expiration dates and service phone numbers so that when something does break down, you have all the information possible to assist with arranging the service call. It's far cheaper to have enough information at hand for your repair person to figure out a problem with a machine than have him or her come out to see it, go back for a part, then come out again to fix it.

Franklin Machine Products is the industry leader in parts and accessories for food service equipment. Need a part for that stove? They've got it. They stock over 8,000 items. Call 800-257-7737 or visit **www.fmponline.com**. Their annual catalog (thicker than many phone books) is a great resource with many equipment schematics. You'll refer to it often. The staff is very knowledgeable and is known to go to great lengths to access the item you need. Highly recommended, this company will save you money.

Consider keeping a repairperson on retainer. Paying a flat $100–$250 monthly fee to a person with skills in the electrical, carpentry, landscaping and plumbing areas is a very cost-effective alternative to hiring specialized contractors in each profession.

Timing repairs. Schedule regular maintenance for the late evening hours or early morning when your establishment is closed or, at the very least, slow. Having to close to perform repairs and maintenance will cost you big in terms of lost business and annoyed, turned-away customers.

Preventative Maintenance

A large part of reducing your yearly repair expenses comes from simple preventative maintenance, planning and forethought. If you and your staff are diligent in the maintenance of your major kitchen and restaurant equipment, it's far more likely to last many years without needing major repairs. This includes your stoves, refrigerators and even freezers. Stick to scheduled cleanings, learn simple small-part repairs, and have a repairperson give yearly inspections on all major equipment.

We all know how to dial a phone number and get a repairperson to fix a broken appliance, but most businesses fail to realize that preventative maintenance can be a far more cost-effective manner of keeping appliances not just running, but running to peak efficiency. Here's how:

Repair manuals. Read the equipment manuals. Keep them on file for when things go wrong. Quite often a manual will feature advice for cleaning, preventative maintenance, and small tips that will save you a service call.

Books. In addition to reading all equipment repair manuals, we recommend you pick up two books for your restaurant. They will pay for themselves on the first use. Both books were written by a veteran restaurant repairperson and are available from Atlantic Publishing:

- *Keeping Your Gas Restaurant Equipment Cooking* is a handy reference guide that will save time and money; **www.atlantic-pub.com**, Item # GAS-01, $39.95.

- *Keeping Your Electrical Restaurant Equipment Cooking* covers all types of electrical equipment, with easy-to-follow directions/instructions;

www.atlantic-pub.com, Item # ELE-01, $39.95.

Check your ice machine regularly. Is it working properly? Is there water build-up? Is the machine making more ice than you need and is that ice the right shape to suit your needs? Try to have your water lines run through or past your refrigeration system so that the ice machine doesn't have to work so hard to cool the water.

Ensure that your pipes are cleaned regularly. Dirty or clogged pipes will invariably cause odors and inconvenience that can cost you customers and costly repairs. Make sure that any issues are addressed before they become major problems. Use drain cover baskets for floor drains in the kitchen. They may be purchased online at **www.atlantic-pub.com**.

Schedule the regular cleaning of all equipment as part of your kitchen staffing duties. While fryers and hoods need to be cleaned more often, the inside of your stoves need scheduled cleaning on a weekly basis, either before or after your regular business hours.

Create a checklist outlining maintenance schedules. Take note of equipment capacities and which items are most likely to break down under stress. A well-maintained kitchen unit will last longer and keep replacement expenses low.

Buy a toolbox and fill it with the basic maintenance supplies. Small and basic repairs can often be performed by management staff or a knowledgeable employee, saving a service call and a great deal of money.

Replace burners, handles and timers as needed. Check these not only for the prevention of food burns and spoilage through improper cooking times and methods, but also to prevent any workers from getting injured on the job, which will save you money on insurance costs.

It may seem obvious, but check that any malfunctioning equipment is actually plugged in before you start calling for service repairs.

Web site sources. For plenty of advice on maintaining your equipment, extending the life of utensils, and kitchen remodeling ideas, visit TapDirect, **www.tapdirect.com**; The Home Store, **www.homestore.com**; and Leather Man, **www.leatherman.com**.

Painting Expenses

Your walls do far more than simply keep the roof up. They lend a tone and ambience to your restaurant that can either add to your diners' experience or subtract from it, in a big way. If you ignore your walls for years on end and never count a repaint as an expense, you may well be losing business and gearing up for a major repaint down the road. The following suggestions will keep painting expenses to a bare minimum:

If you ignore your walls for years on end and never count a repaint as an expense, you may well be losing business and gearing up for a major repaint down the road.

Keep up on your in-house painting needs. Letting your restaurant colors go drab can leave your customers with the feeling that your dining area is unclean or less customer-friendly.

When considering using a local painter, ask for references. While an individual with a brush and ladder can be a very inexpensive option compared with a large painting contractor, a bad paint job can end up costing you a lot of money to fix.

Paint. Consider buying the paint yourself if you are hiring a local repairperson for your painting needs.

Smoke and grease. Wiping the smoke and grease from your walls once a month, including the actual dining areas, will keep the paint job fresh and lessen the chances of a repaint being necessary for some time. An additional plus is that clean walls won't smell, leaving your establishment looking and feeling good for your clientele.

Liability Expenses

Legal action from a customer, a fire, a catastrophic equipment failure or an employee accident can send your business into financial peril, so it's imperative that you take as many proactive measures as possible to protect yourself. Here are some examples:

Reduce the risk of a fire starting in the kitchen. Keep grease and food from building up within your oven and fry hoods, thereby significantly reducing the chances of a fire engulfing your kitchen.

Introduce an in-depth cleaning schedule. Utilize your labor to its fullest potential, and make sure that your business is always in health-inspection order.

Inspect your furniture. Have regular inspection schedules for your furniture as a means not only of keeping your insurance premiums low, but also of reducing the potential for lawsuits filed against your business.

Wires and cables. To reduce the potential for lawsuits, keep your building safe by ensuring all cords and wires are tightly secured and out of the path of anyone walking by. If you must run a wire over a portion of floor space, ensure that it is taped down from end to end and that it is marked with brightly colored tape so that even if someone doesn't spot the wire, they're unlikely to trip over it. If this wire is to be there on a permanent basis, run it along a wall or underneath carpeting.

Avoid sharp-edged furniture. If you're creating a new restaurant, you may want to consider furniture with rounded edges, including tables, bar counters, serving counters and even the cash register.

Walk around the exterior of the building. Does everything appear safe? Check all of your walkways. Could a customer trip easily? Would people with disabilities have problems entering your building? Walk through the interior of the restaurant. Are all the lights working and are they bright enough? Can two people pass between your tables without any trouble?

Staff responsibility. Organize a safety and labor committee where employees help each other identify the restaurant's "problem areas."

Restaurant Law Basics. Atlantic Publishing offers a book called *Restaurant Law Basics* that can be an excellent resource for figuring out how to handle situations involving liability. It can be ordered on the Internet at **www.atlantic-pub.com**. This small investment can save you a lot in legal fees.

Furnishing Maintenance

When a table gets a shaky leg, what do you do? Throw it out? Hire a repairperson? Whichever you choose, you could be throwing away good money after bad, not to mention damaging the customer experience. While you shouldn't take shortcuts, nor should you pay through the nose. Here's how:

Spare furniture. Keep a couple of extra chairs and tables in storage in case you need a replacement in the future. When you buy in quantity, you should see a discount on your purchase price, which creates a savings on the price of the furniture and allows you to maintain uniformity in your furnishings, and make replacement costs a non-issue for a long time to come.

Invest a few dollars in scratch-repair polish. This is an easy and effective measure to keep up with the wear and tear on your dining furniture and the overall appearance of your restaurant. For a host of ideas and tips on do-it-yourself repairs, visit Refresh Furniture at **www.refinishfurniture.com** or Furniture Wizard at **www.furniturewizard.com**.

Chapter 12

Security and Theft Prevention

Explore the Underlying "Excuses" for Theft

Take a step back and explore why thieving is rife in the beverage industry. Your motives may not be entirely altruistic for doing so, but the fact remains: If you're trying to reduce costs, you need to know what you're up against. An informed manager is in a much stronger position to take steps to control and reduce "wastage" due to theft.

Rationalizing theft. Employees contemplating theft will first have to "justify" the risks to themselves. They will have to weigh the possibility of getting caught compared with the potential gains. Don't put temptation in their way. Keep high-value inventory under lock and key.

Greed. Some thieves simply enjoy the challenge of "getting one over" on management. They're bored and looking for excitement.

Resentment. Sometimes staff resent taking orders and believe, for whatever reason, that they're being "picked on." In the interests of the overall success of the operation, managers must appear, at all times, to be acting fairly and reasonably.

Reducing Employee Theft

Sometimes the best way to improve your bottom line doesn't include making cost reductions, it involves keeping a better eye on money you've already made. Theft reduction is an incredibly important area to keep an eye on, as one sticky-fingered employee can cost you big. Internal theft is a massive area of expense in many businesses, and, though you don't want to spend more on security and precautions than you save, an ounce of prevention is worth a pound of cure. To keep employee theft to a minimum, you'll need to concentrate on the following areas of your establishment:

Staff rotation. If practical, try to rotate your employees so that they are not working with the same people constantly, minimizing the opportunities to collude and steal from the business.

Routine inspections. Using daily inspections is much more likely to spot an employee being dishonest or a system that isn't working well than waiting for a catastrophe to happen. Have management conduct regular surprise inspections throughout the facility, with a goal to becoming more aware of what's going on throughout the premises.

Watch the bar area. You can tell if money is being spent or not. If you don't see money being exchanged, it's a safe bet that your bartender is giving free drinks. Reduce your bar expenses by keeping a watchful eye, perform spot checks on the register at unexpected times. Also, don't allow underage persons to work or be seated around the bar area.

Are your bartenders or servers over-pouring drinks? Implement portion-control pourers on your liquor bottles. Your pricing is based on a "per shot" basis. If your bartender or server is providing a "shot and a half" in every drink, they're in effect giving away one in every three bottles of liquor, for free.

Are your employees failing to charge for items, such as coffee and tea? If you notice that a certain employee's customers never buy items that other servers' customers buy, investigate further and take appropriate action if you find any deception taking place.

Mistakes? Have your employees place any "mistakes" on a shelf for management review and notate as to why and how the mistake occurred. Using (and sticking to) this method will make certain that employees and managers take spoilage and waste seriously, as well as deter theft.

Do you monitor employee meals? All employee meals should be paid for at the time of ordering, unless you offer them for free, in which case they should be signed for and noted by a manager.

If you wanted to serve a meal without ringing it up, how easy would it be? Consider the ability of your servers to get food from the kitchen without recording sales and then give those items to the customers or friends.

Giveaways

Many establishments give food and drinks away to customers as part of their promotional expenses. A two-for-one deal or a free drink for every main course is a great incentive to get people through the door, but make sure you're not being ripped off in the process. Here's how:

Use a separate key. If you occasionally give customers free drinks or meals, either as complimentary gifts or as part of a promotion, use a separate key on your register to ring up those giveaways and ensure a manager knows about every incidence, either by signing for it or by receiving a voucher. This tightens control on giveaways, maximizes your profits, and allows you to maintain incentives.

Monitor coupon usage. Destroy all complimentary meal and discount coupons you receive to ensure that the same vouchers aren't being used twice. Handing a used promotional voucher back to friends is a common ploy used by unreliable employees to defraud your establishment.

Employees often enjoy free or reduced meals while they're working, but you still need to account for these expenses in order to keep accurate tabs on your inventory and to be able to forecast your purchasing needs.

Are your employees consuming too many free drinks at the bar after work? Many restaurants have a "one free drink after work" policy, which may become a two- or three-drink policy without you realizing it. Consider implementing a rule whereby only management can dispense the free drink.

Guest Checks

Keep a close eye on your guest checks and have a system in place for issuing and monitoring them. Here are a few tips:

Ensure all guest checks are numbered and the numbers are kept on file alongside the server's name. If checks don't match the total rung up on the register, you want to have as much hard evidence as possible should you decide to terminate an employee.

Any guest check voided because of error still needs to be accounted for. This will allow you to spot when any check goes "missing" and make sure that the payment for every check makes it into the register and not into an employee's pocket.

Have all guest checks accounted for before an employee leaves. Keeping strict control of the money within your business will significantly lower theft opportunities, not to mention man-hours spent trying to figure out shortages.

Register Practices

Your earnings go through a number of steps before they make it into your checking account. The first of those steps is the journey it makes from the customer to the cash register. It is vital that you have rigorous register procedures in place and that all staff is fully aware of the importance of sticking to the rules. Here are a few essential guidelines:

Position of cashier. Having your cashier located at the only non-alarmed exit door will not prevent customers from leaving without paying, but it will certainly make such a move more risky for them. If your hosting employees are alert and attentive, your customer walkouts should be kept to a minimum.

Leaving the cash register unattended. Unavoidably, there are often times when employees have to leave their cash register unattended—a situation that almost invites dishonesty. Create a system where either your staff shouldn't have to leave the drawer unattended or they must log on with a pass code to open the drawer. Not only does this prevent theft, but it also allows you to instill confidence in your staff that any errors (or thefts) by someone else won't be attributed to them.

Ensure that your cashiers call out the total amount of a transaction. They should also call out the amount tendered to the customer. This communicates what you are doing with the customer; it also reduces the risk that the customer will claim he or she handed across a larger note than was actually the case. By the same token, make certain your cashier doesn't put any notes into the cash drawer until after the transaction is complete.

Train employees to count aloud any change they're handing to the customer. This ensures that the change is counted three times—once when your cashier takes it out of the drawer, once again when it's being handed to the customer and finally, by the customer while it's being handed to them. This reduces the incidence of costly mistakes, misunderstandings and employee theft.

Monitor all voids and over-rings. If an employee makes a lot of "mistakes," they may be taking cash out of their drawer after a customer has paid and left the premises. The same goes for under-ringing of checks. Always watch and match your checks to your register rolls.

Remove cash from the register throughout the night. At various times throughout the night, under the supervision of the cashier involved, have your manager "bundle" any notes that number 12 or more in the cash drawer into bundles of 10, and then move them to the safe, replacing them in the drawer with signed requisition slips. This keeps the end-of-the-night count simple, and it keeps large amounts of cash out of the place where it's most vulnerable.

Cashiers should never have access to the keys you use to display and print your end-of-day sales reports. Any incidence where a cash register is "rung off" should be noted and performed by a manager. A new cash drawer should be used from that point onwards.

Bank Deposits/Accounts Payable

Proper auditing of bank deposits and charges slips must be conducted to ensure all deposits were made and to account for missing checks. Upon receipt of the bank statement, don't put it aside for your accountant; reconcile it yourself and you will gain new insight into the business and close the last loophole where money could escape. Use the form on the back of your bank statement or use your computer software program and follow this step-by-step method:

1. Check addition and subtraction in your checkbook through the end of the month.

2. Compare each canceled check with your cash disbursements journal to be sure the amounts agree. Check them off as you go.

3. Mark the check stub for each check you have received.

4. Mark each amount on the bank statement to indicate you have compared the check.

5. Compare deposit slips with your checkbook.

6. If you have deposit slips for deposits not marked in your checkbook, add the amount at the end of the month with the date of the deposit.

7. Mark your checkbook and/or cash receipts journal for each deposit slip you have received.

8. Mark each deposit slip to indicate you have compared it.

9. Mark each deposit amount on the bank statement to indicate you have compared the deposit.

10. Record any bank notices or charges (e.g., new checks, returned checks, etc.) in the checkbook and cash disbursements journal at the end of the month.

11. If a check you deposited was returned:

    a. Subtract the amount from your balance at the end of the month.

    b. Note on the deposit and on the end-of-the-month statement why you are subtracting this amount, who the check was from, and why it was returned.

    c. Make a copy of the check and return notice to keep with your records.

    d. Send the original check back to your bank for recollection efforts.

Voided checks. If you have voided a check, keep the defaced original with your check stub and cross out the amount in your checkbook and disbursements journal so that it is not treated as a check amount.

Identify and Prevent Bookkeeper Theft

Accounting (bookkeeping) theft is a major concern within the food service industry. From falsifying daily inventory records to complicated auditing abuse, this area of theft is often the most difficult to detect. Sometimes, it is the managers themselves who are behind the scams. Owners need to be aware of the following possibilities:

Sales records. Falsifying daily sales records and stealing the difference between recorded and actual cash received.

Inflating overtime. Adding overtime or extra hours to payroll records in order to increase wages.

Discounts. Recording higher-than-actual discounts when reimbursement checks from credit card companies are deposited.

Forging signatures. Making checks payable to oneself, forging signatures or using signed blank checks, and then destroying paid checks returned from the bank.

Falsifying bank statement reconciliations. Over-recording deposits that have not been recorded, under-recording outstanding checks, or even deliberately miscalculating reconciliation worksheets with the intention of covering cash shortages.

Overpaying suppliers' invoices. Then converting the suppliers' refund check for personal use.

Resubmitting invoices. Duplicating requests for payment and splitting the difference with dishonest suppliers.

Dummy companies. Setting up "dummy" companies and using them to submit invoices for payment.

"Padding" the payroll. Issuing checks for fictitious members of staff or employees who no longer work for the company.

Manager Theft—The Danger Areas

Managers are in powerful positions; they are trusted. A dishonest manager can easily conceal fraudulent activities until it is too late to rescue the business. The scope for dishonesty amongst middle management, in particular, should never be underestimated. No one is in a better situation to defraud the operation than a thieving middle manager. Beware of the following examples of manager theft:

Stealing cash receipts and inventory. In most operations, managers are responsible for removing cash from the register at the end of each shift and preparing the opening banks and daily deposits. A dishonest manager could easily take a premature "Z" reading, or steal cash receipts and claim that the bartender's cash drawer was short.

Collusion. Teamwork involving thieving employees and managers is common, so be sure to monitor all employees.

Inventory abuse. A manager is in the ideal position to offset previous theft without raising suspicion by simply altering the records and perpetuating fraud.

Defrauding bank deposit funds. An interesting solution to the problem is for the owner to allocate this particular task to junior members of staff on a rotational basis. The secret is not to give any one person overall responsibility for depositing cash in the establishment's bank account.

"Spotters." If you suspect theft by management, employ a professional "spotter" or mystery-shopping service to scrutinize your operation. Spotters will have an in-depth knowledge of prices, procedures and policies. They will "infiltrate" your establishment, as plain-clothes detectives, and assess the honesty of your employees, from management downward. Search the Internet using the keyword "mystery shopping service" for one in your area.

Reducing Customer Fraud

Your customers can also be a prime source of loss, especially if your employees are less than careful. Here are some common pitfalls:

The letter scam. The customer is always right, yes, but use caution. This scam appears every few years. A letter arrives in the mail or over the fax telling you what a great evening they had at your restaurant. "Food, wine, service; everything was great. We can't wait to come back." The zinger: "The only problem was, of course, when the busboy spilled some wine on my jacket, so enclosed is the bill for $30 for the cleaning."

Bad checks are a major source of customer theft. Try to avoid accepting checks unless you know the customer well. If you absolutely must take a check, be sure to check the ID of the person signing it.

Credit cards. When accepting credit cards, always have your employees check the signature on the card against the signature on the receipt. To ensure they do this, have them write "verified" on the receipt afterwards.

Property theft. Guests often view stealing glassware or decorative furnishings from beverage outlets as a harmless prank. Turn this around. Offer embossed or customized items for sale at a modest price. Everybody wins. The establishment generates extra income and at the same time reduces the potential for theft-incurred costs.

Walkouts. In order to prevent customer walkouts, after presenting the bill the server should return to the table promptly for payment or at the very least keep a constant eye on the customers. Having your cashier located at the only non-alarmed exit door will not prevent customers from leaving without paying, but it will certainly make such a move more risky for them. If your staff is alert and attentive, your customer walkouts should be kept to a minimum.

Taking advantage. Customers will often take advantage of staff errors in calculating guest checks. A practical tip is to provide employees with calculators with printing tape for non-automated transactions. A hard copy of the figures can provide useful evidence.

Transfer charges. Dishonest guests may disclaim beverage charges incurred in other areas of the establishment. Make it a routine procedure for guests to sign all transfer checks upfront.

Keeping Your Own House in Check

It's all well and good to keep an eye on everyone else, but you need to ensure that your own practices are as secure as everyone else's—this means putting office procedures in place that will limit the chance of theft. The following practical procedures can make a big impact on reducing the operating costs of your restaurant:

Never make an outgoing check to "cash," and don't accept them either. With a "cash" check, anyone could deposit the check as his or her own, or worse: the receiver of the check could bank it and claim it never arrived. Your check is always your last chance for a receipt, and security of that check is paramount.

Keep all unused checks locked in a safe.

Keep tabs on all check number successions. Take immediate action if checks go missing. You always have the option of stopping payment if need be, but if you don't spot a problem quickly, you may never get that chance.

Limit all access to petty cash. Petty cash is the number-one area of office fraud. If your petty cash isn't under lock and key, you can almost guarantee it will find its way out the door.

The person who signs your company checks should also be the person who mails them. This ensures that your checks find their way to the company for which they're intended; it also makes certain you don't pay any "fake" invoices.

Double-check. The manager responsible for writing deposit slips, counting money and marking the deposit entry in your books should always be "seconded" by another person, especially when it's being deposited, to ensure that nothing goes missing between the office and bank.

Reconcile all bank statements as quickly as possible. If bank reconciliations are delayed and there is a major error in the checkbook, you could end up bouncing checks or being told by the bank that a problem cannot be corrected. Do you need help in learning how to reconcile your bank statement? The following links provide ideas and tips in keeping your financials in order: Quick Books at **www.quickbooks.com/support/faqs/qbw2001/122131.html** or Mumssie Online at **http://hometown.aol.com/mumssie/bankstatement.html**.

Night drops. If employees have to make night bank drops, make sure that they're accompanied by another employee.

Security

Money isn't the only thing you need to worry about being stolen. Inventory and supplies are an internal thief's "bread and butter"—a steak, a few knives and spoons, a bottle of champagne or two. Everything you own needs to be watched and secured whenever possible. Safeguard the following vulnerable areas of your establishment:

Always be sure to lock your bar inventory when the bar is not open for service. This will actively deter employees and wandering customers from engaging in petty theft. It will also allow you to identify exactly when and where any losses occur.

Make sure you have locks on all of your storage areas. Establish rules as to who can get their hands on the keys. Your local locksmith can help you not only with the locks, but also with more sophisticated measures, such as closed circuit cameras and card swipe systems.

Lock the office. Limiting access to your office areas will prevent theft of valuables as well as confidential information.

Kitchen layout. When designing or refitting a kitchen, locate your freezers and walk-in coolers as far from the back door as possible. Making it harder to sneak out high-cost items can only benefit your fight to avoid loss through theft.

Implement a robbery plan for your employees. If the unthinkable should occur, you want to ensure that both your employees and customers are as safe as possible and that your cash is hard to get. Talk to a security expert and your local law enforcement officials to determine the best plan of action in the event of a robbery.

Electronic Security

In the restaurant industry, electronic security is a necessity. Consider the following essentials:

Back-door security. Have your back door hooked up to a small buzzer so that anytime it's opened, a small noise sounds letting anyone in the kitchen and office know. Using this feature will also keep customers, inspectors and even the competition from sneaking a peek into your kitchen. Also remember that a wide-open door invites bugs, rodents and outside noise into your kitchen.

Utilize an employee login system into your POS wherever possible. Make sure employees know that these numbers are for their own good and that sharing their numbers puts their safety in jeopardy. Systems like this not only let you keep track of who is opening a register, but also which employees are busiest, fastest, and make the least number of mistakes.

Install alarms on exit doors marked for "emergency use only." This will keep your clientele and employees from walking out when they're not supposed to, as well as keeping outsiders from sneaking into your establishment. For more information on door chimes and alarms, take a look at these online alarm retailers: Chime City at **www.chimecity.com** or Drive Alert at **www.drivealert .com**.

Security cameras. Consider installing security cameras or, at the very least, "fake" cameras at exit doors and cash areas. This will keep your staff on their toes and your customers from getting sneaky.

Chapter 13

Breakage, Spoilage and Storage

Breakage Prevention

By following a few simple rules, you can greatly reduce losses from breakage and keep your glassware, tableware and equipment supplies from turning over unnecessarily:

Hot pads. Always have your employees use hot pads when serving meals, thereby reducing breakage incidents when a plate is "too warm."

Cooling time. Ensure that all employees using dishwashing machines give your glassware and tableware ample time to cool before they start moving them around the kitchen. When glassware or ceramics are heated, they have a far lower breakage point and are much more likely to develop small cracks or break.

Correct usage. Make it clear to your kitchen staff that ceramic bowls are not to be used for things like whisking of eggs or stirring of contents. Such actions will damage your tableware and dramatically lessen their usable lifespan. Provide Tupperware or metalware for these sorts of activities.

Silverware. Have employees dry all silverware before putting it away for an extended period. This simple activity will ensure that every piece of cutlery is actually clean and will also cut down on rust over a long period.

General glassware. Make sure that all glassware properly fits your glass racks, especially in the dishwasher. If they don't have a snug fit, glasses will do a lot of bouncing around during the wash cycle and while being transported. This will bring their "failure date" a long way forward.

Stemmed glassware. Stemmed glasses are far more susceptible to breakage than most other types of glasses, not to mention generally more expensive. All staff should take extra care in the handling of these items, perhaps even to the point of washing them only by hand.

Are your dishes and bowls easy to handle? Quite often what looks great on a table can be hard for an employee to handle, leading to breakages. Similarly, if your plates aren't easily stackable and thick enough to take the wear and tear of daily restaurant life, you could be wasting money. When choosing dinnerware for your restaurant, take more than just looks into account.

Never allow your bar staff to use glasses as ice scoops. Obvious as this is, we often see this happen. A tiny chip of glass falling into the ice bin can cause a great deal of injury. Bar glassware certainly isn't designed to shovel rocks of ice. Along the same lines, any time a glass breaks in or near an ice bin, the entire ice bin needs to be emptied and the contents disposed of before it can be used in the preparation of another drink. Always line the bin with a plastic bag to make emptying it easier. Use a Saf-T-Ice Scoop Caddie to keep the ice scoop safe from bacteria, dirt and ice burial, available from **www.atlantic-pub.com**, 800-814-1132, Item # ST-2000, $23.95.

Staff should never touch the upper half of a glass in the act of serving a drink. It's unhygienic and it looks terrible to the customer. Also, the glass will be much more susceptible to breakage if it's being regularly handled in this manner.

All glasses and plates need to be inspected, if only briefly, before they're used to fill an order. A lipstick smudge, chip, crack or remnants of a previous meal or drink are not only off-putting to a customer, but also hazardous to the customer's health.

Limit the number of dishes stacked on the warming table, by the dishwasher and in storage areas. Placing large stacks of dishes on top of each other causes great stress on those at the bottom of the pile. It will also result in your tableware breaking far sooner than it should. Try to avoid piling them any more than a dozen high.

Avoid unnecessary handling and transportation of dishes and glassware. If the journey your dishware takes from the dishwasher to the warmer to the counter to the table is a long one, think about ways to eliminate steps from the process. Is the warmer next to the washer? Does your staff stack loaded dishracks when they're just out of the washer, adding another step to the process? Use your space to your advantage.

Spoilage Prevention

Spoiled food is money thrown out the window. Here's how to reduce spoilage to the bare minimum:

List all spoiled food on a form. This allows you to make inventory adjustments, noting whether you're ordering too much of an item or have an equipment problem; for example, an ineffective cooler.

Color code, label and date all food. Using older food before newer food will ensure you keep losses to a minimum and can see any problems coming in advance. You can also use date stickers so employees know how long an item has been stored. Use dissolvable labels so that the label and adhesive dissolve in any water temperature. DayMark Food Safety Systems manufactures a line of biodegradable labels that will dissolve in under 30 seconds, leaving no sticky residue. These labels will adhere to hard plastics and stainless steel containers. The labels are FDA approved for indirect food contact. These food rotation labels may be purchased at **www.dissolveaway.com**, 800-847-0101.

Are your coolers too cold? Freezing, frost and freezer burn is a major source of spoilage in the kitchen. Make regular inspections of your cooler's temperature. Keep a written chart of when the last checks were performed. Use specialty thermometers for these areas (see **www.atlantic-pub.com**). Look for fluctuations or "cold points" in the cooler that differ in temperature from the rest of the area.

Different qualities and brands of food may spoil at different rates. If you happen to change your brand or supplier on a particular line of food, make sure to keep a closer eye on the condition of your stock, taking note of any changes in freshness so that you can alter your purchasing to suit.

Eggs at room temperature. To keep the yokes of your eggs from breaking easily, have any eggs to be used in the coming hours set at room temperature before they're used. This simple piece of advice will keep your eggs in perfect "cracking" condition and keep your wastage to a minimum.

Don't refreeze foods. This will take away from the taste of the food. Sometimes you may have no choice, but if you can keep food in a cooler at a refrigerated temperature and reuse it quickly, you'll be far better off.

Spices, sauces and marinades can be pre-prepared and stored for long periods without spoiling if kept at the right temperature. If a sauce or marinade requires an item with a high spoilage rate, make a large batch and freeze it in small containers to be used as needed, saving on time and money. It also ensures that every meal has a consistent taste.

Backup generator. If your electricity supply went down for half a day, what would happen to your inventory? Save yourself the heartache of watching your food go to waste in the event of a utility problem by purchasing a backup generator. A small generator powerful enough to keep your walk-in cooler up and running at all times could save you thousands of dollars in lost assets if the unthinkable happens.

Monitor your walk-ins and freezers. Your alarm monitoring company may have a program to monitor the temperature in your freezers and coolers. Or you could hire a company such as Food Watch, **www.foodwatch.com/foodwatch.htm**. Their systems accurately and remotely measure the refrigeration efficiency of walk-ins, stand-alone refrigerators or food cases. The patent-pending Compressor Watch sensor attaches to the outside of the compressor motor. The system can also record the amount of time the walk-in door is left open. The system is operated via a telephone line.

Electrical failure. If the power fails to resume within 1–2 hours or if a mechanical problem hasn't been fixed, keep the freezer closed. Use dry ice to keep the freezer temperatures below freezing and to prevent spoilage. Locating where dry ice can be purchased now will save valuable time later. Consider calling other restaurants, your vendors or cold-storage companies should the problem involve further delays. Plan ahead now.

Storage

A well-organized storage system and clearly defined procedures can significantly reduce your restaurant's operating costs. Consider the following possibilities:

Correct stacking. The improper stacking of storage containers can result in spills, breakage and accidents. Ensure that if you use storage containers, they stack properly and are easy to handle. Stacking items on top of one another in your cooler might seem to be the most productive way to utilize your limited space, but such a system makes cleaning and access to certain items very difficult.

Shelving. A good shelving system that is flexible enough to allow you to change shelf heights is essential. It makes the most of the available space, allows easy access to every item in your fridge, and makes cleaning a breeze.

Reuse containers. When you receive deliveries like flour, sugar and salt in large five-gallon buckets, you might be able to reuse them for storing dry materials. Buckets like these are usually airtight and designed for maximum protection of the contents, so rather than tossing them, clean them, re-label them and utilize them. Do not, however, use them for ice storage. (Check with your health department concerning regulations on this topic.)

Use a designated ice transport container such as Saf-T-Ice Tote. Ice transfer is a cross-contamination disaster waiting to happen in most food service operations. Saf-T-Ice Totes help you control this serious food safety danger. The units are made of tough, transparent, durable polycarbonate. The six-gallon size keeps the carrying weight at safe levels. Features include a stainless steel bail handle for easy carrying/emptying. Saf-T-Ice Totes are dishwasher safe, meet health department requirements for dedicated food service containers, and are available from **www.atlantic-pub.com**, 800-814-1132, Item # SI-6000, $79.95 for a pack of two.

Canned versus fresh. Don't automatically use fresh fruit and vegetables if canned alternatives can be used without cutting back on meal quality. Canned tomatoes, artichoke hearts, chili peppers, pears, etc., can all be used in many meals without a big loss in flavor. The trade off is easier storage and a big drop in price and spoilage rates.

Rotate stock when receiving deliveries. There's no better time to perform a stock rotation than when you're first putting away fresh items. Failure to do so can make it harder to differentiate what's new and what's old.

Hygiene

In financial terms, poor hygiene can seriously damage your operation. Even a single incidence can ruin your good reputation and force you out of business. Insist on the following preventative measures:

Kitchen staff should always wear hats and gloves and keep hair tied back when working with food. Failure to use preventative measures such as these can see you losing big money when an expensive meal is returned because of a single hair being where it shouldn't.

Storing leftovers. When storing leftovers, make certain to wrap items tightly in Saran Wrap or in airtight Tupperware. For example, keeping cut tomatoes and onions in airtight containers will go a long way towards preserving freshness. If food is stored using non-airtight methods, it will dry out and quickly become unusable. Also, exposed food invites germs, bugs and spills.

Storing hot food. When putting away hot food, such as soups and stews, divide the food into smaller batches and allow to cool in shallow pans. Alternatively, place the pans in a shallow ice bath. This will help cool the food quickly and avoid the possibility of contamination. Consider a blast chiller unit or small, easy-to-use plastic "Flash Chill" containers designed to reduce the core temperature of the content (available at **www.atlantic-pub.com**).

Rodent and Bug Prevention

One mouse. That's all it takes to send your customers running. No matter how clean you think your kitchen is, it only takes one bug to classify it as a failure in the eyes of your patrons. Take measures to prevent the unthinkable.

Receipt procedures. Bugs and rodents can come into your kitchen in many ways, particularly under doors, through cracks in the walls and, most often, inside deliveries of fruit and vegetables. Ensure that each and every delivery of produce is checked outside the kitchen, if possible, so that any insects or rodents aren't brought into your food prep area.

You don't always need to spend a lot on an exterminator for your premises. For information on do-it-yourself pest control, try the following Web sites: Do Your Own Pest Control at **www.doyourownpestcontrol.com** or Pest Control Supplies at **www.pest-control-supplies.com**.

Bug-free kitchen. The only way to ensure bugs and rodents don't enter your kitchen is to make it clean enough to starve them out. This means no food left on floors and surfaces and regular pest-control visits. The use of roach traps is another good hidden, preventative measure.

Don't store dry foods in boxes or out in the open. Rather, use sealable, clear, plastic storage containers to prevent mice, worms, cockroaches and ants from finding their way in. Cambro manufacturing, **www.cambro.com**, makes a complete line of these products for food service use.

SECTION III

Controlling Labor Costs:
Strategies and Tips

SECTION III

Table of Contents

Chapter 14—Building Your Team—The
Foundation of Success................................ 159

Chapter 15—Saving Payroll Dollars 187

Chapter 16—Training Employees................. 197

Chapter 17—Employee Supervision 209

Chapter 18—Scheduling Your Staff.............. 221

Chapter 19—The Productive Workplace 229

Chapter 20—Productive Buildings 237

Introduction

From the parking attendant to the chef, the people who serve your customers are your restaurant. You can have a prime location, a beautiful dining room, and impeccably prepared food and have it all spoiled by a rude server, sloppy busperson, or an inattentive janitor. Your restaurant's success is based upon your ability to locate, hire and solidify a group of people into your Customer Service Team.

The food service industry has long been plagued with an inadequate workforce and exceptionally high turnover rates. The increased demand for service workers and culture changes within the workforce means less educated recruits, more non-English-speaking employees, and fewer younger people interested in restaurant work.

Whether you own a celebrity-filled, trendsetting establishment or a truck-stop diner, the situation is the same. Where do you find good employees? How do you keep good employees?

How can you get your money's worth?

Labor costs typically run 25–35 percent of your budget and, depending upon your menu offerings, can equal or exceed your food costs. Keeping your prime costs (food and payroll) in the 60–69 percent range is your profit-making goal. Simply cutting staff won't do it, though. Your aim should be to get the highest productivity possible for your money. But to save money without losing quality of service, you have to start at square one.

Chapter 14

Building Your Team— The Foundation of Success

Good food and good service are the foundation of a successful restaurant. As a service industry, restaurant profit margins are notoriously slim. Your restaurant's profitability is a direct result of your ability to control your service costs without sacrificing your customers' needs and expectations.

Service Is Paramount

Keep firmly in mind that service is paramount. Surveys show that 83 percent of customers would not return to a restaurant if they experienced poor service. Sixty-one percent mentioned slow service as a factor. However, we aren't just talking about the front-of-the-house staff—every employee plays a vital role in good customer service. If your customer finds better service elsewhere, what do you lose? Just one customer, right? But if that customer spent $10 in your establishment twice a week: $10 x 2 = $20 x 52 weeks = $1,040 a year! What if you lose five customers or even ten? One server with a bad attitude can cost you their salary or more in lost revenue and permanently damage your reputation within the community. Good service is a combination of:

Strong commitment by management. Standards and expectations backed by a respect and partnership attitude.

Positive employee attitudes and motivation. A desire and willingness to serve others and good communications.

Good training methods. Top-notch employee skills and abilities.

Practical approaches and procedures. To work together efficiently.

Labor-saving devices. An environment filled with tools and equipment that promote good ergonomics and maximum productivity.

Profits Are Everyone's Business

As a restaurant owner you have a strong personal motive to be profitable—and so do your employees! Reducing your labor costs wisely and compassionately balances the needs of the organization with the needs of its team members. Reducing your labor costs requires:

Good hiring practices. Search for the right person to fill the job. Look beyond the basic skills for a person that fits your restaurant's personality. Learn more about interviewing employees by reading *501+ Great Interview Questions For Employers and the Best Answers for Prospective Employees*. To order call 1-800-814-1132 or visit **www.atlantic-pub.com** (Item # 501-02 • $24.95).

Balanced staffing levels. Schedule ample people to get the job done and satisfy customers without wasting resources.

Greater employee productivity. Teach them how to work smarter, not harder.

Excellent people skills. Communicate well with managers, line supervisors, support staff and customers. Loyal employees create loyal customers.

Sound financial decision making. Analyze and invest in labor-savers. Research and utilize tax breaks and business support programs.

People Are Assets

You probably wouldn't think too highly of someone who bought a beautiful automobile and then never bothered to clean it, change the oil, or tune it. Who would spend so much and not protect their investment? Well, employing one person can cost as much as a car and unless you are diligent, you, too, could be wasting your money!

Invest wisely. Every dollar you spend (directly and indirectly) to "purchase" and maintain an employee is an investment in your business. Protecting your human assets and securing your investment is integral to your labor-saving efforts. Are you investing wisely?

High Turnover Rates

Employees leave after three months; why should I spend the money only to have them move to a competitor? Because the industry creates high turnover rates and you have a responsibility to your business to provide a solution. Exceptionally high food service turnover rates are deeply rooted in historical attitudes and a business model based upon spending as little as possible for workers and your "factory." By ignoring workers' physical and emotional needs, restaurant owners have created an industry filled with some of the "worst jobs."

Address problems. Certainly you cannot solve these industry problems single-handedly; however, you can play an active role and reap the benefits of addressing such factors as low pay, excessive stress, inferior work conditions, limited career potential, poor economic security, and overwhelming physical demands.

Costs. "I cannot afford to pay more!" But you already are. You're paying for it through costly recruiting and training, reduced productivity, increased food costs, inconsistent customer service and larger overhead. By redirecting these dollars towards maintaining and enhancing your human assets, you'll be investing in your business instead of just paying to keep the doors open.

Employee satisfaction. Employee satisfaction isn't just a touchy-feely goal—it's a key to your success. To learn more about building happy and productive employees, read:

- *How to Hire, Train & Keep the Best Employees for Your Small Business* by

Dianna Podmoroff, available at **www.atlantic-pub.com**.

- *365 Ways to Motivate and Reward Your Employees Every Day—With Little or No Money* by Dianna Podmoroff, available at **www.atlantic-pub.com**.

- *Keeping Your Employees* at **www.keepemployees.com**.

- *First, Break All the Rules: What the World's Greatest Managers Do Differently* by Marcus Buckingham and Curt Coffman.

- *Follow This Path: How the World's Greatest Organizations Drive Growth by Unleashing Human Potential* by Curt Coffman and Gabriel Gonzalez-Molina.

Reducing Your People Costs

Notice we said PEOPLE costs. Why? Because if you only think about cutting labor-hours, you'll lose site of your objective: to please your customers and be rewarded with profits! Your business success is based upon your success at gathering together a group of workers with different skills and experiences to produce a quality product. Your most valuable asset—your employees—is filled with personal desires and expectations. You must tap into their need to be valued and respected. Here are three outstanding resources on people management, mentoring and building partnerships with your employees:

1. *Mind Your Own Business—People, Performance, Profits* by Jim Sullivan. This restaurateur-written book offers excellent advice on hiring and leading employees. For more personnel and customer service advice, visit **www.atlantic-pub.com**.

2. *Managers as Mentors* by Chip R. Bell, a nationally recognized customer service guru. This book explains creating strong employee relations; available on the Web at **www.chipbell.com**.

3. **Restaurantowner.com.** This site provides extensive guidance for restaurant owners. A "Food for Thought" passage sums up their "people business" philosophy: "Your effectiveness as an owner or manager is directly related to your understanding of people and the quality of your interactions with your staff."

Management Commitment

Your commitment to quality service is reflected in how you and your management staff conduct themselves. Take a look at your behaviors and actions. Are they how you'd want your employees to act? Below are some though-provoking questions on leadership. A "yes" answer to any of these means you should invoke the first rule of good leadership—leading by example.

Do you come to work grouchy? Your employees will copy your mood. Greet your employees with a happy, friendly attitude; the way you want them to greet your customers.

Are you sloppy or careless in your work habits? Are you late for appointments or forget to follow-up on their requests?

Is your appearance unprofessional? If you dress sloppily, your employees will resent having to meet higher standards and will slowly begin to ignore your dress code.

Do you disobey your own established standards? If you pour doubles for your friends at the bar, your bartenders will start to do the same for their friends. If you ladle on extra portions, look for rising food costs because your kitchen staff will stop measuring too.

Do you avoid addressing problems when they arise? When you see someone skirting established standards, promptly and tactfully remind them (but never in front of customers). If you let mistakes slide, soon your standards will be nothing but "hot air."

Do you ramble or lecture when answering questions or giving directions? Keep it short and simple or your employees will "zone out" and miss the point. Always make sure they understand.

Do you feel they should do whatever you ask because you're the boss? Mutual respect plays an enormous role in good leadership. Respect is something you earn, and not just because you sign the paychecks.

Do you share your goals with your employees? Help reduce employee discontent by sharing your short- and long-term business goals. They'll feel more valued and in greater control of their work.

Formal written policies and procedures are very important for setting standards. However, a large part of setting standards is done through leading by example.

Hiring Team Members

Hiring is the start of a long-term relationship between employer and employee. Or at least it should be. Can you imagine hiring a full staff of qualified workers and having them stay with you for years? This is rare in the restaurant business, but it isn't an unattainable goal. Hiring is more than just finding warm bodies to fill positions. You need to find competent, hard-working people who are a good fit for your restaurant personality. Hiring the "best" applicant, even if they don't meet your standards, will cost you in the long run.

Your Challenge

Your challenge as a restaurateur is to balance your business needs with the needs of the people who will spend the majority of their day in the service of your customers. Perhaps your greatest challenges as an employer are the economic realities of a service industry where the majority of jobs are low paying with low social status. Federal reports show food prep and serving wages average $7.72 an hour, and 75 percent make less than $8.50 an hour—the lowest wages among the major occupational groups studied. The result is a shortage of service workers and turnover rates of 250 percent for line staff and 100 percent for managers.

Restaurant Employee Classifications

Your mix of employees will include seasonal, part-time, full-time and career-oriented employees. The list below is in pyramid order—with the top level being the smallest number within an organization and by highest to lowest salary.

Executive careers. Comprehensive fiscal responsibility, college educated, may report to owner and/or stockholders (President or CFO).

Managerial careers. Manages people and/or things, college educated (General Manager or Human Resources Director).

Artisans. Creative talent may be self-taught based on natural abilities, on-the-job training or career training (Lead Chef or Pastry Chef).

Skilled workers. Valuable skills acquired from work experience or schooling (Bookkeeper, Wine Steward).

Semi-skilled workers. More complex task with indirect supervision, some prior experience or training (Server or Baker).

Unskilled laborers. Manual tasks with direct supervision, no special training (Janitor or Busperson).

The Right Person for the Job

Finding the right person for the job starts with a solid understanding of what your business team needs. As the saying goes "You can't get what you want if you don't know what it is."

Before you start recruiting, you need to make some decisions that will become the basis for a written job description. The following sections will help you gather your thoughts and prepare for the writing process.

Clarifying Your Needs

Whether you are hiring your first employee or adding to a staff of 75, there are five primary areas you should consider before you place that classified ad.

1. Tasks employee(s) must accomplish.

2. Skills and experience employee(s) must possess.

3. Training levels you must or are willing to provide.

4. Personality and attitude your customers expect.

5. Budget available for salary, taxes and benefits.

Tasks

Identify the tasks (duties) that must be completed during the shift, week, month and beyond. Categorize each activity by:

- What will they do? Detail action (e.g., clean, cut and store salad ingredients; accept food delivery, compare to packing list, sort and store; or answer phone, accept and schedule reservations).

- Where will they do it? Front- or back-of-the-house.

- When will they do it? Before, during or after active serving times.

- How often must they do it? Daily, weekly, monthly or other.

- What is a success? What is acceptable performance? What is award-winning performance?

Skills and Responsibilities

Classify each task by skills required and level of responsibility. Typically, the greater the skills and responsibility level required, the higher the salary you'll pay. Identify areas where less costly labor can be used or whether you should reward someone for accepting more responsibility.

Skill Level	Responsibility Level
Management Skills • Dining room supervisor • Beverage manager	**Profit and Loss Responsibility** • Executive chef • Banquet manager
Prep Skills • Pastry chef • Sauce cook	**Reports "As Needed" To Superior** • Soup cook • Baker
Customer Service Skills • Server • Bartender	**Empowered To Act on Behalf of Restaurant** • Hostess • Dining room manager
Support Staff Skills • Busperson • Receiving clerk	**Direct Daily Supervision** • Server • Bartender
	No Significant Decision-making Duties • Dishwasher • Janitor

Skill and Experience Training Expectations

All good companies train constantly. Learning is a never-ending process that enhances employee skills and your service quality.

Consider comprehensive training. Comprehensive job training programs and perhaps even life-skill training may be needed. New hires with little to no prior work experience or no food service history can be developed into loyal employees through in-house mentoring and training or work-study programs.

Trainee jobs. Some restaurant positions are, by nature, trainee jobs. In this case, your job description will also include an outline of the training program that the new hire must complete before moving beyond their probationary period.

Developing skilled workers. With restaurant owners nationwide routinely reporting a shortage of skilled workers, you may be forced to develop your own experienced workers. This means many positions may have to be filled by trainees.

Above all, train your employees properly. *The Encyclopedia of Restaurant Training* (available at **www.atlantic-pub.com**) is an encyclopedic, out-of-the box employee training program for all food service positions. From orientating the new employee to maintaining performance standards to detailed training outlines and checklists for all positions, this book will show you how to train your employees in all positions in the shortest amount of time. One of the best features of this book is the companion CD-ROM, which contains the training outline for all positions in MS Word, so you can easily customize the text. There are numerous training forms, checklists and handouts. There are job descriptions for all positions including General Manager, Kitchen Manager, Server, Dishwasher, Line Cook, Prep Cook, Bus Person, Host/Hostess, and Bartender.

Training videos are also a good investment. *The Complete Waitstaff Training Course Video* is a 53-minute, high-quality waitstaff training video, where your staff learns how to consistently deliver quality service that makes customers come back and tell others about their memorable experience. Study guide and tests are included. Topics covered include: alcohol sales and wine service; preparing for service; taking beverage orders; hosting and greeting guests; correct service procedures; taking, placing and picking up the order; serving food; and completing the service. Available at **www.atlantic-pub.com** or by calling 800-814-1132.

Your Budget

Employee wages are influenced in each community by the cost of living, available workforce, competition and social status of the position. Your financial ability to pay for certain skills and training may limit your expectations for a position. Your compensation package (salary and benefits) must be appropriate for the duties and responsibility outlined in the job description.

Whether you've written several pages of job tasks or just scribbled some thoughts on a napkin, it's time to start writing an overview of the job you seek to fill.

Writing Job Descriptions

A job description is a detailed definition of a job and a list of the specific tasks and duties the employee is responsible for daily, weekly and monthly. The more complete the job description, the simpler the task of training. A good job description will help you and your staff to:

- Hire the best candidate for the job.

- Understand required job skills and expected responsibility levels.

- Develop and complete training programs.

- Create goals for employee growth and potential salary increases.

Job Description Tips and Resources

Below are some ideas and resources to help you create useful job descriptions.

Ask your staff. Their input can be invaluable. You'll also discover opportunities to redistribute duties and reward better employees with "prized" assignments.

Incorporate attitude standards. Descriptions should include attitude standards such as, "Will answer phone with cheerful voice within three rings."

Hire a human resources expert. Find expert help from the Human Resources Consultants Association (**www.hrca.com**) and the Society for Human Resources Management (**www.shrm.org**).

Have an attorney or human resources consultant review for legality. Well-written job descriptions can help you defend yourself in wrongful termination or other employee litigation.

Review job descriptions posted on the Internet. Use keywords "restaurant job description" and "[insert job title] job description" to see how other restaurant owners explain the position.

Buy a book. Contact the National Restaurant Association at 800-482-9122 and request publication MG999, *Model Position Descriptions for the Restaurant Industry*.

Buy a pre-written job description. Jump-start the process by purchasing job descriptions from sites like HR Net at **www.hrnet.net**. American Express offers a handy interactive tool at the Small Business Resource site **http://www133 .americanexpress.com/osbn/tool/hiring/intro.asp**.

Read about creating job descriptions. National Restaurant Association articles at **www.restaurant.org/business/ bb/2000_05.cfm** and **www.restaurant.org /rusa/magArticle.cfm?ArticleID=754**.

Your Employee Package

Employees are "paid" in a variety of ways: wages, tips, meals, profit sharing, bonuses, commissions, insurance coverage, vacations, tuition reimbursement, childcare assistance, transportation subsidies, retirement plans and family leaves.

Paying minimum wage and offering no benefits is one way to keep your labor costs low, but rarely will you be hiring the best available, and you'll constantly be dealing with high turnover and employee dissatisfaction. Although money isn't the only motivator, it certainly is an important factor in attracting and retaining quality employees. You've got to think creatively and act aggressively to design a cost-effective yet valuable employee package.

Wages

No other industry has such divergent wage standards between federal, state and local jurisdictions. The Fair Labor Standards Act (FLSA) establishes federal work standards. However, these do not apply if state or local laws are more stringent.

Federal law. Federal law requires that you pay the minimum wage ($5.15 per hour as of 2002) for all hourly employees (except those who receive more than

$30 a month in tips) and youth wages ($4.25 per hour as of 2002) for the first 90 days. Superseding laws may require that the prevailing minimum wage be paid even if the worker earns tips; others allow for a reduced hourly rate for tip earners. To learn more about wage regulations:

Visit the Department of Labor site at **www.dol.gov** for current wage and hour laws and links to state information or contact your local State Employment Division.

State minimum wage rates at **www.dol.gov/esa/minwage/america.htm**.

Tipped employee wages by state at **www.dol.gov/esa/programs/whd/state /tipped.htm**.

National Restaurant Association. Read what the National Restaurant Association has to say about minimum wages at **www.restaurant.org/legal/law _minwage.cfm**.

Gratuities

In recent years, IRS and court rulings have created a lot of headaches for the restaurant industry in regards to taxing tips. With ongoing litigation, your best bet is to read the current legal bulletins produced by state and national restaurant associations. The National Restaurant Association provides tip resources for employers and employees at **www.restaurant.org/legal/tips /resources.cfm**. To protect your business from IRS audits and tax liabilities, encourage your employees to accurately report tips and hold employees responsible for tip income by having them read and sign a form that explains tipping rules.

You should also consider reading *The Complete Guide to Tips & Gratuities: A Guide for Employees Who Earn Tips & Employers Who Manage Tipped Employees and Their Accountants.* This new book deals with all aspects of tips and gratuities. For the employee or self-employed, learn how to earn more tips and how to properly account for and pay taxes on them. For the employer: learn how to manage and properly account for the taxes on tipped employees. For the bookkeeper and accountant: get the latest on tax and withholding laws. Available at **www.atlantic-pub.com** or by calling 800-814-1132.

Employee Benefits

Fringe benefits are an important part of compensating your employees. These are all voluntary rewards and enticements, as the law does not mandate them. Don't overlook the emotional impact (self-esteem, peace of mind, confidence, security and safety) these have on employees when developing your package.

Web sites. To learn more about employee benefits, visit BenefitNews at **www.benefitnews.com**, BenefitsNext at **www.benefitsnext.com** or CCH Business Owner's Tool Kit at **www.toolkit.cch.com**.

Holidays. Pay for closed holidays or offer comp time for open holidays.

Sick days. Grant a set number of annual sick days. But to encourage attendance, offer a cash bonus for unused days. Allow staff to convert sick days to family leave or vacation days.

Vacations. How employees take their vacation can create some unnecessary payroll costs. Learn about potential savings at **www.toolkit.cch.com/text/P05_4385.asp**.

Family leave. Help reduce employee stress by offering family leave options. You might offer short leave periods for bereavement and funerals and extended leaves for maternity/paternity/adoption or long-term family care. For information on family leave under the Family and Medical Leave Act (FMLA), see the Department of Labor information at **www.dol.gov/elaws/fmla.htm**.

Other time off. Jury duty, voting and military leave may be required by law in your state.

Offer discounted meals for employees dining with immediate family members. Thank workers and their families who may dine out infrequently.

Costly but Valuable Benefits

Employers who provide the "costliest" benefits are providing employees peace of mind and security. Although these benefits can escalate your total payroll costs, their value can be significant. Many of these benefits simply would be financially unattainable without even limited employer support. By having these benefits, you will reduce turnover, and the cost of benefits is usually less than turnover costs.

Invest in health insurance coverage. Unless it's financially prohibitive, health insurance coverage should be your most touted benefit. Employer-paid premiums are rare, but sharing the cost and exploring partially self-insured plans can make this more affordable for everyone. This is the most desired benefit for job applicants.

Talk to your accountant and financial advisor about retirement plans. Stock options, 401(k) plans and IRAs can be created to attract career-minded individuals. Visit **http://www.dol.gov/ebsa/compliance_assistance.html** for information on federal pension plan laws under the Employee Retirement Income Security Act of 1974 (ERISA).

Offer life and long-term care insurance. Employees can benefit from tax-free life insurance coverage (up to $50,000) and long-term care insurance.

Where to Find Your Next Employees

Many owners will tell you the hardest part of operating a restaurant is finding enough good employees. Searching for new employees can become almost a full-time job. Don't wait until you have a vacancy to develop contacts and personnel resources to draw from at a moment's notice. Building your team members requires a continual proactive search effort. Overall, it's most cost effective for a business to hire a fully qualified and experienced employee. So how do you find one? Below we've outlined a variety of places and ways to find loyal, hard-working employees.

Employee referrals. Personal referrals can be strong candidates, as your reliable employees will typically have good friends. Offer a referral bonus of $50 to $300 (perhaps even more for managerial hires).

Your competitors and peers. If you encounter an experienced worker when dining out, discreetly give them your card and let them know you are hiring and thought he or she might be a good candidate.

Your customers. Another reliable referral. Long-term customers have a good feel for your environment and are great "word-of-mouth" advertising.

Headhunters. Top managerial and "talent" positions may require a headhunter. These employment specialists typically have connections and contacts within specific industries. Expect to pay up to 33 percent of the new hire's first year salary.

Employment agencies. Semi-skilled workers can be found through employment agencies, but fees typically can outweigh benefits.

Trade organizations. State and national hospitality and food service organizations offer employment services.

Employment open house. Creating an open and friendly atmosphere puts potential employees at ease, builds great word of mouth, and establishes your business as a desirable workplace.

Job fairs. Set up a booth at community job fairs. Sell your restaurant as a great place to work with great people.

Unions. Many restaurateurs are "fearful" of unions, but quality employers who offer competitive compensation packages and good working conditions shouldn't hesitate to take advantage of their job banks.

Advertising for People

"Help wanted" advertising is a common method for locating unskilled and semi-skilled food service employees. However, classified ads won't typically attract sufficient candidates for skilled, artisan and managerial positions. The key is to select a medium (print or Web) and publication where your potential employees will be looking.

Classified ads. Place text or display ads in print and electronic publications. Local newspapers, school papers and ethnic (native language) newspapers for your entry-level/trainee, unskilled and semi-skilled positions.

Your Web site. Include a link on your restaurant Web site to a "We're Hiring" page, detailing job opportunities and application procedures.

Trade associations. Post jobs and search résumés at state and national restaurant associations' and hospitality associations' online job banks, newsletters and magazines. Many hospitality and food service organizations also offer personalized recruitment services and training support.

The National Restaurant Association offers links to industry-specific employment sites such as **www.restaurant.org/careers/jobs.cfm**, as well as job search information at **www.restaurant.org/careers/employers.cfm**, and food service publications at **www.restaurant.org/business/resources_magazines .cfm**.

Job site listings. For skilled and executive staff, tap into the workforce around the world at general sites: Monster.com at **www.monster.com**, FlipDog at **www.flipdog.com**, America's Job Bank (national and state) at **www.ajb.dni .us**, EmploymentGuide at **www.employmentguide.com**, CareerBuilder at **www.careerbuilder.com** and LatPro (for Spanish- and Portuguese-speaking managers and professionals) at **www.latpro.com**.

Industry-specific job sites. Search Web directories and search engines by such keywords as "restaurant jobs," "food service career" and "chef" for employee/employer matching sites.

Summer job sites. Connect with students and recent graduates seeking summer work: A+ Summer Jobs at **www.aplus-summerjobs.com**, Seasonal Employment at **www.seasonalemployment.com/summer.html** and Summer Jobs at **www.summerjobs.com**.

Tips for Writing Powerful Ads

Want to write the ad yourself? Consider these resources:

Learn ad-writing techniques from JobsOnline at **www.jobsonline.com /how_to_write_job_ad.asp** and TotalJobs.com at **recruiter.totaljobs.com /forrecruiters/knowyourstuff/getstarted/index.asp**.

Hire an expert writer at **www.drnunley.com/drnad.htm** or search the Web for "freelance copywriter."

More Places to Find Help

State employment divisions. Every state maintains a job bank of potential workers. Some states work like a private employment agency (but with no costs to you) to actively match employees and employers.

Cable TV. Cable advertising can be surprisingly inexpensive. Your initial ad development cost can be amortized over several ad campaigns. Your local cable company can assist with ad production.

At the movies. On-screen advertising can be a great way to connect with potential employees as most moviegoers are in your targeted age group.

Billboards. Although not inexpensive, billboards can potentially reach thousands every day with your "help wanted" message.

Radio. Ask your best employees for their favorite radio stations to reach potential team members. Radio stations can handle everything in-house for you.

Résumé "archives" and rehires. High turnover rates means workers are frequently shopping for another job. "Leftover" or rejected applicants may be the right match now! Former employees (providing they left in good standing) may have found "the grass isn't greener" elsewhere and be interested in returning.

Senior centers. Need mature part-time support? Many active seniors are seeking to reenter the workforce.

Foreign worker agencies. Some service industries have discovered the benefits of hiring experienced foreign workers. More details on hiring foreign workers can be found at the Department of Labor at **www.workforcesecurity.doleta.gov**

/foreign/hiring.asp.

Human resource sites such as **www.safehr.com/hiring_foreign_nationals_and _imm.htm**.

Trainees for Hire

What do you do if you cannot find the right person for the job? Create one! Here are some ways to locate and develop people with potential:

High school and community college career centers. Develop relationships with career counselors who can direct potential part- and full-time employees to you.

Trade schools (food service, hospitality and restaurant management). Work with guidance counselors to find students needing financial assistance. Participate in work-study programs.

Students. Start your outreach before the student graduates. Offer tuition reimbursement or full sponsorship in exchange for guaranteed employment.

U.S. Armed Services. Thousands of well-disciplined and dependable people leave active duty every year seeking civilian employment. See Corporate Gray Online at **www.corporategrayonline.com**, Transition Assistance Online at **www.taonline .com** and Department of Defense at **www.dmdc.osd.mil/ot/linkpage.htm**.

Federal, state and local full-employment programs. Government, non-profit and faith-based programs offer employees a helping hand. Employers benefit from financial subsidies (reimbursement and tax credits), counseling and off-site training.

Displacement, relocation, internship and school-to-work programs. Reach out to laid-off workers, rural areas (with typically higher unemployment) and high school and college students seeking a direct career path.

Special-need labor pool. Reentry programs for the disabled, single mothers, welfare recipients, retirees, high-risk youth, Veterans and non-English speakers.

Foreign-born (non-English speaking) job placement services. English as a Second Language (ESL) training for workers and cultural advice for employers.

Ticket to Work and Work Incentive Improvement Act (employing the disabled). Department of Labor at **www.dol.gov/odep/pubs/ek00/ticket.htm**.

Social Security Administration at **www.ssa.gov/work/Employers/employers .html**.

Veteran employment. Department of Labor at **www.dol.gov/vets**.

Welfare-to-Work at **www.mnwfc.org/wotc/empacket.pdf**.

Overlooked labor pools. Thousands every year needing a second chance and "life saving" can be loyal and dependable workers, if given a chance. Like the "special-need" work pool, there are numerous programs that provide financial, educational and transition support for employers and employees. Contact such groups as United Way of America at **www.unitedway.org.**

Outsourcing, Temps and Leasing

Have an occasional need for a specialist? Need extra hands for a banquet or large event? Don't want to waste your time on personnel matters?

Seek out consultants to provide you with decorating, floral arranging, bookkeeping, marketing and other "as needed" activities. Check your local Yellow Pages, Business-to-Business Directory, Better Business Bureau membership roles or restaurant association.

Explore independent contractors. These freelancers are responsible for all of their employment taxes, workers' compensation insurance, etc. Be aware of the regulations on using independent contracts by visiting Nolo Law for All at **www .nolo.com/lawcenter/index.cfm** or speaking with a legal advisor.

Borrow an employee. In developing good relationships with other restaurant owners, you should explore referrals for workers who are looking to moonlight or pick up a few hours of extra work.

Lease an employee. No hassles here as the leasing firm handles all human resources activities. This isn't typically a cost-effective option, but circumstances may warrant it. Beware of "hiring" clauses that penalize you for direct hiring of placed individuals. For more information on employee leasing firms, also known as a Professional Employer Organization (PEO), visit PEO.com at **www.peo.com /peo**; National Association of Professional Employer Organizations at **www .napeo.org**, 703-836-0466; and National Association of Temporary and Staffing Services at **www.natss.org**, 703-549-6287.

A Diverse Workforce

When hiring and keeping food service employees turns into a full-time job, nurturing and growing dependable employees from diverse backgrounds becomes a necessity. Creating a diverse workforce is good for society and it's good for business. Below are some helpful suggestions and resources on creating a strong and diverse staff that includes the disabled, elderly, minorities, homosexuals, women and people from various cultures and ethnic backgrounds.

Buy a book such as:

- *Workplace Diversity: A Manager's Guide to Solving Problems and Turning Diversity into a Competitive* by Katharine Esty.

- *The Diversity Toolkit: How You Can Build and Benefit from a Diverse Workforce* by William Sonnenschein.

- *Peacock in the Land of Penguins* by B. J. Gallagher Hateley and Warren H. Schmidt.

Take a class on diversity. Contact local universities and community colleges for management to learn how to smoothly transform a group of individuals into a cohesive team. For online classes at World Learning, see **www.worldlearning .org/solutions/index.html**. Research videos on diversity from Newsreel at **www.newsreel.org/topics/diversity.htm**.

Take time to learn about other cultures. Sometimes language isn't the only barrier. Cultural differences may cause miscommunication, hard feelings, and work problems. Working with people from specific cultures and ethnic groups requires patience and a willingness to learn.

Search the Internet and read articles using keywords like "diverse workforce," "diversity" and "equal opportunity." Look for articles like Supervising Across Language Barriers at **http://agecon.uwyo.edu/RiskMgt/humanrisk /SupervisingAcrossLanguageBarriers.pdf**.

Explore local minority-support organizations for English as a Second Language (ESL) classes, diversity programs, and educational support.

Work with non-profit organizations to develop equal opportunity and diversity programs. Good places to start are Goodwill Industries at **www.goodwill.org**, National Business and Disability Council at **www.business-disability.com**, National Adult Literacy at **www.nala.ie**, American Association for Affirmative Action at **www.affirmativeaction.org**, and National Organization for Women at **www.now.org/ issues/wfw/index.html**.

Employee Search Resources

Dozens of national employment and food service industry sites can be excellent places to search or advertise for future employees. Below you'll find industry-specific sites to start your outreach.

- American Culinary Federation: **www.acfchefs.org**

- Bartending Jobs: **www.bartendingjobs.net**

- Careers in Food: **www.careersinfood.com**

- Chef 2 Chef: **www.chef2chef.net/pro/jobs**

- Chef Jobs: **www.chefjobs.com**

- Chef Jobs Network: **www.chefjobsnetwork.com**

- ChefJob.com: **www.chefjob.com**

- Chefs Employment: **www.chefsemployment.com**

- Culinary Job Finder: **www.culinaryjobfinder.com**

- Entrée Job Bank : **www.entreejobbank.com**

- Escoffier: **www.escoffier.com/classifieds.html**

- Fine Dining Jobs: **www.finediningjobs.com**

- Food Industry Jobs: **www.foodindustryjobs.com**

- Food Work: **www.foodwork.com**

- Hospitality Career Net: **www.hospitalitycareernet.com**

- Hospitality Careers Online: **www.hcareers.com**

- Hospitality Classifieds: **www.hospitalityclassifieds.com**

- Hospitality Link: **www.hospitalitylink.com**

- Hospitality Online: **www.hospitalityonline.com**

- Hotel and Caterer Jobs: **www.hotelandcaterer.com**

- HotelRestaurantJobs.com: **www.hotelrestaurantjobs.com**

- I Hire Hospitality Services: **www.ihirehospitalityservices.com**

- Just Restaurant Jobs: **www.justrestaurantjobs.com**

- Management Search Associates, Restaurant Division: **www.best -restaurant-jobs.com**

- My Food Jobs: **www.myfoodjobs.net**

- Nation Job Network: **www.nationjob.com/restaurant**

- National Restaurant Association: **www.restaurant.org/careers/jobs.cfm**

- Need Waitstaff: **www.needwaitstaff.com**

- On The Rail: **www.ontherail.com**

- Pastry Whiz: **www.pastrywiz.com/talk/job_toc.htm**

- Resources in Food: **www.rifood.com**

- Restaurant Jobs: **www.restaurantjobs.com**

- Restaurant Jobs Store: **www.restaurantjobstore.com**

- Restaurant Manager: **www.restaurantmanager.net**

- RestaurantBeast.com: **www.restaurantbeast.com**

- RestaurantManagers.com: **www.restaurantmanagers.com**

- Sommelier jobs: **www.sommelierjobs.com**

- WineWingsWaitStaff.com: **www.winewingswaitstaff.com**

Selecting the Right Candidate

If you've done a good job in attracting qualified candidates, you should have a stack of résumés and applications. Unlike other fields, well-qualified workers may struggle with the written word and multiple jobs are typical. Below are some tips on how to select the best candidates for face-to-face interviews.

Read between the lines. Does this person have the right experience? Spot-check references for red flags.

Why are they leaving their current position? Applications should ask the reason for leaving. When checking references, verify why the employee left. Conflicting stories isn't a reason to toss the application, but it is a red flag needing attention.

Is the application neat and legible and filled out properly? If they can't fill out an application properly, how well will they do with writing guest checks, ringing up sales, or following recipe directions?

Are they a short-timer? If they change jobs every few months, they will most likely do the same with you. If everything else looks good, you may want to interview them anyway, but keep it in mind and explore why they move around so much.

Conduct phone screenings. You can learn a lot from a two-minute phone call. Always ask questions that require more than yes or no answers.

- What are your career goals?

- What income level do you expect?

- What kind of career growth would you like?

- Ask one to three questions that verify a person's knowledge and skills.

- Ask about work history gaps.

Listen carefully and use your instincts. Is the person articulate and friendly? Are they hard to reach? Be careful what you ask. Many traditional interview questions are no longer legal or wise.

Getting Ready to Interview

Your next step is to schedule face-to-face interviews.

Choose from three to six candidates.

Set interview dates at least two days in advance for local applicants and two weeks in advance for out-of-state applicants.

Explain when, where and how long the interview will be, format of the interview, and what, if anything, they should bring with them.

Tell them if you'll be conducting tests.

Provide adequate directions along with a contact name and phone number.

Set aside ample time for each interview and a half-hour break between. The break will give you time to rest (interviewing can be an intensive process) and to jot down notes and reminders.

Be prepared. Put together handouts and company introduction materials to present your restaurant as a great place to work. Create a quick tour to show off your facility and introduce candidates to key employees.

Improve your interview skills. There are plenty of good books, classes, videos and Web sites to help. If you are nervous or inexperienced at conducting interviews, practice. Role-playing can be a great way to improve your interview skills. Rent tapes on learning how to improve interviewing skills and techniques from Web sites like **www.interviewing-skills.com/gutfeeling.html**. Job Interview (**www.job-interview.net/index.htm**) is a great site for interview advice, or read one of these books:

- *501+ Great Interview Questions for Employers and the Best Answers for Prospective Employees* by Dianna Podmoroff. Available at **www.atlantic-pub.com** or by calling 800-814-1132.

- *High-Impact Hiring: How to Interview and Select Outstanding Employees* by Del J. Still (2001).

- *Hiring the Best: A Manager's Guide to Effective Interviewing* by Martin Yate (1993).

- *96 Great Interview Questions to Ask Before You Hire* by Paul Falcone.

The Interview Process

The interview process can be stressful and nerve-racking for everyone! Your job as an interviewer is to elicit information from an uncomfortable interviewee while being a mind reader, psychologist and salesperson. You'll be asking probing questions, listening intently, judging attitudes and appearances, and trusting your managerial instincts. Below are some helpful resources for interviewing and selecting qualified employees.

Web resources. For restaurant-specific advice, visit consultant Simma Lieberman Associates at **www.simmalieberman.com/articles/interviewemp.html**. For hiring systems, visit Unicru at **www.unicru.com**.

Understand what characteristics, skills and experiences you need and what you can live without. Refresh yourself by reading through the job description and preparatory notes.

Record your notes immediately. Remember, just like the employee, you're under stress and your memory can falter. Also, don't take any notes that might appear to be discriminatory. These are all fair game for opposing attorneys!

Be prepared to answer the tough questions. You should be able to answer salary, benefit and advancement questions along with work expectations and your business stability.

Never over-promise. Don't indicate there are advancement opportunities when none exist.

Give them your full attention. Emergencies happen, but as opposed to conducting an interview on the run or while you are distracted, reschedule it.

Create an interview team. Include supervisors and team leaders in the interview process. They can help you select people who not only have the skills but also the attitude your restaurant needs.

Ask Probing Questions

Be careful what you ask. Some questions are against the law, while others should be avoided to protect you and your business from discriminatory claims. For a list of illegal interview questions, visit Office.com at **http://www.office .com/templates/page1.asp?docid=34**.

Ask all your questions at once. This puts the burden on the interviewee instead of on you. It will also keep you from talking too much or leading the interviewee to the answers you want to hear.

Ask essay-style questions that can't be answered with yes or no. Use your own style of speaking, but ask questions such as:

- What would your former employer or coworkers have to say about you?

- Who was your best boss and why?

- Describe your favorite job.

- Was there anything at your last job that you didn't get a chance to do or learn?

- Describe a disagreement you had with a supervisor and how you resolved it.

- If I were your boss, what would be the most important thing I could do to help you be successful?

Make interviewees feel comfortable. Some back-of-the-house staffers may be too nervous to ask questions. Beware of servers or front-line people that have a problem speaking up.

Bring the interview to a close with, "We have about five more minutes." When people know they're running low on time, they get down to what is really important to them. Often this last-minute exchange can cement your impression of the candidate—sometimes positively and sometimes negatively.

Listen Intently

Watch the interviewee. Do they fidget and constantly change position? If you're hiring for a high-energy position, this might be the right person. If what you are looking for is a calm, controlled employee, they might not be the best choice.

Improve your listening skills with help from the International Listening Association at **www.listen.org**.

Learn to interpret body language. Read about the signs in *Interview Body Language: It's Not What You Said* at MBA Jungle, **www.mbajungle.com**.

Judging Attitudes and Appearances

Did they show up on time? Someone who is late for an interview has a good chance of being late for work. Of course, if they have a flat tire, be reasonable. How they handle being late is equally important.

How are they dressed? You wouldn't expect a prospective server to show up in a suit, unless you have a very high-class establishment. But a sloppy, slovenly interviewee will surely be a sloppy, slovenly employee. Are fingernails clean, hair washed, and clothes neat?

Do they look around and show interest during your tour? If they have no interest in what may be their future place of employment, how much interest will they have if you hire them?

Does the interviewee respond in a friendly manner when introduced to other employees? A friendly attitude and outgoing personality is vital for good customer service.

Pre-Employment Reviews

Screening and assessment tests and checks are frequently used during the pre-employment stage to unearth high-risk, unqualified or dishonest candidates. Investing in pre-employment screening helps to reduce turnover, protect your business, and select qualified candidates. Here are an assortment of resources and articles to help you decide whether your restaurant could benefit from pre-employment procedures:

Skill and aptitude tests. See Hire Success at **www.hiresuccess.com/aptitude .htm**; Employee Selection and Development, Inc. at **www.employeeselect.com /basicAptitude.htm**; Psychological Services, Inc. at **www.psionline.com**; or Reid London House at **www.reidlondonhouse.com**.

Assessment products and services. See Saterfiel at **www.saterfiel.com** or Evaluations at **www.evaluationslc.com**.

Restaurant manager test from Pan Testing at **www.pantesting.com/products /ResourceAssociates/rma.asp**.

Personality tests. See Personality Tests for Business Management at **www.personality-tests-personality-profiles.com**; or 123 Personality Tests at **www.123-personality-tests.com**.

Background checks. See U.S. Search.com, Inc. at **www.ussearch.com**; or Privacy Rights Clearinghouse (Fact Sheet #16) at **www.privacyrights.org**.

Drug screening. See Employment Drug Testing at **www.employmentdrug testing.com**; or National Drug Screen at **www.nationaldrugscreen.com**.

Hiring the Best Person for the Job

Unfortunately, there is no exact science for making your final choice. However, you can improve your chances for success with good hiring practices. We've gathered some informative sources for tools and guidance to help you choose your next employee.

Research. Read an excellent article on selecting the right employee at My Web (The Site for Small Business Owners)—*Choosing Between Two Equally Qualified Candidates* at **www.mywebca.com/infolibrary/staffing/staffing7.htm**.

Conduct multiple interviews if necessary. First impressions can be deceiving and second (or even third) interviews can reveal new facts. Use the second interview to bring in other interviewers and to discuss wages and benefits.

Check references thoroughly. Failing to check references can be a costly mistake. You could be hiring a poor worker or someone with excessive absences. You could be risking a negligent hiring lawsuit where an employer can be held liable when they knew, or should have known, that an employee presented a foreseeable risk of harming others. Monster.com offers excellent advice to employers on reference checking at **http://hr.monster.com/archives /hiringprocess/reference**. Career Know-How, **www.careerknowhow.com /resumes/fibs.htm**, reports these job-seeker statistics:

- 51 percent falsify length of past employment and salary.

- 45 percent falsify criminal records (remember, you can only ask about convictions, not arrests).

- 33 percent lie about driving records.

Non-work-related references. Entry-level workers, with little or no prior work experience, should provide teachers, pastors, Scoutmasters, or other responsible adults as references.

Hire a reference-checking company. Companies like HRPlus, **www.hrplus .com**; Employment Screening Services, **www.employscreen.com**; and Info Link Screening, **www.infolinkscreening.com** can get the full scoop and save you hours of phone calls.

Don't tell all the candidates of your decision until your new employee starts. You may find that the chosen candidate changes his or her mind at the last moment. This way your second choice doesn't feel like one!

"Help wanted" advertising is a common method for locating unskilled and semi-skilled food service employees. However, classified ads won't typically attract sufficient candidates for skilled, artisan and managerial positions. The key is to select a medium (print or Web) and publication where your potential employees will be looking.

Chapter 15

Saving Payroll Dollars

Saving Payroll Dollars

Savvy entrepreneurs never overlook allowable tax deductions, credits, government programs, business subsidies, or other money-saving opportunities. Some will be easy to take advantage of, while others will require some diligence and extensive paperwork. However, the direct and indirect savings can go a long way to balancing your budget. Below you'll find some valuable resources and ideas on trimming payroll costs. The information provided here is for your educational benefit. Please consult with your accountant, tax advisor or attorney for current information and applicability to your situation.

Pay employees with benefits. The more cash wages you can move into exempt and pre-tax categories, the less payroll taxes you and your employees will pay.

Benefits fall into three categories: taxable, exempt and pre-tax. Taxable benefits are subject to federal income tax withholding, Social Security, Medicare or federal unemployment tax. They are reported on Form W-2. Exempt benefits are excluded from employee withholdings and employer contributions (with some exceptions) and are not reported. Pre-tax benefits feature flexible benefit plans that allow employees to design and pay for customized benefit packages with nontaxable employer dollars. They can cover accident and health costs, adoptions, dependent care, and life insurance.

Create charts and employee guides to demonstrate how employers can "earn" more by saving tax dollars. Use these tools during the hiring process and employee orientations to help employees to understand the advantages of receiving benefits over a larger paycheck.

Properly calculate overtime pay for tipped workers. To verify whether you are accurately calculating overtime rates, review the information available from the National Restaurant Association at **www.restaurant.org/legal/law _ot.cfm#meals**. (The Department of Labor Web site at **www.dol.gov** offers up-to-date information on current and pending overtime laws.)

Review your workers' compensation premiums. Studies show many businesses routinely overpay for workers' compensation. A very informative article can be found at **www.bizjournals.com/denver/stories/2000/11/13 /focus3.html**. Search for assistance at sites like Cut Comp, **www.cutcomp.com**; and Workers' Comp Info, **www.workerscompinfo.com**.

Keep track of time. Good recordkeeping can trim payroll costs up to 7 percent. Check out manual, electronic and computer-based time clocks with thumbprint ID sign-in at Time Centre, **www.timecentre.net**; and Time Clock Plus, **www. timeclockplus.com**.

Offer the Right Benefit Package

Employee compensation packages are comprised of taxable wages (employee and employer paid) and taxable (employee) and non-taxable benefits.

Implement pre-tax benefit plans that save everyone money. A variety of benefits can be packaged where deductions would be pre-tax (prior to withholding calculations). Retirement, commuting, dependent care and medical savings plans can all be paid with pre-tax dollars, such as section 125 Plans ("cafeteria" or "flex" plans).

Explore benefits that cost almost nothing, but save you payroll dollars. Although many employers contribute to benefit plans, you can set up 100 percent employee-paid plans where your only costs would be to administer the plan and file IRS Form 5500. See BenFlex, Inc. at **www.beneflexinc.com**; My Cafeteria Plan at **www.mycafeteriaplan.com**; U.S. Health Plans at **www .ushealthplans.com/medsavings.shtml**; or learn more about 401(k) plans at **www.401khelpcenter.com**.

Hire a benefit consultant. Companies like Broad Reach Benefits, Inc., **www .brb1144.com/index.html**, can guide you through establishing voluntary benefit programs and expand your benefit choices.

Offer tax-exempt employee benefits. Explore with your tax advisor the benefits of offering these fringe benefits (wage deduction figures given are per employee per year):

- Achievement awards—personal property award up to $1,600 tax free.

- Adoption assistance—$10,000.

- Athletic facilities—value to employees.

- Dependent care assistance—up to $5,000.

- Education assistance—up to $5,250.

- Employee discounts—formula based on cost.

- Group-term life insurance—contact the IRS for current regulations.

- Meals—up to 100 percent of costs. Read about de minimus (little value) meals and workplace meals at **www.5500accountant.com/meals-and-lodging.htm** and in IRS Publication 15-B.

Tax Deductions and Credits

We've outlined some potential wage and tip tax-saving ideas that you should discuss with your business advisors:

Let an expert guide you! Your first step to savings should be to hire a qualified CPA. Many payroll-related activities require strict compliance with court rulings, IRS opinions and state and federal laws that change frequently.

Keep current on tip tax laws and court rulings. The restaurant industry continues to tackle the issue of tips and their tax obligations. Recent rulings have been in the IRS's favor, but the discussion continues. Your local restaurant association can keep you and your accountant up to date. For current information and tip-reporting guides, visit the National Restaurant Association's tip reporting page at **www.restaurant.org/legal/tips**; call the IRS at 800-TAX-FORM; or download **www.irs.gov/pub/irspdf/p1872.pdf**.

Protect yourself from an audit by agreeing to a standard tip calculation method. The IRS agrees not to audit your tip records if you agree and comply with either the Tip Rate Determination Agreement (TRDA) or the Tip Reporting Alternative Commitment (TRAC). For more information, visit the *Restaurant Report* at **www.restaurantreport.com/departments/ac_tiptactics.html**.

Take a 45(B) credit. The IRS allows businesses to take a credit against Social Security and Medicare (FICA) taxes paid on tips. To learn more, read the National Restaurant Association's article at **www.restaurant.org/legal/law_fica.cfm**.

Claim wage credits and deductions for employees' meals. Meals provided in your restaurant for your convenience are not taxable. If your staff must remain on-site during their shift, meals provided are not taxable as wages. Meals used as rewards or outside of the employees' scheduled work period are typically taxable. Meals provided at no charge may be credited against your employer's minimum wage obligation. Some states set specific values for meal credits while the Fair Labor Standards Act (FLSA) allows the "reasonable" cost as an offset.

Claim wage credits and pay exemptions for extended breaks. Typically, rest periods longer than 30 minutes and where no work duties are required, are not compensable. Check the following Department of Labor links for information on your state's rules: For state laws on rest periods, see **www.dol.gov/esa /programs/whd/state/rest.htm**. For state laws on meal periods, see **www.dol.gov/esa/programs/whd/state/meal.htm**.

Take Advantage of Benefit Discounts and Subsidies

Join trade, business or community organizations to lower benefit costs. Many offer reduced pricing on insurance, wellness programs, incentive plans, training, and retirement packages. Contact your state's restaurant association and the National Restaurant Association at **www.restaurant.org/join/services .cfm** to learn more about industry offerings. Small business organizations can provide reduced rates for members. Try one of these to reduce your employee benefit costs: National Business Association at **www.nationalbusiness.org** or Small Business Benefit Association at **www.sbba.com**.

Offer discounts for lifestyle and health needs like prescriptions, vision, dental, and cosmetic surgery.

Create a carpool and ride-share program. Employers' subsidies promote the reduction of urban traffic and energy usage. Information is available through federal, state and local government energy and transportation departments.

Barter with local merchants for pizza, movie passes, theater tickets, and other items suitable for employee rewards. Consult your tax advisor regarding your tax obligation and recordkeeping requirement.

Contact your bank for employee-banking services including free checking, discounted loan services, and automatic payroll deposit.

Enroll your business with a credit union. Credit unions offer employees excellent discounted financial services. Convenient on-site enrollments are available.

Set up a U.S. Savings Bond program. Funds are deducted from each paycheck, held until the purchase price is accumulated, and then the employee's bond is ordered. For information, visit **www.savingsbonds.gov**.

Explore employee discounts on auto and home insurance. An example can be found at Broad Reach benefits at **www.brb1144.com/auto_home.htm**.

Offer no-cost life-skills classes. Seek out bankers and investment counselors to provide free financial advice on savings, borrowing, investing, retiring, and owning a home. Nonprofit and government organizations can be good sources for free classes on topics like parenting, choosing a child care provider, and health concerns.

Government Employment Programs

Government agencies frequently take active roles to help high-risk and disadvantaged people become employed by offering payroll subsidies, tax breaks, and training programs. There are also financial-support programs based on where your business is located and the type of benefits you offer.

Search out work programs, subsidies, and tax breaks by contacting your local chamber of commerce, small business associations, and State Departments of Welfare, Commerce and Employment, and your accountant. Ask about your state employment division about "empowerment or enterprise zone" tax credits.

Read IRS Publication 954 "Tax Incentives for Empowerment Zones and Other

Distressed Communities" to learn about federal wage (salary plus company-paid health insurance costs) credits.

- Distressed communities (up to $3,000 per employee).

- Native American employment credits (up to 20 percent credit).

- Work opportunity credit for high unemployment groups; for example, felons, veterans, and food stamp recipients (up to $2,400 per employee/$1,200 summer youth employee).

- Welfare-to-Work (up to $8,500 per employee).

Help the disadvantaged and your business. Training programs and tax credits and deductions are available. Disadvantaged—CCH Inc. (**www.cch.com**) has an informative article on the four federal tax credits listed above at **http://taxguide .completetax.com/text/Q16_3214.asp**. Contact Disadvantaged—U.S. Work Force at **www.usworkforce.org**, 877-US2-JOBS.

Disabled Worker Programs

The federal government defines "disability" as a physical or mental impairment that substantially limits one or more of the major life activities; for example, walking, seeing, speaking or hearing. Under the Americans with Disabilities Act (ADA), employers are to make "reasonable accommodation" to facilities, job duties, work schedule, equipment, and other accommodations. A "qualified individual with a disability" means an individual with a disability who, with or without reasonable accommodation, can perform the essential functions of the employment position that such individual holds or desires.

Learn more about the financial benefits of hiring the disabled under the Ticket to Work and Work Incentive Improvement Act (TWWIIA) at the Department of Labor, **www.dol.gov/odep/pubs/ek00/ticket.htm**.

Improve your accommodations for disabled workers and accessibility for disabled employees and/or customers. The Disabled Access Credit (IRS Code Section 44) grants small businesses a tax credit (a 50 percent credit up to $5,000 annually). Details are available from the Department of Labor at **www.dol.gov /odep/pubs/ek97/tax.htm**. Expenses covered include:

- Sign language interpreters for employees or customers with hearing impairments.

- Readers for employees or customers who have visual impairments.

- Purchase of adaptive equipment or the modification of equipment.

The Architectural/Transportation Tax Deduction (IRS Code Section 190), **www.dol.gov/odep/pubs/ek97/tax.htm,** grants small businesses up to $15,000 a year for expenses incurred in removing barriers for persons with disabilities. Amounts above the $15,000 maximum annual deduction can be depreciated. Expenses covered include:

- Accessible parking spaces, ramps and curb cuts.

- Telephones, water fountains, and restrooms accessible by wheelchairs.

- Walkways at least 48-inches wide.

Businesses may take both the Section 44 credit and the Section 190 deduction in the same year providing the activities qualify.

Other Helpful Tax-Savers

Share credit card fee costs. Before disbursing tips added to credit card charges, you may legitimately deduct the credit card company's processing fee on the tip portion. Be certain to verify if this is allowed in your state.

Hire family members to eliminate some tax obligations. Many restaurants are unincorporated family businesses where everyone capable of working does. If your children or spouse aren't on the payroll and they can legitimately handle some type of work, you may be eligible for a variety of tax breaks. For example, hire your under-18 child and don't pay Social Security or federal unemployment taxes. Speak with your tax consultant for specifics. Read the Motley Fool article at **www.fool.com/taxes/2002/taxes020628.htm**.

Explore other tax deductions and credits related to benefits. Many are tax-free to employees and all are legitimate business deductions. Below are a few tax-savers:

- Up to 50 percent of employee pension plan set-up costs.

- Up to $100 a month per employee for public transportation discounts or passes.

- Up to $180 per month per employee for parking.

- Clothing (uniforms, aprons, hats) imprinted with the name of your business can be considered an advertising expense.

Hidden Payroll Expense Savings

You'll also have other costs associated with payroll. It takes time and money to maintain time slips, calculate taxes, write payroll checks, keep payroll records, administer benefit programs, and make tax deposits. To help you with the paperwork hassles and reduce these costs, we've compiled some practical ideas and useful resources.

Hire a local payroll service firm. Even if you handle your own bookkeeping, outsourcing payroll can be a wise decision. You won't have to worry about the right tax table or when to deposit withholdings. One advantage of hiring a professional is that they frequently assume all liability for filing errors and pay for all penalties or interest on late or inaccurate filings. Be certain to ask about liability issues.

Try online payroll services. Search the Internet under the keyword "payroll service" for banks, national service firms, local consultants, and Web-based solutions. Ask about liability issues. See Wells Fargo Bank at **www.wellsfargo .com/biz/products/payroll/payroll.jhtml**; Paychex at **www.paychex.com**; or Automatic Data Processing **at www.adp.com**.

Buy payroll software and do it yourself. Popular accounting packages have add-on modules and stand-alone software programs. Remember, you assume all liability for errors. See QuickBooks at **www.quickbooks.com/services /payroll**; Peachtree at **www.peachtree.com/epeachtree/payroll.cfm**; Pensoft (restaurant versions) at **www.pensoft.com**; or Restaurant Technology Inc. at **www.internetrti.com/ProductTours**.

Use human resources software, online services and downloadable human resources forms. See Trak It Solutions (HR software) at **www.trak-it.com /welcome.html**.

Find someone to do the human resources support and paperwork. Human resource consultants and personnel service providers can handle every aspect from advertising to interviewing to overseeing your benefit plans.

Eliminate writing payroll checks. Direct deposit paychecks into employee bank accounts. Some banks even offer free checking for employees needing to open a bank account associated with your direct deposit participation.

Consider lengthening your payroll periods. You can reduce your payroll accounting costs (check writing, recordkeeping) by up to 70 percent by switching from weekly to monthly. If employees find the monthly cycle difficult, try offering a less costly procedure like a scheduled draw mid-month. To verify your state's pay period requirements, see the Department of Labor's chart at **www.dol.gov /esa/programs/whd/state/payday.htm**.

Other Payroll Resources

Tax Tip Calculator at **www.paycheckcity.com/TipCalc/tipCalculator.asp**.

Time and attendance software listings at **www.hr-software.net/pages/211.htm**.

Days off calculator at **www.daysoffcalculator.com/web.htm**.

Pay raise calculator at **www.payraisecalculator.com**.

Bill Volk, owner and head chef of the **Camp Robber Café** *in Montrose, Colorado, opened the business in 1994 with his wife Kim. The Camp Robber Café will move to a new location in the near future that will triple its size. In preparation for the move, Volk has been exploring ways to increase the business profitability.*

I've been doing research, reading magazines like *Restaurant Hospitality* and *Restaurant News* to get ideas. I've also talked with electricians, plumbers and other tradesmen about the most efficient ways of doing things. Space is definitely a concern in big cities, but it has also become important in rural areas like ours. We're trying to fit in our equipment so that it takes up the least amount of room. That way we can use more space for seating.

In the new restaurant, for example, we'll be able to control the refrigerator compressors with remote controls. The actual compressors will be outside the building. That will save both space and the cost involved with dispersing all the heat the compressors generate. I've also talked with tradesmen about which kind of refrigerant gas is the most efficient. Another area where I'm looking for a significant reduction in operating costs is in the light fixtures we'll use. Some of the new bulbs will at least double the efficiency of standard fluorescent lights.

Chapter 16
Training Employees

Teaching Success

Accepting the responsibility for training is expensive, so your first choice should be to hire people with experience. Paying more than the prevailing wage and offering a comprehensive benefit package may cost you less in the long run. If you are lucky enough to have an ample well-educated workforce in your community, your employee training may only consist of orienting new hires to your own procedures and establishing personal goals and employer expectations. However, if trained workers aren't readily available, your only option may be to accept the responsibility of bringing their skills up to your standards.

Allocate work time to properly train your employees. Their increased productivity will pay for your time and investment.

Invest in Training

Invest time and money in training to improve productivity, increase sales and enhance quality.

Allocate work time to properly train your employees. Their increased productivity will pay for your time and investment.

A good job description = better training = more productivity.

Reasons for Training

- Unprepared employees are unhappy employees, resulting in high turnover.

- Unskilled or untrained employees will cost you more in low productivity, poor service, waste and inefficiency.

- Lack of training creates employees with poor attitudes and bad work habits.

Train the Trainer

If you didn't hire someone for their training abilities, don't expect them to be a natural at it. Simply handing over a new employee to a coworker may work, but most often it won't. Your first step is to train the trainer.

Teach employees to be trainers with help from Workforce.com at **www .workforce.com/section/11/article/23/24/25.html** and **www.atlantic-pub .com**.

Food safety training tips and techniques from Food Safety Training and Education Alliance at **www.fstea.org/resources/training.html** and **www .atlantic-pub.com**.

Find a "Train the Trainer" seminar. Restaurant management-specific classes and seminars are available through your state's restaurant association.

Your Training Needs

You pay for training, whether it is done right or wrong. Protect your investment by developing a program that meets the needs of your organization and brings you the greatest benefits.

Look at your current employees. What natural talents do they have that need to be enhanced? What would they like to learn? Talk to them and review their current skills against their assigned job description. Which tasks were still as difficult for them as when they started their job? These tasks should move up higher on your training schedule.

Start cross-training. Cross-training is teaching your employees how to do a job (or even specific tasks) other than their own regular job. This can be very valuable, especially to a smaller operation. Cross-trained employees can fill in when others are absent and jobs can be combined during slow economic times. Cross-training can also be used to prevent boredom for employees with routine jobs. Rotating positions can make the work more interesting.

Specific Training Areas

Below are some training areas from which your employees and restaurant might benefit:

Computer. Personal computer hardware, computerized systems (sound and lighting systems), computerized equipment.

Software. Point-of-sale systems, time management, scheduling, inventory control, reservation system.

Language. English for immigrants or foreign languages to converse with non-English-speaking employees or customers.

Safety. Food and alcohol, personal and workplace safety (accident prevention, injury, ergonomics), theft and robbery.

Legal. Discriminatory practices, sexual harassment.

Purchasing. Inventory control, waste management.

Leadership. Problem solving, motivational.

Personnel management. Problem employees, disciplinary, hiring, firing, sexual harassment, discrimination prevention, diversity.

Time management. Productivity improvements through time management.

Communication skills. Peer-to-peer, employee-to-employer, customer contact, phone skills, grammar, vocabulary.

Customer service, sales techniques. How to increase ticket sizes without offending customers, handling difficult customers, building customer relationships.

Etiquette. Personal, phone, cultural differences.

Setting Goals and Expectations

New employee orientation is where you'll lay a foundation for success by establishing your expectations of their performance and set productivity and performance goals. These aren't just something you announce and then never revisit. Goals and expectations are benchmarks for future employee reviews, bonus systems and salary increases. Here are some practical suggestions and resources to help you explain your performance standards and set success goals.

Read an e-book from Restaurant Trainers at **www.restauranttrainers.com /html/goal_setting.html**.

Work with employees to discover their career path. Goal setting is more than just stating someone must cover 7 tables and serve 24 customers an hour or they won't get a raise. It's also working together to develop a career. Many food service careers are based on advancing through the ranks and on-the-job training. You have a personal opportunity to transform a trainee into a talented chef or valuable manager.

Build in rewards and incentives.

Explain how their success relates to the success of their department and your operation. Employees that understand how they can make a difference accept increased responsibility and think more often about the common good. Personnel motivators call this "owning" the job.

Establish schedules and deadlines whenever possible. It's only human nature to delay actions until the very last minute. By setting deadlines and regular performance reviews, you'll keep the goals active.

Provide the tools and resources to reach goals. This can be something as simple as a book to read or as comprehensive as an educational subsidy.

Develop goals together and ask for a commitment. Give employees a copy of agreed-upon goals and expectations. Place a signed copy in their employee file.

Establishing Quality, Productivity and Performance Standards

For proper training and performance evaluation, you need to have established standards for each job description. These become your training, proficiency and motivational guidelines.

Quality standards. Quality standards can be difficult to express. You should do your best to illustrate these in words (job descriptions) and demonstrations (on-the-job training). Show servers what the dinner salad should look like (along with appropriate weights, measures and other food-control specifications) rather than just telling them.

Performance standards. The information you gather becomes the basis for your training, motivational and employee review efforts. These standards also take into account human factors. Only machines can be expected to consistently perform each task exactly the same way in the same amount of time.

Not a weapon. Work standards shouldn't be used as a weapon or threat but as a guideline. You cannot reduce a warm smile or a melt-in-your-mouth dessert to a standard.

Write them down. These standards should all be in writing. Besides including them in operational manuals and job descriptions, create and display wall charts. Use performance improvements between employees or shifts as the basis for a contest or bonus program.

Productivity Standards

The fast-food industry has become exceptionally adept at calculating down to the second how long it takes from the moment the customer walks up until they leave with bag in hand. In a single quick-service restaurant, 30 seconds can translate into thousands of dollars annually. To follow are some helpful tips on setting your restaurant's productivity standards.

Gather and analyze data. The better your data, the more accurate your standards will be. Take time and elicit your staff's assistance in setting productivity standards.

Conduct studies using actual real-world situations. You or a productivity consultant should do time and motion studies. This is also an excellent time to review ergonomics and procedures for wasted time and motion.

Gather data from other sources. A wide variety of data may already be available from credit card transaction time stamps, POS and inventory reports, equipment timers and usage calculators, and time clocks. Hosts/hostesses, servers and cooks can gather information during their days. For example, to calculate steps taken, purchase inexpensive pedometers.

Don't rely on "industry standards." Food prepared and served, facility size, layout, and equipment factors are different for every operation.

Set realistic minimum activity levels. This is your benchmark figure. Remember that trainees and experienced staff members cannot be expected to perform at the same level. However, everyone must be able to meet the minimum activity level.

Created tiered performance standards. Start with your minimum standard level and then add an "experienced" level and an "expert" level. These additional levels can be used in incentive programs.

Use your most productive employees to set optimal standards. No employee can or will perform at 100 percent capacity 100 percent of the time. Your goal is to average as high as possible as compared to the optimal productivity standards. Depending on the task and employee experience, acceptable levels will range from 75 percent and up.

Express all standards by the amount of work that can be completed within a set time and the qualitative level of performance required. For example, 25 racks of dishware, flatware and glassware to be washed, dried, sorted and returned to storage area "C" in two-hour off-peak periods of 8:30 a.m. to 10:30 a.m., 2:30 p.m. to 4:30 p.m., and 11:30 p.m. to 1:30 a.m.

Hire an expert. ProSavvy at **www.prosavvy.com** or Food Consultants Group at **www.foodconsultants.com** can help you locate a consultant.

Training Plans

Take your standards and job descriptions and develop a training plan for each job. This will make it clear to a new employee the skills, tasks and behaviors that they must master by the end of their training period.

Analyze the job description. Identify the specific duties to be done and the skills needed to do them. List the duties from the most basic to the most specific.

Don't think of it as school. Your training shouldn't resemble a high school class where everyone would rather be somewhere else. School means memorizing facts and figures, not learning practical skills. Hands-on and face-to-face is the best way to teach because we master skills better by doing.

Use hands-on training and practice sessions. The quickest way for an employee to learn new tasks is through on-the-job demonstrations and immediate practice.

Use role-playing for new employees who will be dealing with the public. You want to make sure they understand their duties and can perform them before you send them out to take care of actual customers. For example, have someone play the part of a customer to test a new server.

Test employees on a few critical issues. Some food-handling and safety facts should be tested to ensure that your employees understand and can comply with regulations. As the cliché goes: Ignorance is no excuse, but it can be quite costly!

Ask them. "Any questions?" is a simple and powerful way to determine what people need to know. Also try, "Is there anything we haven't addressed?" or "Should we go over that again?" Reward people who speak up and encourage all questions.

Starting Off Right

Even experienced employees need training to start them on a good path. Employee retention starts from day one. Don't just expect them to show up on Monday morning and be ready for work. You must be ready to start them off right.

Orientation. Orientation is your first training session. Don't just hand them a W-4 to complete and a policy manual. Good employer/employee communication starts here!

Tell them. Tell them what you and your company stand for and how important their success is to you and your team. Tell them what you're willing to do to make them a better employee and the benefits of building a future with your company.

Make it memorable. Don't drone on and on. You can even break the orientation into segments to be held over several days.

Inject some humor. Try these tapes and books for ideas: *The Big Book of Humorous Training Games: Dozens of Games for Popular Training Topics, From Customer Service to Time Management* by Doni Tamblyn and Sharyn Weiss.

Avoid technical words or jargon. New employees are less likely to ask questions, so your point may be lost unless you keep it simple.

Demonstrate whenever possible. Miscommunication can reduce productivity or create unsafe situations.

Cover the important topics first. Think about what you'd want to know and cover those first.

- How do I get paid? Make certain people understand how to complete and turn in time cards. Explain pay cycles, draws and benefit deductions.

- To whom do I report? Clearly identify direct and indirect supervisors and explain the relationship.

- Whom do I ask? Tell new hires about each person's expertise and duties through personal introductions.

- How do I work it? Allow ample time for equipment training. Lack of training directly impacts employee and equipment productivity.

- Don't overlook common items such as phone systems and time clocks.

- Create cheat sheets and reminders for quick reference.

- Concentrate on ergonomics and safety training.

Meetings

A quick meeting before the shift starts gives you an opportunity to teach and listen. You can also use this time to recognize individual accomplishments and share personal updates, improve communications and reduce gossip, give pep talks and announce contests, and make everyone feel included. Feeling "in on things" is very important to employees.

Don't try to solve the world's problems. But do listen to what your people have to say. You don't have to come up with a solution on the spot.

Make problem solving a team project. Implement solutions to previously voiced problems during these meetings. When your employees know that you are listening and trying to make their job better, you may be amazed at the solutions they can suggest themselves!

Create an atmosphere of trust. If you ask for input but your people have nothing to say, then you don't have their trust, especially if you overhear mumbled complaints after the meeting is over. To be effective, listen to their complaints and suggestions with an open mind and to come up with a fair and reasonable solution.

Culinary and Hospitality Programs

Building a relationship with one of the 1,700 culinary and hospitality trade schools nationwide can mean you'll get "first pick" from the most talented students. However, these graduates are still trainees in the sense that they have yet to perform day in and day out. You'll also find high school, community college and university programs to help you develop your own employees. Also, contact your state Employment Division for other employee-development programs. To follow are several resources for locating schools and programs dedicated to the culinary arts.

Trade schools. National Restaurant Association at **www.restaurant.org /careers/schools.cfm**; Star Chefs at **www.starchefs.com/helpwanted.html**; Culinary Education at **www.culinaryed.com**; Cooking Culinary Arts Schools at **www.cooking-culinary-arts-schools.com**; CookingSchools.com at **www.cookingschools.com**; and Culinary Training at **www.culinary-training.com**.

Industry programs. Sponsor a student. A CookingSchools.com article aimed at potential culinary students has some great ideas for potential employers. Go to **www.cookingschools.com/articles/scholarships** to learn more.

Learn about apprenticeship programs from the American Culinary Federation at **www.acfchefs.org** or HospitalityCampus.com's online training at **www .culinaryconnect.com**.

In-House Training Programs

Below are resources and tools for enhancing your in-house training programs.

- *The Encyclopedia of Restaurant Training, The Complete Waitstaff Training Course—Video* and *The Waiter & Waitress and Waitstaff Training Handbook: A Complete Guide to the Proper Steps in Service for Food & Beverage Employees.* These are all available from Atlantic Publishing, **www .atlantic-pub.com**, as well as other videos and training programs.

- *The Waiting Game: The Ultimate Guide to Waiting Tables* by Mike Kirkham.

- *The Restaurant Training Program: An Employee Training Guide for Managers* by Karen Eich Drummond and Karen A. Drummond.

- Trade Secret training products from Bill Main at **store.yahoo.com /tradesecrets/index.html** and online consulting at **www.profittools.com**.

- Food safety and skills training from Restaurant Workshop, **www.restaurantworkshop.com**.

- E-Learning and CD-ROM food service courses from Tap Series, **www.tapseries.com**.

Adult Education

Adult illiteracy costs U.S. businesses an estimated $225 billion annually in lost productivity. Workplace literacy isn't just an issue for non-English-speaking workers; American born-and-raised adults also lack the training to read written instructions, do basic math calculations, or complete a job application properly. Many restaurateurs have discovered the benefit of supporting, sponsoring and offering adult education classes: greater productivity, fewer errors, and increased workplace safety. To support employer efforts, a variety of private and public funding, tax benefits, and wage subsidies are available.

Literacy. Visit the National Institute for Literacy organization at **www.nifl.gov**. Watch an interactive presentation on adult literacy in the restaurant industry by the state of North Carolina at **www.ncrtec.org/pd/cw/rest/start.htm**. Develop a workplace literacy program. For information, visit the Adult Literacy Organization at **www.adultliteracy.org/wpl.html**.

The General Educational Development (GED) credential was created as a solution for adults who did not graduate from high school for one reason or another.

English as a Second Language. Adult ESL is the term used to describe English instruction for non-native-speaking adults. The goal of ESL instruction is English language (speaking, writing, reading and comprehension) and literacy proficiency. Unlike general adult educational programs, ESL programs may be offered to highly educated learners who simply lack English proficiency. Read *Communicating in a Melting Pot* from Restaurants USA at **www.restaurant.org /rusa/magArticle.cfm?ArticleID=106**. Learn more from the National Association for Bilingual Education (NABE) at **www.nabe.org** or call 202-898-1829.

Life-skills training. Life skills represent the knowledge and aptitudes necessary for a person to function independently and to keep a job. Workers lacking economic and educational opportunities may not have developed these basic skills and may struggle to meet employer expectations. Helping your workers develop life skills can be a wise investment. To learn more, Work Shops, Inc. has a manual online at **www.workshopsinc.com/manual/TOC.html**.

*As general manager of **Andiamo's** restaurant in Dearborn, Michigan, Tony Gagnon has 55 to 60 servers and 10 bartenders working under him.*

With that many people working on different shifts, it's difficult to communicate with all of them, so we had mailboxes made for each employee. They check them when they come in to start their shift. This way, if I've got a new drink promo or a dinner special, I can be sure everyone knows about it.

I'm also optimistic about a new loyalty program we've started recently. It's a way to give back to customers who have been loyal and increase our business at the same time. It's much like the frequent flyer miles that airlines award to their customers. We call it *Milli Graci* (that's "a thousand thanks" in Italian). For a one-time fee of $25, our customers can become members. They will receive a point for each dollar they spend with us. They can redeem those for discounts on food—after three visits they should have their $25 back—but they also become eligible for all kinds of prizes. One of the prizes is having one of our chefs come into your home and cook dinner, but we're even giving away free trips to Las Vegas and Italy.

It's an expensive program—less than 1 percent of restaurants in America are doing this—but because there are 10 Andiamos in the Detroit area, we think this is economically feasible. We've got a long way to go, but we're happy with what we've seen so far. Cost cutting is great, but when you have people coming through the door, that solves a lot of problems.

Chapter 17
Employee Supervision

Leadership

It takes a leader to "create" and maintain productive employees. Do you see employees as diamonds in the rough, ready to be polished? Or are they just warm bodies that meet an immediate need for a short period of time?

Being a good boss. The two commonly sited reasons why employees leave are they feel unappreciated or they hate their boss. These don't have to be employee issues in your business. Being a good boss doesn't come naturally to some people, but the good news is that you can learn how by reading books, taking classes and watching training videos.

Improve your leadership skills by reading. *The Gifted Boss: How to Find, Create and Keep Great Employees* by Dale A. Dauten. *How to Become a Great Boss: The Rules for Getting and Keeping the Best Employees* by Jeffrey J. Fox. Discover what employees say makes a good boss at Business Research Lab's Web site, **www.busreslab.com/bosses /goodboss.htm**.

Selecting other good leaders. As your business grows, you'll be increasing your management staff. In doing so, you should be looking for good leaders. A good leader is a good teacher.

Lead by Example

Leadership begins with your own actions and attitude. Below are some simple actions you can take to show your commitment to your goals. Your number-one goal should be good customer service. Second should be productivity. Here are a few simple ways to impress this standard on your employees:

Walk through the dining room regularly. If a customer needs something, get it for them. You will impress the customer that they have been taken care of by the owner, and if your server is too busy to get it, they will remember your willingness to help. If the server was slacking off, and you have hired good people, they will double their efforts so that you don't have to do it again.

Jump in and help if food is coming from the kitchen slowly. If this is a common problem, find out what is causing the slowdown and fix it.

Supervise your host/hostess. Make sure they are aware of the workload on each server and seat people accordingly. Not by number of people, necessarily, but by the difficulty of serving each group. A rowdy group or a group with small children would be more difficult to take care of than the same number of casual adults.

Give your help a challenge. See if you can clear a table before they get to it. Again, if you have hired correctly, they will do everything in their power to clean those tables before you get to them.

Replace people who just can't meet acceptable performance standards. Train them properly and give them encouragement. Counsel them if they fall short. But if they can't make the grade, you have to let them go. The counseling shows your fairness, but removing an employee who isn't doing their job shows your commitment to your business and to your other employees. Good employees shouldn't have to cover the workload for employees who can't make the grade.

Empowering People

One of the most powerful tools you have is to empower your people. Employees that act like owners are more profit-motivated and more productive. Create a team by empowering employees to work for the common good. Create a profit-based incentive program and teach them how inattentiveness and waste costs everyone.

Learn how to create a team. Here are some excellent articles and books on team building, empowering and delegating:

- *Customers as Partners (Building Relationships That Last)* by Chip R. Bell.

- *Knock Your Socks Off Service Recovery* by Ron Zemke and Chip R. Bell.

Help your staff understand what it costs to run a restaurant. Show them your invoices for utilities, rent, insurance, food, and beverages. If they understand just how expensive it is to do business, they'll be better prepared to make cost decisions.

Review time-saving procedures and ideas with your management and service staff to determine whether they make economic sense for your restaurant. Remember that the best way to get these changes to pay off is to get everyone to buy into them.

Employee Motivation

Employee motivation is an ongoing process that starts at the first interview. As a leader, you are responsible for discovering what motivates your employees. As a businessperson, you are responsible for increasing productivity and spending your resources wisely.

Motivating your employees means you are developing a partnership attitude; creating camaraderie and team spirit, improving attitudes and resulting behaviors, stimulating and challenging employees to grow, rewarding positive behaviors, mentoring and enhancing lives, and building dedication and loyalty. Keep Employees (**www.keepemployees.com**) is an excellent site detailing motivational factors.

What motivates people? In a national survey, hundreds of employers were asked, "What motivates your employees?" The majority answered "More money." But when their employees were queried, money ranked in the middle. Employees listed their morale boosters as: interesting work, appreciation and recognition, feeling "in on things," job security, and good wages. Notice that all of these are subjective. Remember, it's how they feel about a situation (as opposed to the facts) that counts. So how do you figure that out? You ask them!

Also, read the following:

- *365 Ways to Motivate and Reward Your Employees Every Day—With Little or No Money* by Dianna Podmorrof.

- *Motivating at Work: Empowering Employees to Give Their Best (a Fifty-Minute Book)* by Twyla Dell and Michael G. Crisp.

Employee Attitudes

Some employers take on the role of Ringmaster when dealing with employees. They wear the uniform and weld the whip as if they were orchestrating a three-ring circus. As lion tamers soon learn, motivating with a whip is short-lived and they are often growled at! Nor do you have to be the head clown to keep people happy. There are times where you'll be wearing your Ringmaster hat and other times when the big clown feet are more appropriate.

As Ringmaster, your job is to oversee an employee's attitude (good or bad) and be aware of how it affects the organization. Determine whether it's a training or attitude problem. Guide people to better attitudes. Reprimand or terminate someone for a bad attitude when it becomes a bad behavior.

Evaluate employees on an informal basis regularly. Your staff needs to hear what they are doing well and how to improve their weak areas. A major source of stress is not feeling in control. Use this process to help them feel in control of their work lives.

Watch for a change in attitude. A change (for the worse) in attitude is your signal to pay attention now. Attitude problems can quickly decrease productivity and invite theft or sabotage.

Listen carefully and don't ignore the signs. You may have been taught to ignore gossip, but in this case it can give you a heads-up. A poor attitude is a red flag signaling a problem. Take time to isolate the source of employee frustration.

Figure out the basis for productivity issues. Some attitude problems are really training issues. A wise manager once said, "If she could do it when you put a gun to her head, it's an attitude problem. If she can't, it's a training issue."

Act decisively. As the cliché goes: It only takes one bad apple to spoil the barrel. Poor attitudes can "spoil" an organization, so don't hesitate to control the situation with a reprimand or termination.

Challenge Your Employees

Highly productive and service-conscious employees are made, not born. They are a product of their work environment. Hire the right attitude, train properly, reward outstanding performance, and guide them in the right direction to build a successful team.

Expect the most from people. People will often surprise you (and themselves) by rising to the occasion when expectations and standards are set high.

Make change a priority. Making at least one change every month shows your employees that you are actively working to make your business better. Even small changes can accomplish this end. If your employees are expecting and used to changes, they will accept bigger changes more readily.

Have a "no stupid questions rule." Encourage employees to ask plenty of questions. You'd be surprised at how often a "stupid" question is the one everyone is afraid to ask. These are also signals that your training is insufficient.

Reward thinking. Encourage and reward creative problem-solving and cost-saving solutions.

Be able to explain why. As any small child knows, "because" isn't an answer. You must be able to explain the reasons for procedures to your employees. If they don't know why things are to be done a certain way, they will take shortcuts. In some cases this can improve productivity, so be open to suggestions. But some shortcuts will reduce your standards.

Learn how to create challenge programs from Dr. John Sullivan (San Francisco State University) at **http://ourworld.compuserve.com/homepages/gately /pp15js34.htm**. Read *Peak Performance: Aligning the Hearts and Minds of Your Employees* by Jon R. Katzenbach.

Leadership Tips

There are dozens of leadership gurus, business experts, and motivational consultants to assist you in improving your people skills. Every major bookstore has an aisle full of the latest and greatest ways to "shape" people into great employees. The thousands of ideas espoused in these books and in the resources here won't be any good if you don't respect your employees first. As we discussed in "What Motivates People," some basic human needs must be met before you buy any inexpensive prizes or get out the clown suit! Below are more useful tips and resources for leading and motivating your team to success.

Learn how to manage and motivate all types of employees. Learn how to manage Generation X from consultant Judy Cox at **www.media3pub .com/usbank/articles/genx.html**; older workers from Hard at Work at **www .hardatwork.com/Stump/ME/OlderWorkers.html**; and short-term workers from Hard at Work at **www.hardatwork.com/Stump/ME/ShortTerm .html**.

Is poor performance your fault? Find out from Business Know How at **www .businessknowhow.com/manage/poorperf1.htm**.

Don't spend anything. Learn cashless ways to motivate from BizTraining.com, **www.biztrain.com/motivation/stories/cashless.htm**.

Try some of these books on motivating employees:

- *1001 Ways to Energize Employees* by Bob Nelson and Kenneth H. Blanchard.

- *Recognizing and Rewarding Employees* by R. Brayton Bowen.

- *The X-Factor: Getting Extraordinary Results from Ordinary People* by Ross R. Reck, Ph.D.

- *From Turnover to Teamwork: How to Build and Retain a Customer-Oriented Foodservice Staff* by Bill Marvin.

- *Playing Games at Work: 52 Best Incentives, Contests and Rewards for the Hospitality Industry* by Phil Roberts and T. J. McDonald.

- *Coaching and Mentoring for Dummies* by Marty Brounstein.

Employee Policies

An employee manual addresses a wide variety of employment issues. A good manual explains:

Hire an expert to create your employee manual. Companies like Literary

Technologies, **www.literarytechnologies.com** and Personnel Policies, **www .personnelpolicies.com**, can handle everything from gathering information to printing. Or see the *Employee Handbook Creator Guide* from Atlantic Publishing at **www.atlantic-pub.com**.

Get expert advice. Employee manuals can be considered contracts by the courts. An attorney should review your manual BEFORE you distribute it. The National Restaurant Association can help you with How to Write an Employee Manual at **www.restaurant.org/business/howto/eemanual.cfm**.

Get a signature. Obtain a signature confirming employees received a copy and accept responsibility for reading and complying with its contents. Some HR experts advise that you have employees read the manual immediately and return with questions.

Avoid legalese. Your manual should be written in conversational English. Your employees need to understand it more than your lawyers do!

Address specifics. For help in writing policies on important issues, check out the following Web sites and online articles: For dress codes (including tattoos, piercings) see Personnel Policy Service, Inc. at **www.ppspublishers .com/dresscodepolicy2.htm**. For a drug-free workplace policy from the U.S. Small Business Administration, see **www.dfwp.utsa.edu**.

Alcohol abuse. Alcohol use and abuse in establishments selling alcohol can be a larger issue than for other businesses. In most states, you can be held liable for the actions of employees who consume alcohol provided by your business.

Watch your alcohol inventory. *The New York Times* addresses alcohol theft at **www.bevinco.com/spirits.htm**.

Gone but Not Forgotten

Employee absenteeism is technically an unscheduled failure to report to work. Because these events cannot be planned for, productivity and morale are immediately impacted and chaos can rein. Scheduled or not, absenteeism occurs for physical and emotional reasons. It is a barometer of employee morale and costs your business! Your first five steps in combating excessive absences should be to:

Calculate the cost of absenteeism to your business. Use the calculator provided by Harris, Rothenberg International at **www.harrisrothenberg.com/vc /vc-comp-abs.htm**.

Invest these losses into prevention.v

Discover the true reason for the absence. Benefits.org can guide you with their Attendance Management Program at **www.benefits.org/interface/cost /absent2.htm**.

Create an absenteeism policy. Review tips and a policy sample at Business Owner's Toolkit Web site, **www.toolkit.cch.com/text/P05_5325.asp**.

Take proactive steps. Employer-Employee.com addresses employer concerns and employee needs at **www.employer-employee.com/absent.html**.

Drug and Alcohol Problems

Drug- and alcohol-related issues cause U.S. companies over $100 billion annually. One in five workers report that they have had to work harder, redo work, cover for a coworker, or have been put in danger or injured as a result of a fellow employee's drinking. Almost 68 percent of illegal drug users are employed either full- or part-time according to the National Institute on Drug Abuse. To learn more, read *Uncovering the Hidden Signs of Workplace Substance Abuse* by the Department of Labor at **www.dol.gov/asp/programs/drugs/workingpartners/uncover.htm**.

Employee Problems

Disruptive behaviors, dishonesty, poor work performance, and absenteeism are problems that create destructive ripples and affect your staff and business. One reason good employees leave is that management doesn't properly or promptly address problems with other employees. Good people want to work in an environment where professionalism, hard work, honesty and service are rewarded—not where the opposite exists by default! Here are a few tips on handling employee problems to keep productivity and morale high:

Don't bury your head. Ostrich-style management is frequently based on an erroneous belief that you must keep the restaurant staffed at any cost. Ignoring problems could mean the only employees you'll be keeping are the problem ones!

Discourage gossip. Gossip is destructive, and workplace gossip can cause enormous employee stress and dissension.

Protect your employees. You have a responsibility to provide a safe and secure environment. This includes sexual and religious harassment and workplace conflicts. Even seemly routine employee problems can transform a peaceful workplace into a scene of violence.

Don't let employees use the threat of quitting as a weapon. This is a poor management style and gives others the impression that you're playing favorites.

Give "negative" feedback in private. Workers often feel a bond with peers and consider management the "opposition." Keep disciplinary actions private to avoid fueling these beliefs.

Manage employee conflict. To learn how, see Management Association Program for Nonprofits' Conflict Management Guide at **www.mapnp.org/library/intrpsnl /conflict.htm**. Get advice on handling problem employees from Business-Town.com at **www.businesstown.com/people/employees.asp**.

Pay attention to employee stress. Stress Directions can give you some valuable insights into the importance of monitoring and reducing employee stress at **www .stressdirections.com**.

Understand the legal issues relating to problem employees. Attorneys Amy Delpo and Lisa Guerin can help with the book, *Dealing with Problem Employees: A Legal Guide.*

Disciplinary Action

Disciplining employees is an unpleasant duty for supervisors. But failing to do so undermines management and disrespects your other workers.

Act early before problems become severe. *A Check-up for Under-Performing Employees* by Dave Anderson at Golden Nuggets Software at **www.bss-gn.com /nl/july2000/art003.htm**.

Be consistent and fair. Video and workbooks to teach proper (legal) disciplining methods is available from Management Training Videos at **www.management-trainingvideos.com**.

Handle with care. Union workers, employees covered by the American

Disabilities Act (ADA), and others may be covered by contracts and/or laws that establish how you can discipline and terminate. We recommend that you have a labor attorney guide you through these issues.

Document well. Business Owner's Toolkit offers comprehensive guidance on documenting disciplinary actions at **www.toolkit.cch.com/text/P05_7230.asp**.

Coach for improvement. See *10 Keys for Successfully Coaching Employees* by Mark Campbell (article available at Society of Professional Consultants' site at **www.spconsultants.org/articles/mcampbell.htm** or the Employee Development and Coaching Guide) from Accel-Team at **www.accel-team.com/human _resources/coaching.html**.

Make the "punishment" fit the crime. Progressive discipline is common personnel practice. Many labor experts advise that this is the only way to protect your business against possible wrongful termination claims and lawsuits. Also, hospitality workers' unions may spell out your disciplinary requirements in contracts.

Terminate when warranted. *When You Can Legally Fire Employees*, an All Business educational article at **www.allbusiness.com/articles/content/HR _article24.asp** will help you make this critical decision.

Terminate Wisely

You owe it to your business and your other employees to remove disruptive, non-productive or insubordinate employees from your staff. Keeping "bad" employees affects your entire team's productivity. To follow are additional resources.

National Restaurant Association addresses termination issues. For how-to and legal issues, see **www.restaurant.org/legal/law_termination .cfm**. For tactful terminations, see **www.restaurant.org/rusa/magArticle .cfm?ArticleID=423**.

Be careful when firing a popular employee. If the grounds are fair, your staff is probably more aware of the problems than you realize. Because the employee is well liked, managers often hesitate to discipline and delay terminating the employee until the behavior becomes severe. This delay increases the stress among the remaining staff and undermines your authority. Don't ignore other performance problems, as this can fuel any claims of unfair treatment.

Build support. Although you cannot share confidential information about employee terminations, you can build support within your staff and encourage them to pick up additional responsibilities while you restaff.

Investigate thoroughly. You may even have to question other employees. HRZone offers advice on this step at **www.hrzone.com/topics/firing.html**.

Be prepared for a negative reaction. Even if you have been coaching and counseling the employee on their unacceptable behavior or inadequate performance, you should be prepared for an emotional response.

Terminate immediately (without disciplinary action) when employee safety is an issue (conflicts, threats, violence), when employees are carrying contraband (drugs, weapons), when employees commit illegal acts (theft, embezzlement), or when employees are under the influence of alcohol or drugs.

Employee Turnover

With restaurant turnover rates running as high as 250 percent annually, no other personnel issue is as costly. Turnover increases your costs for employee searching, hiring and training. Restaffing and training can also cost your business thousands annually in productivity losses and customer service declines.

They'll always leave. You'll never eliminate employee turnover. And, in fact, you don't really want to. Turnover is what brings you fresh faces, innovative methods, youthful exuberance, wisdom and experience, trendsetting ideas, and new skills. Your goal is to reduce it, manage it, and transform it into new opportunities.

Why They Leave

You'll lose employees because of poor training, retirement, physical and mental health concerns, graduation, competition, poor wages/benefits, burnout, stress, transfers, poor attitudes, family needs, desire for personal growth, and death. Some are not in your control; however, you can positively influence many of these factors. Understanding why your employees leave is your first step to reducing turnover.

Listen and learn. We don't just mean staff meetings or boss-to-employee lectures. Take time to ask and listen about their families, expectations and dreams.

Survey them. Employee satisfaction surveys are one way to head off problems. See Business Research Lab at **www.busreslab.com/consult/empsat.htm** or Employee Surveys at **www.employeesurveys.com**.

Interview them. Exit interviews are valuable information-gathering opportunities. If you find that your departing employees aren't forthcoming, you might try hiring a consultant to follow up with surveys, interviews or questionnaires. Financial incentives can improve your success rate and can pay off. To learn more about conducting exit interviews, visit Bill Marvin, The Restaurant Doctor at www.**restaurantdoctor.com/articles/exit.html**.

The Cost of Turnover

The National Restaurant Association puts the average cost of losing a minimum-wage hourly employee at $2,494 and a manager at $24,000. Using these statistics, a restaurant with 75 hourly employees and three managers, a 90 percent turnover rate translates into over $203,000 lost each year. With numbers like these, even small operations should "invest" in creating a work environment that provides stability, financial security and emotional support to its employees. Invest your time and money in retaining valued employees. To learn more about turnover costs:

Use the turnover calculator at **www.uwex.edu/ces/cced/publicat/turn.html** to learn how turnover affects your business. These cost figures don't take into account the productivity and quality factors that indirectly impact customers, employees, and your bottom line.

Chapter 18

Scheduling Your Staff

The Eight Basic Scheduling Steps

There are eight basic steps in the scheduling process:

1. **Developing work production standards.** Calculate the amount of work (covers, meals, place settings) that an individual employee with a specific job (server, cook, dishwasher) is expected to accomplish in a set time period.

2. **Plotting patterns of activity in various units of the operation.** Food service facilities usually have different patterns of activity during the day that requires different levels of scheduling.

3. **Forecasting levels of activity.** Shift, daily, weekly and monthly customer/sales cycles should be factored in. These can be broken down into quarter, half and hourly segments within each day.

4. **Determining the number of workers and/or hours needed.** Divide the work production standards into the anticipated number of covers (customers) and the number of personnel required can be calculated.

5. **Considering employee time and assignment requests.** Job assignments; skills, abilities and experience; scheduled absences; desired rotation; wage rates; and legal considerations such as hours for minors and overtime are all important considerations.

6. **Approval by management after the schedule is written.** Evaluate by criteria such as labor cost per hour, customers served per hour, or any other appropriate criteria.

7. **Distributing approved schedule to employees.** Employee handouts, breakroom and office postings, Web site postings, e-mail broadcast, and "call-in" systems are all ways to ensure staff members have ample notification of shift assignments.

8. **Recapping and reviewing the historical schedules** by management to discover problems, explore solutions, and improve processes.

Scheduling Truisms

Your goal is to complete all necessary work using the least number of labor hours possible while maintaining an outstanding level of service.

Establish a baseline for a minimally acceptable service level. Then analyze how each additional worker impacts service quality and productivity. Remember, employees appreciate getting more help but become irritated when they "lose" help.

Absenteeism will play havoc on your fine-tuned schedule on a regular basis. Controlling unplanned absences is critical to maintaining adequate productivity and service levels. See the section on "Absenteeism" for more information.

Good forecasting requires good data. Historical and current data must be accurately gathered and easily assessable.

Outside factors are important forecasting issues, such as seasonal demands, weather conditions, special events, and competitive issues.

You must understand your team's capabilities and capacities. Consider individual skills and abilities to balance scheduling. People have active/sleep cycles and are more productive during specific times of the day. Some servers cope with noisy children better, so schedule them during family times. Family needs create unplanned absences and distract workers. Whenever possible, you should consider these during scheduling.

Overworking (physically and emotionally) staff members can significantly lower productivity, increase absenteeism and escalate turnover rates. Frazzled employees are potential customer-service nightmares. Inattentive service, inaccurate orders, spills, and angry encounters lower your service quality and chase away customers. Tired employees can cut corners—increasing food safety problems, food waste, equipment and dishware damage, accidents, and injuries.

Overstaffing doesn't just inflate your payroll, it can decrease your overall productivity. Congested serving and kitchen areas makes everyone's job more difficult and lowers service quality.

You must balance quality and quantity. A fast cook who makes mistakes and turns out sloppy meals is not up to your quality standards. A slow cook who turns out perfect meals is not up to the quantity standards.

Schedule Types and Patterns

There are different types of schedules that can be used in a food service operation.

Scheduling by production requirements for individual items. Determine what has to be produced for the meal, period or day. You may include items that will be produced for future meals.

Scheduling by station production. Items from the production schedule are assigned to a workstation (e.g., bakery, salads, etc.). Smaller operations may combine a production schedule and a station work guide.

Scheduling by staff coverage (individual schedules). This provides coverage for the various units within the operation. Production schedules should be coordinated with individual scheduling. Dining room scheduling is based on the forecasted number of patrons divided by the work production standards of the dining room personnel.

There are three common scheduling patterns:

1. **Block or stacked schedule.** Everyone on a shift starts and stops

working at the same time. This makes it easier to check that everyone is present and on time and share common information. This works best for operations closed between meal times as customers aren't directly affected by any staff changes.

2. **Staggered arrivals and departures.** Employee schedules correspond to the work pattern and customer flow. More efficient than block scheduling, as the number of employees gradually increases during the peak volume periods and decreases towards the end of the day.

3. **Spanner shifts.** Overlapping coverage for a smooth transition between shift changes. Overlap times range from 30–60 minutes, depending upon the job category and duties. It eliminates staff working past scheduled departure times to "finish up."

Other Possible Scheduling Methods

Forecasting can be difficult, especially for newer establishments without any historical data from which to draw. This can cause scheduling inaccuracies that inflate your labor costs or result in substandard service. You'll find that unplanned events can directly impact your staffing requirements. There are other scheduling procedures to help you through unpredictable times. Below we'll discuss six ways you might consider. Although federal wage and hour laws do not address these issues, you should be aware of union contracts, local labor practices, corporate policies, and state laws that may govern your use of flexible scheduling practices. Meal and rest periods may also be mandated by your state even if workers are on the clock for less than eight hours.

On-call scheduling. Hourly employees remain at home until you call them into work. Quick response can be critical so employees can be given pagers or cell phones so they aren't "trapped" at home. Employees can rotate being on-call to give them additional free time without significantly affecting their paycheck. On-call periods would be scheduled like any other work duty. Trainees and new hires can be used for on-call coverage during probationary periods. Minimum hours may be mandated by union contracts and other labor practices.

Send-home-early scheduling. The reverse of on-call scheduling, employees are sent home when work slows. With good forecasting and intelligent scheduling, this would typically be used for unusual circumstances, such as bad weather. Employees can rotate, draw straws, or volunteer to go home early. Trainees and new hires (seniority) can be chosen.

Part-timers. Schedule part-timers for additional coverage during peak periods and seasonal influxes. Post a roster of workers interested in part-time or temporary work. This can be a good choice for people seeking part-time work with exceptional flexibility. High school and college students who need to work around class schedules or during summer, spring and winter breaks, retirees needing to supplement Social Security, or parents interested in working during school hours.

Split shifts. Similar to part-timers but where employees would work multiple, non-consecutive mini-shifts totaling up to 40 hours a week. Employees clock out between scheduled work periods. Workers would cover specific meal periods or required prep and clean-up times (before and after peak periods).

On-break schedules. When it isn't practical to send someone home, you can put them on an extended break. A 30-minute off-the-clock break and employer-provided meal means you can deduct the cost of the meal against the minimum wage requirement and save half an hour of pay.

Short-term overtime. Overtime is costly but sometimes necessary when unforeseen emergencies arise and short-term coverage is required. Beware of burnout and stress when employees are working extra hours to help out.

The Negative Impacts of Understaffing

Unskilled managers can be too zealous in keeping labor costs low. A shortage of workers and/or relying primarily on inexperienced, lower-paid workers will initially reduce your costs. However, the long-term impact on service, morale and productivity could mean a slow and painful death for your business. Below are some useful resources and ideas on how to measure whether your staffing levels are creating problems.

Ask your customers. Tour the dining room throughout the meal, asking about their dining experience. Conduct customer service surveys. For information on surveys, visit The Business Research Lab at **www.busreslab.com/consult /restcslg.htm** or Mercantile Systems and Surveys at **www.mercsurveys.com**.

Hire a "mystery shopper." Professionals visit your restaurant to gather information and report on your customer service. Check the Mystery Shopping Providers Association at **www.mysteryshop.org**, 972-406-1104, for a local consultant.

Employees suffer. You risk losing your most productive employees, as they will probably be the ones working longer hours. Overworked employees can quickly become unhappy and unproductive employees. Some employees won't complain; they'll just lose their incentive to work hard—then they'll leave. Others will develop a disruptive attitude—then they'll leave.

Costs soar. Instead of saving money, you'll be spending more through lost productivity and lost customers! Other potential liabilities could be costly. As detailed in Nation's Restaurant News (July 20, 1998), cumulative fatigue can become a financial burden. A McDonald's restaurant was held responsible for $400,000 in personal injury damages after an employee, who had worked three consecutive shifts in 24 hours then fell asleep at the wheel, was involved in a serious collision.

Business declines. How long customers will wait varies from establishment to establishment. Customer expectations during a workday lunch are significantly different than at a leisurely resort. In our fast-food nation, waiting is a major issue for diners. Customers will only put up with slow service for so long.

The Negative Impact of Overstaffing

Having too many people on hand can affect your bottom line in more ways than just wasting your payroll budget!

Don't forget Parkinson's Law: "Work expands so as to fill the time available for its completion." If you give someone two hours to do a one-hour job, it will take two hours. Or, if two people are scheduled to do a one-person job, it will take both of them to get it done.

Poor work habits and attitudes will rise as employees slow down. Employees will resist an increase in their workload after being overstaffed for a while. They will have adapted their performance levels to a lower productivity standard. They will even feel overworked and find it difficult to "speed up."

Unneeded workers with idle time become distractions. Water cooler chit-chat begins to interfere with customer needs. The atmosphere becomes too relaxed and service declines due to the resulting apathy.

Physical and mental fatigue becomes an issue because of boredom and time-wasting habits. Morale drops because management must eventually reduce their labor costs. But before they do, tips will suffer, which also creates motivational problems.

Scheduling Tips and Hints

We've put together some useful scheduling tips, hints and resources:

Develop a manpower plan to determine hiring needs. Restaurantville.com tells you how to calculate whether you need to increase your staff at **www.restaurantville.com/sc/hr/recruiting/needs.cfm**.

Study your volume. Schedule labor to match volume needs (level of activity).

Study the level of activity breakdowns by area. For example, kitchen help needed before the busy period (9 a.m.–1 p.m.), waitstaff during the busy period (11 a.m.–2 p.m.) and cleaning after (12–3 p.m.).

Remember that different work units have different patterns of activity throughout the day. Normally, activity is highest in the kitchen before it is in the serving areas. The dishwashing units' activity peak may be 15–45 minutes after the serving area peaks.

Schedule according to your customer flow. You need more employees on hand during peak times, and fewer employees when you have fewer customers.

Plan for shift changes to minimize service disruptions. Take into consideration the layout of your establishment and the total duties of each position.

Employees should be given enough flexibility to ensure that transitions are handled smoothly and tasks completed to the customers' satisfaction. But set some limits to keep overtime in check.

Computerized Scheduling

Restaurants of all sizes can successfully implement computerized employee-scheduling systems and software. Employee scheduling can be handled by a Web site, an uncomplicated Windows program, or linked directly to "time clocks."

Below are a few sources for computerized scheduling:

Optimal Solutions at **www.optimal-solutions.com**. They offer online solutions that run through your browser and desktop programs.

Schedule for Restaurants at **www.aschedule.com**. The program can automatically calculate your labor costs per cover and has an "Overtime Alert." Two versions are available for small or multi-store operations.

Asgard Systems Inc. at **www.asgardsystems.com**. The "Time Tracker" system also keeps track of vacation time, sick time, etc. It can review past activity and prepare payroll data.

Restaurant Technology, Inc. at **www.internetrti.com**. Management, scheduling and accounting software for the food service industry.

Staff Schedule at **www.staffscheduling.com** is a free Web-based scheduling program and can be accessed by management and employees from any Web-accessible computer to set and check work schedules.

Open Wave at **www.open-wave.com** offers various Web- and PC-based programs.

Explore software that captures data directly from your time clock. These programs automatically track employee hours, let you know if someone is late or early, warn you of possible overtime, and even send the information directly to your payroll software.

Chapter 19

The Productive Workplace

Productivity

Profits are simply the difference between what you sell and what it costs you to sell it. To increase profits, you can increase sales or decrease costs. Your serving staff should all be trained to "sell" more—larger tickets lower your cost per cover. However, an extra $150 per shift doesn't increase profits by $150. After costs and taxes, you might be lucky to net $20! But saving $150 by operating more efficiently increases your bottom line by $150. Improved productivity can be defined as working smarter, not harder, to achieve more. To increase your staff's productivity, changes can be:

- **Simple.** Buying extra trashcans.

- **Complex.** Commissioning work-motion studies.

- **Free.** Overcoming poor work habits.

- **Costly.** Remodeling the entire kitchen.

- **Physical.** Building a facility with no stairs.

- **Psychological.** Creating an "ownership" attitude.

Productivity Is Also a Quality Goal

If the quality of your food and customer service declines, you have hurt your business, not helped it. The most important factor in improving productivity is smart management.

Don't compromise your quality standards. A change that noticeably lowers your quality will also noticeably lower your sales! Beware of changes done for the sake of "efficiency" that cause employee morale to decline.

Invest in your business's productivity. Invest in training. Well-trained employees are happier, more productive, less prone to job stress, and less likely to be lured away by your competition. Or invest in equipment that pays for itself in labor-savings or in a worker-friendly building. Make it easier for your staff to do their jobs with proper ergonomics and well-designed rooms.

Productive People

There are three basic ways to make employees more "cost effective." First, get more work from the employees you have in the same number of hours. Second, get the same amount of work from fewer employees in the same number of hours. Third, get the same amount of work from fewer employees in fewer hours. To help your employees reach their productivity potential, we've outlined some business concepts and suggestions on implementing them.

Make it important. Being profitable is important to everyone! It's important to your customers, your staff, your management, your community and you—the owner. Getting everyone to share this never-ending goal is your first step in directing people to be more efficient. Employees that see a direct correlation between their work performance, the customers' satisfaction, and your restaurant's success are going to work harder.

Don't waste a minute. Have time cards initialed by the manager on duty upon arrival and departure. You'll know exactly when the employees arrive and start to work, but your manager also gets the chance to check the employees' appearance. If there are special instructions to be given to an employee, the manager doesn't have to go looking for anyone. At the end of each shift, the manager has an opportunity to thank the employee and privately address problems.

Listen to your employees. No one knows better what it takes to improve a job than the person doing it. The most valuable "boss" has the ability to listen.

Always follow up somehow. The quickest way to create unhappy employees is to "forget" to handle suggestions and complaints. When asking for input, remember that it always requires some "output" by management. This doesn't mean you have to implement every one or "solve" every complaint—it means that you take them seriously and act accordingly. Your actions tell your employees that their ideas and opinions have value!

Make it clear. Detail tasks in writing. Write job descriptions and break down tasks into simple steps. This will help you set time and performance standards and make it easier to train employees. Plus, it lets employees know what needs to be done.

Give employees benchmarks and guidelines for improvement. Don't just set minimum standards. Tell them what they can do to be a top performer, and then reward them!

Assign tasks based on skill level and ability. Match the job with the right person. Tasks should be assigned to the lowest-paid employee capable of successfully handling the job.

Share information regularly and consistently. Good communication is critical to creating a productive service team. Schedule daily orientation meetings to review specials and menu changes, set sales goals and incentives, review procedural changes, and address potential problems. Schedule weekly meetings to recap your restaurant's production and employee performance. Thank and reward people. Address customer problems and complaints. Schedule monthly or quarterly meetings with your full staff. These team-building sessions are where you reinforce good behavior and attitudes and develop strong bonds.

Reinforce your message with handouts, diagrams and illustrations. Post information on an employee-only Web page and breakroom bulletin boards.

Stimulate, but don't stifle. Some employees are "naturally" productive. Their personal work ethic and positive attitude make them self-motivated and productive. Sometimes it can seem as if these are "problem" employees, as they tend to be more independent and headstrong. Your job is to harness and direct their energies without stifling them.

Create productivity incentives. Beyond rewarding your most productive employees with higher wages, consider bonus programs and profit sharing to make everyone personally connected to and responsible for productivity.

Consider sharing ownership. Studies have shown that when employees own a "piece of the pie," they increase their productivity. This could be accomplished literally by creating employee ownership programs, forming partnerships, offering share options or giving stock bonuses, or figuratively by linking pay structures and bonuses to profitability.

Create a reward program. You can offer fun prizes monthly for the best laborsaving suggestion. Or go all out and create a "share-the-wealth" program where employees are rewarded a percentage of the documented savings.

Make it easier. Watch your employees at work. Silent observation can reveal inefficiencies in your system. Mentally break down their activities into small segments to see where you can add laborsaving equipment, rearrange the work center, or save steps between work areas.

Train and supervise. Untrained employees are not working up to their potential. Unsupervised employees won't do their job quickly and accurately unless they clearly know what their job is! *Chapter 16–Training Employees* provides you with more in-depth information.

Reduce employee stress and fatigue. Working people harder will increase productivity but only to a point! Employee burnout is 60 percent emotional and 40 percent physical.

Cross-train and rotate staff. Monotony and repetition can "burn out" employees and decrease their output. Changing duties can provide an emotional and/or physical lift.

Make it last. Build in checks and balances to see that shortcuts aren't being taken that compromise your performance, quality or safety standards. Assign team leaders to supervise implementation of productivity changes.

Create a follow-up plan to verify that employees haven't fallen back into old habits. Don't let turnover degrade good habits and efficient procedures.

Streamlined Tasks

Manufacturing productivity experts can spend hours analyzing what's the fastest and most efficient method for inserting Part A into Part B. You should be looking at your daily operations from the same point of view: How can we do it better? To follow are some suggestions to get you started in reviewing tasks and establishing better procedures and methods.

There usually isn't just one right way to do something.

It's easier to replace a bad habit with a good one than to try to break it!

Target specific activities for time and performance studies one at a time. Don't overload yourself and your staff by trying to improve everything at once!

Tackle the obvious first. A few positive changes can stimulate your team to work together to find other areas for improvement.

Analyze production standards on a daily basis. It takes some time and analysis to determine standards, but it's worth the effort. See the Chapter 2 for more information.

Advance planning is the key to controlling costs. Plan production activities in advance. Group together like activities in specific timeframes to minimize cleanup.

Review your menu choices. Are you selling enough of a specific item to warrant the labor required to prep, prepare and serve it? Will altering a recipe slightly allow you to do more advance prep? Does purchasing fully prepped ingredients or pre-processed entrées cost less than handling it in-house?

Provide less service. If your restaurant style lends itself to self-serve salad bars, buffets and self-bussing, you can cut your staffing needs and your labor costs. When reviewing the cost-benefit analysis, be certain to consider the cost of equipment, shrinkage/waste and customer perception. Remember, many people eat out because they are waited on.

Make use of new, more efficient equipment. Conveyer-style dishwashers can eliminate a part-time dishwasher.

Work Smarter, Not Harder

To unlock productivity in your team:

Read a book. *Work Smarter, Not Harder! The Service That Sells! Workbook for Food Service*, available from Atlantic Publishing at **www.atlantic-pub.com**.

Hire an efficiency consultant like Peggy Duncan, **www.duncanresource.com**.

Learn how Pal's did it. This Tennessee fast-food chain, **www.palsweb.com**, won the prestigious 2001 Malcolm Baldridge Quality Award, **www.nist.gov/public _affairs/pals.htm**.

Give small, unexpected rewards. A job well done should never go unnoticed. An inexpensive reward like a quick-pick lottery ticket or movie pass.

Conduct memorable meetings. Routine meetings become routine. Keep employees on their toes with humor, silly costumes, magicians, humorous training videos, and other attention-getters. To learn how to have fun meetings, see EffectiveMeetings.com at **www.effectivemeetings.com/meetingplanning /fun/meetinglite.asp** or Patricia Fripp at **www.fripp.com/art.makefun1.html**.

Work ahead. The more activities you can combine before serving times, the more prep labor you'll save.

Adopt Technology

The importance of technology to the restaurant industry cannot be understated. For an industry with steady but unspectacular growth of 1–3 percent annually since 1991, technology offers one of the few opportunities for cutting costs, improving efficiency, and affecting the bottom line. Restaurateurs have been slow to adopt technological advances for a wide variety of reasons, from not enough buying power to the feeling restaurants should be run by people, not computers. The broad acceptance of computers in our daily lives, from ATMs to the Internet, has taken away much of the apprehension. The food service industry began looking to technology for cost-cutting assistance in the 1990s. From 1992 to 1997, computer-related expenses more than doubled in our industry. "Early adopters" supported the evolution of technologically based advancements making them more user-friendly, dependable and affordable.

The right computer system can help you reduce both labor and food costs. Computers can reduce your paperwork, allowing your managers to spend their time managing people instead of paper. The efficiency of computerized systems can also help you to maximize your people resources through better scheduling and communications.

Invest for today and tomorrow, but don't overbuy. Your equipment should meet your current needs and be able to handle your growth. Conversely, don't overbuy "just in case." If you can stand in the corner and see your entire establishment, then your needs are much less complex than if your establishment has 300 seats spread over two or three floors.

Hire an expert. Unless you've got a lot of time on your hands or are already a computer whiz, you can actually save money by hiring an expert to research, purchase and implement complex systems.

Establish what you want to accomplish before you buy. This will help you focus on solutions and not toys! It's easy to get caught up in a salesperson's pitch and forget your objective.

Other Ways to Save Labor Costs

Use disposables. If the ecological concerns of disposables aren't a concern, disposables can be a labor-saver when it comes to those nasty cleanups.

Label and color code. Create a color-code system to quickly identify items at a glance. Colored labels can help people return items to their proper storage area or let them know if it needs to be refrigerated. See **www.daymark.biz**.

Use napkin rings. Build wrapped napkin/silverware sets ahead of time to save table-setting time. You'll also reduce storage handling and rewashing. Add your restaurant logo for a personal touch. Bands are available from ColorKraft at **www.colorkraft.com**, 866-382-4730.

Use Griptite™ serving trays. Available from local suppliers, these metal trays have a non-slip surface for easier carrying. The 31-inch oval tray can hold 8 dinners!

Eliminate clutter. Clutter is defined as anything that has no immediate use or value. Everything else should be tossed or properly stored. Hire an organizational expert to review your storage systems and suggest ways to reduce handling costs.

Eliminate pot and pan cleanup with PanSaver, available at **www.atlantic-pub .com**. PanSaver is a high-temperature (400°F/204°C) material designed as a commercial pot and pan liner that keeps pans clean and can be used to store leftovers.

Use pre-prepared products. There's almost no ingredient that doesn't come prepped, portion-controlled or prepared for reheating. Not all are good candidates for your restaurant, but many can be incorporated into your food offerings, without any noticeable quality decline. Food that is eaten in its most natural state—washed, cut and ready to serve, like fruit and vegetables—is an obvious choice. Bread products that are proof and bake- or brown-and-serve are another option. Tea and lemonade concentrates are very common and taste better than powdered versions.

Chapter 20

Productive Buildings

Building in Efficiency

In building or remodeling your restaurant, you have the opportunity to build in labor-savers. From the building's infrastructure to the decorative touches, you should review the form, function and material choices for potential time savings. Your restaurant is your factory and, like any good factory, it needs to be designed with your workers and their productivity in mind. This chapter will explore construction, design and decorating issues and how they affect labor costs.

Site Selection

Select land/buildings with sufficient exterior space for waste/recycling activities and deliveries. You'll need good access, wide doors, and ample ramps. Avoid sites that would require time-consuming hand offloading. If you'll be receiving palleted goods, be certain you'll be able to accommodate a small forklift and/or lift trucks.

Be careful when considering retrofitting buildings. Buildings that weren't originally built as restaurants can pose some real challenges. Carrying a heavy tray up a small stairway or dozens of small isolated rooms will increase your servers' workload. Inadequate kitchen space or inconvenient storage can significantly slow your kitchen productivity.

Hide the wires! Not only are exposed wires unsightly, they can also be potential safety hazards.

Deaden, mask or enhance sounds. Excessive noise creates stress, increases fatigue, and causes headaches.

Create a building that promotes productivity and safety. Failing to properly address cleanliness, safety, workflow, and ergonomic issues can put your customers, employees and business at risk.

When making construction and design choices, don't forget:

- Suitable work areas that eliminate potential cross-contamination.

- Ample storage that promotes good food-handling procedures and eliminates cluttered floors.

- Ample lighting in common areas, workstations and "danger zones" to minimize accidents.

- Proper drainage in wet areas (prep, restrooms) to prevent slip-and-fall injuries.

- Appropriate non-slip or slip-resistant flooring material in high-traffic and wet areas.

Select Materials That Do the Work

Some materials are obviously easier to clean, like cold, hard plastic, but unless you're building a kid-proof joint, your restaurant probably needs some softer, warmer touches to make it feel inviting. Your goal should be to incorporate as many easy-to-clean-and-maintain materials as possible. Here are some practical ideas for easy-care building materials. Entrances, waiting areas, dining rooms and restrooms can all benefit from materials that do the work!

Determine the area's "dirt" level. The more potential dirt, the more important your material and color choices become. Front entrances and entries must be scrubbable, non-skid surfaces. Add mats inside and out to catch water, mud, sand and tar. Rent mats for more savings. Restrooms must be able to withstand heavy-duty cleaners, disinfectants and hot water.

Use color, texture and patterns to "hide" dirt and wear. Make certain normal wear and tear (shoe scuffs, carpet wear, high-heel damage) and daily activities aren't visual negatives. In dining areas, select carpets/flooring that won't show footprints and crumbs.

Seal surfaces whenever possible. Porous materials, like your concrete walk and wood floors, should be professionally sealed to reduce stains and cleaning times.

Explore "self-cleaning" materials and products, such as Self-Cleaning Glass from Pilkington Activ™, **www.activglass.com**. Bathrooms can feature automated public toilets from Exceloo, **www.automatic-toilets.com**. You may want to look into self-cleaning air cleaners from Peak Pure Air, **www.peakpureair.net/aqe .htm**.

Choose commercial-grade building materials. Many building products have industrial grades that are designed for heavy-use environments. Be sure to read the warranty. Some building products have shorter warranty periods and/or limited coverage for commercial applications.

Look for materials/products that have antimicrobial agents to prohibit microorganism growth. These shorten cleaning times by inhibiting the growth of bacteria, spores and molds. To learn more, visit Abiotics Online at **www .geocities.com/hotsprings/6869/industrial.htm**.

Healthy Environments

Healthy environments are productive environments. On-the-job injuries, workplace stress and unhealthy atmospheres are significant factors in high absenteeism and employee turnover. Your goal should be to create a pleasant work environment that minimizes employee stress, protects their health, and promotes safety.

Ergonomics

Ergonomics is the study and engineering of human physical interaction with spaces and objects during activities. A prep area that requires workers to repeatedly stretch across to reach ingredients or a broiler unit that only very tall workers can safely reach is "poor" ergonomics. Good ergonomics, such as well-fitting tables and comfortable chairs, can also enhance your diners' experience. Here are some valuable tips to help you "engineer" your restaurant to work well with people.

Create mini-work stations where all necessary food, utensils and prep spaces are close at hand.

Eliminate excessive bending, lifting and reaching while encouraging proper prep and storage procedures.

Provide stools or chairs to give backs and feet a rest if the work being done doesn't require standing.

Make certain your tools and equipment weren't designed for only men. Although more and more women are donning toques, tools and equipment haven't necessarily been redesigned to accommodate their shorter frames or differing physical characteristics.

Provide stable, heavy-duty work ladders for accessing top shelves and deep storage units.

For left-handed employees, purchase a supply of special tools and utensils.

Arrange seating to minimize steps and reduce cross-traffic patterns.

Make a point to minimize your guests' exposure to glare, drafts and noisy areas, and create easy entrances and exits.

Choose fixtures and equipment that can be easily moved from work area to work area when needed.

Protect employees from injury by placing heavy items closest to waist height as possible. Provide sturdy stepstools, ladders and rolling carts nearby. Except for rarely accessed areas, keep shelving shallow enough for easy reach.

The Air We Breathe

Healthy air is a concern that impacts restaurants legally and morally. "Poor air" contributes directly to employee absenteeism and workers' compensation claims. Many communities have rigid air emission and work environment regulations relating to proper ventilation, wood burning, grease and smoke. Unpleasant odors also contribute to "poor" air quality.

Physically separate smoking and non-smoking dining areas and/or direct airflow away from non-smoking tables. Ban employee smoking in the kitchen, dining room and bar. Visit the Phillip Morris USA's Options Web site at **www .pmoptions.com**, dedicated to indoor air-quality issues. You'll also find free assessment tools and an HVAC referral service.

Indoor air. Wood-burning ovens, charbroilers, fryers and "sealed" buildings can also create unhealthy or unpleasant air conditions. Indoor air quality requires bringing sufficient outdoor air in, properly filtering the outdoor and re-circulated air and directing airflow.

Improve indoor air quality by installing a whole-building air cleaner/filtration system that also reduces airborne particles and dust. Also, check for radon, mold spores and biological dangers when converting older or long-vacant buildings. Read what the EPA says about indoor air quality at **www.epa.gov/iaq/pubs /insidest.html**. Be aware of unhealthy emissions from carpeting, paint and cleaning products. Sick Building Syndrome is explained at the National Safety Council site at **www.nsc.org/ehc/indoor/sbs.htm**.

Productive Environments

The layout of your establishment may be costing you money. Wasted movement is wasted time, which is a waste of your labor dollars.

Rearrange the work area. The fewer steps your people have to take, the faster they can do their job.

Review your walkways and halls. Have room for employees to move without bumping into others.

Study how your staff moves through the active and passive work areas. Watch the traffic patterns. Do people have to stop to let others pass? Do they have to circle a dining room to get to the kitchen?

Increase productivity by creating three types of storage: active, backup and long-term. Active storage is accessed repeatedly throughout the day and should be located closest to the active work area. Backup storage is used to refill (bulk) items for active areas and items used occasionally during the week. It should be located further from the active work area but easily accessible. Long-term storage is for nonperishable special-use and seasonal items. Locate it in an out-of-reach, less accessible area.

Eliminate unnecessary bending, stooping and reaching. Simple, low-tech innovations can cut costs too. Try putting a shelf above the prep table for condiments. No turning or reaching. The preparer doesn't have to move to finish the plate.

Beautiful and Carefree

Without interior decorating, you'd be serving meals in a warehouse. The beautiful touches you add to make the environment more attractive, more entertaining or more relaxing should also be practical and low maintenance. Decorative items shouldn't get in the way of good service or create work obstacles for servers. Here are several suggestions on how to keep your restaurant beautiful:

Rent greenery. Your staff won't have to worry about regular care, plant rotation, and seasonal updates.

Install quick-connect water valves/faucets to water interior and exterior plants and trees. Access to water will make after-hours mopping and hosing quicker.

Install plenty of electrical, phone and sound system outlets. No crawling under tables and over cabinets to plug in something.

Incorporate skylights, light tubes and windows to bring in more natural lights. Studies show natural light increases productivity and reduces stress.

Explore full-spectrum lighting (which reportedly makes people feel healthier) for work areas.

Make it easier for spur-of-the-moment room changes with chairs that are easy to move, stack and store. Choose round table tops in various sizes and separate legs/stands to mix and match. Utilize divider doors, screens and walls on rollers/casters/wheels.

Eliminate tablecloths. Placemats take less time for setup. If your restaurant theme is very informal, go bare! Tame table toppers. Don't overload the table, slowing down setup and bussing.

Traffic and Workflow

A well-designed restaurant makes it easier and faster to serve meals. Improper workflow and poor traffic patterns mean thousands of wasted steps and movements every day. Analyzing your layout and equipment needs from the viewpoint of the user will increase productivity, decrease employee stress and injuries, and improve your customers' service. To follow are some areas of traffic within your restaurant and how you might eliminate excess steps and waiting while increasing productivity.

Restrooms. Place restrooms at the front of the restaurant to minimize traffic around the kitchen.

Hire a traffic/workflow expert. A food service consultant specializing in traffic analysis and workflow streamlining can help you maximize your space while improving employee productivity.

Listen to your staff. Service personnel, chefs and assistants with hands-on experience can help you create layouts that help them respond quicker and improve morale.

Make the self-service counter easy to access. Allow 4.5 feet for counter workers and 2.5 feet for back bar workers. Be certain trays, bins and service carts can fit between aisles and counter sides.

Help your servers and buspeople. Table layout can affect the speed diners are served and tables are cleared. If faster service is your goal, make certain servers aren't battling your table placement. Don't use fussy tablecloths and napkins, and make sure all surfaces can be cleaned quickly and efficiently.

Diagram the room. Seeing where every table and workstation is placed in relationship to each other, and how they relate to the active food prep areas and kitchen, will help you eliminate unnecessary steps, cross-traffic and backtracking. Some designers can create helpful diagrams detailing the number of steps between tables and work areas. Or try floor planner software. You can find information at OnTheRail.com, **www.ontherail.com/site/news /floorplanner.asp**.

Place banquet and large party areas closest to the kitchen to improve service and food delivery times.

Enhance communication to reduce steps and speed service. Centrally located or multiple-station POS equipment. Even more efficient is handheld order-entry systems that allow the waitstaff to move directly to the next customer. Use vibrating pagers and two-way radios to signal that tables are cleared or meals are ready.

Determine the activities your staff will be doing in the dining room and at tableside. Plus, make certain staff can rearrange tables quickly and easily to accommodate the party's size.

Front-of-the-House Support Stations

Realistically, not all food prep and service work can be accomplished behind closed doors. To do so would exhaust your waitstaff unnecessarily, slow down your service, and create a workflow nightmare in the back-of-the-house.

The front-of-the-house may have a reception to meet and greet, take reservations, and assign customers to servers. It would also have a cashier area to receive meal payments, process credit card charges and sell retail items. A food service area for beverage centers, salad prep and dessert service may also be practical. Finally, dinnerware and utensil storage with a place for setups, additional napkins and specialty utensils can be helpful. Depending upon your restaurant layout, service methods, etc., some workstations may have multiple functions.

Don't forget to build in floor drains, use scuff-resistant baseboards, and add casters to equipment that must be moved for quick cleaning.

Reduce lifting and carrying with mobile carts and rolling waste receptacles. Also, use anti-fatigue mats and non-slip flooring.

Use properly aimed task lighting to avoid glare while allowing staff full visibility of the work surface.

Separate "wet" and "dry" tasks to avoid damage, food contamination and electrical accidents. Incorporate hand and/or utility sinks whenever possible to save steps and promote cleanliness.

Provide ample counter space below pass-throughs to add garnishes, verify orders, and fill trays.

Consider incorporating a small (and quiet) under-counter glass washer for thorough cleanup of critical tools and utensils.

Back-of-the-House—Your "Factory"

Too many people, too little space, too much work to get done in too short of a time. Sounds like a busy restaurant! Good traffic patterns and workflow make it easier for your chef and support staff to be productive.

Add traffic aisles. Thirty inches is the minimum to allow traffic to move around the kitchen without interfering with active workspace. Be certain aisles are wide enough for mobile carts. Heavy traffic areas or aisles with workers on each side may require 48 inches or more.

Add extra doors for direct bar access. Concentrate on straight-line production whenever possible.

Install separate kitchen access doors. Separate doors should be 2 feet apart. Doors should only swing one way with large, clear, unbreakable windows in each. Clearly mark the doors—IN or OUT—on each side. Doors should be at least 42 inches wide. If separate doors aren't possible, use double-swinging doors (at least 84 inches total).

Employee Energy Boosters

Create rest areas. Rest areas for employees should consist of something more than a back step. A peaceful area is a great way to rejuvenate employees and let them know how important they are.

Don't overlook music in the kitchen and staff areas. Music has proven to enhance productivity and reduce stress. Just make certain that it doesn't overwhelm normal voice-level conversation.

Provide employee-only restrooms. Employees will be able to feel more relaxed and get in and out quicker.

Create a covered employee-only area outside. A bit of sun can be a great refresher. Also, smokers have a private area to smoke even during bad weather.

Kitchen Design

Good kitchen design is an art and a science. Hire a talented consultant to balance space limitations, safety issues, food prep needs, and budgets without sacrificing food quality, productivity and your staff's sanity! Here are some suggestions on how you might make your kitchen layout work for your chef and support staff.

Know what you'll serve (raw ingredients and prepared foods) and how you'll serve it to determine your prep, assembly, storage and serving needs.

Break your kitchen activities into self-contained workstations where ingredients, tools, equipment and supplies are within easy reach.

Include plenty of waste receptacles. Divide by type of waste if you will be implementing recycling programs.

Create work triangles. Triangle or diamond layouts give quick access to prep tables, sinks and cooking equipment. Straight-line layouts work best for assembly line-style prep and cooking where more than one person participates.

Draw out traffic maps to minimize unnecessary steps, crisscrossing paths. Then locate your cooking and final prep areas near dining areas to shorten kitchen trips.

Allow for ample open space. People need to pass, carts need to be rolled, shelving needs to be moved, buckets need to be wheeled, and trays need to be lifted.

Place your volume cooking areas towards the back of the kitchen and your to-go order needs nearest dining areas. Production that requires little tending shouldn't take up precious high-activity space.

Laborsaving Equipment

In a restaurant you are starting with raw material, creating a finished product, and supplying it straight to the consumer, all on the same premises. From start to finish, machinery can help your employees do their job faster. However, restaurants don't just sell food; they sell service, convenience and entertainment. It can be a mistake to replace people with self-service machines in some environments. You must balance your profit needs with your customers' expectations. From simple, little items that save a minute here and there to fully computerized and integrated kitchens, there is a plethora of equipment available to help you cut your costs and enhance your service. Here are helpful resources and practical ideas for every area of your operation.

Spending $10,000 on equipment could pay for itself in less than a year. Equipment covered by IRS Code Section 179 (100 percent deductible in acquisition year) that eliminates one minimum-wage employee saves you thousands over the equipment's life.

Consider the equipment's length of service and maintenance costs when calculating your savings.

Understand your customers' expectations. Self-service is fine for fast food and family restaurants, but are a poor idea when people want to be waited on.

Test equipment with staff before buying. Many distributors and local utility companies operate full test kitchens for demo purposes. Certainly an experienced factory rep can easily operate the stove, but if it is hard to operate or difficult to understand, it won't make things easier for your people.

Don't overbuy. Do you need all those features? Would a more basic model suit your needs?

Take time to train. Many manufacturers or distributors offer training for your staff. Don't be afraid to ask for support.

Make certain it's easy to clean and sanitize. Prep and cooking time savings can be wiped out if the equipment or tool takes too long to clean.

Front-of-the-House Labor-Savers

Equipment, fixtures, furniture and decorative items are all potential labor-savers. Yes, even a chair can save you time if it's quick to clean, easy to move, and convenient to store.

Create a communication station for your receptionist by including a multi-line phone system, fax machine, POS system, guest and server paging, and computer reservation systems. Don't forget network and Web access to monitor online reservations and to-go orders. Video camera systems can also help in seating patrons in larger or multi-story establishments.

Explore computer reservation and customer data systems. Computerized reservation systems range from simple scheduling software for $150 to complex systems for $5,000 that can track your valued patrons' personal preferences and contact information. To learn, more visit JCR System at **www.jcrsystems.com /rsvip.htm** or MicroCafe at **www.microcafe.net** for Reservation Pro.

Move some reservation functions to the Web. Your Webmaster can assist you with scheduling via your Web site or you can use directory-style sites or three-party services. In major cities, you can list your restaurant on Web sites like Open Table at **www.opentable.com** and Food Line at **www.foodline.com**. CyberWhiz, **www.cyberwiz.com**, will host your reservations on the Web with SimpleREZ or you can purchase standalone applications.

Communication Systems

Wireless headsets can save thousands of steps a day by connecting your front-of-the-house staff with your bar and kitchen staff. Combined with a POS system, wireless technology can speed service and improve communications—even in noisy kitchen environments. To learn more about wireless communications, contact HM Electronics, **www.hme.com**, for a variety of wireless systems and pagers. Panasonic, **www.panasonic.com/pos/ultraplextxt.htm**, offers complete license-free 900MHz systems.

Silent pagers. Hand waving, finger snapping and whistling for a server are a thing of the past. Never again will your customers be frustrated by an "invisible server." Silent pagers are the high-tech solution. One-button pagers are placed on the table. If the customer needs anything, they simply press the button. The appropriate waitperson is notified instantly and silently. A glance at the vibrating personal pager lets them know exactly which table needs their attention, no matter where in the building they may be. Pagers can also be used to let diners know their table is ready (even if they have wandered to the mall next door), signal a busy busperson, or let the manager know they are needed tableside. JTECH, **www.jtech.com/hospitality/hosp_index.htm**, carries guest, manager and staff paging systems. Advanced Communications Equipment, **www.advanced-ce.com**, sells the Server Wireless Calling System for guests to signal servers. E-POS, **www.eposonline.com/lrs.html**, offers guest and server pagers to enhance communications and keep seats filled.

POS Systems

POS systems can allow servers to concentrate on customer needs without running back and forth to the kitchen. They also shorten wait times at every stage of service. You'll reduce guest check errors because there's no more messy handwriting to decipher or math errors. You can monitor sales and productivity by food category, shift or table and enhance inventory-control systems. Plus, you can gather data to improve your scheduling procedures and adjust staffing levels based on accurate reports—even during mid-shift.

Purchasing a POS system. Seek out real-world experiences and recommendations. Ask vendors for local references and repair service contacts. Restaurant Report gives suggestions in their Q&A at **www.restaurantreport.com/qa /possystem.html**. The POS Help Desk, **www.poshelpdesk.com**, states, "We don't sell POS systems... We help you buy them!" Also, visit state, regional and national restaurant shows. You'll be able to demonstrate and compare hardware, software and features at vendor booths. Finally, ask about report sharing and data exporting. To share statistics with your accountant, be certain that reports and/or raw data can exported or electronically linked with other systems.

Front-of-the-House Tools

Here are some practical ideas and helpful resources for labor-saving tools from the front door to the kitchen door.

Outfit workstations throughout larger dining rooms and exterior dining areas to reduce trips to the kitchen. A self-contained workstation could include serving utensils and bowls; extra place settings and glassware; extra aprons and laundry bags; hot/cold beverage dispensers and coffeemakers; waste receptacles on wheels and mobile carts; under-counter dishwasher; salad and dessert assembly and service; POS systems, computer network and phone systems; hand sink and/or utility sinks; ice machines and/or storage units; and emergency clean-up supplies.

Incorporate self-service activities whenever possible. Take care, as these may "turn off" customers or be negated by increasing food/beverage costs. Try placing menus in holders on each table. Create a beverage bar with hot and cold drink dispensers. See the Espresso Specialists Inc. at **www.esi-online.com/Product /prod_frankesaphira.html** for the Saphira unit; perfect for self-service.

Back-of-the-House Equipment

Behind the swinging doors is your greatest opportunity for incorporating laborsaving equipment and tools. There are computerized ovens that can be programmed to bake and hold entrées without anyone watching; conveyer belt dishwashing systems that carry dishes from the serving area to a fully automated dish room; and compact, multi-purpose units that can be placed within easy reach.

Look for equipment that is easy to move, easy to clean and easy to operate. Since looks aren't important in the kitchen, go for functionality over appearance.

Invest in quality materials so your staff doesn't waste time tinkering, adjusting, operating, scrubbing or waiting for a repairperson.

Buy user-friendly. Are the knobs placed within easy reach? Are labels, controls and instructions in plain view and easy to understand? Are emergency shut-offs well marked? Check the buying guides and articles at FoodServicesSearch.com, **www.foodservicesearch.com/Well_Equiped/index.cfm**. This site requires free registration for full access.

Purchasing Inventory-Control and Kitchen Equipment

Consider computerizing your purchasing and inventory control. Companies like Crunchtime, **www.crunchtime.com**, and Food Trak, **www.foodtrak.com**, offer software solutions. Many popular POS systems have inventory/purchasing capabilities or add-on modules.

Barcode systems using hand-held printers and readers can streamline inventory management. Check out MRA Technologies at **www.mra-tech.com** to learn more. For wine inventory-control systems in upscale establishments, see

Wine Seller Pro, **www.winesellerpro.com**.

Prep Equipment

Saving even 30 minutes a day pays off! Here are some proven time-savers:

Toss the Ginsu knife and find a better way to peel, chop, dice, slice and shred.

Chop like a maniac with an electric vegetable processor. Read what Foodservice Equipment Reports has to say at **www.fermag.com/sr/v3i6_sr _fp.htm**.

Peel a melon in 15 seconds with the Univex PerfectPeeler, **www.univexcorp .com**. Peel and seeds are automatically separated from the melon. Quick-change blades adjust to accommodate everything from small cantaloupes to large honeydew.

Buy wedgers, cutters and slicers in a variety of sizes with quick-replace blades and place them on a convenient workstation. Inconvenient, hard-to-use and out-of-sight equipment won't get used!

Produce up to 300 cookies per minute with the Kook-E-King, **www.kook-e -king.com**, an automatic cookie depositer. The hopper can hold up to 90 pounds of dough, and more than 60 different dies are available.

Purchase combination prep machines for greater efficiency. Is it a mixer that blends or a blender that mixes? Robot Coupe USA, **www.robotcoupeusa.com /d1.html**, produces a variety of food processors with multiple functions.

"Flatten and par-bake pizza crusts in seconds without skilled labor." That's the claim of the PizzaPro by ProProcess Corporation, **www.doughpro.com**. Crusts can be prepared in less than 60 seconds and hold for hours for the lunch crowd. Crusts can also be frozen for later use.

Eliminate tears with an onion slicer. Nemco Food Equipment, **www.nemco-foodequip.com**, specializes in food-prep equipment like the Easy Onion Slicer and the Green Onion Slicer Plus.

Cleaning Equipment

Dry dishes faster. High-velocity air-driers meet sanitation codes which means staff can be reusing or storing dishes faster.

Add a conveyer system to make it easier to move soiled dishware to the kitchen. Adamation, Inc., **www.adamationinc.com**, manufacturers standalone conveyors and continuous-conveyor dishwashers.

Waste and Recycling Equipment

Place wet and dry waste receptacles and recycling bins near every work area. These should be clearly marked and color coded for quick recognition. For faster handling, they must have casters or be placed on mobile carts.

Install indoor trash compactors. Manufacturers state compactors can hold the equivalent of 15–20 trash bags (55-gallon) before emptying.

Set up a self-contained recycling system. Waste Away Systems, **www.waste-awaysystems.com**, sells a compact, no-lift, no-touch reduction/recycling unit. Ver-Tech, **www.ver-tech.com/select.html**, manufacturers recycling equipment for baling cardboard, compacting plastic bottles and aluminum cans and handling other common restaurant waste products.

Switch to an outdoor trash compactor. Manufacturers specializing in recycling and waste disposal management and equipment can be found at the Open Directory Project, **www.dmoz.org**, under the keywords "waste management" and "recycling."

Storage Fixtures

Use see-through storage containers with spigots and drop-down doors or sliding lids for quicker access and inventorying and less handling.

Purchase refrigeration units capable of accommodating deliveries on pallets. Walk-in cooler doors should be 4- to 5-feet wide for easy access.

Specify self-closing doors or use a Thermal Flex Swing Door, **www.walkin-refrigeration.com/ThermalFlexSwingDoor.html**.

Cut chilling times to speed handling steps. Kolpak's, **www.kolpak.com**, Polar-Chill system blast chills products from above 140°F to 40°F in 2 hours.

Install a strip door to improve access and visibility in storage rooms and walk-in coolers. Visit Strip Door World at **www.stripdoorworld.com** to learn more.

Cooking Equipment

Cook faster. Microwave, conveyor, convection and impingement (pressured hot air) ovens are all energy and labor-savers. Match your needs with the proper equipment. Some high-speed methods handle specific cooking and baking tasks better than others. Explore combination ovens that combine microwave technology with convection or impingement. These ovens provide the speed of microwaves without the taste and appearance negatives often associated with microwave cooking. Investigate lightwave/microwave countertop ovens from the Vulcan-Hart Company, **www.vulcanhart.com**. Speed claims of 50–75 percent, compact size (30" x 16"), and programming capabilities make the VIVA model worth considering.

Make your cook super-human. Conveyor cooking technology and Blodgett's, **www.blodgett.com**, 36-inch Magigrill means one person can cook up to 250 burgers or 200 pieces of fresh chicken per hour.

Research air-door ovens. Lang Manufacturing, 425-349-2400, builds "doorless" energy-efficient pizza ovens. Forced air keeps the heat in and gives operators quick access and easy product viewing.

See the Microwave Association, **www.microwaveassociation.org.uk /factsheets/caterers.htm**, for commercial microwave oven information Lincoln Products, **www.lincolnfp.com**, has impingement oven information.

Cool and cook in one unit. Minimal service and display kitchens frequently have space limitations. Even in large kitchens, combination equipment can save unnecessary steps, lifting and reaching.

Search for equipment that satisfies multiple functions such as Imperial Commercial Cooking Equipment's Sizzle 'n Chill™ stovetop/refrigeration unit, **www.imperialrange.com**. Investigate Rankin-Delux's hot plate/wok combo, 800-345-4752, West; 800-338-4325, East. Look into Thermomix USA's 12-in-1 appliance that whips, blends, chops, kneads, steams and cooks, **www .thermomix.com**.

More Cooking-Equipment Tips

Free up employees with built-in temperature probes and loud notification buzzers.

Increase productivity, food quality and safety with accurate thermometers.

Use portion-control dispensers for everything you can. You'll not only trim food costs, but your staff will be working more efficiently.

Move the kitchen out front. Display kitchens aren't just popular with customers; they are great fun for show-off chefs and free up space in the back. Food is cooked in full view and within steps of diners.

Reduce grease-handling activities. Install a central grease collector. Contract with a company that delivers oil to remote tanks. Clean oil is piped directly to fryers and used fat is piped out for recycling. Or purchase an "oil-free" fryer, where "frying" is done through infrared technology or flash heat activates the oil already in frozen, pre-browned foods.

Add a refrigerated base to the workstation. Silver King, **www.silverking.com /cb.shtml**, makes models that hold six or ten full-size pans.

Use Sterno's Smart Can™ **for buffet and chafing dishes.** The built-in heat indicator tells workers at a glance that the can needs changing.

Beverage Tips

Select ice machines and bins that can be filled, emptied and cleaned easily. Add long-handled food-safe scoops to help shorter workers access ice.

Invest in a gravity-fed ice system. No more wasted labor lugging and loading ice with Follet's Ice Storage and Transport systems, **www.follettice.com**. Follet anticipates a typical restaurant can save up to one full-time worker per month every year!

Other Cooking Innovations

Don't wrap and rewrap pans. Use see-through lids for steam-table pans from Cambro, **www.cambro.com**.

Tired of waiting for the pot to fill with water? Wall-mounted flow fillers are available from Fisher at **www.fisher-mfg.com**, 800-421-6162.

Need a sharp edge fast? Edgecraft's, **www.edgecraft.com**, Chef's Choice knife sharpener can hone a razor-sharp edge in 60 seconds and re-sharpened knives in less than 15 seconds.

Never scrape off a steam-table pan label again. Buy wash-off labels from DayMark Food Safety Systems, 800-847-010, **www.dissolveaway.com**.

Install an air door between hot and cold areas to preserve energy and improve traffic flow. Visit Air Door World at **www.airdoorworld.com** for information.

Laborsaving Equipment Resources

Food service equipment manufacturers are constantly introducing models designed to save you floor space and labor, energy and service costs. We've put together a brief list of commercial cooking equipment manufacturers to get you started towards working smarter, not harder.

Ask your local food service equipment distributor about the brands most commonly used in your community. Visit your local test kitchens at trade schools, utility companies and equipment resellers.

Select a model that suits your needs and budget. Many manufacturers offer a broad range of equipment and models from which to choose.

Manufacturer Lists, Articles, Reviews and Other Resources

- Food Service Central: **www.foodservicecentral.com**

- Supply and Equipment Food Service Alliance: **www.sefa.com**

- Food Service Equipment Reports: **www.fermag.com**

- FoodService.com: **www.foodservice.com**

- Food Service Equipment Magazine: **www.fesmag.com**

- Kitchen-Today (small equipment, tools): **kitchens-today.com**

SECTION IV

Controlling Food Costs: Strategies and Tips

SECTION IV

Table of Contents

Chapter 21
The Basics...259

Chapter 22
Essentials of Controlling Food Costs............273

Chapter 23
Reducing Food Costs 279

Chapter 24
Food-Cost Problem Areas.............................289

Chapter 25
The Menu, Standardized Recipes and
    Menu Pricing...297

Chapter 26
Purchasing, Receiving and Storage 313

Chapter 27
Production and Service 337

Chapter 28
Kitchen and Food Safety.............................355

Chapter 29
Technology 367

Introduction

If you manage a food service operation, you have to buy food products; that's the reality. The largest expenditure for most food service operations is the cost of food. However, in this book we will show you many ways to reduce your food costs. Even a 3 percent reduction in food costs for a restaurant grossing $1,000,000 with food costs of $400,000 means an approximate savings of $12,000, which will go straight to your bottom line.

In order to control food costs effectively, there are four essential things that you need to do:

1. Forecast how much and what you are going to sell.

2. Purchase, receive and prepare according to these forecasts.

3. Portion effectively.

4. Control money, waste and theft.

Thankfully, improvements in technology and

management techniques allow smart restaurant operators to keep food costs within the boundaries needed to generate a profit, while still providing their customers with the level of service that they need to generate repeat business. A restaurant manager must be prepared to develop and monitor cost-control programs, particularly food cost, to maintain profitability.

Unless you make changes, this book is of no use to you. You must begin to change your thinking and your methods. Take them one at a time, and make them a part of your business. Many of these tips will not only cut your food costs, but will also enhance your finished products. Better food brings more business, which brings more money. A reduction in your food costs means that you can keep more of that money. Armed with the information in this book, you will find actual tips that produce profitable results, without consuming all your time in unnecessary research or experiencing painful trial, risk and error.

Chapter 21

The Basics

Controlling food cost is basically about two concepts: First, ensuring that all food and revenue is accounted for and utilized in the most efficient manner. Second, ensuring that every ounce of food purchased is sold at the maximum allowable price. The following sections will present a system of cost controls. Combining these controls with basic procedures and policies as outlined in this book will enable you to establish an airtight food cost-control system.

Getting Organized

Organization is the easiest and cheapest manner of generating productivity and reducing food costs. The mere act of putting instructions on paper or giving your staff a checklist, instead of having to hold their hand through a process, can save your company thousands.

Organizational and structure component charts. Use organizational charts to know and understand who does what in your restaurant on a daily, weekly and monthly basis. How can this structure improve? Are jobs allocated in the most productive manner possible? Written job descriptions are good tools to use for this. You can find examples of job descriptions and a questionnaire for writing job descriptions at **www.hrnext .com**. Atlantic Publishing offers a complete set of restaurant job descriptions available on CD-ROM at **www.atlantic-pub.com**.

Use checklists for yourself. Create a checklist of tasks you perform every day and organize your time. Of course, variations from this checklist will always occur, but you will cover the basics a lot faster with a guide in hand. This will save you and your staff time and confusion.

Where to find forms and checklists. This book utilizes forms and checklists for cost-control procedures. You can certainly create your own forms based on the templates provided in this book using a computer or manual system; however, all of these forms and many more (over 80 total) are available on CD-ROM with the purchase of *The Restaurant Manager's Handbook (3rd Edition)* by calling 800-814-1132 or visiting **www.atlantic-pub.com** (Item # RMH-02).

Food Sales and Costs Survey

Before you can determine the best ways to reduce your food costs, you to need look at your sales and cost figures. Take a look at the following food sales and costs statistics. How does your operation compare?

What Does Your Food-Cost Percentage Really Mean?

Johnny's steakhouse has a food cost of 38 percent; Sally's steakhouse has a food cost of 44 percent. Which is a more efficient operator? Which is more profitable? Your restaurant has a food cost in January of 38 percent; in February it is 32 percent. Did you operate more efficiently the second month? The answer to these questions is: We just don't know. There is not enough information to determine this from the figures; we need to know what the food-cost percentage should have been as well.

Importance of food-cost percentages. Don't become overly concerned over food-cost percentages; they are truly meaningless unless you know what your food-cost percentage should be for the given time in question. Remember, you get paid in and deposit dollars into the bank, not percentages.

Weighted food-cost percentage. Once your food cost is calculated, you must determine your weighted food-cost percentage. A weighted food-cost percentage will tell you what your food cost should have been over a given period of time if all procedures and controls in place operated at 100 percent efficiency. We will show you how to determine a weighted food cost in a later section.

The Key to Controlling Food Cost Is Reconciliation

The key to controlling food cost is reconciliation. Every step or action in the cost-control process is checked and reconciled with another person. Once these systems are set up, management's responsibility is to monitor them with daily involvement. Should all the steps and procedures be adhered to, you will know exactly where every dollar and ounce of food went; there are no loopholes.

Teach them. Management must be involved in the training and supervision of all employees. For any cost-control system to work, employees must be trained and know what actions are expected of them. It is management's responsibility to supervise employees and see that they receive this training.

Communicate. Daily involvement and communication is needed in order to succeed. Employees must follow all procedures precisely. If they do not, they must be informed of their specific deviations from these procedures and correct them. This is a daily task that involves a hands-on management style.

Enforce. Any control initiated is only as good as the manager who follows up and enforces it. The total amount of time a manager needs to complete all of the work that will be described in this section is less than one hour a day. There is no excuse for not completing each procedure every day. A deviation in your controls or involvement can only lead to a loss over the control of the restaurant's costs.

Tracking. Although a simple manual system is detailed here, many of your cost-control procedures can be tracked through your computerized accounting system and/or POS system. Many of the basic purchasing and receiving functions are found in virtually all off-the-shelf accounting programs.

Practical Examples

The kitchen controls section combines all the personnel and procedures previously described into a system of checks and balances. This section will enable the restaurant manager, through the use of the sample forms and simple procedures, to know exactly where every food item and every cent the restaurant business spent.

To enable you to envision precisely how the personnel procedures and controls combine to control the restaurant's food cost, a summary of the key points are listed in this section in a sequence of events.

In the example, you will trace 25 pounds of shrimp through a typical day's operation, from the initial purchase to reconciling the revenue. The first column in each of the example forms are filled out so you will be able to see how they are used and why each one is a critical part in the overall control system. We would recommend that the manager put the following list in the form of a check-off sheet for his or her own organizational purposes.

Sample sequence of events:

1. Determine the need to purchase shrimp.

2. Purchase the amount needed. Example: 25 pounds.

3. Shrimp is delivered. Follow the receiving and storing procedures.

4. Enter the amount delivered on the Perpetual Inventory Form. Example: 5 boxes of 5 pounds each.

5. Preparation cooks compute the opening counts from the previous evening. Example: 25 shrimp dinners is the beginning count.

6. The minimum amount needed as determined by sale history is 33. The preparation cooks need to prepare 9 more dinners for that night.

7. Cooks remove 5 pounds, or 1 box, of shrimp from the freezer.

8. Cooks sign out the 5 pounds of shrimp on the Sign-Out Sheet.

9. The amount, 5 pounds, is placed in the "Amount Defrosted or Ordered" column on the Preparation Form.

10. The shrimp is prepared as prescribed in the Recipe and Procedure Manual.

11. The cooks prepare nine 8.5-ounce dinners; enter this figure in the "Amount Prepared" column. The starting total would be 9 + 25 = 34. Enter these figures on the Preparation Form.

12. The Preparation Form is completed and given to the kitchen director or manager. All storage areas are locked before leaving.

13. The invoices are brought to the manager's office.

14. The kitchen director computes the yields.

15. The cooks come in for the evening and count all the items for the Starting Total.

16. The manager verifies that the Starting Total on the Preparation Form is the same as on the Cook's Form.

17. The manager issues the tickets to the waitstaff. The manager issues the cashier drawer to the cashier and verifies the starting amount.

18. The manager checks the perpetual inventory (the daily usage of your main entrée items).

19. The waitstaff gives the order tickets to the kitchen expediter.

20. The expediter reads off the items to the cooks who start to cook the menu items.

21. When completed, the waiter/waitress takes the dinner to the customer.

22. The bill is totaled and given to the customer.

23. The cashier verifies the amount and collects the money or charge.

24. The cooks count the ending balance. Example: Starting total is 34; ending balance is 21; 13 were sold.

25. The expediter itemizes the carbon copies. Thirteen shrimp dinners were sold.

26. The manager cashes out with the cashier. Ticket itemization shows 13 shrimp dinners sold.

27. All three figures are verified: cooks to expediter to cashier.

28. The following morning the manager verifies the ending balance of the Cook's Form (21) to the beginning count of the Preparation Form.

29. The bookkeeper rechecks and verifies all the transactions of the previous night, ensuring that 13 shrimp dinners were sold and the money was accounted for.

You will find a blank copy of all these sample forms in Chapter 39 and also on the companion CD-Rom.

PERPETUAL INVENTORY FORM

ITEM	1	2	3	4	5	6	7	8	9	10	11	12	13	14	15	16	17	18	19	20	21	22	23	24	25	26	27	28	29	30	31	
	+	5																															
	-	1																															
Shrimp (20) (5 lbs.)	=	24																															

SIGN-OUT SHEET

ITEM	DATE	AMOUNT/WT.	EMPLOYEE
Shrimp-box	11-30	1 5-lb. box	Joe B.

DAILY PREPARATION FORM

ITEM	MINIMUM AMOUNT	AMOUNT DEF./ORD.	BEGINNING AMOUNT	AMOUNT PREPPED	STARTING TOTAL
Shrimp	33	5 lbs.	25	9	34

MINIMUM AMOUNT NEEDED FORM

ITEM	MON	TUES	WED	THURS	FRI	SAT	SUN
Shrimp						33	

COOK'S FORM

ITEM	START	ADDITIONS	STARTING BALANCE	BALANCE ENDING	# SOLD
Shrimp dinners	25	9	34	21	13

DAILY YIELDS FORM

ITEM	STARTING WEIGHT (OZ.)	# OF PORTIONS	TOTAL PORTION WEIGHT (OZ.)	YIELD %	PREP/ COOK
Shrimp dinner	*80.0*	*9*	*9 X 8.0 oz. ≈ 72 oz.*	*90%*	*BOB S.*

TICKET ISSUANCE FORM

WAITPERSON	INITIALS	TOTAL #	#THRU	RETURN # VERIFIED

TICKET ITEMIZATION FORM

ITEM	USE A ✓ MARK TO DESIGNATE ON SOLD	TOTALS
Shrimp dinners	✓✓✓✓✓✓✓✓✓✓✓✓✓	13

CASHIER'S REPORT FORM

Prepared By: _____

Date: _____ **Day:** _____ **Shift:** _____

		BAR REGISTER		SERVICE REGISTER		TOTAL
		Day	Night	Day	Night	All Shifts
1	**BANK DEPOSIT** Part I					
2	Currency					
3	Silver					
4	Checks					
5	**SUB TOTAL**					
6	**CREDIT CARDS:**					
7	MasterCard/Visa					
8	American Express					
9	Diner's Club					
10	Other					
11	**OTHER RECEIPTS:**					
12	**TOTAL BANK DEPOSIT**					
13	**CASH SUMMARY** Part II					
14	Sales per Register					
15	Sales Tax per Register					
16	**ADJUSTMENTS:**					
17	Over/Under Rings					
18	Other: Complimentaries					
19	Other					
20	**TOTAL ADJUSTMENTS**					
21	Sales to Be Accounted For					
22	Sales Tax to Be Acctd. For					
23	Accounts Collected					
24	Other Receipts:					
25						
26						
27	**TIPS CHARGED:**					
28	MasterCard/Visa					
29	American Express					
30	Diner's Club					
31	Other					
32	House Accounts-Tips					
33	**TOTAL RECEIPTS**					
34	**DEDUCT: PAID OUTS**					
35	Tips Paid Out					
36	House Charges					
37	Total Deductions					
38	**NET CASH RECEIPTS**					
39	**BANK DEPOSIT** (Line 12)					
40	**OVER or SHORT**					

Chapter 22

Essentials of Controlling Food Costs

In order to control food costs effectively, there are four essential things that you need to do. First, forecast how much and what you are going to sell. Second, purchase and prepare according to these forecasts. Third, portion effectively. Finally, control waste and theft. Consider the following:

Standards. In order to do these effectively, you must have standards to which you rigorously adhere. Here are several standards that will help you sustain quality, consistency and low cost:

Don't allow chefs to determine pricing. The plates your chefs create are their pride and joy. But don't let them set prices. As you are the manager or owner with specific profit goals in mind, allowing a chef to set prices may mean your targets aren't reached. Discuss menu pricing parameters and costs with your chefs so that they are dreaming of hamburgers instead of filet mignon, but keep the menu pricing a management function.

Standardized recipes. Since the recipe is the basis for determining the cost of a menu item, standard recipes will ensure consistent quality and cost. Standardized recipes include ingredients, preparation methods, yield, equipment used and plate presentation. You will find a sample standardized recipe below, as well as various standized recipe forms in *Chapter 39–Essential Cost-Cutting and Time-Saving Forms.*

BLUE RIDGE JAMBALAYA		Recipe No. 126
Portion Size: 1.5 cups	Yields: 40 portions	COST PER PORTION: $0.90

INGREDIENTS	WEIGHT/ MEASURE	COST
Chicken, boneless breast cut in 1-inch pieces	4 lbs	$8.00
Andouille sausage, sliced	2 lbs	$5.58
Celery, chopped	16 cups	$3.16
Red peppers, chopped	8 each	$6.00
Onions, chopped	4 each	$0.40
Garlic cloves, minced	8 each	$0.17
Short-grain brown rice, dry	6 cups	$4.74
Beer	32 oz	$3.50
Chicken stock	60 oz	$1.72
Canned diced tomato	60 oz	$2.12
Tabasco sauce	4 tsp	$0.03
Parsley (garnish)		$0.04
Cornbread (side)		$0.58
	TOTAL COST	$36.04

Directions: Trim chicken, and cut into 1-inch pieces. Heat vegetable oil in a large sauté pan. Add chicken and cook through. Add sausage and heat through.

In a large stockpot, sauté onion, garlic, celery and red pepper in oil. Add rice, and coat rice with oil. Turn heat down to low, add beer and broth a little at a time, allowing the rice to absorb the liquid before adding more. When rice has simmered about 15–20 minutes, add tomato, chicken and sausage. Continue cooking until done and rice is tender (about 1 hour). Add Tabasco, salt and pepper.

Portion out the jambalaya into smaller containers to cool. Can refrigerate or use immediately for service.

Serve: Serve in a dinner bowl with a piece of cornbread on the side. Top with parsley.

Standardized purchase specifications. These are detailed descriptions of the ingredients used in your standardized recipes. Quality and price of all ingredients are known and agreed upon before purchases are made, making the recipe's cost consistent from unit to unit and week to week.

Yield Costs

Once you have standardized recipes in place, you can determine the per-plate cost of every dish. In order to do this, you need to know the basic ingredients' cost and the edible yield of those ingredients for each dish. There are a number of necessary terms for this process:

As-Purchased (AP) Weight. The weight of the product as delivered, including bones, trim, etc.

Edible-Portion (EP) Weight. The amount of weight or volume that is available to be portioned after carving or cooking.

Waste. The amount of usable product that is lost due to processing, cooking or portioning, as well as usable by-products that have no salable value.

Usable Trim. Processing by-products that can be sold as other menu items. These recover a portion or all of their cost.

Yield. The net weight or volume of food after processing but before portioning.

Standard Yield. The yield generated by standardized recipes and portioning procedures—how much usable product remains after processing and cooking.

Standard Portion. The size of the portion according to the standardized recipe, also the basis for determining the cost of the plated portion.

Convenience Foods. Items where at least a portion of the preparation labor is done before delivery. These can include pre-cut chicken, ready-made dough, etc. To cost convenience foods, you simply count, weigh or measure the portion size and determine how many portions there are. Then divide the number of servable portions into the AP price. Even with their pre-preparation, a small allowance for normal waste must be factored in, often as little as 2 percent per yield.

These factors allow you to calculate plate costs. The cost of convenience foods are higher than if you made them from scratch, but once you factor in labor, necessary equipment, inventories of ingredients, more complicated purchasing and storage, etc., you may find that these foods offer considerable savings.

Costing items from scratch is a little more complex. Most menu items require processing that causes shrinkage of some kind. As a result, if the weight or volume of the cooked product is less than the AP weight, the EP cost will be higher than the AP price. It's a simple addition of the labor involved and the amount of salable product being reduced. Through this process, your buyer uses yields to determine quantities to purchase and your chef discovers optimum quantities to order that result in the highest yield and the least waste.

Menu Sales Mix

The menu is where you begin to design a restaurant. If you have a specific menu idea, your restaurant's location must be carefully planned to ensure customer traffic will support your concept. This also works the other way: If you already have the location, design your menu around the customers you want to attract. Consider the following basic requirements:

Functionality. Once your concept is decided, your equipment and kitchen space requirements should be designed around the recipes on your menu. Once a kitchen has been built, there is, of course, some flexibility to menu changes, but new pieces of equipment may be impossible to add without high costs or renovations. To design correctly, you need to visualize delivery, processing, preparation, presentation and washing. To do this, you must be intimately familiar with each menu item.

Fit for purpose. When shopping for equipment, choose based on the best equipment for your needs, not price. Only when you have decided if you need a small non-vented fryer or an industrial one, two ovens or five, and then which specific brand will meet your needs, should you begin to find the best price. This is true for equipment all the way down to pots, pans, dishes and utensils.

The Menu

Your menu should not just be a list of the dishes you sell, it should positively affect the revenue and operational efficiency of your restaurant. Start by selecting dishes that reflect your customers' preferences and emphasize what your staff does well. Attempting to cater to everyone generally has you doing nothing particularly well and doesn't distinguish your restaurant. Your menu should be a major communicator of the concept and personality of your restaurant, as well as an important cost control. Bear in mind the following:

Menu item placement. Where you place an item on your menu is important in determining whether or not the customer will order the item. Customers are most likely to remember the first and last things they read. By placing the items you want to sell (the items that yield the highest profits) first or last, you increase the chance of selling them.

Design. A well-designed menu creates an accurate image of the restaurant in a customer's head, even before the customer has been inside. It also directs the attention to certain selections and increases the chances of them being ordered. Your menu also determines, depending upon its complexity and sophistication, how detailed your cost-control system needs to be.

An effective menu does five key things:

1. Emphasizes what customers want and what you do best.

2. Is an effective communication, merchandising and cost-control tool.

3. Obtains the necessary check average for sales and profits.

4. Uses staff and equipment efficiently.

5. Makes forecasting sales more consistent and accurate for purchasing, preparation and scheduling.

Plan to have a menu that works for you. The design of your menu will directly affect whether it achieves these goals. Don't leave this to chance. Certain practices can influence the choices your guests make. Instead of randomly placing items on the menu, single out and emphasize the items you want to sell. These will generally be dishes with low food cost and high profits that are easy to prepare. Once you have chosen these dishes, use design—print style, paper color and graphic design—to direct the readers' attention to these items. In general, a customer's eye will fall to the middle of the page first. This is an important factor; however, design elements used to draw a reader's eye to another part of the menu can be effective as well. Also, customers remember the first and last things they read more than anything else, so drawing their eyes to specific items is also important.

Print the menu in-house. With today's desktop publishing technology, you can easily produce your own menus. All you need is a software program like Menu Pro, available at **www.atlantic-pub.com**. Choose from a selection of menu papers at **www.ideaart.com** or **www.armesco.com**.

Tell your story on the back of the menu. People always want to know more. Use this chance to increase their value and perception of your restaurant quality. Tell them how your staff prepares fresh salad ingredients on a daily basis, never using pre-made items or canned goods. Let them know that you grind fresh gourmet coffee beans each morning before coffee is brewed. Tell your story and your guests will be impressed.

Provide clean, presentable menus. Ensure that your menus are always clean and appear to be as good as new, otherwise throw them out. Greasy, sticky, soiled menus with bad creases, dog-ears and stains are not very appealing to people who are preparing to dine. If a server hands a sticky, dirty menu to a customer, what kind of impression do you think that customer will have of your restaurant?

Menu "Do Nots"

Don't charge extra for the small items. Some restaurants will charge an additional $0.30 for a slice of cheese on their hamburger or $0.40 for blue cheese dressing. While it may cost you a bit extra for these items, you should cover the cost by averaging it in on the overall cost of the meal. When you break down charges like this, people get the impression that you are being petty.

Don't tell your guests that you've run out of a particular item. You've sold out, not run out. That makes it sound as if the restaurant is poorly managed and unprepared. Instead, make sure you tell them that you've sold out of that item because it has been so popular. Selling out is a good thing, not a bad thing. It means business is good and food is fresh.

Chapter 23

Reducing Food Costs

Setting Menu Prices

This manual is, of course, devoted primarily to operating costs. However, food costs are such a large part of your expenses that we should at least take a quick review. To follow are some important considerations when setting your menu prices.

Ideally, for every dollar that you earn, you should aim for 10–12 cents as a profit. Once you figure out your food cost, multiplying it by 3.3 will give you about a 10 percent profit per item, factoring in food cost, labor cost and overhead. Do realize that some items will have to have a slightly higher cost structure, and others will have a lower cost structure, giving you, overall, a 10 percent profit.

Keep in mind that factors other than direct costs will influence your menu prices. Indirect factors, such as how a customer perceives quality, your location, the restaurant's atmosphere, and the competition will also play a role in your menu-pricing decisions.

You can buy software that will facilitate the costing procedures. Atlantic Publishing offers once such program called NutraCoster. NutraCoster will calculate product cost (including labor, packaging and overhead) and nutritional content. The program can be ordered online at **www.atlantic-pub.com**

Try to price your menu so that the food cost and labor cost of each meal is about 70 percent of the sales price. In other words, try to price your menu items so that direct expenses run about two-thirds of the sale price. If you can bring other expenses down and do a good job of up-selling to your customers, you should be able to make a good profit while providing your customers with great meals at a great price—a win/win situation. Up-sellling can be accomplished in a number of ways. Coach your waitstaff on suggestive selling. By having servers ask if a customer wants appetizers or desserts, the customer is more likely to order these extra items.

Change your menu to accommodate large price shifts. When the price of beef soars, consider raising your main menu prices to accommodate. Change your menu items to use pork, chicken or another meat with an acceptable price level.

Menu Costs

Use your menu as a means for reducing your operating costs:

Menu sales analysis. A menu sales analysis is a good tool to use to track what you are selling. Keeping track of this information will enable you to identify areas where you can reduce costs, such as labor, waste, rising food cost or over-portioning. A menu sales analysis will tell you three things:

1. How much of a particular item was sold.

2. The cost of the item.

3. The profitability of the item.

Produce reports. Many restaurants have computerized cash registers, so getting a report on what items sold nightly, weekly or monthly is easy. If your restaurant does not have a computerized register, you can track a period of time and get this information by pulling it off guest checks.

Pull all this information into a simple table so you can compare it easily. See the example below:

Item	Popularity*	Cost	Menu Price	Profit Margin
Pork tenderloin	42/100	$0.62	$12.50	$4.88
Spaghetti & meatballs	12/100	$1.79	$8.25	$4.46
Shrimp scampi	46100	$3.40	$15.95	$7.55

*42/100 means 42 tenderloins were sold out of a total of 100 entrées served in that time period.

What do you do with this information once you have it? What does this information tell you about how you can reduce costs? Looking at your table, you see that your pork tenderloin is almost as popular as your shrimp dinner, but it costs a good deal less to make. You can summarize that by focusing on such lower-cost items. You can also increase your profit margin by decreasing your food cost. Keep in mind, however, that by only focusing on low-cost items, you will lower your guest check average and this will lower profits. To reduce costs and remain profitable, you should emphasize a mix of high- and low-cost food items on your menu.

Menu costing software. There are many software packages available to help you with menu costing. CostGuard's Web site, **www.costguard.com**, offers a product called Menu/Sales Engineering that tracks your sales mix information and provides analysis of your most and least popular and profitable items. The product currently sells for $495. Calcmenu is another software product you can use for menu costing, inventory management, menu planning and nutrition analysis. You can find Calcmenu at **www.calcmenu.com**. There are various versions that are priced between $580 and $950. The site also offers a free trial version.

Calculating Food and Drink Costs

The following guidelines will help you calculate food costs for your restaurant:

Inventory. Start by calculating the value of your beginning inventory. Then add your purchase costs over the course of the month. At the end of the month, subtract the value of your remaining inventory from that figure to produce your monthly food expenses. Divide this figure by food revenue for the month and you'll know exactly the food-cost percentage of sales.

Cost of sales is the cost of the food or beverage products sold.

Drinks. Beverage cost of sales and operating supplies would be calculated in a similar manner. Wine and beer should also be separated into another cost of sales category.

Standardized Recipes

Using standardized recipes helps control costs and ensures quality and consistency of menu items. By providing your cooks and bartenders with this necessary information, you can retain control over portioning. Keep these in the kitchen and bar so your kitchen and bar staff will use them. You can store them on index cards and in an index cardholder or use a three-ring binder with recipe sheets inserted into transparent envelopes that can be easily wiped clean. Information to include on your kitchen recipe form follows:

Name of item and recipe number.

Yield—the total quantity the recipe will prepare.

Portion size—this may be listed by weight or number of pieces. You may want to include what size of utensil to use for serving. For example, use the 6-oz ladle for a cup of soup.

Ingredients—make sure to list quantities of ingredients used.

Preparation instructions.

Garnish—you may want to draw a diagram or include a photograph to show your staff how the item should look when it leaves the kitchen.

Finishing—describe any finish the product needs, such as brushing with oil or melted chocolate drizzled on top. Also include how to cool and at what temperature the product should be held. Can it sit at room temperature or does it need to be refrigerated?

Cost—include every ingredient and every garnish for accuracy. You will need to look at product invoices to get unit prices, then determine the ingredient cost from this. Total the cost of each ingredient for your total recipe cost. This figure can then be divided by the number of portions in order to arrive at a portion cost.

There is an example of a standardized recipe in Chapter 22 on page 274. You will also find Standardized Recipes Forms in Chapter 39.

How to Economize Without Reducing Quality

Try the following food/ingredient cost-reducing tips. They could make a big difference to your overall expenditures.

Extend the life of oil or fat for the deep fryer. By following these six simple steps, you can almost eliminate the need to discard old fry oil or fat:

1. Thoroughly clean fryer baskets and the fryer elements with a mild detergent rinse at least once a week.

2. Filter with the Fry-Saver, from **www.espressoplusmore.com**, one to three times per day or after each shift.

3. After one week, remove 50 percent of the filtered oil or fat and store in a clean container to be used for daily "top off" oil.

4. Refill fryer with 50 percent new oil and continue using.

5. Add used, aged, filtered oil or fat for upkeep to refill fryer back to fill line.

6. Repeat steps on a regular schedule.

Use air pots for coffee. They are sealed and insulated like a thermos and can hold temperature and coffee quality up to eight hours.

Bread baskets. The potential for waste in bread baskets is large. Most of these come back from the table partially eaten at best. You may want to consider providing bread baskets only if requested or you may want to cut down on the amount served. You could also consider including packaged items since these can be reused. Some operators are now serving bread only by request and one roll or breadstick per guest served from a bread basket with tongs at a time.

Cut kitchen waste. One of the major culprits in high food costs is waste. Put a new garbage can in the kitchen. This can is for wasted product only, such as wrong orders, dropped food, etc. By giving your kitchen staff this visual aid, you can reinforce the amount of money that gets spent on such product waste.

Substitute pre-made items for some items you have been making from scratch. You don't have to sacrifice quality; many pre-made items are particularly high standard. You can also start with a pre-made item and add ingredients. For instance, you can buy a pre-made salad dressing and add blue cheese or fresh herbs. Using these items will lower your food and labor cost and you can still put out a quality item.

Use industry information. Check out **www.restaurantnews.com/foodcost .html** for other restaurateurs' tips on how to lower food costs.

Portion Control

Ensure all employees adhere to portion standards. If the portions your staff is serving are just 10 percent more than you're budgeting for, you're losing a lot of money every month. This holds true from the size of a slice of meat to the amount of salad and dressing served with each meal. Bear in mind the following:

Weights and measures. Ensure your kitchen staff weighs all portions and ingredients before cooking them so as to meet recipe specifications on every meal. Often when you purchase from suppliers, you're paying by the pound, so if your portions are too large, you're losing money on every meal. Trim where necessary and maintain consistency wherever possible.

Established recipes. Restaurant recipes have two purposes: to ensure consistency and control costs. Following these practices will keep food costs from getting out of control. Also, having a consistent quality for all your meals won't hurt the way your establishment is perceived by customers.

No "free handing it." Be sure your staff is using scales, measuring cups, measuring spoons and appropriate ladles. Often cooks will "free hand it" after a while. This usually results in over-portioning.

Does your staff use trim items from meal preparations in other meals? For example, meat trimmings can be used for soups to great effect, celery leafs can be used as garnishes, and pastry off-cuts can be re-rolled and used.

Fixed menu. Maintain a fixed menu for your business, one that allows you to keep a smaller inventory and a fairly simple price list for employees to remember. When you do offer daily specials, fashion them around whatever ingredients you managed to buy for a great price that week or items in your inventory that you would like to move. If you do use a seasonal menu, try to use local growers for lower produce prices and design seasonal menus that allow you to use ingredients in several dishes so you can order in bulk.

Side dishes. Soups, breads and salads have a far lower fixed per-plate cost than your entrée meals, so make your soups and salads available with a variety of meals and ensure they're of high quality. Your customers will notice how good these meals are, and you can keep your entrée portions to a manageable size without leaving customers hungry.

Portion out all condiments, sauces and breads according to the number of guests at a table. If servers put more bread on the table than is needed, your patrons will inevitably eat more and order less. Similarly, if the bread is thrown away and not used, it is simply wasted money.

Plate size. Be certain your kitchen staff uses the correct-sized dish for each menu item. If they are serving a salad on a dinner plate, they will probably serve too much since the prescribed portion will look small on a large dinner plate.

Train your staff. Train all new employees and spend time retraining existing staff at regular intervals.

Manage Costs—Increase Sales

Managing business costs such as inventory, supplies, labor and other services takes focus and consistency, but there are also a few easy tips that can help you keep such costs to a minimum. Utilize existing resources, such as:

Expand sales without additional investment. Provide a display case selling specialty items that can last for a few days or even weeks. Have your chef prepare these items during the slow hours. Many guests would love the idea of purchasing items "to go" that they can't purchase in a store or anywhere else. Utilize existing resources and create additional sales on the side.

Gourmet Display offers a wide array of food and beverage display equipment. Visit **www.gourmet-display.com** to see the wide selection. To capitalize on growing off-premise sales opportunities, package your desserts or carry-outs attractively. Sabert, **www.sabert.com**, has many cost-effective disposable solutions. Sabert's elegant product styling makes food look great. Platters, bowls and utensils are available in an extensive selection of styles and sizes. All products are food service tested for superior performance and designed with food service operators' needs in mind.

This three-tiered tray from Gourmet Display is an excellent way to display desserts or other items. Visit www.gourmetdisplay.com or call 1-800-767-4711 to order.

Sabert's FastPac three-compartment tray is an excellent to-go solution. Available from www.sabert.com or call 1-800-SABERT1 (1-800-722-3781) for more information.

Virgin drinks. Offer a wide selection of virgin specialty drinks for children, non-drinkers and designated drivers. This saves you the expense of providing free refills on coffee, tea and sodas.

Sell water. Offer customers a choice of bottled water such as spring water, still water, sparkling water or even flavored water, before you simply pour them a glass of ice water from a pitcher. You'll be amazed at how much this simple act will increase your sales figures.

Reduce waste. Remove all garbage cans from the kitchen and instead place plastic tubs throughout the prep area. At the end of each shift, the tubs' contents can be checked to ensure the proper procedures are being followed for preparation and trimming raw products. Make workers accountable for the quality of their work.

Other Cost-Saving Tips

You may well have trimmed your inventory and staffing costs, but in a restaurant environment, many other possibilities exist for cost control. Consider the following opportunities:

Lease icemakers. Icemakers are costly to purchase and repair. Rent or lease icemakers on an as-needed basis instead. However, if you already have an icemaker, be sure to install appropriate filters in the unit to enable it to last longer. Contact the following companies for leasing restaurant equipment and supplies:

- Arctic Refrigeration and Equipment, **www.arcticfoodequip.com**, 866-528-8528

- Easy Lease Company, **www.easyleasecompany.com**, 800-514-4047

- Global Restaurant Equipment and Supplies, **www.globalrestaurantequip .com**, 800-666-8099

Install electric hand dryers. Not only do they save on costs, they are also better for sanitation purposes. Contact:

- ASI Electric Dryer, **www.cescompany.com**, 707-664-9964

- Stielbel Eltron, **www.stiebel-eltron-usa.com**, 800-582-8423

- World Dryer, **www.worlddryer.com**, 800-323-0701

Return pallets and crates to vendors. Pallets and crates take up valuable space, as they are bulky items requiring labor to manage them. By making vendors responsible for taking pallets away and reusing them, the burden on your staff is reduced as well as the costs of waste management.

Save on table-top items. To eliminate the use of individual wrapping, use straw and toothpick dispensers. Also consider using drink coasters that can be reused instead of cocktail napkins. Decorations do not have to be expensive. Consider browsing through online party and decoration sites:

- 123 Party, **www.123party.com**

- D and D Design, **www.ddchili.com**

- Grab A Bargain, **www.grababargain.com**

Offer discounts for mugs. Offer discounts to customers who bring in reusable mugs for refills. Several restaurants have similar programs that encourage customers to reduce unnecessary waste. The incentive to bring in their own mug works when they receive beverages at reduced prices. Contact:

- Advertising Magic, **www.advertisingmagic.com**, 800-862-4421

- Ceramic Mugs, **www.ceramic-mugs.com**, 305-593-0911

- DADEC Photo Mugs and Gifts, **www.dadec.com**, 866-853-3257

- Gift Mugs, **www.giftmugs.com**, 321-253-0012

- My Promo Store, **www.mypromostore.com**, 877-838-3700

Use cleaning rags instead of paper towels. Encourage staff to use cleaning rags instead of high-quality napkins and paper towels to mop up a spill. The purchase of disposable towels and napkins can be more expensive than laundry service.

Install thermal strips over cooler and freezer doors. Keep cold air in and warm air out. This increases efficiency and reduces unnecessary electricity usage so that the compressor doesn't have to work as hard. Here are a few companies that provide seal-tight doors and replacement parts:

- Arrow Restaurant Equipment, **www.arrowreste.com**, 909-621-7428

- Commercial Appliance, **www.commappl.com**, 800-481-7373

- Loadmaster, **www.loadmaster.com**, 514-636-1243

Separate hot and cold appliances. Separate the locations of hot and cold appliances. It will increase efficiency and temperature regulation. Draw out an organizational diagram of your kitchen. The one-time effort will be worth it.

Chapter 24

Food-Cost Problem Areas

Math and Cost Ratios

Owners and managers need to be on the same page in terms of the meaning and calculation of the many ratios used to analyze food costs. It's important to understand how your ratios are being calculated so you can get a true indication of the cost or profit activity in your restaurant. Cost control is not just the calculation of these numbers; it's the interpretation of them and the appropriate (re)actions taken to bring your numbers within set standards.

Beginning Inventory

The beginning inventory is the total dollar value of food supplies on hand at the beginning of the accounting period. This figure represents the starting point from which you can then compute total food cost each month.

Computing the beginning inventory is a simple calculation. If you are purchasing all new food products, simply total all your food purchases prior to opening day. This figure will be the beginning inventory.

Opening an old restaurant at a new location. If you are opening an existing restaurant and will be using some of the old supplies, first take an inventory of the old supplies. Add the dollar value of these supplies with all your new food purchases prior to opening day.

Ending Inventory

An ending inventory is taken for a complete and accurate count of the food stock on hand at the end of an accounting period so that the remaining amount may be used in projecting the total cost for each category. When conducting the ending or physical inventory:

Use scales for the most accurate determination.

Stocking order. Place inventory sheets in the same order that the room is stocked.

Separate sheets. Use a separate sheet for each area.

Include the following on the form: your inventory unit, units per case, pack or size, par, and vendor code.

Use two people: one to count (a manager) and one to record the figures (preferably an employee from a different area). For example, have the bar manager assist in the food inventory. One will count while the other writes. The person counting states each item, its unit and its total amount. The other person enters the figure on the inventory sheet on the correct line.

Partial items. If there is a partial item, such as half a case of tomatoes, estimate how much is remaining on a scale from 0.1 to 0.9 (0.5 being half of a container). Make sure there is a figure on either side of the decimal point (e.g., 0.5, 1.3).

Counting order. Count shelves all the way across. Do not jump around.

Fill in all columns. Put a zero (0) in columns where there is no item to be counted.

Use pound and unit costs. Convert all items that are in prepared form into pound and unit costs. For example: 15 fish dinners at 12.5 oz = 11.72 lbs.

Multiples. For items with multiple weights, such as different-sized cans of crushed tomatoes, use a separate pad for your addition, and enter your total on the inventory form.

Double-check. Make sure there's an entry for each item.

Be thorough. Complete each area before moving on to a new one and check for blanks and possible mistakes.

Estimating. When estimates must be made, they should be made with sound reasoning, not guessing.

Food-Cost Percentage

This basic ratio is often misinterpreted because it is calculated in so many different ways. Basically, it is food cost divided by food sales. Whether your food cost is determined by food sold or consumed is a crucial difference. For your food-cost percentage to be accurate, a month-end inventory must be taken. Without this figure, your food-cost statement is inaccurate and, therefore, basically useless because your inventory will vary month to month, even in the most stable environment.

Distinguishing between food sold and consumed is important. Food consumed includes all food used, sold, wasted, stolen or given away to customers and employees. Food sold is determined by subtracting all food bought (at full price) from the total food consumed. (See the example on the following page.)

Employee meals, complimentary food and manager-consumed food are removed from the food-cost equation as these costs should be reclassified on the P&L. Employee meals are an employee benefit, complimentary meals are considered promotional costs, and manager meals are a management benefit.

Cost Calculations—The Basics

Maximum allowable food-cost percentage (MFC). This is the most food can cost for you to meet your profit goal. If your food-cost percentage is over your maximum allowable percentage at the end of the month, you won't meet your profit expectations. This is how you calculate it:

1. Write your dollar amounts of labor costs and overhead expenses (subtract food costs). Refer to past accounting periods and yearly averages to get realistic cost estimates.

2. Add your monthly profit goal as either a dollar amount or a percentage of sales.

3. Convert dollar values of expenses to percentages by dividing by food sales for the periods used for expenses. Generally, don't use your highest or lowest sales figures for calculating your operating expenses. Subtract the total of the percentages from 100 percent. The remainder is your maximum allowable food-cost percentage (MFC).

100 – (monthly expenses – food costs) + monthly profit goal = MFC %

Actual food-cost percentage (AFC). This is the percentage at which you're actually operating. It's calculated by dividing food cost by food sales (only food sales, not total sales). If you are deducting employee meals from your income statement, then you are calculating cost of food sold. If there is no deduction of employee meals, which is true for most operations, then the food cost you're reading is food consumed; this is always a higher cost than food sold. If inventory is not being taken, the food cost on your income statement is just an estimate based on purchases and isn't accurate.

Potential food-cost percentage (PFC). This cost is sometimes called the theoretical food cost. PFC is the lowest your food cost can be because it assumes that all food consumed is sold and that there is no waste at all. Calculate this cost by multiplying the number sold of each menu item by the ideal recipe cost.

Standard food cost (SFC). This is how you adjust for the unrealistically low PFC. The percentage includes unavoidable waste, employee meals, etc. This food-cost percentage is compared to the AFC and is the standard that management must meet.

The prime cost includes the cost of direct labor with food cost. This cost includes labor incurred because the item is made from scratch (labor from baking pies and bread, trimming steaks, etc.). When the food cost is determined for these items, the cost of the labor needed to prepare them is added. This costing method is applied to every menu item needing extensive direct labor before it is served to the customer. Indirect labor cannot be attributed to any particular menu item and is overhead.

Beverage exclusions. Beverage sales should not include coffee, tea, milk or juice, which are usually considered food. If you include soft drinks in your food costs, be aware that it will reduce the food cost, since the ratio of cost to selling price is so low.

Ratio of food to beverage sales. This is simply the ratio of the percentages of your total sales. In restaurants with a higher percentage of beverage than food sales, profits are generally higher because there is a greater profit margin on beverages.

Sales mix. Sales mix is the number of each menu item sold. It's crucial to cost analysis because each item impacts food cost and food percentages differently.

Daily Food-Cost Analysis

Traditionally, food cost is calculated once a month. There is no reason, however, why you cannot compute a daily food cost and a daily weighted food cost to analyze problem areas. Much of the inventory counting can be eliminated by moving only the products used for production into the kitchen at the beginning of the shift. In this way, you can pinpoint problem areas, problem employees or problem shifts. You can also calculate a separate food cost for breakfast or lunch.

Weighted Food-Cost Percentage

Once your food cost is calculated, determine weighted food-cost percentage. A weighted food-cost percentage will tell you what your food cost should have been had all procedures and controls operated at 100 percent efficiency. The schedule on the following page summarizes sales information from the restaurant's POS system or from other bookkeeping records. Basically, you are recreating the food cost for each item based on the standard recipe costs to determine what your food cost and, thus, food-cost percentage should have been. For this example we will pretend that only four menu items are served in this restaurant. From this example you can see that $7,000 of food costs have slipped away (assuming all calculations are accurate). The restaurant should have actually had a 34.28 percent weighted food-cost percentage.

WEIGHTED FOOD-COST CHART

Menu Item	Cost per Meal	# of Meals Served	Cost per Menu Item
Chicken Kiev	$5.00	2,000	$10,000.00
Steak Oscar	$8.00	4,000	$32,000.00
Stuffed Flounder	$9.00	1,000	$9,000.00
Hamburger Platter	$3.00	3,000	$9,000.00
Weighted Total Cost			**$60,000.00**
Actual Sales			$175,000.00
Weighted Food-Cost Percentage			34.28%
Variation Over Actual Food-Cost Percentage			4% or $7,000.00

Raising Prices

Want to immediately lower your food-cost percentage? Raise your prices. At some point in your career as a food service manager, you have to deal with the issue of raising prices.

Reasons for raising prices. Make an overall review of your establishment. You may be experiencing higher food costs because food prices have risen significantly since your last price review. Perhaps you have just undergone major renovation and have upgraded the atmosphere of your restaurant. Competition may have changed since the last increase, or you may have decided that you need to make a bigger profit in order for it to be worthwhile to stay in business. All of these are valid reasons for price increases. The way to implement increases, however, should be considered carefully.

Target certain items first. If you do an across-the-board price increase, you may scare off some customers. You may want to consider increasing the price on a certain number of key dishes and leaving other price increases for a later date.

Decide how to communicate these increases. Should you print a new menu or devise a way to increase the price on existing copies of the menu? It's never a good idea to simply cross out the old price and write in the new, but many food service managers also feel that it is a bad idea to increase prices when you print new menus that have changes in the items being offered. Whatever you decide, don't alert customers to price increases!

Test market. It may be best to reprint old menus with new prices and save any changes to the bill of fare until a later printing. This strategy will also let you "test market" the new prices. If you're not seeing the sales you need from the new prices, you can adjust them with a second printing.

Remember, it's never a good idea to simply cross out the old price
and write in the new. Consider redesigning or reprinting your menu.

Chapter 25

The Menu, Standardized Recipes and Menu Pricing

Menu Sales

The menu is where you begin to control food costs. Consider the following basic requirements:

Functionality. Once your concept is decided, your equipment and kitchen space requirements should be designed around the recipes on your menu. Once a kitchen has been built, there is, of course, some flexibility to menu changes, but new pieces of equipment may be impossible to add without high costs or renovations. To design correctly, you need to visualize delivery, processing, preparation, presentation and washing. To do this, you must be intimately familiar with each menu item.

Food-Cost Tracking

Cost is the basic building block of menu pricing, so you need to understand how to track food cost in order to price your menu for maximum profits. Before you price your menu, you need to cost out each menu item. This information can come from your standardized recipe or you can create a separate cost sheet that lists all the items on the menu.

Costs should be based on a standardized recipe. Consistency in operations, costs and customer expectations are why all recipes must be standardized. Take the example of a "little" restaurant chain called McDonald's. What do they do best? They serve consistent, hot food fast, whether you order a Big Mac™ hamburger in London, Tokyo or Chicago. When you order, you know exactly what you are going to receive. You want your customers to know what they are going to receive each and every time.

Standardized recipes. What would be your reaction if you went to a favorite restaurant for their huge prime rib and you received a much smaller portion than usual? Marketing surveys indicate that 60–90 percent of the revenue of independent restaurants is generated from return business. Standardized recipes are the only way you can have accurate costs and portions and a viable business. Think of your business as a manufacturing plant. Every toaster that GE produces is identical regardless of the employee assembling the unit. You need a standard recipe for every item you prepare: bread, salad dressings, sauces, garnishes, side dishes, etc.

Here are some of the advantages of using standardized recipes:

- Customers will communicate to others about your great food, generous portions and terrific service.

- It ensures product consistency, uniform quality and taste.

- The waitstaff will know what dish they will receive and can communicate that to the customer.

- The customer will know what to expect.

- It improves cost control by controlling portion size.

- It lists each item's costs, which makes it easy to access and use this information for pricing.

- It helps make the kitchen run smoother and more efficiently.

- It helps create inventory and purchasing lists.

- It helps with employee training.

- Less supervision is needed during preparation.

- You will need less highly trained (and highly paid) staff.

- You will have better food-cost control.

- It will be possible to calculate the cost of each meal accurately.

Menu item cost information. Bear in mind that while the standardized recipe is an obvious place to list menu item costs, it may not be the only place. More than likely, you and your kitchen staff aren't keeping current with cost changes. Try keeping menu item cost information on a separate sheet with your invoices and other purchasing paperwork. This way you can easily monitor your food costs and keep track of any changes.

Laminate your standard recipe cards and place them in several locations in the kitchen. Use a Polaroid or digital camera to record how the finished dish should look, including the correct plate and garnish to use. Place this photo on the recipe card.

Chefs and experienced line cooks may be resistant to following standard recipes. In your restaurant you can only have one way to prepare each menu item.

Consider the following when developing your recipe file:

- Test all recipes in your kitchen.

- Have ingredients listed in the order they are used.

- Check for correct ingredient amounts.

- Make sure the sequence of activities is clear.

Make sure you have all the necessary equipment to prepare the recipe. If your staff is using various pans to cook something because you don't have the correct size, the item will not turn out the same each time and you are forfeiting consistency.

Give dry ingredients' measure by weight and liquid ingredients' by volume. Be sure you have a scale to measure the weighed amounts.

Make sure that you or a designated person records any changes to the

recipe over time.

Use it! Make sure you enforce the use of standardized recipes with your kitchen staff.

List the appropriate plate and garnish and, if at all possible, include a photo.

Recipe holders. Use index cards and an index cardholder to hold your recipes. Alternatively, use a three-ring binder with recipe sheets inserted into transparent sleeves that can be easily wiped clean.

Organize your file in a meaningful way. Group all the appetizers together, all the soups, all the entrées, all the salads and all the desserts.

Recipe Information

Although your recipe file will change over time, it should always contain certain basic pieces of information. Make sure that you keep track of these changes and keep your file up to date. The following is a summary of the essential information you need to include on your recipe form:

- **Name of item.**

- **Recipe number**/identification within the file system.

- **Yield.** Record the total quantity that the recipe will yield.

- **Portion size.** List portions by weight or number of pieces. You may want to include what size of utensil to use for serving. For example, use the 6-oz ladle for a cup of soup.

- **Garnishes.** Be specific and make sure every plate goes out looking the same. This includes plate setup. You may want to draw a diagram or include a photograph to show your staff how the chicken should lean up against the polenta squares and how the asparagus should sit at an angle on the other side of the chicken.

- **Ingredients.** List ingredients in order. Make sure to list quantities of ingredients used, and keep the abbreviation used for quantities consistent. If you use "oz" for ounce in one recipe, make sure you use it in all your recipes. Give the physical state of ingredients: Are the nuts whole or chopped? Is the flour sifted?

- **Preparation instructions.** Be sure to include any preheating instructions. Use the correct terms for instructions. Do you want the eggs mixed into the batter or folded into it? Should the employee stir or mix with an electric mixer? Be sure to include any precautions or special instructions. If someone is preparing caramel, for example, caution the individual that the sugar water is extremely hot and that they should take the mixture off the heat before adding the cream. This section should also include pan sizes, preparation time, cooking temperature, cooking time, how to test for doneness, and instructions for portioning.

- **Finishing.** Describe any finish that the product needs, such as brushing with oil or melted chocolate drizzled on top. In addition, include how to cool and at what temperature the product should be held. Can it sit at room temperature or does it need to be refrigerated?

- **Cost.** Not all restaurants include cost on the recipes. If you do, the recipe can be used as a resource for everyday ordering as well as menu design. Include every ingredient and every garnish for accuracy. You will need to look at product invoices to get unit prices, then determine the ingredient cost from this. Total the cost of each ingredient for your total recipe cost. Divide by the number of portions to come up with the portion cost.

You can find an example of a standardized recipe card in Chapter 22 on page 274.

Menu Pricing

Menu pricing is a major component of your food-cost equation. The more you can charge your customers, the lower your food-cost percentage. Pricing may seem like a mathematical exercise or a lucky guess, but it is neither of these. Pricing is based on a markup of cost, which is figured by determining food cost, sales history, and profit margin. But pricing strategy does not end there. Consider the following:

Pricing decisions. They are influenced by indirect factors such as:

- Human psychology

- Market conditions

- Location

- Atmosphere

- Service style

- Competition

- Customers' willingness to pay

Never forget that prices are demand or market driven. When the economy is poor, restaurants are likely to see reduced profits because people may be eating out and traveling less. The market will ultimately be a large determinant of your prices. In the end, what it costs you to produce a particular menu item will not matter if the price is so high that no one will buy it. Make sure that your prices reflect not only the cost of the item but also what the competition is charging and what the customer is willing to spend on an item.

Price competitively. Market-driven prices are more responsive to competition. Menu items that are common in an area (hamburgers, chicken sandwiches, prime rib, French fries) and can be purchased at many restaurants and have to be priced competitively.

Signature dishes. Focus on prices that are demand driven; your profitability will be higher. Dishes that have demand-driven prices may be signature items or simply items that are hot food trends.

Location and atmosphere are also important in determining menu prices. If you buy red snapper in Seattle, the price you expect to pay as a customer is greater than what you would expect to pay for the same dinner in Athens, Georgia, simply because in Georgia, red snapper is more readily available and therefore cheaper to purchase. Likewise, if you purchase a grilled chicken sandwich at a restaurant with table service, you expect to pay more than if you get this meal at a drive-through restaurant.

Keep an eye on the competition. Check out what the competition is charging. If you are serving the exact same item as the diner down the street for $3 more, you will invariably lose customers to the other diner, all other things being equal.

Customers' willingness to pay. This is very important when making pricing decisions. All the other factors make no difference if your customers think your prices are too high for what they are receiving. Remember, your customers aren't concerned with your costs. They are concerned with getting their money's worth when they dine out.

How Indirect Factors Can Help Increase Profits

Certain factors can give you a competitive edge, allowing you to charge more than the competition for your products. For instance, if you operate a steakhouse that serves prime beef and all the other steakhouses in town serve choice and select, you are able to charge more for your product because of the higher quality. Other factors may allow you to charge more (or less) as well. If your steakhouse has lush decorations and the service is impeccable or if you have off-street or valet parking, you offer amenities that allow you to charge higher prices than some of your competition may be able to. Make the most of the following:

Plate presentation. Introduce flair! Good plate presentations will allow higher prices than a plate that was given no thought as to its appearance. If the customer is served a plate that looks good, with thought given to garnishes, arrangement and color, he or she will be willing to pay more than if the food is scattered on the plate and hurried out of the kitchen.

Serve food on china and use nice glassware. It will add value to the meal, enabling you to charge more than if you serve meals in baskets or use plastic or Styrofoam.

Atmosphere and décor. Consider remodeling your restaurant if it has not been updated for a number of years. Would just a fresh coat of paint spruce up your dining room and make it an attractive, comfortable place for a meal?

Cleanliness. Customers do not want to eat in a restaurant that is dirty, nor do they want to eat with utensils that have not been properly cleaned. Keep a regular cleaning schedule (and pest-control schedule!). Make sure your restaurant is an attractive venue.

Service. What type of service do you offer? While your customers definitely want quality food, good service is just as important.

Table service. Focus more on table service. It always allows you to charge higher menu prices than carryout or self-service.

Location. Where are you located? This is an important factor in determining what you will be able to charge. If you are in a middle-class neighborhood, you won't want your prices to be on the cutting edge, even if your food is.

What is your customer base? If your customers are college students, you know they have limited spending budgets. Don't price yourself out of the market.

Calculating Entrée and Meal Food Cost

Armed with cost information, you are now in a position to establish your menu prices. Remember, however, that prices will also have to take indirect factors into consideration.

Calculate food costs. Usually food cost is expressed as a percentage of the menu price or of overall sales. Food cost of a specific menu item is figured by dividing the cost of the ingredients for the item by the menu price. This figure is expressed as a percentage. For example: $3.80 (ingredient food cost) ÷ $12.50 (selling price) = $0.30 (30% food cost).

Record overall food costs on a monthly income statement. These numbers will help you decide how well your restaurant operation is doing.

Use your monthly figures. High monthly food costs can be an indication of many things: the need for employee training, the need to better adjust menu prices to reflect costs, over-purchasing, waste, and theft to name but a few.

Set targets. Define realistic food-cost targets for your establishment.

Determine the revenue you can make from an item. Look at the cost, the menu price, and your sales history. If you divide the total income into the total cost of the item, you can determine food cost for a particular period of time. For example, if you sold 200 items during a month that had a cost of $3.80 and price of $12.50: $760 (cost of $3.80 multiplied by 200) ÷ $2,500 (sold 200 at $12.50) = 30%.

Use your sales history to forecast which items will sell in the future. It can help you evaluate how much to purchase and prepare. It can even help you reduce kitchen labor costs.

Poor menu design? If you're not reaching your food-cost goals or are not achieving as high a profit margin as you would like, it may be because of your menu design. Are you emphasizing high-food-cost or low-profit items? Change the design of your menu. It will help decrease food cost and increase profits. Remember, if you sell too many high-cost items, your food cost will go up because many of these (such as beef and seafood) have a high cost. On the other hand, if you sell too many low-cost items, your check averages and gross profits will decline. When designing your menu, you will want to have a mix of both of these types of items.

Keep in mind that there's a difference between actual food cost and target food cost. Every restaurant has a food-cost percentage or a food-cost percentage range that they strive to obtain based on a determined weighted food-cost calculation. Often, managerial bonuses are tied to reaching such food-cost goals.

Moving targets. It's a month-to-month battle to keep your ever-changing food costs in your target area. Just remember, your actual food cost is what you actually spend on ingredients. While your target food costs may be 32 percent, last March your actual food costs might have been 38 percent. Identify the reasons for this difference; it's an important factor in controlling food costs.

Math and Costing Software

The industry generally uses five different pricing methods. The pros and cons of each method are discussed below.

The five methods are as follows:

1. Food-cost percentage pricing.

2. Factor pricing.

3. Actual-cost pricing.

4. Gross-profit pricing.

5. Prime-cost pricing.

What you'll need. To use these methods you will need to gather certain pieces of information from the following sources:

• Sales history and daily receipts.

• Production sheets.

• Profit and loss statements.

Costing software. Software will make all of your calculations easier and more accurate. Atlantic Publishing offers a program called NutraCoster. NutraCoster will calculate product cost (including labor, packaging and overhead) and nutritional content. The program costs about $300 and can be ordered online at **www.atlantic-pub.com** or by calling 800-814-1132. In addition, Atlantic Publishing offers a software program called ChefTec, software for inventory control, recipe, menu costing and nutritional analysis.

Food-Cost Percentage Pricing

This is probably the most widely used method of menu pricing and more than likely it will be the way you price the majority of your menu items. To calculate cost percentages, use target food-cost percentage and actual item food cost.

How it works. With the food-cost percentage method, you determine what percentage of sales will be taken by overhead, labor and food cost and what percentage can be profit. Most restaurants want to realize a profit between 10 and 20 percent, but each establishment is different so you'll need to determine what your actual and target percentages are.

The calculation. To determine prices with this method, you must know your actual food cost and your target food-cost percentage: Food cost ÷ target food-cost percentage = menu price.

> *Example:* Let's say you have Chicken Caesar Salad on your menu. Its food cost is $1.84 and your establishment's target food cost is 35 percent. $1.84 ÷ 0.35 = $5.25

Round up or down. The price in the above example is actually $5.26, but round to 5 or a 9 when setting your prices. You could also round up to $5.35, if you feel your customers will pay this amount for this item. Most restaurant mangers tend to round figures up.

Pros. It's an easy formula to use.

Cons. It doesn't take labor or other costs into consideration.

Factor Pricing

As with food-cost percentage pricing, factoring also uses your overall target food cost (as a percentage) and the particular item's food cost to determine price. To calculate the price factor, use target food-cost percentage and actual item food cost.

How it works. This method uses a factor that represents food-cost percentage. To determine prices with this method, the food cost is multiplied by the pricing factor. The factor will always be the percentage of your desired food cost divided by 100.

The calculation. Let's say your target food cost is 35 percent. Divide 35 into 100, and you get 2.86 as your factor: 100 ÷ 35 = 2.86. By multiplying this number by your food cost, you come up with a price.

> *Example:* If the food cost on a dish is $2.67:
> $2.67 x 2.86 = $7.65 (food cost x pricing factor = menu price)

Pros. It's an easy method.

Cons. Each individual item will not meet your overall target food cost. Some of your menu items will have a higher cost and some will have a lower cost. Factoring will overprice high-cost items and underprice low-cost items.

Actual-Cost Pricing

This method is used when the menu price is established before the food cost is known. By looking at all other costs, it determines what can be spent on food cost. This method includes profit as part of the menu price. Catering operations use it when working with a customer who has a definite budget that they have to meet. By working back from what the person can spend, the manager can determine what can be spent on food and, in turn, what kind of menu they can offer the customer. To calculate actual costs, use menu price, overhead costs (as a percentage), labor costs (as a percentage), and desired profits (as a percentage).

How it works. First, you need to determine what percentage of your costs go into overhead and labor and what percentage of sales need to go to profit. Since this equation is expressed as a percentage, overhead, labor, food cost and profit must equal 100 percent: 100% – overhead % – labor % – profit % = food cost %.

The calculation. By looking at your profit and loss statement, you see that your labor is 30 percent of your sales, overhead is 20 percent, and you know you are aiming for a 15 percent profit. Therefore, you can spend 35 percent of the price you establish on food cost.

> *Example:* Look at your sales history. You earned $100,000 in a 6-month period. Of that $100,000, $20,000 was spent on overhead expenses, $30,000 was spent on labor, and $15,000 was allocated to profit. That leaves you $35,000 to spend on food.
> 100% – 20% – 30% – 15% = 35%.

Let's look at a specific menu item now. Your lasagna sells for $11. Of that $11, $2.20 is spent on overhead, $3.30 is spent on labor, and $1.65 is profit. That leaves you $3.85 to spend on food.

Pros. It includes profit in the calculation of the price of each menu item.

Cons. You are working backward from menu price to food cost, so this method may not be helpful if your goal is to come up with menu prices in the first place.

Gross-Profit Pricing

The gross-profit method is designed to enable you to make a certain amount in profit from each customer. To calculate gross profits, use past revenue in dollars, past gross profit in dollars, past number of customers, and item actual food cost.

How it works. Let's say your food service operation looks at its past year's sales and you find that you made $80,000 in sales. Food cost was $25,600, so your gross profit was $54,400 (no costs other than food have been subtracted at this point, so this is not net profit). From your guest check tally, you can conclude that you served 25,000 customers during that time period.

The calculation. Divide the gross profit by the number of customers; an average gross profit of $3.20 per customer is established: Gross profit ($54,400) ÷ number of customers (25,000) = average gross profit per customer ($2.18).

Next, establish your food cost from your standardized recipe. Add this to the gross profit to determine your selling price: Food cost + average gross profit = selling price.

> *Example:* Your lasagna's food cost is $3.85:
> $3.85 + $2.18 = $6.03.

Pros. You are assured of making a predetermined amount of money on each customer. It works well when customer counts are predictable.

Cons. It is hard to adjust for any major changes in business or customer counts; it may be more adaptable for institutional operations like hospitals and schools than for commercial establishments. It does not take the cost of labor into account.

Prime-Cost Pricing

Items on your menu will differ with regards to how much labor is involved in their production. Homemade soups and desserts, for instance, involve quite a bit more labor than pre-made items. This method allows the price to reflect this labor cost.

Calculate labor costs. Labor expenditure can be determined by noting the length of time that each item takes to prepare. This labor figure should include the time it takes to assemble ingredients and utensils, washing, chopping, peeling, mixing, preliminary cooking (such as blanching) and cleanup time. The labor cost is determined by taking this amount of time and multiplying it by the employee's hourly wage: Employee wage x amount of time to prepare = labor cost of producing item.

Labor cost of individual servings. In order to determine a labor cost for each serving of a particular item, simply divide the above number by the number of portions. When this amount is added to the food cost, you come up with your prime food cost.

To calculate prime costs, use the following figures: Total labor cost as a percentage, labor cost for preparing item, actual item food cost and target food cost as a percentage.

How it works. Look at your menu and determine which items require an extensive amount of labor in the production process. Then determine the labor used to prepare the specific menu items and add the items' food cost to the labor cost to get a total: Food cost + labor cost = item cost.

Next, determine what percentage the labor cost for preparing the item is of your total labor percentage. This number will be expressed as a percentage. Add the item's labor percentage to your target food cost (expressed as a percentage) to come up with the prime food-cost percentage.

The last step. Divide the total item cost by the prime food-cost percentage and you get the menu selling price.

Example: Your menu includes a meat lasagna. It takes your prep cook 1.5 hours to prepare 2 trays of 12 servings, for a total of 24 servings. Your prep cook is paid $8 an hour (since the line cook does not have to do anything but reheat the lasagna, that labor does not have to be figured in). Labor for this item is $12. For each portion, the cost is 50 cents: $8 x 1.5 = $12; $12 ÷ 24 = $0.50.

Item labor cost. By looking at your financial statements you know that your total labor is 25 percent, so you figure out that the labor for this item is 8 percent. Add this percentage to your desired food cost (say 37 percent) for the prime food-cost percentage: 8% + 37% = 45%.

Suggested menu price. Direct labor percentage + desired food-cost percentage = prime food-cost percentage. Now, add the direct labor per portion (50 cents) to the food cost (say $4) and divide this by the prime food-cost percentage (45 percent). This will give you a suggested menu price: Direct labor per portion + food cost per portion ÷ prime food-cost percentage = suggested menu price: ($0.50 + $4 ÷ .45) = $10. In reality, this would probably be adjusted to $9.95.

Pros. You can include cost for labor on items that require a significant amount of labor in the preparation.

Cons. It is a complicated method to use. It should only be used on items with a high labor cost.

Menu Sales Analysis

Menu sales analysis, or menu scores, track how many of each menu item is sold.

Looking at this information, together with food cost and menu prices, can give the food service manager a great deal of information. Look at the following:

Sales mix. Study the menu sales mix. Determine which menu items should be emphasized.

Emphasize the mix of items and keep your food costs under control. Concentrating on the mix is one of the best ways to realize the highest profit possible. Rather than focusing on the profit of individual menu items, you should concentrate on what kind of profit you are achieving from your menu as a whole.

Avoid negatively impacting your check average. In an attempt to contain food costs, don't emphasize only low-cost items. Usually items that have a low food cost also have a low menu price (items such as chicken and vegetarian meals). If your customers predominantly are buying these items, your check average will be too low to realize the profit you desire.

Analysis Simplified

Managers have different ways of analyzing their sales mix. This may range from simply looking at a cash register report at the end of each night, to having an intuitive feeling for which items are selling, to creating a complicated way of categorizing each menu item in order to analyze the sales mix. Some of these methods focus on controlling food costs to increase profitability and others focus on increasing sales of more profitable items. While the more complicated methods have their advantages, most food service managers are hard pressed for time and more than likely you can't squeeze even one more hour out of their week to analyze menu sales. The following guidelines represent a middle ground. You can still get the information you need from a sales analysis, but you don't have to devote a great deal of time to computation:

Menu sales mix. When you're looking at your menu sales mix, you are interested in three things:

1. How many of an item is sold.

2. Item cost.

3. Item profitability.

Why is the sales mix so important? Assume a restaurant serves only two products:

1. Shrimp with a total food cost of $5 and a selling price of $12.

2. Chicken breast with a total food cost of $2.50 and a selling price of $8.50.

WEEK 1 (1,000 Entrées Sold) **NET PROFIT = $6,900 AND 40% FOOD COST**	
900 Shrimp Dinners	
Sales	(900 x $12) = $10,800
Cost of Sales	(900 x $5) = $4,500
100 Chicken Breasts	
Sales	(100 x $8.50) = $850
Cost of Sales	(100 x $2.50) = $250
Total Items Sold	= 1,000
Total Sales	= $11,650
Total Cost of Sales	= $4,750
$4,750 ÷ $11,650 x 100	= 40% Food Cost

Now examine the second week with the reverse sales mix.

WEEK 2 (1,000 Entrées Sold **NET PROFIT = $6,100 AND 31% FOOD COST**	
900 Chicken Breasts	
Sales	(900 x $8.50) = $7,650
Cost of Sales	(900 x $2.50) = $2,250
100 Shrimp Dinners	
Sales	(100 x $12) = $1,200
Cost of Sales	(100 x $5) = $500
Total Items Sold	= 1,000
Total Sales	= $8,850
Total Cost of Sales	= $2,750
$2,750 ÷ $8,850 x 100	= 31% Food Cost

In the previous example, Week 1 had a 12 percent higher profit margin with the same number of customers served, yet the food-cost percentage was 9 percent higher than in Week 2. Thus, in this simplified example, you can clearly see the effect the weighted average sales has on food-cost percentages and overall profitability.

Food-cost percentage meaning. Don't become overly concerned over food-cost percentages; they are truly meaningless unless you know what your food-cost percentage should be for the given time in question. Remember, you get paid in and deposit dollars into the bank, not percentages.

Food-costs percentages are different at individual establishments. There are establishments in this country that can run a 50 percent or higher food-cost percentage and still be very profitable because of the high sales volume.

Analyze and Classify Your Menu Sales Mix

Once you have an effective menu design, analyzing your sales mix to determine the impact each item has on sales, costs and profits is an important practice. If you have costs and waste under control, looking at your menu sales mix can help you further reduce costs and boost profits. You will find that some items need to be promoted more aggressively, while others need to be dropped altogether. Classifying your menu items is necessary for making those decisions. Here are some suggested classifications:

MENU CLASSIFICATIONS		
PRIMES	**STANDARDS**	**SLEEPERS**
These are popular items that are low in food cost and high in profit. Have them stand out on your menu.	Items with high food costs and high profit margins. You can possibly raise the price on this item and push it as a signature.	Slow-selling, low food-cost items with low profit margins. Work to increase the likelihood that these will be seen and ordered through more prominent menu display, featuring on menu boards, lowered prices, etc.

Problems. High in food cost and low in profits. If you can, raise the price and lower production cost. If you can't, hide them on the menu. If sales don't pick up, get rid of them altogether.

You need to know the answers to these questions:

- What is the most popular entrée served?

- What is the most profitable entrée served by dollar amount?

- What is the lowest food-cost item served by percentage of food cost?

Chapter 26

Purchasing, Receiving and Storage

Food Purchasing

Does it sometimes feel like you are constantly ordering food for your restaurant? Where is your inventory going? How much have you invested in the stock room this month? How much did that dropped chicken breast, which was just thrown away, actually cost you? The goal of purchasing is to obtain wholesome, safe foods to meet your menu requirements. The operation must have food to serve customers when needed. The food needs to be the right quality consistent with the operation's standards and purchased at the lowest possible cost. Here are some essential purchasing tips:

Consider buying in bulk. When purchasing food and supplies, buy in bulk if it can save you money. Items like spices have a very low spoilage rate and can be stored for a long period without losing quality.

When you find a great price, don't over-purchase. A long-term saving may be offset by additional storage costs, spoilage, and by having your finances tied up in stock that won't give you a return on your investment for some time.

Name brands. When purchasing food, avoid more expensive "name brands" wherever possible. Of course, you want to make sure you're buying quality ingredients for your food, but are your customers really likely to tell the difference between a name brand as opposed to an industrial brand?

Buy local. Talk to local fresh-produce suppliers to see if you can't get fresher, cheaper, better-quality produce direct from the grower. Why pay a supplier to get the fruit and vegetables, ship them to their central warehouse, then ship them back to you, when you can just drive ten minutes down the road and enjoy food right off the tree or vine?

Include menu items that are essentially made with similar ingredients to other items on the menu. For example, a shrimp cocktail and shrimp pasta are two very different meals, but the ingredients are simple, inexpensive and don't take up a lot of storage space. Having five or six other pasta sauces offered likewise loads up your menu with choices, without excessively increasing your inventory. Not only will this allow you to buy in bulk and keep costs down, but it will also lighten the load on your kitchen staff.

Test sample. When considering the purchase of a new food or beverage product, ask if you can test a sample before you make your decision. Not only is free stock always a nice thing to have, but also testing a new item properly is essential if you don't want to deal with unforeseen problems later.

Check deliveries. Who checks your purchase orders when food is delivered to you? If the answer is nobody, then you may well be getting fleeced and not even know it. It's an all-too-common practice either to send more than was ordered, charge a higher price than quoted, or under-pack a box.

Lists. The person who handles your inventory counts of food and beverages should also be responsible for creating lists of what needs to be ordered. Keeping the main responsibility of deciding purchasing quantities with the person closest to the inventory assures that you won't go overboard with your buying habits. Also, two people should double-check what is in stock. One of them may be the person who does the ordering, as long as the second person changes on a regular basis to prevent collusion and theft.

Inventory tracking. Use custom-made restaurant purchasing and inventory software. With inventory-control software, managers can use a laser scanner, similar to the ones used in grocery stores, to scan bar codes. The software can also be linked to your distributors and you can place your orders electronically, based on the inventory. ChefTec, software for inventory control, recipe, menu costing and nutritional analysis, is available at **www.atlantic-pub.com**, 800-814-1132.

Another Web site of interest is www.foodprofile.com. This site was established for the collection and distribution of product information for the food industry and is part of an initiative called Efficient Foodservice Response (EFR). Distributors pay to list their products on this site. It provides over 65,000 items and has the most up-to-date product information available, including serving suggestions, nutritional information, cooking instructions and ingredient statements. EFR is an industry-wide effort to improve efficiency in the purchasing process. To find out more about EFR, log on to **www.efr-central .com**.

Failing to stock enough supplies to last you until your next delivery is a big waste of money. Having to pick up supplies from the supermarket across the street might be an easy fix, but it's also very expensive compared to your normal supplier.

Dealing with Suppliers

Your suppliers are an aspect of your business that can be of great assistance to you, if you know how to deal with them. Good relationships with vendors can greatly reduce your operating costs. Try the following approach:

Do you have poor relationships with your suppliers? Take the time to talk with your delivery person and order-taker. Try to speak with the same people every time you deal with them and build a relationship of trust.

Strike a bargain. Ask what items they have in stock that are an exceptionally good deal this month or are of greater quality than normal. Ask suppliers if you can do a deal, if they'll knock a few dollars off an item if you buy a larger quantity, or if they'll throw you a discount (or a bonus) if you settle your invoice early.

Do you use fixed orders? Often a fixed order will see you granted a small discount because it allows the vendor to plan their own purchases accurately. But if you're buying more than you need over the long run, this deal might cost you more than it saves you. Review all standing orders at least every quarter, reducing or increasing where necessary and keeping your inventory at a productive level.

Use your suppliers' Web sites. Many of the larger food suppliers, such as SYSCO, have Web sites on which you can place and track orders. Like SYSCO, they may also have links to current market reports and information on new products. You can visit SYSCO's Web site at **www.sysco.com**.

Do you monitor markets regularly for lower prices? Perform monthly price checks for food, beverages and supplies. If you spot someone selling cheaper than your supplier, ask them to match the price. A supplier trying to get, or keep, your business may offer discounts, bonuses and incentives that can save you a bundle.

Vendors and food safety. Food safety at this step is primarily the responsibility of your vendors. It's your job to choose your vendors wisely.

Suppliers must meet federal and state health standards. They should use the HACCP system in their operations and train their employees in sanitation.

Delivery trucks. Delivery trucks should have adequate refrigeration and freezer units, and foods should be packaged in protective, leak-proof, durable packaging. Let vendors know upfront what you expect from them. Put food-safety standards in your purchase specification agreements. Ask to see their most recent board of health sanitation reports, and tell them you will be inspecting trucks on a regular basis.

Delivery schedules. Good vendors will cooperate with your inspections and should adjust their delivery schedules to avoid your busy periods so that incoming foods can be received and inspected properly.

Inventory Levels

Your inventory system is the critical component of purchasing. Before placing an order with a supplier, you need to know what you have on hand and how much will be used. Allow for a cushion of inventory so you won't run out between deliveries. Once purchasing has been standardized, simply order from your suppliers. Records show supplier, prices, unit of purchase, product specifications, etc. This information needs to be kept on paper and preferably computerized. Purchase food items according to usage. For example, if you plan to use tomatoes by blending and mixing them with other ingredients to make a sauce, purchase broken tomatoes as opposed to whole tomatoes. However, if you intend to use tomatoes to decorate a dinner plate or as a topping, opt for high-quality produce, such as baby plum vine-grown tomatoes.

The first step in computing what item to order and how much you need is to determine the inventory level, or the amount needed on hand at all times. This is a simple procedure, but it requires order sheets. To determine the amount you need to order, you must first know the amount you have in inventory. Walk through the storage areas and mark in the "On Hand" column the amounts that are there. To determine the "Build To Amount," you will need to know when regularly scheduled deliveries arrive for that item and the amount used in the period between deliveries. Add on about 15 percent to the average amount used; this will cover unexpected usage, a late delivery, or a backorder from the vendor. The amount you need to order is the difference between the "Build To Amount" and the amount "On Hand." Experience and food demand will reveal the amount an average order should contain. By purchasing too little, the restaurant may run out of supplies before the next delivery. Ordering too much will result in tying up money and putting a drain on the restaurant's cash flow. Buying items in large amounts can save money, but you must consider the cash-flow costs.

A buying schedule should be set up and adhered to. This would consist of a calendar showing:

- Which day's orders need to be placed.

- When deliveries will be arriving.

- What items will be arriving from which company.

- Phone numbers of sales representatives to contact for each company.

- The price the sales representative quoted.

Post the buying schedule on the office wall. When a delivery doesn't arrive as scheduled, the buyer should place a phone call to the salesperson or company immediately. Don't wait until the end of the day when offices are closed.

A Want Sheet may be placed on a clipboard in the kitchen. This sheet is made available for employees to write in any items they may need to do their jobs more efficiently. This is a very effective form of communication; employees should be encouraged to use it. The buyer should consult this sheet every day. A request might be as simple as a commercial-grade carrot peeler. If, for example, the last one broke and the preparation staff has been using the back of a knife instead, the small investment could save you from an increase in labor and food costs.

Purchasing and Ordering

What exactly is the difference? Purchasing is setting the policy on which suppliers, brands, grades, and varieties of products will be ordered. These are your standardized purchase specifications; the specifics of how items are delivered, paid for, and returned. These specifications are negotiated between management and distributors. Basically, purchasing is what you order and from whom. Ordering, then, is simply the act of contacting the suppliers and notifying them of the quantity you require. This is a simpler, lower-level task. Here are the basics:

Develop a purchasing program. Once menus have been created that meet your customers' satisfaction and your profit needs, develop a purchasing program that ensures your profit margins.

An efficient purchasing program incorporates standard purchase specifications based on standardized recipes and standardized yields and portion control that allow for accurate costs based on portions actually served.

Keep in mind that purchasing more than you need usually results in poor portioning, excess spoilage, waste, and theft. Not buying enough can mean paying retail prices or using a more expensive substitute.

Purchasing procedures. These procedures should include creating written purchasing specifications for every product and selecting good, reliable purveyors.

Your purchasing program should do three things:

1. Allow you to purchase the required items at prices that meet your food-cost goals.

2. Maintain control over your existing inventory.

3. Establish a set of procedures to be sure that you receive quality product at the best price.

Price checks for different vendors. Sometimes you may find that one vendor is less expensive than another for a while, and then this may shift. Keep current with competing vendors' prices.

Purchasing Specifications

By creating purchasing specifications, you control which items you purchase and maintain product consistency. This information is extremely important if you have more than one person that does ordering in your operation. You need to record the following basic information:

Purchasing specifications. They state the exact requirements for the amount and quality of items purchased. These specifications should include:

- Product name.

- Quantity to be purchased (designated with correct unit such as pounds, can size, etc.).

- Indication of grade, if applicable.

- Unit by which prices are quoted.

- What the product will be used to produce.

Meats. Meats should be inspected by the USDA or other appropriate agency. The parts or packaging should carry a federal or state inspection stamp.

Eggs. Eggs should have a USDA grade; frozen and dried eggs should be pasteurized.

Shellfish. Shellfish should be purchased from suppliers that appear on public health service Food and Drug Administration's list of Certified Shellfish Shippers or on lists of state-approved sources. The control tags must be available if live shellfish are used.

Introduce a record sheet. Make it readily available for all your employees. They need to be sure that they're ordering the correct items in the correct amounts. You're also more likely to attain your desired food cost by keeping these records and maintaining purchasing controls. Keeping your food cost down will help you to maximize profits from your menu prices.

Purchasing and Inventory Software

Purchasing and inventory software is readily available to restaurant operators. Many larger organizations are using inventory-control software that saves a significant amount of time and money. Most managers are used to the monthly grind, standing in the walk-ins counting eggs, butter pats and frozen chickens. With inventory-control software, managers can use a laser scanner, similar to the ones used in grocery stores, to scan bar codes. The software can also be linked to your distributors and you can place your orders electronically based on the inventory. Check out the following software vendors:

Atlantic Publishing (www.atlantic-pub.com; 800-814-1132) offers a software program called ChefTec, software for inventory control, recipe, menu costing, and nutritional analysis.

Visit the National Restaurant Association's Web site at **www.restaurant.org** for vendors of this software (as well as many other products). Take a trip to their annual National Restaurant Association Exhibit each year in Chicago to see all the latest products available in the restaurant industry.

Another Web site of interest is **www.foodprofile.com**. This site was established for the collection and distribution of product information for the food industry and is part of an initiative called Efficient Foodservice Response (EFR). Distributors pay to list their products on this site. It provides over 65,000 items and has the most up-to-date product information available, including serving suggestions, nutritional information, cooking instructions, and ingredient statements. EFR is an industry-wide initiative to improve efficiency in the purchasing process. To find out more about EFR, log on to **www.efr-central.com**.

Consider placing your orders online. Almost all distributors now have systems in place to order online. The advantages are numerous: it reduces ordering errors, it's convenient, there may be discounts, and most systems build a customer database based on what you have previously ordered, making re-orders easy. A list of vendor Web sites follows:

- **www.usfoodservice.com**

- **www.sysco.com**

- **www.seafax.com/cgi-bin/WebObjects/Seafax**

- **winebusiness.com**

- www.tampamaid.com

- www.foodservicecentral.com

- www.foodservice.com

- www.agribuys.com

- www.gfs.com

- www.nugget.com

- www.pocahontasfoods.com

- www.whitetoque.com

Use purchase orders (PO). A PO is a written authorization for a vendor to supply goods or services at a specified price over a specified time period. Acceptance of the PO constitutes a purchase contract and is legally binding on all parties. Utilizing POs will enable you to know what was ordered, the quantity, and the price. If you are using software to record the invoice and receipt of inventory, the program will restock and adjust pricing automatically. In addition, your perpetual inventory will be updated. Purchase orders from software programs can easily be faxed or e-mailed into the vendor, saving time and money.

When purchasing food, avoid more expensive name brands wherever possible. Of course, you want to make sure you're buying quality ingredients for your food, but are your customers really likely to tell the difference between a name brand and an industrial brand?

Local growers. Talk to local fresh-produce suppliers to see if you can't get fresher, cheaper, better-quality produce direct from the grower. Why pay a supplier to get the fruit and vegetables that are shipped to their central warehouse, then shipped back to you, when you can just drive ten minutes down the road and enjoy food right off the tree or vine? You can also use this as a promotional device. If you use local produce, let your customers know!

Cooperative purchasing. Many restaurants have formed cooperative purchasing groups to increase their purchasing power. The cooperatives purchase items that are commonly used by all food service operators. By joining together to place large orders, restaurants can usually get substantial price reductions. Some organizations even purchase their own trucks and warehouses and hire personnel to pick up deliveries. This can be advantageous for restaurants that are in the proximity of a major supplier or shipping center. Many items, such as produce, dairy products, seafood and meat, may be purchased this way. Chain restaurants have a centralized purchasing department and, often, large self-distribution centers.

Make sure you shop for purveyors. Don't rest once you've found one. Comparison shop on a continual basis.

Look at vendors' product labels. This will tell you where the product came from. Most manufacturers won't ship more than 100 miles away from their plants. The further away that a supplier is located, the more shipping will cost.

Consider planting your own herb and/or vegetable garden. Great food starts with using the freshest herbs and vegetables, and the best way to do that is to grow them yourself! The techniques for growing your own are not difficult. With a little planning, you can build your own 24-hour supply of garden-fresh herbs. Even a small garden can infuse your kitchen with heavenly aromas and striking flavor. What a great way to lower your food cost and separate yourself from the competition! You can buy seeds online at:

- **www.burpee.com/main.asp**

- **www.dansgardenshop.com**

- **www.johnnyseeds.com/catalog/index.html**

- **www.richters.com**

- **www.parkseed.com**

Inventory, Storage and Accounts Payable

Ordering effectively is impossible unless you are completely familiar with the inventory items. Prior to orders being placed with vendors, counts of stock need to be established. Software programs are able to determine order quantities based upon par balances and sale figures; we highly recommend this implementation. Whether your ordering system is performed with a pencil and paper or by computer, its purpose is to:

- Provide reports of what is needed.

- Provide reports of the specified products.

- Provide reports of vendors and contact information.

- Provide reports of prices.

- Provide a historical report of prices.

- Provide a method for the ease of order placement.

Keep these critical points about inventory in mind:

Inventory amounts. The more you have in inventory, the harder it is to control.

Shelf life for perishables. Meat, produce and seafood will only last 2–3 days, so do not order too much of these products at a time.

Excessive inventory ties up your cash, hindering cash flow.

Extra food on hand tends to lead to over-portioning and is easier for theft.

Inventory turnover. Ideally, the entire food inventory should be turned every 5–8 days.

Vendors. Schedule vendor representative visits so you are not interrupted.

Standing orders. Consider placing standing orders for regularly used items.

Check trade magazines and **www.foodbuy.com** for rebates available from manufacturers.

Join a buying group such as the one at **www.foodservice.com**. They have pre-negotiated manufacturer allowances available on over 10,000 food and food-related products from over 125 network suppliers from manufacturers like Sweetheart, Ecolab, Sara Lee and General Mills.

Warehouse buying clubs. Check out warehouse buying clubs such as Sam's Club, **www.samsclub.com**, Costco, **www.costco.com** and Restaurant Depot, **www.restaurantdepot.com**.

Cash discounts. Many purveyors provide cash discounts if payment is made early, such as "2/10, net 30." With this, a 2 percent discount may be taken if payment is made within 10 days. Cash discounts are worth taking; a restaurant that purchases $500,000 per year and takes a 2 percent discount will save $10,000.

Alternatives. Don't automatically use fresh fruit and vegetables if canned alternatives can be used without cutting back on meal quality. Canned tomatoes, artichoke hearts, chili peppers, pears, etc., can all be used in many meals without a big loss in flavor, and the trade off is a big drop in price and spoilage rates.

Purchasing Kickbacks and Gifts

Unfortunately, the food service industry is notorious for kickbacks. It is even more unfortunate that these kickbacks or gifts are essentially paid for by you in the form of higher prices. Here are some ideas to help keep kickbacks out of your store:

Purchasing and receiving must be done by different employees. The person ordering should not be the same person receiving and checking the items.

Kickback policy. Develop a general policy and list it in your employee handbook that employees cannot receive anything for free from a vendor or potential vendor.

Change positions. People become complacent over time; move positions around.

Check on prices of expensive items like meat and seafood yourself.

Purchasing Ideas

There are many ways to curb costs. Here are a few ideas:

Inexpensive fish. Turn your customers on to seafood alternatives and lower your food cost. Consider using some alternatives such as Tilapia, farm-raised salmon, fresh-water perch, Alaskan halibut, mahi-mahi, shark, or skate.

Shelled eggs. If the recipes allow, consider buying shelled eggs if your restaurant uses more than three cases of eggs per week. This will reduce the amount of cardboard and other packaging that must be disposed or recycled. Shelled eggs are often packaged in five-gallon buckets that can later be reused for cleaning or maintenance.

Condiments. Use refillable condiment dispensers instead of individual condiment packets for dine-in customers.

Cost-Watch Web site. This site, **www.cost-watch.com**, helps restaurant management control labor, utility, and food and beverage costs. It also offers regional reports to compare expenses and food costs in similar restaurants as well as price trend forecasts. It is a great resource for purchasing managers.

Join a barter club. Bartering allows you to buy what you need and pay for it with otherwise unsold products, such as food and beverages or even catering services. Almost anything and everything can be purchased with barter services. Nationally, over 250,000 businesses are involved in barter. Check out **www.barterwww.com** and **www.barterbrokers.com.**

Similar ingredients. Include menu items that are essentially made with similar ingredients as others on the menu. For example, a shrimp cocktail and shrimp pasta are two very different meals, but the ingredients are similar. These ingredients are simple and inexpensive and don't take up a lot of storage space. Having five or six other pasta sauces to offer also loads up your menu with choices without excessively increasing your inventory. This will not only allow you to buy in bulk and keep costs down, but will also lighten the load on your kitchen staff.

Substitute pre-made items. Substitute pre-made items for some items you have been making from scratch. You don't have to sacrifice quality to do this; many pre-made items are very good. You can also start with a pre-made item and add ingredients. For instance, you can buy a pre-made salad dressing and add blue cheese or fresh herbs. Using these items will lower your food and labor costs, and you can still put out a quality item.

Receiving Goals

The goals of receiving are to ensure foods are fresh and safe when they enter your facility and you are receiving what you ordered and are paying for. Transfer items to proper storage as quickly as possible.

Let's look more closely at two important parts of receiving:

1. Getting ready to receive food.

2. Inspecting the food when the delivery truck arrives.

Receiving Policy

Introduce a receiving policy. Remember, it's easy to "lose" products in this part of your operation. Let's say, for example, you have no one specifically assigned to check in orders. Normally one of your line cooks will do it. Let's also say that one day your order is late and arrives in the middle of lunch rush. No one can check the order for accuracy, so they just sign for it in a hurry. If this happens, it is virtually impossible to correct any mistakes at the time. Furthermore, if your line cooks don't get to put the order away until several hours later, you will lose product because it has sat out too long and is now unsafe to serve.

Receiving Tips

There are several important guidelines to keep in mind and tasks to complete as you get ready to receive food:

Calibration. Make sure all scales and thermometers are in place and calibrated.

Sanitary carts. Make sure your receiving area is equipped with sanitary carts for transporting goods.

Plan ahead for deliveries to ensure sufficient refrigerator and freezer space.

Mark all items for storage with the date of arrival or the "use by" date.

Lighting. Keep the receiving area well lit and clean to discourage pests.

Remove empty containers and packing materials immediately to a separate trash area.

Keep all flooring clean of food particles and debris.

Delivery truck. When the delivery truck arrives, make sure it looks and smells clean and is equipped with the proper food-storage equipment. Then inspect foods immediately.

Check expiration dates of milk, eggs and other perishable goods. Make sure shelf-life dates have not expired.

Frozen foods. Make sure frozen foods are in airtight, moisture-proof wrappings.

Reject foods that have been thawed and refrozen. Look for signs of thawing and refreezing, such as large crystals, solid areas of ice, or excessive ice in containers.

Rejecting canned goods. Reject cans that have any of the following: swollen sides or ends; flawed seals or seams; dents; or rust. Also reject any cans whose contents are foamy or smell bad.

Check the temperature of refrigerated and frozen foods, especially eggs and dairy products, fresh meat and fish, and poultry products.

Look for content damage and insect infestations.

Dirty crates. Reject dairy, bakery and other foods delivered in flats or crates that are dirty.

Weighing items. Meats, fish and most items ordered by the pound must be weighed and tagged. Food items purchased by count need to be checked and counted. All items received must be counted, weighed and date stamped. Don't deviate from this critical step.

Invoice accuracy. Check the accuracy of the invoice against the purchase order, specifically price, damage, quality, quantity, brand, grade and variety. Items that are not correct need to be noted and returned before the driver leaves and the driver must sign the form.

Don't let delivery people into your storage areas.

Items packed in ice need to be removed from the ice prior to weighing.

Check animal cavities in fish and poultry for ice.

Delivery personnel should be professional, not rushed, and friendly, but not too friendly. Ensure they know that it doesn't matter if they are in a hurry; you are going to check everything in and count and weigh everything prior to their leaving.

All food products must be date coded, rotated and put away immediately.

Placed in order. Products should be placed on the shelves in the same order as the inventory sheets and purchase order forms. This will help in inventory counting and control.

Determine which employees are allowed to access the storage areas. Storage areas are prime targets for theft. Not only employee theft, but if areas aren't kept locked and secure, outside people will be able to get in and help themselves to your products.

Getting What You Paid For

Keep an eye on the deliveries coming through your back door. Don't pay for other people's mistakes; keep an eye out for inconsistencies, mistakes and outright fraud. Here's how to make sure that you get what you paid for:

Never pay for any shipping invoice that has not been signed for by an employee from your establishment. Inform your sales rep and delivery driver that when deliveries are scheduled to arrive, a member of your staff must be available to check the goods and sign the invoice.

Let employees know that they're responsible for whatever they signed. If a box is supposed to contain 20 pounds and it only contains 19, that should be pointed out and noted when the delivery first comes in.

Returns. Insist that returned or refused items are marked and initialed by the delivery person on the packing slip and then put back on the truck before the driver leaves your establishment. It's far harder to send goods back and be credited for them when they've been sitting in your establishment.

Purchasing and Storage Policies

Make sure you have purchasing and storage specifications in place for your staff to follow. Specifications should include:

- Specific product information for placing orders.

- Correct storage temperatures.

- Rotation policy for stock.

Minimize food loss in storage by keeping frozen foods at 0°F and food in dry storage areas at temperatures around 50°F. Keep food in dry storage, on shelves, at least 6 inches from the floor and the wall. Make sure the staff is storing raw meat on shelves below raw produce, and ensure that fresh fish is being kept on ice in the refrigerator to maintain the proper temperature of 30°–34°F.

Check expiration dates. Anything with a suspect date should be refused or sent back.

Check scales for accuracy. How often are kitchen scales checked for accuracy?

Your scales need to be checked and calibrated on a weekly basis to ensure complete accuracy so that you are not billed for product you haven't received.

Make sure your scales are adequate to check the weight of incoming orders. You should be able to check, quickly, if you are receiving 50 pounds of hamburger or only 45 pounds. If you don't have scales, consider purchasing them. To purchase kitchen scales online, visit Scale World at **www.scaleworld .com**, Scale Man at **www.scaleman.com** or Itin Scales at **www.itinscale.com**.

FIFO and Labeling

All food items need to be rotated to ensure that the oldest items in inventory are used first. The first in, first out (FIFO) method of rotation is used to ensure that all food products are properly rotated in storage. Label all boxes, cans, containers, bags and shelves. It is a good idea to enforce these procedures with your employees by displaying posters. Atlantic Publishing offers a "First In, First Out" reminder poster for $8.95 (Item # FSP10-PS). Available at **www.atlantic-pub.com** or by calling 1-800-814-1132.

The FIFO method uses these principles:

1. New items go to the back and on the bottom.

2. Older items move to the front and to the left.

3. In any part of the restaurant, the first item used should always be the oldest.

4. Date and mark everything.

Any food operator using the FIFO method of food rotation and operators who are following a HACCP program needs to use labels. Labeling reduces spoilage and food costs when products are dated correctly and staff becomes accountable for managing food storage and preparation. Labeling also ensures product freshness and flavor. Properly documenting prep dates and use-by dates allows an operator to identify which foods need to be consumed by a specified date, thus eliminating the discard of food.

DayMark (**www.daymark.biz**) offers a variety of labels to be used in food rotation that comply with the FDA's storage requirements:

- Dissolve-A-Way (DissolveMark™)

- Removable (MoveMark™)

- Freezable (CoolMark™)

- Permanent (DuraMark™)

- Repositionable (ReMark™)

Storage

In general, there are four possible ways to store food: First, in dry storage for longer holding of less-perishable items. Second, in refrigeration for short-term storage of perishable items. Third, in specially designed deep-chilling units for short periods. Finally, in a freezer for longer-term storage of perishable foods. Each type of storage has its own sanitation and safety requirements.

Dry Storage

There are many items that can be held safely in a sanitary storeroom. These include canned goods, baking supplies (such as salt and sugar), grain products (such as rice and cereals), and other dry items. In addition, some fruits ripen best at room temperature, such as bananas, avocados and pears. Some vegetables, such as onions, potatoes and tomatoes, also store best in dry storage. A dry-storage room should be clean and orderly with good ventilation to control temperature and humidity and retard the growth of bacteria and mold. Keep in mind the following:

Temperature. For maximum shelf life, dry foods should be held at 50°F, but 60°–70°F is adequate for most products.

Wall thermometer. Use a wall thermometer to check the temperature of your dry-storage facility regularly. See **www.atlantic-pub.com** for a complete selection of thermometers.

First in, first out (FIFO). Use the FIFO rotation method, dating packages and placing incoming supplies in the back so that older supplies will be used first.

Pests. To avoid pest infestation and cross-contamination, clean up all spills immediately and do not store trash or garbage cans in food storage areas.

Keep it up. Do not place any items—including paper products—on the floor. Make sure the bottom shelf of the dry-storage room is at least 6 inches above the ground.

Avoid chemical contamination. Never use or store cleaning materials or other chemicals where they might contaminate foods. Store them, labeled, in their own section in the storeroom away from all food supplies.

Refrigerated Storage

Many commercial refrigerators are equipped with externally mounted or built-in thermometers. These are convenient when they work, but it is important to have a backup. It's a good idea to have several thermometers in different parts of the refrigerator to ensure consistent temperature and accuracy of instruments. Record the temperature of each refrigerator on a chart, preferably once a day. Here are more facts about refrigerated foods to keep in mind:

Fresh products. Keep fresh meat, poultry, seafood, dairy products, most fresh fruit and vegetables and hot leftovers in the refrigerator at internal temperatures of below 40°F.

Shelf life. Although no food can last forever, refrigeration increases the shelf life of most products.

The colder the better. Because refrigeration slows bacterial growth, the colder food is, the safer it is.

Shelves. Your refrigeration unit should contain open, slotted shelving to allow cold air to circulate around food. Do not line shelves with foil or paper.

Circulation. Do not over-load the refrigerator, and be sure to leave space between items to further improve air circulation.

Date everything. All refrigerated foods should be dated and properly sealed.

Dairy products. Store dairy products separately from foods with strong odors like onions, cabbage and seafood.

Cross-contamination. To avoid cross-contamination, store raw or uncooked food away from and below prepared or ready-to-eat food.

Containers. Use clean, nonabsorbent, covered containers that are approved for food storage.

Raw meat. Never allow fluids from raw poultry, fish or meat to come into contact with other foods.

Perishable products. Keeping perishable items at the proper temperature is a key factor in preventing food-borne illness. Check the temperature of your refrigeration unit regularly to make sure it stays below 40°F. Keep in mind that opening and closing the refrigerator door too often can affect temperature.

Stock tags. Fresh shellfish always arrives with an identity stock tag. This information is recorded and kept on file for 90 days.

Deep Chilling

Deep chilling, storing foods at temperatures between 26°F and 32°F, has been found to decrease bacterial growth. This method can be used to increase the shelf life of fresh foods, such as poultry, meat, seafood, and other protein items, without compromising their quality by freezing. You can deep chill foods in specially designed units or in a refrigerator set to deep-chilling temperature.

Frozen Storage

Frozen meats, poultry, seafood, fruits and vegetables and some dairy products, such as ice cream, should be stored in a freezer at 0°F to keep them fresh and safe for an extended period of time. As a rule, you should use your freezer primarily to store foods that are frozen when you receive them. Freezing refrigerated foods can damage the quality of perishable items. It's important to store frozen foods immediately. It's also important to remember that storing foods in the freezer for too long increases the likelihood of contamination and spoilage. Like your refrigeration unit, the freezer should allow cold air to circulate around foods easily. Be sure to:

Use moisture-proof containers. Store frozen foods in moisture-proof material or containers to minimize loss of flavor as well as discoloration, dehydration and odor absorption.

Monitor temperature regularly. Monitor temperature regularly using several thermometers to ensure accuracy and consistent temperatures. Record the temperature of each freezer on a chart. Remember that frequently opening and closing the freezer's door can raise the temperature, as can placing warm foods in the freezer.

Cold loss. To minimize heat gain, open freezer doors only when necessary and remove as many items at one time as possible. You can also use a freezer "cold curtain" to help guard against heat gain.

Organize Your Storage Areas

Set up your areas (dry storage, refrigerated and freezers) so that there is a specific place for everything. Items that move quickly should be near the door if possible. Keep the door locked. Expensive items such as exotic mushrooms, saffron and wine or alcohol used in the kitchen could be stored and locked in a separate cabinet inside the store room.

Label the shelves. Ordering and checking inventory will be much easier.

Stacking. The improper stacking of storage containers can result in spills, breakage and accidents. Ensure that if you use storage containers, they stack properly and are easily handled.

Shelving. Stacking items on top of one another in your cool room might seem to be the most productive way to utilize your limited space, but such a system makes cleaning and access to certain items very difficult. A good shelving system that is flexible enough to allow you to easily change shelf heights will not only help you make good use of space, but also make every item in your refrigerator easier to access. In addition, cleaning will be a breeze.

Five-gallon buckets. When you receive deliveries like flour, sugar and salt in large five-gallon buckets, you might be able to reuse them for storing dry materials. Buckets like these are usually airtight and designed for maximum protection of the contents. Rather than tossing them, clean, re-label and utilize them. Do not use them for ice storage, however.

Ice is food too. Use a designated ice transport container such as Saf-T-Ice Tote. Ice transfer is a cross-contamination disaster waiting to happen in most food service operations. Saf-T-Ice Totes help you control this serious food-safety danger. It is made of tough, transparent, durable polycarbonate and the unit will not nest, so dirt and bacteria cannot be transmitted by stacking. The six-gallon size keeps the carrying weight at safe levels. It also features a stainless steel bail handle for easy carrying/emptying. It meets health department requirements for dedicated food service containers and it is dishwasher safe. Saf-T-Ice Totes (Item # SI-6000, $79.95 for a pack of two) can be ordered from Atlantic Publishing at **www.atlantic-pub.com** or by calling 800-814-1132.

Storage Spoilage Prevention

List all spoiled food on a form; detail the date spoiled, item description and the reason that it is being tossed out. This allows you to make inventory adjustments, noting whether you're ordering too much of an item or have an equipment problem, such as an ineffective cooler.

Are your coolers too cold? Freezing, frost and freezer burn are a major source of spoilage in the kitchen, so make regular inspections of your cooler's temperature, and keep a written chart of when the last checks were performed. Use specialty thermometers for these areas. Atlantic Publishing carries these specialty items which you can order online at **www.atlantic-pub.com**. Look for fluctuations or "cold points" in the cooler that differ in temperature from the rest of the area.

Spoilage rates. Different qualities and brands of food may spoil at different rates from what you're used to. If you happen to change your brand or supplier on a particular line of food, make sure to keep a closer eye on the condition of your stock, taking note of any changes in freshness so that you can alter your purchasing to suit.

Eggs. To keep the yokes of your eggs from breaking easily, put out any eggs to be used in the coming hours to sit at room temperature before they're used. This simple piece of advice will keep your eggs in perfect "cracking" condition and keep your wastage to a minimum. Check with local health regulations first and remember that eggs are a highly perishable item.

Refreezing. Don't refreeze foods; this will take away from the taste of the food. Sometimes you may have no choice, but if you can keep food in a cooler at a refrigerated temperature and reuse it quickly, you'll be far better off.

Spices, sauces and marinades can be pre-prepared and stored for long periods without spoiling, if kept at the right temperature. If a sauce or marinade requires an item with a high spoilage rate, make a large batch and freeze it in small containers to be used as needed, saving on time and money and ensuring that every meal has a consistent taste.

Consider a generator. If your electricity supply went down for half a day, what would happen to your inventory? Save yourself the heartache of watching your food go to waste in the event of a utility problem by purchasing a backup generator. A small generator powerful enough to keep your cooler could save you thousands of dollars in lost assets if the unthinkable happens.

Electrical failure. If the power does not resume within 1–2 hours, or if a mechanical problem hasn't been fixed, keep the freezer closed and use dry ice to keep the freezer temperatures below freezing to prevent spoilage. Locating dry ice sources and determining your needs now will save valuable time later. Consider calling other restaurants, your vendors, or cold-storage companies should the problem require further delays. Plan ahead now.

Monitor your walk-ins and freezers. Your alarm monitoring company may have a program to monitor the temperature in your freezer and coolers, or you can hire a company such as Food Watch, **www.foodwatch.com/foodwatch.htm**. Their system will accurately and remotely measure the refrigeration efficiency of walk-ins, stand-alone refrigerators or food cases. The patent-pending Compressor

Watch sensor attaches to the outside of the compressor motor and monitors the amount of time it runs by sensing the field that surrounds the motor. The system can also record the amount of time the walk-in door is left open. The system works via a telephone line. You can even review the data on your own Web site.

Issuing

Procedures for removing inventory from storage are an integral part of the cost-control process. Here are some tips on issuing. For an example of a Sign-Out Sheet and Preparation Form, see Chapter 39.

Raw food. All raw material from which entrées are prepared, such as meat, seafood and poultry, must be issued on a daily basis.

Signing out. Whenever one of these bulk items is removed from a freezer or walk-in, it must be signed out.

Who should issue stock? Managers or kitchen managers should be the only ones to issue stock from storage. When a part of a case or box is removed, the weight of the portion removed must be recorded in the "Amount" column. The Sign-Out Sheet should be on a clipboard affixed to the walk-in or freezer. Once the item is signed out, the weight must be placed in the "Amount Used or Defrosted" column on a Preparation Form. This will show that the items signed out were actually used in the restaurant. From this information, the kitchen director can compute a daily yield on each item prepared. This yield will show that the portions were weighed out accurately and the bulk product that was used to prepare menu items. At any one of these steps, pilferage can occur. The signing-out procedure will eliminate missed pilferage.

WANT SHEET

ITEM	EMPLOYEE	APPROVED	ORDERED ON	RECEIVED

Chapter 27

Production and Service

Precise portion and menu control is crucial in controlling food cost. Physical production also should be considered when looking at cost controls and menu changes. Watch your kitchen operation to see how things are working. You may need to buy some new equipment or rearrange your labor schedule to implement some of the changes that you want. Focus particularly on the following:

Labor. Are you scheduling the appropriate amount of labor for shifts and prep work?

Recipes. Be sure staff members are using the standardized recipes and production sheets.

Inventory controls. Do you have strict inventory controls in place? Is your staff familiar with inventory procedures?

Invest in laborsaving equipment. You'll be able to pay for the equipment in no time with the money that you will save on labor.

Involve the Crew

A good way to lower food costs is to involve your kitchen crew in your efforts.

Visual aid. One of the major culprits in high food costs is waste. Put a new garbage can in the kitchen. This can is for wasted product only, such as wrong orders, dropped food, etc. By giving your kitchen staff this visual aid, you can reinforce the amount of money that gets spent on such product waste. This will help keep your staff tuned in to keeping an eye on kitchen waste.

Pick a month to have the entire staff work to lower food cost. If you're running a 38 percent food cost, tell your employees you want to try to lower it to 36 percent that month. Give them an incentive—throw a party at the end of the month if the goal is achieved. Create T-shirts and prizes to give away at the party. For example, offer a prize for the server who sold the most desserts that month or the cook who came up with the best new cost-saving measure. Not only will you cut your costs, you'll build employee morale and loyalty at the same time.

Make sure your cooks are using scales and measuring ingredients. Often cooks will "free-hand it" after a while, sure that they can eyeball the correct proportions. Set up a scale. After the cook prepares an item the usual way, have the same cook prepare the item using a scale and/or measuring devices. Show the staff the difference in ingredient amounts.

Kitchen Space

The control process allows managers to establish standards and procedures. It is used to train all employees to follow those standards and procedures, monitor performance, and take appropriate action to correct any deviations from the established procedures. Kitchen organization is a major consideration when setting up operational controls and standards.

Review the available facilities. Before you create or redesign a menu, you should take a good look at your kitchen and analyze exactly what it can provide. Look at the following aspects:

- What is the kitchen size?

- How many stations are there?

- How many kitchen employees do you have working the dinner or lunch rush?

- How much and what types of equipment do you have?

- How much storage room do you have?

- Is your kitchen getting orders out in a timely manner?

Review your menu to make the most of your facilities. If employees are getting in each other's way at certain work stations during rush periods, consider a serious menu overhaul. Perhaps your menu is appetizer heavy and you only have one employee at that station who also has to help the grill cook. If you want to keep all the appetizers, you may need to think about adding additional staff.

Extra staff during busy periods. If, after reviewing the menu, you need to bring in extra staff, you may want to raise your appetizer prices to compensate. If you think your appetizer sales will decrease with a price increase, you may want to eliminate some of the choices. This way your appetizer cook can get things out correctly and on time. This more efficient service may even increase your appetizer sales even though there are fewer choices.

Monitor current procedures. When contemplating a menu change, first watch your kitchen as they prepare the current menu. Are there ways in which you could change an item's preparation or ingredients that would strengthen the menu? Are there ways to simplify preparation procedures in order to lower costs? All of these questions need to be considered when designing or redesigning a menu.

Kitchen Design

Poorly designed kitchens and equipment are a major complaint of busy chefs and assistants. Inefficiency breeds waste. Poor planning decreases productivity, increases wait times, contributes to employee turnover, and distracts busy workers. Good kitchen design is an art and a science. An experienced consultant can help you balance space limitations, safety issues, food prep needs, and budgets without sacrificing food quality, productivity, and your staff's sanity!

Workflow. There are several of different workflow patterns that can be used to create a balance between passive storage and active work areas. You'll need to accommodate areas for:

- Hot and cold foods—prep and assembly.

- Beverage—dispensing and storage.

- Storage—food and non-food items.

- Sanitation—ware washing and front-of-the-house cleaning equipment and supplies.

- Receiving—off-loading space and inventory systems.

Break your kitchen activities into self-contained work stations. Make sure that ingredients, tools, equipment, supplies and storage are within easy reach.

Create work triangles. Triangle or diamond layouts give quick access to prep tables, sinks and cooking equipment. Straight-line layouts work best for assembly line-style prep and cooking where more than one person participates.

Draw out traffic maps. Draw a map of your space to determine how to minimize unnecessary steps.

Strategic locations. Locate your cooking and final prep areas closest to the dining room.

Consider placing your volume or batch cooking areas towards the back of the kitchen and your to-go order needs nearest the dining room. Production that requires little tending shouldn't take up precious high-activity space.

Isolate dishwashing tasks. The noises and chemical smell shouldn't mingle with your dining room ambiance.

Allow for ample open space. People need to pass, carts need to be rolled, shelving needs to be moved, large buckets need to be wheeled, and trays need to be lifted.

Coordinate placement of all equipment that requires venting to share a single ventilation system and reduce costs. Check your local code requirements on ventilation of heat- and moisture-producing equipment.

Include plenty of waste receptacles. Divide your receptacles by type of waste if you will be implementing recycling programs. Check with your waste management company on local requirements for segregating glass, metal, paper, etc.

Design kitchens with multiple sets of "IN" and "OUT" doors. Examples are doors that go directly from the dining area to the dish room (bypassing food prep) and doors from the bar to the dish room, ice machine and/or barware and liquor storage.

Ask your staff. Take advantage of their daily experiences and enhance their work areas during a kitchen renovation.

Cooking Procedure Tips

The manner in which food items are cooked can have a significant effect on food yields.

Adhere to the proper temperatures; high temperatures increase shrinkage and reduce yield.

Use accurate thermometers and calibrate them weekly.

Grades of meat will have different levels of shrinkage due to fat percentages.

Use convection ovens whenever possible; they decrease cooking time and, thus, shrinkage.

Cooking in small batches provides the best quality and food turnover.

Pot-scrubbing machine. Continuous pot-scrubbing machines reduce the time spent on scrubbing. Power-soaking equipment will virtually eliminate the time and hassle spent scrubbing burnt or baked-on food. See **www.natconcorp.com**. The NC-880-GWP cleans food service pots and pans with a combination of high-power water flow and specially designed granules. A single cycle will wash and sanitize all types of cookware and serving pans in less than five minutes, without pre-soaking or scrubbing!

Storage boxes. Cambro's storage boxes, **www.cambro.com**, feature a sliding lid. No need to move the box; just slide the lid back and remove what you need. Save time and strain on employees' backs. Staff also don't have to worry about finding a clean place to lay the lid while they get what they need from the box.

See-through lids. Cambro's see-through lids for steam-table pans are another innovation you may want to consider. Labor is saved by simply snapping on a lid instead of covering and wrapping pans. More time is saved because you don't have to unwrap the pan to see what is inside. The lids fit tightly, preventing food from spilling or slopping out of the pan, and less cleanup is required.

Coffee. Bunn-O-Matic uses technology to ensure that your coffee will always be brewed to specifications. The machine itself makes sure that the grounds-to-water ratio is perfect every time. Future innovations will let the machine analyze and adjust the coffee as it is being brewed. For more information, visit **www.bunnomatic.com**.

PanSaver®. PanSaver is an interesting concept for food service operations. It is a high-temperature-resistant (400°F/204°C) material which has been specifically designed to fit the standard-size pots and pans used in commercial kitchens. Simply line your pans with PanSaver and cook as usual. At the end of the night, toss the liner or use it to store leftovers. No pan scrubbing, soaking or scouring needed. No problems with fat-laden waste going down your drains to cause clogs or hassles with your local municipalities. Straight into the trash and you are ready to start fresh the next day. Food doesn't dry out or burn as easily since it isn't in direct contact with the hot metal of the pan, resulting in less food waste. PanSaver has a line of oven bags for baking, boiling, steaming and freezing. Another line of containers is used for cook/chill, where you can prepare food ahead of time and chill it in these special containers that seal the food from contamination and dissipate heat more quickly than conventional methods. Visit Atlantic Publishing's Web site at **www.atlantic-pub.com** to order.

Keep in mind the following safe cooking tips as well:

Stir. Stir foods cooked in deep pots frequently to ensure thorough cooking.

Deep frying. When deep frying potentially hazardous foods, make sure fryers are not overloaded, and make sure the oil temperature returns to the required level before adding the next batch. Use a hot-oil thermometer designed for this special application.

Cooking procedures. Be aware that conventional cooking procedures cannot destroy bacterial spores nor deactivate their toxins.

Cook/chill systems. Use the modern cook/chill systems for advance food preparation and portioning. The cook/chill system is a manufacturing process. Food is cooked to a "just done" status, then immediately chilled (not frozen) for storage and reheating. The basic cook/chill concept is based on the fact that foods are cooked to the proper temperatures, killing most organisms and microbes, then the food is stored as close to the freezing point as possible without allowing it to actually freeze. These systems are very popular in school, prison, and cafeteria food service environments, but they lend themselves well to a traditional restaurant situation. For more information, visit **www.nafem.org** and **www.useco.com/html/flowchart.html**.

Cook/freeze systems. Cook/freeze systems follow the same principles as cook/chill, but rather than being rapidly chilled, the food is rapidly frozen to -20°C. This allows storage of the food for a number of months rather than five days, as in the cook/chill system.

Thermometers and Cooking Temperatures

Calibrating a Thermometer

Using a food thermometer is the only reliable way to ensure safety and determine the doneness of meat, poultry and egg products. To be safe, these foods must be cooked to an internal temperature high enough to destroy any harmful micro-organisms that may be in the food. Doneness also refers to food cooked to a desired state, including the desired texture, appearance and juiciness. Unlike the temperatures required for safety, these sensory aspects are subjective. There are two ways to check the accuracy of a food thermometer. One method uses ice water, the other uses boiling water. Many food thermometers have a calibration nut under the dial that can be adjusted. Check the package for instructions.

Ice water. To use the ice-water method, fill a large glass with finely crushed ice. Add clean water to the top of the ice and stir well. Immerse the food thermometer stem a minimum of 2 inches into the mixture. Wait a minimum of 30 seconds before adjusting. (For ease in handling, the stem of the food thermometer can be

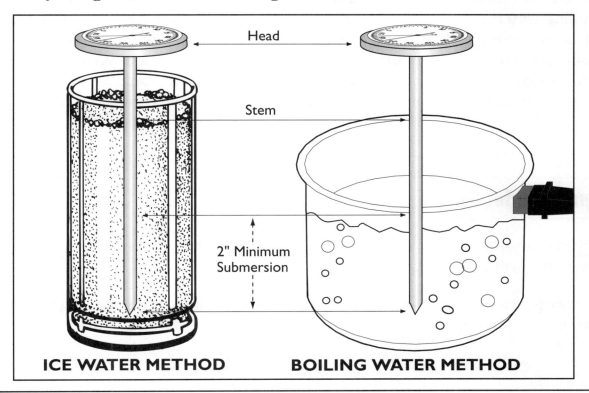

Head

Stem

2" Minimum Submersion

ICE WATER METHOD   **BOILING WATER METHOD**

placed through the clip section of the stem sheath and, holding the sheath horizontally, lowered into the water.) Without removing the stem from the ice, hold the adjusting nut under the head of the thermometer with a suitable tool and turn the head so the pointer reads 32°F.

Boiling water. To use the boiling-water method, bring a pot of clean water to a full rolling boil. Immerse the stem of a food thermometer in boiling water a minimum of 2 inches, touching neither the sides nor the bottom of the pan. Wait at least 30 seconds. (For ease in handling, the stem of the food thermometer can be placed through the clip section of the stem sheath and, holding the sheath horizontally, lowered into the boiling water.) Without removing the stem from the pan, hold the adjusting nut under the head of the food thermometer with a suitable tool and turn the head so the thermometer reads 212°F.

Accuracy. For true accuracy, distilled water must be used and the atmospheric pressure must be one atmosphere (29.921 inches of mercury). A consumer using tap water in unknown atmospheric conditions would probably not measure water boiling at 212°F. Most likely it would boil at least 2°F, and perhaps as much as 5°F, lower. Remember that water boils at a lower temperature in a high-altitude area. Check with the local cooperative extension service or health department for the exact temperature of boiling water in your area.

Inaccuracies. Even if the food thermometer cannot be calibrated, it should still be checked for accuracy using either method. Any inaccuracies can be taken into consideration when using the food thermometer or the food thermometer can be replaced. For example, water boils at 212°F. If the food thermometer reads 214°F in boiling water, it is reading 2 degrees too high. Therefore, 2 degrees must be subtracted from the temperature displayed when taking a reading in food to find out the true temperature. For safety, ground beef patties must reach 160°F. If the thermometer is reading 2 degrees too high, 2 degrees would be added to the desired temperature, meaning hamburger patties must be cooked to 162°F.

Preparation for Service

There are several actions you and your kitchen staff can take when preparing for service that will help control costs.

Uniform portions. Regulate the size and thickness of each portion to make cooking time predictable and uniform.

Allow cooking equipment to heat up between batches.

Monitor the accuracy of heating equipment with each use by using thermometers. In addition, always use a thermometer to ensure food reaches the proper temperature during cooking. Use a sanitized metal-stemmed, numerically scaled thermometer (accurate to plus or minus 2°F) or a digital thermometer. Check food temperature in several places, especially in the thickest parts, to make sure the food is thoroughly cooked. To avoid getting a false reading, be careful not to touch the pan or bone with the thermometer.

Roughly prepared ingredients are finished prior to plating. The quality and care with which this is done determines the amount of waste generated in preparation of standard recipes.

Portioning

Pre-portioning is a very simple way to make sure that portions are always standard. Pre-portioning can be done during slow periods, saving time when there is a rush.

Measure everything. Everything must be measured and portioned; this includes not only entrée portions but side dishes, sauces, condiments, garnishes, salads, salad dressings, etc. Most items will be proportioned in the preparation process. Many items will be weighed, but liquids will be measured using specified ladles, spoons and cups. Items such as eggs and baked potatoes should be counted.

Consistency. In addition to a crucial element of cost control, accurate portioning ensures food consistency. Have you ever been in a restaurant when a waiter brings to another table the prime rib hanging off the plate, only to later receive your average-size order?

Quality. Final food preparation procedures must be studied constantly to ensure quality and quantity standards. Portion-controlling all food items is an effective way to control food costs, but it also maintains consistency in the final product.

Follow standardized recipes. Once the precise recipe is developed, the completed menu item should look and taste exactly the same regardless of who prepared it. A dinner presented to a customer on Tuesday must be exactly the same as it was on Saturday night.

Portion variance. Portions may have a variance of up to, but not exceeding, half an ounce. Thus, if the set portion size for a steak is 12 ounces, the steak may range from 12–13 ounces. Any amount over 13 ounces must be trimmed. A light steak should be utilized for something else. Although a 1/2-ounce variance may seem like a small amount, it will actually add up very quickly. In fact, many restaurants allow a variance of only 1/8 of an ounce. If every steak with a portion size of 12 ounces is 1/2 ounce overweight, you will lose one whole steak on every 24th steak that is prepared (24 x 1/2 ounce = 12 ounces).

Scales. Since portion controlling is such a vital kitchen function, purchase the best scales available. A good digital ounce scale will cost upwards of $200. However, this investment will be recouped many times over from the food-cost savings it will provide. Purchase at least two ounce-graduated scales for the kitchen and always keep a third available in reserve. One floor-type pound scale with at least a 150-pound capacity will be needed as well. This scale will be used to verify deliveries and raw yields. All scales should have a temperature-compensating device. Maintain these scales per the manufacturers' instructions; clean them periodically and oil when necessary, and they will provide years of service. To ensure the accuracy of the scales, test them periodically with an item of known weight. Most good scales come with a calibration kit. New digital scales have automatic counting functions and many are hand-free operated.

Portion-control bags. Use portion-control bags and day-dated bags to control food items prior to use. These bags are ideal for all foods but can be particularly effective for items that are hard to bundle and store. For example, a side order for sautéed mushrooms can be portioned into 6-ounce portions, or an 8-ounce scallop entrée can be bagged and stored; these items can be portioned and stored in the bag ahead of cooking time, dated and rotated properly, ensuring perfect control. Contact DayMark Food Safety Systems at 800-847-0101 or **www.dissolveaway.com** for more information.

Scales must be checked weekly. Visit the Scale Buyers' Guide, a great source for all scale manufacturers' calibration systems. Locate calibration system manufacturers and calibration system distributors at **www.scalebuyersguide.com**.

Get your employees involved. Explain to the staff, for example, how wasting 1 ounce of shrimp on each dinner portion translates into a tremendous loss of money. If 1 ounce of shrimp costs 60 cents: 60 cents/ounce x 50 dinners a day = $30 a day x 365 days = $10,950 per year.

Pre-portioned items. Purchase as many items as possible from your vendors pre-portioned. Virtually all meat, chicken, pork, fish, condiments, etc., can be purchased pre-portioned. The food cost is higher but your labor cost will be lower, and costs and consistency are ensured.

Spatulas. Ensure your staff uses spatulas and spoons to scrape pans, bags, etc. New high-heat spatulas can be used effectively on heated pans, pots, etc. See **www.atlantic-pub.com** for high-heat spatulas.

Plate size. Be certain your kitchen staff uses the correct-size dish for each menu item. If they are serving a salad on a dinner plate, they will probably serve too much, since the prescribed portion will look small on the dinner plate, and they will tend to add more food to compensate.

Train your staff. Have standardized recipes, charts and measuring equipment available. Charts should be laminated and posted on all kitchen walls.

Compute Yield Percentages

To properly portion menu items, you will need to learn about yield percentages and yield tests.

1. Compute the total amount of ounces used. Verify the amount in this column against a Sign-Out Sheet. This figure is the starting weight in ounces.

2. The Amount Prepared column contains the number of portions yielded. Enter this figure on a Yield Sheet.

3. To compute the yield percentage, divide the Total Portion Weight (in ounces) by the Starting Weight (in ounces).

Yields should be consistent regardless of who prepares the item. If there is a substantial variance in the yield percentages (4–10 percent) consider these questions:

Are the preparation cooks carefully portioning all products? Over the months have they gotten lax in these methods?

Are you purchasing the same brands of the product? Different brands may have different yields.

Are all the items signed out on the Sign-Out Sheet actually being used in preparing the menu items? Is it possible some of the product is being stolen after it is issued and before it is prepared? Do certain employees preparing the food items have consistently lower yields than others?

Is the staff properly trained in cutting, trimming and butchering the raw products? Do they know all the points of eliminating waste?

Periodically compare the average yield percentage to the percentage used in projecting the menu costs. If the average yield has dropped, you may need to review the menu prices.

Yield Tests

A yield test is used to determine the amount of a product that is edible and the amount that is waste. Inventory yield tests should be carried out on a regular basis, especially on items that have a high perishability rate. Don't waste money on items that yield little edible product! Consider the following:

Quality. Higher-quality items will usually provide more edible product, so it's important to be able to recognize high-quality products. Factors to look out for when deciding on product quality include:

- Weight

- Texture

- Grade

- Odor

- Packaging

- Temperature

- Color

- Size

Two types of yield tests. There are two yield tests: a convenience yield test and a fresh-food yield test. Convenience yield tests are conducted on prepackaged products and generally consist of taking the item out of its packaging and weighing it. Fresh-food yield tests are more complicated and should involve the following steps:

- Weigh the product when it is received and again when it comes out of storage.

- Trim excess fat, bones, etc., and weigh.

- Wash and weigh the item again.

- Prepare the food and weigh again to determine the amount of weight lost during the cooking process.

- Cut the item into portion sizes.

- Weigh the portions.

Record each stage of the yield test. This information will help you decide whether or not you are wasting money on product that contains high amounts of wastage.

Presentation

Plate presentation is an important element of any menu item. Food that is presented well is perceived to have more value by the customer and your prices for well-plated food can be on the higher side of the price continuum. Three elements compose plate presentation: dish type and size, portion size, and garnish. Consider the following:

Provide the appropriate plate sizes for menu items. Otherwise, kitchen staff may be prone to over-portioning. For example, if a salad that should be plated on a salad dish is put on a dinner plate, the pantry person is likely to add more salad so that the item is not swallowed up by the dish. Include plate-size information on your standardized recipe.

Portion size should also be included on your standardized recipe. Consistent portioning is important to customer satisfaction, especially for your regulars. Your customers may order the same dish many times. It's important that each time it comes out of the kitchen, it looks and tastes the same. Since most restaurants have various people working in the kitchen, you must put controls in place so that everyone creates the same dish the same way.

Garnish is often overlooked in recipes and in presentation. For minimal cost, garnish can add to the appearance of your plates. Garnish can be anything from simple chopped parsley to sauces drizzled across the plate in a decorative manner. It's the slice of lemon on top of your salmon or the cheese croutons in the soup.

Plate Arrangement

Along with the actual garnish ingredients, think about how you want the food to be arranged on the plate. Factors to consider when arranging a plate include:

Layout. Think about where you want the customer to focus. Usually a plate consists of a meat, a starch and a vegetable. Most times you want the customer to focus on the most expensive item on the plate (this will enhance the perceived value of the meal). The main element of the plate is usually the meat, so you would usually want your customer to focus on that item.

Balance. Take the balance of the plate into consideration. Balance refers to the weight of the items on the plate.

Line. Line is also important because a strong line has strong eye appeal. A strong line helps to draw the customer's eye to the plate.

Dimension/Height. Dimension or height also adds to a plate's appeal. Use molds to mound potatoes or rice and lean meat up against these mounds to create height and a three-dimensional plate. Don't overdo the height factor, however. You do not want to overwhelm the taste of the food itself by the presentation. Do not over-stack or over-portion a plate.

Color. This is important in plate presentation; try to get maximum eye appeal. Perhaps top your salmon with some red pepper curls or chopped chives.

Maneuverability. Keep in mind that the customer is eventually going to eat the masterpiece that you have just created. Don't make it difficult to reach around garnishes or to cut into the food.

Overall appearance. Rather than just putting the sliced roast pork beside the mashed potatoes and the green beans, tie the pieces together. Place the mound of potatoes in the center of the plate and fan the slices of pork around it leaning against the mound. Tie the green beans into a bundle with a steamed chive and angle them on the other side of the potatoes. Think of the plate as a canvas and see what you can create.

Serviceability. Balance durability with aesthetics.

Guest Tickets and the Cashier

There are various methods of controlling cash and guest tickets. The following will describe an airtight system of checks and balances for controlling cash, tickets and prepared food. Certain modifications may be needed to implement these controls in your own restaurant. Many of the cash registers and POS systems available on the market can eliminate most of the manual work and calculations. With a POS system, the order is entered into the system as it is received from waitstaff. With a manual system, the sale isn't recorded until the customer pays. In addition, with a POS system, the check can't be lost. The systems described in this section are based on the simplest and least expensive cash registers available.

Write it down. All food or bar items must be written down in ink before the cook or bartender prepares them.

Guest checks. Guest checks, when properly accounted for, will provide an audit trail to food and sales.

Register keys. The register must have three separate subtotal keys for food, liquor and wine sales, and a grand total key for the total guest check. Sales tax is then computed on this amount. The register also must calculate the food, liquor and wine totals for the shift. These are basic functions that most machines have.

Guest tickets must be of the type that is divided into two parts. The first section is the heavy paper part listing the menu items. At the bottom is a space for the subtotals, grand total, tax and a tear-away customer receipt. The second section is a carbon copy of the first. The carbon copy is given to the expediter, who then issues it to the cooks so they can start the cooking process. Some restaurants utilize handheld ordering computers and/or the tickets may be printed in the kitchen at the time of entry into the POS system or register. Regardless, the expediter must receive a ticket in order to issue any food.

Guest check numbers. The tickets must have individual identification numbers printed in sequence on both parts and the tear-away receipt. They must also have a space for the waitperson's name, date, table number, and the number of people at the table. This information will be used by the expediter and bookkeeper in tracking down lost tickets and/or food items.

Issuing checks. Each member of the waitstaff is issued a certain number of tickets each shift. These tickets are in numbered sequence. For example, a waitperson may be issued 25 tickets from 007575 to 007600. At the end of the shift, he or she must return to the cashier the same total number of tickets. No ticket should ever become lost; it is the responsibility of the waitstaff to ensure this.

Mistakes. Should there be a mistake on a ticket, the cashier must void out all parts. This ticket must be turned in with the others after being approved and signed by the manager.

Giveaways. In certain instances, the manager may approve of giving away menu items at no charge. The manager must also approve of the discarding of food that cannot be served. A ticket must be written to record all of these transactions. To follow are some examples of these types of situations:

- **Manager food.** All food that is issued free of charge to managers, owners and officers of the company.

- **Complimentary food.** All food issued to a customer compliments of the restaurant. This includes all food given away as part of a promotional campaign.

- **Housed food.** All food which is not servable, such as spoiled, burned or incorrect orders.

Cashier report form. All of these tickets should be filled out as usual, listing the items and the prices. The cashier should not ring up these tickets, but record them on the Cashier Report Form (see example on the following page). Write the word "manager," "complimentary" or "housed" over the top of the ticket.

Cash drawer. The manager issues a cash drawer, or "bank," to the cashier. The drawers are prepared by the bookkeeper. Inside the cashier drawer is the Cashier Report itemizing the breakdown of the money it contains.

Accuracy of Cashier's Report. The accuracy of the Cashier's Report is the responsibility of both the cashier and the manager. Upon receiving the cash drawer, the cashier must count the money in the cash drawer with the manager to verify its contents. After verification, the cashier will be responsible for the cash register. The cashier should be the only employee allowed to operate it.

Each member of the waitstaff will bring his or her guest ticket to the cashier for totaling. The cashier must examine the ticket to ensure:

- All items were charged for.

- All items have the correct price.

- All bar and wine tabs are included.

- Subtotals and grand total are correct.

- Sales tax is entered correctly.

Cashier's Report Form

Charge card forms. The cashier is responsible for filling out the charge card forms and ensuring their accuracy. The cashier will return the customer's charge card and receipt to the appropriate member of the waitstaff.

Cashing out. At the end of each shift, the cashier must cash out with the manager. List all the cash in the "Cash Out" columns. Enter the breakdown of sales into separate categories. Do not include sales tax. Enter all complimentary, housed and manager amounts. Itemize all checks on the back. Itemize each ticket for total sales and total dinner count. Break down and enter all charged sales.

The total amount of cash taken in plus the charge sales must equal the total itemized ticket sales. Itemize all checks on the back of the Cashier's Report and stamp "FOR DEPOSIT ONLY." The stamp should include the restaurant's bank name and account number.

Charged tips. Should a customer charge a tip, you may give the waiter or waitress a "cash paid out" from the register. When the payment comes in, you can then deposit the whole amount into your account. Miscellaneous paid-outs are for any items that may need to be purchased throughout the shift. List all of them on the back and staple the receipts to the page.

When everything is checked out and balanced, the sheet must be signed by the cashier and manager. The manager should then deposit all tickets, register tapes, cash, charges and forms into the safe for the bookkeeper the next morning. The cash on hand must equal the register receipt readings. The bookkeeper will perform an audit and prepare the bank deposit.

POS training. Ensure all employees are trained on the computer POS system. Poor training will result in incorrect orders, add-ons not being charged for, and cooking instructions being neglected. Many systems allow a ticket to be voided instead of housed or comped, which means you will lose a credit in the monthly food-cost calculation.

*Jerry Frazier and his wife, Anna, run **Anna's Restaurant** in Narrows, Virginia. It's a small restaurant with about 20 employees. As with any small business, insurance costs have the potential to eat up a nasty percentage of the profits.*

Safety is my big concern. I like to hold a meeting every four to six weeks just to refresh everyone's memory as to what our employees need to be aware of. We have tile floors that get slippery when wet, so spills need to be cleaned up right away. I try to remind people the proper way to do things, like how to handle knives, for example. And, if something heavy needs to be lifted, I tell employees to get help instead of doing it alone. We've gone two years now without any accidents, and I like to think that part of the reason is our focus on safety.

Chapter 28

Kitchen and Food Safety

Ensuring your patrons and staff aren't injured on the premises is more than a matter of caring for their well-being, it's an essential part of avoiding a business-threatening lawsuit and lengthy downtime. Laborsavings, insurance savings, workers' compensation reductions, and sick pay savings, not to mention staying out of civil court, all come from putting safety procedures in place—and sticking to them. Here's how:

Keep equipment in working order. Make sure that equipment, tools, machinery and substances are in safe condition.

Talk to your workers about safety in the workplace. Encourage open discussion.

Hygiene. Maintain safe and hygienic facilities including toilets, eating areas and first aid.

Staff training. Offer information, training and supervision for all workers.

Involve your staff. Implement processes to inform workers and involve them in decisions that may affect their health and safety at work.

Safety procedures. Implement processes for identifying hazards and assessing and controlling risks.

Accident book. Record work-related injuries and illnesses.

Be observant. Pay attention to safe work. Your business will not only become more competitive, but you can help stop the pain and suffering from workplace injury or fatality.

Post safety signs. Ensure safety signs, usually available for free from your local Department of Health or Labor or your appliance manufacturers, are posted about your kitchen. These will include details on how to safely lift heavy items, directions on proper signage for slippery floors and dangerous equipment, as well as rules on who handles jobs like lighting gas pilots, changing light bulbs and sharpening knives.

Atlantic Publishing offers a 10-poster set of workplace safety posters in both English and Spanish. Communicate important information to your employees by posting these colorful, four-color informative Safety and Human Resource posters throughout your workplace. Each poster is 11" x 17" and is laminated for long-term protection. Topics include: First Aid For Burns, First Aid For Cuts & Wounds, First Aid For Choking, Proper Lifting, Emergency Phone Numbers, Drug-Free Workplace, Fire Extinguisher Use, CPR Guidelines, Falling, and Sexual Harassment. To order visit **www.atlantic-pub.com** or call 800-814-1132 (Item # WPP-PS, $79.95).

Basic Knife Safety

A study by the National Safety Council states hand lacerations cost employers an average of $3,337 in expenses and lost productivity. Yet so much can be done to avoid both the personal and financial pain involved. Consider the following possibilities:

Keep knives sharp and handle them carefully:

- Don't cut with the edge toward you or your fingers.

- Don't leave sharp knives loose in a drawer.

- If you're working with or handling a knife and you drop it, stand back. Let it fall; don't try to catch it.

- If you have a dirty knife, don't toss it in the dishwater. You don't want the dishwasher to come up with a handful of sharp knifes.

- Don't lay a knife down with the edge pointing up.

Gloves cost about $15 per hand. Knit-type cut-resistant gloves give greater levels of dexterity and comfort. They are made with fabric reinforced with a combination of strong fibers including stainless steel. Metal mesh gloves, made of double-interlocked welded rings (think of a suit of armor) are used by butchers, meat processors, chefs and ice carvers. They provide the highest level of cut resistance.

Cut gloves are available in four sizes from www.daymark.biz or call 800-847-0101 for more information.

Knife handling. Videos and books are available on proper knife handling and safety at **www.atlantic-pub.com**.

Tips for a Burn-Free Kitchen

Steam, oil and grease, boiling soups, hot grills and ovens can all result in workplace burn injuries. The Burn Foundation has found that such injuries tend to occur when managers don't enforce safety rules or when workers themselves are careless about safety. The potential for accidents is also greater when workers are worn out, on drugs or alcohol, or are simply taking unnecessary risks. Every restaurant is fast-paced and generally congested, providing all the needed ingredients for a disaster. The following tips can make a big difference to maintaining a burn-free kitchen:

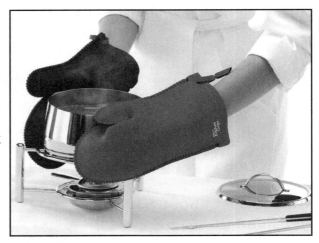

Mitts. Wear protective gloves or mitts when handling hot pots or cooking with hot deep-frying oil. Duncan Industries, **www.kitchengrips.com**, offers a complete line of cooking mitts and tools.

Footwear. Wear non-skid shoes to prevent slipping on wet or greasy tile floors.

Nip small fires in the bud. Extinguish hot oil/grease fires by sliding a lid over the top of the container.

Avoid reaching over or across hot surfaces and burners. Use barriers, guards or enclosures to prevent contact with hot surfaces.

Equipment instructions. Read and follow directions for proper use of electrical appliances.

First aid. Keep first-aid kits readily available and make sure at least one person on each shift has first-aid training.

Keep fire extinguishers accessible and up to date.

"AWARE." The National Restaurant Association's Educational Foundation offers an educational program called "AWARE: Employee and Customer Safety." The nine modules offered include sections on ensuring fire safety in the kitchen and preventing burns. The Educational Foundation also offers videos that promote workplace safety, which focus on how to prevent on-the-job injuries, along with an interactive CD-ROM.

Other Avoidable Kitchen Hazards

However busy you are, you simply cannot afford to ignore the following danger zones:

Hot oil. Transporting hot waste oil from the fryer is very dangerous. Very serious accidents have occurred as the night crew changes the oil at the end of the shift. They are tired and want to go home and may be rushing. Consider purchasing Shortening Shuttles, **www.shortening-shuttle.com**, 800-533-5711. These inexpensive devices make hot-oil transfer safe and easy and virtually eliminate the dangers and liability of exposure to hot-oil burns.

Wet floors. Ensure anyone mopping a floor area puts out ample signage to indicate the floor is wet and may be slippery. This doesn't mean a single yellow cone; it means enough signage so that a person has to make an effort just to get to the slippery floor.

Coolers. Keep any heavy coolers or storage refrigerators located at or above waist level, wherever possible.

Keep your food supply safe. Make sure your employees are trained in food service sanitation. Check with area community colleges for courses in food safety and sanitation. The National Restaurant Association also offers ServSafe certification courses through Atlantic Publishing at **www.atlantic-pub.com**.

Food-Borne Illness

Food-borne illnesses cost lives and money. According to the FDA, millions of people become sick each year and thousands die after eating contaminated or mishandled foods. Children, the elderly, and people with weakened immune systems are especially vulnerable to food-borne illness.

Costly. The National Restaurant Association estimates the average cost of a food-borne illness outbreak at more than $75,000.

Serving safe food has numerous benefits. By preventing food-borne illness outbreaks, establishments can avoid legal fees, medical claims, wasted food, bad publicity, and closure of the establishment.

What Makes Food Unsafe?

Hazards can be introduced into food service operations in numerous ways: by employees, food, equipment, cleaning supplies and customers. The hazards may be biological (including bacteria and other microorganisms), chemical (including cleaning agents) or physical (including glass chips and metal shavings).

Microbiological hazards. Microbiological hazards (bacteria in particular) are considered the greatest risk to the food industry. Bacteria usually require food, acidity, temperature, time, oxygen and moisture in order to grow. Controlling any or all of these factors can help prevent bacterial growth.

Temperature and time. Temperature and time are the two most controllable factors for preventing food-borne illness. The temperature range between 41°F and 140°F is considered the "danger zone" because these temperatures are very conducive to bacterial growth. Within this range, bacteria grow most rapidly from 60°F to 120°F. When the conditions are right, bacteria double in number every 10 to 30 minutes. For instance, in three hours, one bacterium can grow into thousands of bacteria. Cooking food to a safe temperature and cooling food quickly are critical steps in the prevention of food-borne illness.

Weighing the Risks

Certain foods and food service procedures are more hazardous than others. High-protein foods, such as meats and milk-based products, and foods that require a lot of handling during preparation require special attention by food service operations. Roast beef, turkey, ham and Chinese foods, for instance, have been linked with more outbreaks of food-borne illnesses than pizza, barbecued meat or egg salad, yet all of these foods are considered potentially hazardous. Other foods, such as garlic in oil, rice, melon, and sprouts, also have been linked with outbreaks of food-borne illness.

Researchers at the Center for Disease Control (CDC) have identified common threads between outbreaks of food-borne illnesses. Outbreaks usually involve one or more of these factors:

- Improper cooling of foods (the leading cause of food-borne illness outbreaks).

- Advance preparation of food (with a 12-hour or more lapse before service).

- Infected employees with poor personal hygiene.

- Failure to reheat cooked foods to temperatures that kill bacteria.

- Improper hot holding temperatures.

- Adding raw, contaminated ingredients to food that receives no further cooking.

- Foods from unsafe sources.

- Cross-contamination of cooked food by raw food, improperly cleaned and sanitized equipment, or employees who mishandle food.

- Improper use of leftovers.

- Failure to heat or cook food thoroughly.

Common Food-Handling Problems

The following lists some of the most common food-handling problems in restaurants:

- Sink-side nailbrushes are missing or not used. (You can order nail and hand brush kits at **www.atlantic-pub.com**.)

- Failure to change protective gloves between tasks.

- Work tables and cutting boards not properly sanitized between uses.

- Food sitting out for long periods.

- Food such as flour and sugar stored in open containers.

- Deliveries left out too long before being put away.

- Food delivery boxes picked up from the floor and unpacked directly on prep tables.

- Equipment not cleaned.

- Empty soap dispensers in restrooms.

What You and Your Staff Can Do to Prevent Food-Borne Illnesses

An important part of the production process is keeping food safe. Make sure you have HACCP procedures in place and train your kitchen staff in food safety. Here are a few simple things to do now to be sure your employees are keeping your food items safe:

Buy and use separate color-coded cutting boards for all food products to prevent cross-contamination. (See **www.atlantic-pub.com** for these products.)

Use a sanitizer to clean surfaces that come into contact with food.

Keep raw products separate from ready-to-serve foods.

Sanitize cutting boards, knives and other food-contact surfaces after each contact with a potentially hazardous food.

Discard any leftover batter, breading or marinade after it has been used with potentially hazardous foods.

Never interrupt the cooking process. Partially cooking poultry or meat, for example, may produce conditions that encourage bacterial growth.

Hand-Washing Exercise

Make sure employees wash their hands. Hand washing is perhaps the most critical aspect of good personal hygiene in food service. Workers should wash their hands with soap and warm water for 20 seconds. When working with food, they should wash gloved hands as often as bare hands. Hand washing is a simple yet effective method for eliminating cross-contamination. To illustrate the importance of hand washing to your staff, try the following exercise. First,

Hand washing is perhaps the most critical aspect of good personal hygiene in food service. It is a simple, yet effective, method for eliminating cross-contamination.

you'll need a fluorescent substance and a black light. (One possible source for these is Atlantic Publishing's Glo Germ Training Kit. See **www.atlantic-pub .com** or call 800-814-1132.) Using these materials, you can show trainees the "invisible dirt" that may be hiding on their hands:

1. Have employees dip their hands in the fluorescent substance.

2. Tell employees to wash their hands.

3. Have employees hold their hands under the black light to see how much "dirt" is still there.

4. Explain proper hand-washing technique.

5. Have employees wash their hands again, this time using the proper hand-washing technique.

6. Have employees once again hold their hands under the black light.

Thawing and Marinating

Freezing food keeps most bacteria from multiplying, but it does not kill them. Bacteria that are present when food is removed from the freezer may multiply rapidly if thawed at room temperature.

It is critical to thaw foods out of the temperature danger zone. Never thaw foods on a counter or in any other non-refrigerated area!

Some foods can be cooked from the frozen state, such as frozen vegetables, pre-formed hamburger patties and chicken nuggets. It is important to note, however, that this method depends on the size of the item. For example, this method is not recommended for large foods like a 20-pound turkey.

The two best methods for thawing foods are in refrigeration at a temperature below 40°F, placed in a pan on the lowest shelf so juices cannot drip on other foods or under clean, drinkable running water at a temperature of 70°F or less for no more than 2 hours. Even when potentially hazardous foods are properly thawed, bacteria and other contaminants may still be present. Cooking foods to the proper internal temperature will kill any existing bacteria and make food safe.

Always marinate meat, fish and poultry in the refrigerator. Never marinate at room temperature and never save and reuse marinade. As with all methods, be careful not to cross-contaminate!

Cautions for Cold Foods

When you are preparing cold foods, you are at one of the most hazardous points in the food-preparation process. There are two key reasons for this: First, cold food preparation usually takes place at room temperature. Second, cold food is one of the most common points of contamination and cross-contamination.

Chicken salad, tuna salad, potato salad with eggs and other protein-rich salads are common sources of food-borne illness. Sandwiches prepared in advance and held un-refrigerated are also dangerous.

Preparation is key. Because cold foods such as these receive no further cooking, it is essential that all ingredients used in them are properly cleaned, prepared and, where applicable, cooked. It is a good idea to chill meats and other ingredients and combine them while chilled.

Here are several other important precautions to keep in mind:

- Prepare foods no further in advance than necessary.

- Prepare foods in small batches and place in cold storage immediately. This will prevent holding food too long in the "temperature danger zone."

- Always keep prepared cold foods below 40°F.

- Wash fresh fruits and vegetables with plain water to remove surface pesticide residues and other impurities, such as soil particles.

- Use a brush to scrub thick-skinned produce, if desired.

Web Site References

Some sites providing tips in the area of food service hygiene and safety include the following:

- The Minnesota State Department of Health: **www.health.state.mn.us**

- MSU's Insight Into Safety: **msu.edu/student/cteam.html**

- U.S. FDA Center for Food Safety and Applied Nutrition: **vm.cfsan.fda.gov/list.html**

- United States Department of Agriculture's Food Safety and Inspection Service: **www.usda.gov/fsis**

- Gateway to U.S. Government Food Safety Information: **www.foodsafety.gov**

- E. Coli Food Safety News—MedNews.Net: **www.MedNews.Net/bacteria**

- Safe Food Consumer: **www.safefood.org**

- Food Safe Program: **foodsafe.ucdavis.edu/homepage.html**

- The Burn Foundation: **www.burnfoundation.org**

Food Irradiation

Food irradiation is a hotly debated topic right now. The Food and Drug Administration has approved irradiation of meat and poultry and allows its use for a variety of other foods, including fresh fruits and vegetables and spices. The agency determined that the process is safe and effective in decreasing or eliminating harmful bacteria. Irradiation also reduces spoilage, bacteria, insects and parasites. In certain fruits and vegetables, it inhibits sprouting and delays ripening. For example, irradiated strawberries stay unspoiled up to three weeks versus three to five days for untreated berries.

Cost. You should know that if you buy irradiated food, it will cost more. Industry experts currently estimate the increase at 2–3 cents per pound for fruits and vegetables and 3–5 cents a pound for meat and poultry products. But these costs may be offset by advantages such as keeping a product fresh longer and enhancing its safety. However, the treatment will also bring benefits to consumers in terms of availability, quantity, storage life, convenience and improved hygiene of the food. Federal rules require irradiated foods to be labeled as such to distinguish them from non-irradiated foods.

HACCP

Have a HACCP (Hazard Analysis of Critical Control Points) system in place. HACCP was developed by NASA about 30 years ago to keep astronauts' food supply safe. Until recently, HACCP was almost exclusively used in food production plants, but restaurants are beginning to adopt this approach to food safety. Having a HACCP system in place could save you a fortune in liability costs. If a situation arises, you may be able to prove you were using reasonable care and this can go a long way in a liability suit. Here's how it works:

HACCP uses seven basic principles. Basically, these principles indicate that you need to identify all the critical points at which food can become unsafe, such as during cooking, storage and production.

You must put measures in place to ensure that food remains safe. These measures can include actions such as establishing minimum cooking times for menu items and having policies about how long food can remain at room temperature before it must be thrown away.

Monitoring. Additionally, you must establish methods to monitor that these policies are being followed.

Corrective procedures. You must also establish corrective actions if the safety measures have not been used.

Further information. For more information on HACCP, HACCP checklists and HACCP form templates, log on to the Food Safety, Education and Training Alliance's Web site at **www.fstea.org/resources/tooltime/forms.html**.

Atlantic Publishing offers a complete line of HACCP products, including the most comprehensive food service manual available today: *HACCP & Sanitation in Restaurants and Food Service Operations: A Practical Guide Based on the FDA Food Code—With Companion CD-ROM.* It is available at **www.atlantic-pub.com** or by calling 800-814-1132 (Item # HSR-02, $79.95).

Chapter 29

Technology

The introduction of technology to the restaurant industry cannot be understated. With profit margins reported for most restaurants in the 3–5 percent range, the introduction of technology is one of the few opportunities for cutting costs, improving efficiency, and affecting the bottom line. One of the best uses of technology is, of course, the computer and POS systems, but there are others. Technology is transforming food service operations in ways that can greatly reduce dependence on human beings. Less highly skilled (and expensive) employees are needed when the equipment does the work. Pushing a button doesn't take much skill or knowledge.

Electronic Ordering Systems

In recent years many restaurants have switched to an "Electronic Guest Check System" or "Wireless Waiter." These systems use a mobile computer. The waitperson carries the mobile computer pad and places the order on the touch-screen display. The drink order is taken first and sent to the bar. As each dish is entered, this information is transferred in real time to the kitchen where the order is printed out. The waitperson is then notified by a beep or vibration when the order is ready for pickup, or a "runner" delivers the meal.

Multiple orders. The waitstaff can place multiple orders using a "Wireless Waiter" without ever walking into the kitchen or bar to check for previously placed orders or to pick up prepared orders. The waitstaff in the dining area of the restaurant never leaves the sight of their customers, and the bill is calculated automatically, removing the risk of human error. Most systems have an optional snap-on credit card reader, which can be attached to the bottom of the handheld device. Customer credit cards are swiped through the handheld unit and processed. Under this system, customers can feel confident that their credit cards are safe, since they are never out of sight.

Laborsavings. Because waitstaff will always be visible in the dining area, customers will be able to easily get their waitperson's attention. In addition, servers will be able to wait on six or seven tables at a time, twice as many as before. If more tables are waited on, more tables can be turned, providing the opportunity to increase sales volume. You might need fewer waitpersons utilizing this system, since each one will be able to handle more customers. This would, of course, result in a reduction of labor costs.

POS Systems

According to information published by the National Restaurant Association, a restaurant averaging $1,000,000 in food and beverage sales can expect to see an estimated savings of $30,000 per year using a POS system. Understanding the numbers collected by a POS system will give the operator more control over inventory, bar revenues, labor scheduling, overtime, customer traffic, and service.

POS systems reduce the opportunities for employees to pilfer. If your servers or other employees simply can't obtain any food without a hard-copy check or without entering the sale electronically, you have eliminated most of their opportunity to pilfer.

Two parts of a POS system. A point-of-sale system comprises two parts: the hardware, or equipment, and the software, the computer program that runs the system. This system allows waitstaff to key in their orders as soon as the customers give them. Additional keys are available for particular options and specifications, such as "rare," "medium-rare" and "well-done." Some systems prompt the waitstaff to ask additional questions when the item is ordered, such as, "Would you like butter, sour cream or chives with the baked potato?" Some will suggest a side dish or a compatible wine.

Processing the order. The order is sent through a cable to printers located throughout the restaurant: at the bar and in the kitchen and office. All orders must be printed before they are prepared, ensuring good control.

Payment. When a server has completed the ordering, a guest check can be printed and later presented to the customer for payment. Most POS systems allow certain discounts and require manager control over others. Charge cards, cash and checks can be processed separately and then reports can be generated by payment type.

POS enhancements. Many POS systems have been greatly enhanced to include the following: comprehensive home delivery, guest books, online reservations, frequent diner modules, real-time inventory, integrated caller ID, accounting, labor scheduling, payroll, menu analysis, purchasing and receiving, cash management, and reports. Up-and-coming enhancements and add-ons include improved functionality across the Internet, centralized functionality enabling "alerts" to be issued to managers, and voice-recognition POS technology.

Below are POS Web Sites for additional information:

- **www.squirrelsystems.com**

- **www.nextpos.com/english/overtureredirproducts.htm**

- **www.microworks.com**

- **www.bmccomputers.com**

- **www.restaurant-pos.com**

- **www.restaurantpos.com**

- **www.touch2000.com/touchsystems.htm**

- **www.tradewindsoftware.com**

- **www.touchnserve.com**

- **www.radiantsystems.com**

Hospitality Equipment

There is a wide range of restaurant-specific technology equipment available. Here is a brief overview of two systems available from Casio. See **www.casio4business .com** for more details:

- **TE4500F Cash Register.** This machine has a 5.2-inch wide color LCD screen. A scheduler function makes it possible to switch the backlight color, price levels, and automate report printing at different times of the day or week. It offers floating guest checks (up to four machines) and shared remote printers.

- **QT-8000 POS Touch Unit.** With its 1.2GHz CPU and ample memory/hard disk capacity, the QT-8000 is ideally equipped for efficient business operation. A 15-inch touch screen with 1024 x 768 SVGA resolution affords a wider viewing angle and easier entry operation via graphical user interface. IPX1 water splash-proof construction protects the touch panel from damage by wet hand operation or water spills. This system can display data on both the LCD and the expansion PC monitor separately or simultaneously.

Technology Maintenance

Successful restaurateurs realize just what advantages technology can bring to a food operation. By the same token, technology can also hold many traps for the unprepared manager, and the costs involved when you make the wrong decisions can prove perilous. Computers crash for no apparent reason. Make sure you can access your information if this happens. Here are some important guidelines:

Daily backups. Back up your data daily to another hard drive device, to a remote location, or use one of the many Web-based backup services such as **www.dataprotectionsoftware.com**, **www.protect-data.com** or **www.amerivault .com**.

Printout reports. Consider having all financial reports printed weekly, or even daily, from your computer. In the event of a major technical crash, these hard copies will allow you to keep track of your finances, inventory, scheduling and purchasing, and will save you both time and money when things go awry.

Manual records. Consider keeping a Rolodex with your entire collection of important phone numbers, addresses and passwords in case your computer crashes.

Payroll. Ensure that your bookkeeper or office personnel can complete your weekly payroll manually, on paper, so that you do not have to outsource payroll should your computers go down. While outsourcing payroll is an alternative, in times of trouble, it could be very expensive for a one-time processing.

Listen to your staff. If your office staff is telling you that a computer, kitchen scale or phone system is not working properly, have the equipment seen to before the problem becomes a large one.

Always look for the easy answers first. Make sure the fax, copier and/or printer has toner, ink, and any other necessary cartridges before making a service call. Sometimes a problem with a small electronic appliance could be as simple as having a surge protector switched to the "off" position.

Ink jet cartridges. Since almost all ink jet printer cartridges are refillable, you can purchase refill kits rather than incur the high cost of replacements. Costs of black ink can be as low as 40 cents per refill versus $18 for an ink jet cartridge.

For helpful hints on maintenance, try the following site: About.Com at **http://pcsupport.about.com/cs/pcmaintenance**.

*After 30 years in the restaurant business, Peter Kuhr has seen plenty of changes, but one of the biggest is the use of technology to cut costs. Now the executive chef for **Lund's and Byerly** in Minneapolis/St. Paul, Kuhr is enthusiastic about the possibilities.*

In today's world where a restaurant or a company might be handling large volumes of food, technology has become a kind of Holy Grail. It offers ways to monitor costs that were never dreamed of 20 years ago. The concept of "shrink" has been around a long time. The difference between budgeted food costs and actual food costs expressed as a percentage, it can provide a way to get a handle on waste.

A good point-of-sale (POS) system—we use ALOHA, but there are others—can allow managers to determine at the end of the day exactly what that day's food costs were. No longer is it necessary to wait till the end of the month. That enables manager's to be more proactive. They can establish standards and specifications. That means more follow-ups to make sure things are done right, but the extra effort will save you money.

I recently gave a series of PowerPoint demonstrations to our executives. I called it "The French Fry Caper" because I demonstrated how much waste was involved in the oversize portions of french fries our cooks were doling out. The executives were shocked to learn how much the practice was costing us. Cooks had fallen into the habit of filling the plate with more french fries than our customers could eat. It was a case where we had to go back to the basics with our training in order to prevent further losses.

SECTION V

Controlling
Liquor, Wine and
Beverage Costs:
Strategies and Tips

SECTION V

Table of Contents

Chapter 30
Budgeting and Forecasting 377

Chapter 31
Cash Control, Costing and Margins 385

Chapter 32
Beverage Purchasing Strategies That Work .. 395

Chapter 33
Beverage Inventory Control 407

Chapter 34
Portion Control Behind the Bar 417

Chapter 35
Beverage Theft 427

Chapter 36
Drink Selection 433

Chapter 37
Bar Staff Recruitment, Management
    and Training 445

Chapter 38
Other Opportunities to Control Costs
    in the Beverage Industry 455

Introduction

Controlling Beverage Costs: Strategies and Tips

You're busy. You just don't have the time to wade through a pile of "heavy" manuals on how to reduce liquor, wine and beverage costs. But you do need answers and you need them fast! You want instant solutions; practical ideas, tips and suggestions that you can implement now.

Look no further. This section contains a wealth of inspiration and practical advice that can help reduce costs and boost profits in any beverage operation. Implement just a handful of these suggestions and transform your establishment into a thriving and successful enterprise. All it takes is a few simple and quick actions to turn things round!

Worried about cash flow, staff problems, inventory control, theft, or any of the myriad of problems that plague the beverage industry? The pitfalls are many. But so, too, are the opportunities. Accept the challenge and take a few shortcuts to success.

Chapter 30

Budgeting and Forecasting

Grasp the Basics About Budgeting

Don't be put off by all the jargon and terminology associated with budgeting. Oftentimes, a simple overview is all you need to make a big difference in the profitability of your establishment. Consider the following:

Budgeting in a nutshell. All it involves is planning for income, expenses and profit. Simply bear in mind all three aspects of budgeting when making important business decisions.

Establish an operating budget. This is a basic plan that estimates what sales income will be generated and what expenses can be incurred in order to meet profit targets. Choose from a variety of different types of budgets, such as long- and short-term, cash and capital. The short, one-year operational budget is probably best suited to a beverage operation.

Use your budget plan to reduce costs. For example, when sales fall below forecast levels or when expenses exceed budget estimates, do something about it, immediately! Review recent expenditures or consider a sales promotion.

Use your budget plan to establish standards. Consistent quality is one of the surest ways to boost profits. Don't compromise on quality in an attempt to achieve sales goals.

Use your budget plan to establish benchmarks for expenditures. Your budget plan is a useful tool for reviewing general expenditures. Use it. Take a fresh look at other aspects of expenditures, such as labor and energy costs.

Choose the Right Budget Plan for Your Business

No beverage operation can survive without an effective budget plan. It provides more than a useful evaluative tool for management. It is essential for keeping operation costs within budget limits and is a good indicator of which areas of the operation require immediate corrective action. There are three main types of budget: fixed, flexible and zero-based. Each, however, follows the same broad, two-stage procedure.

The two stages. It is well worth following this broad, two-stage outline; it gives structure to your budget. The first stage is known as "descriptive." It deals with assumptions only. These assumptions are then used to develop the second stage of the plan, the financial aspect, which goes into much greater depth.

Fixed budget. Fixed budgets assume that expenses and sales volume will remain stable during the 12-month period. Fixed budgets are useful for evaluating past costs and performance.

Flexible budget. Sales in the beverage industry tend to fluctuate considerably. A flexible budget is useful in this type of situation where, in order for profitability to be maintained, costs need to be re-assessed at frequent intervals.

Zero-based budget. The zero-based budget is a variation on the flexible budget. Although costs are estimated within a range of activities, the starting point for developing costs for the new budget is always zero. This is useful in operations, such as liquor outlets, where accountability is essential.

Don't complicate matters! Only include information in your budget plan that is useful and relevant to your particular establishment.

Adapt Your Chosen Budget Plan to Suit Your Establishment

Having established the need for a budget (there's no getting away from it!) and decided upon which method best suits your establishment, you now need to put some thought into personalizing and adapting your chosen budget plan. Think flexibility, and make your budget work for you.

Keep it simple. For example, if you manage a single-unit operation, concentrate on recording only basic budgetary information. Even if you are responsible for running a multi-unit operation that involves budgeting for several operations, the plan need not be complex. Review current procedures and eliminate any details that are not essential to the smooth running of your operation.

Delegate. In small operations, the owner has little choice but to develop and operate the budget single-handedly. However, if you run a larger establishment, delegate! Assign budget management to specific members of personnel.

Consult. Use budget analysis as an opportunity to consult with other members of staff. Have a brainstorming session. Each employee can offer a different perspective about where and how to trim costs.

Introduce "bottom-up" budgeting. Most employees, from the most junior upwards, prefer to be involved in the company's budgeting strategy, rather than be subject to "top-down" budgeting, where all decisions are made at the corporate level.

Budget Control—Introduce Cost-Effective Initiatives

The budget manager is responsible for developing cost-controlling policies throughout the operation. An effective budget should enable you to control costs and improve overall efficiency. Budgeting solutions need to be easy to apply, suitable and ethical. For optimum results, focus on the following areas:

Financial reports. These are the building blocks of successful budgeting. Consolidate daily, weekly and monthly figures. Ask questions. Investigate, for example, whether certain products are more profitable than others and whether wastage is too high in certain areas.

Labor productivity controls. Within budget resources, now may be the time to introduce productivity improvements. Could you automate inventory, purchasing, requisitioning and issuing procedures? Maybe review employee insurance policies—are you getting the best value for your money?

Maintain company assets. Get the most out of your computer systems, particularly those designed for purchasing, inventory and bar support. Are these systems being used to their full capacities? Seek advice about upgrading.

Protect your establishment from unnecessary exposure. Of course budgetary controls must be cost effective, but beware of overstepping the mark. Any cost-cutting initiatives must comply with IRS legislation, safety laws, and any other labor regulations that may apply to your business.

Develop a Forecasting Strategy That Is Relevant and Realistic

Company forecasts are often unusable for the simple reason that they contain too much irrelevant information. "Blanket" forecasting that is relevant only in parts to your operation often renders the whole report redundant. Devise a forecasting plan that is 100 percent useful to your establishment.

Basic requirements. Forecasts should focus on two main areas only:

1. Operational issues—purchasing and staffing.

2. Financial results—estimated costs and revenue percentages.

Any other figures are of limited value.

Minimum information requirements. All you need to establish any type of budget is the following information:

- Previous period operating figures.

- Assumptions of next period operations.

- Targets.

- Simple monitoring procedures.

Forecasting methods. There are several methods of forecasting available, many of them time-consuming and unproductive. Pause first and ask yourself three simple questions:

1. Is the method practical?

2. Will the end results be reliable?

3. Is this method cost effective?

Choose your method according to your answers.

Analysis. Stick to basics. Successful forecasting is simply a matter of predicting the consequences of certain business decisions over a specific period of time.

Time. In most operations, time is a prime consideration. Make sure that any time spent on forecasting is used constructively. Focus on achieving tangible results, like trimming costs in areas such as inventory, labor and/or operations.

Resources. Does your establishment have the resources to implement your chosen forecasting method? Is data readily available?

Make Forecasting Work for Your Establishment

Forecasting is traditionally associated with the obligatory exercise of producing figures for bank managers or accountants. It need not, however, be unproductive. Turn forecasting into a useful predictor of your operation's future performance. Use it as a tool in the planning process. Make it an integral part of budget strategy. Consider the following possibilities:

Sales team approach. Get sales personnel involved with producing forecasts for their own sections of the operation. Responsibility promotes accuracy and increased employee commitment.

Identify problems sooner rather than later. Use forecasts to alert management to weaknesses in specific areas of the operation. Take action immediately to remedy, for instance, inventory discrepancies behind the bar.

Clientele expectations. An underused yet highly effective approach to forecasting.

Devise customer surveys. Value the opinions of all those who patronize your establishment.

Executive opinion. In large enterprises, forecasting often centers on the collective opinion of top executives from the various divisions including sales, purchasing and accounting. Adopt this approach to forecasting if you want representative, accurate and rapid feedback, as well as workable solutions.

Labor forecasting. Use sales forecasts to establish required labor. Overstaffing, for even a single shift, can considerably reduce profits.

Budgeting and Beyond—Look to the Future

There are those who argue that a budget isn't necessary; that it's too time-consuming, too revealing, that it causes conflict. Many established enterprises, however, are convinced that they would not be in business today if it were not for sound budgeting and, more specifically, long-range budgeting. Adopt a long-term approach.

Achievement budget. This short-term budget covers a brief period, say a week or a month. It includes information such as weekly bar requisition totals and the number of staff required for the seven-day period. But, as the achievement budget is the foundation for long-range budgeting, it is vital to get it right from the start.

Annual budget. Most enterprises that operate a budget do so on a yearly basis. Project ahead, beyond this period's end. Identify long-term trends and make them work for you.

Long-range budget. Devise a three- to-five-year budget (sometimes referred to as a strategic plan). All you need to produce is a brief outline about where the operation should be heading. For example, you may want to add extra operational units to increase sales, or maybe you're planning a construction project that could temporarily restrict sales volume.

Computerized Budgeting and Forecasting

There's no getting away from it, when it comes to budgeting and forecasting, a computer is the backbone of most beverage operations. All you need is an electronic spreadsheet, such as Microsoft Excel. Most small establishments need look no further. However, packages, tailormade to the industry's requirements, have become increasingly popular over the years for both routine and advanced applications. Here are a few pointers to help you choose the system that is right for your establishment:

Basic electronic spreadsheet software. These programs are specifically designed to cope with all types of budgeting and forecasting. They are low-cost and simple in concept. The electronic spreadsheet looks like a traditional worksheet; arranged in rows and columns and is straightforward to use. And, it has powerful computation capabilities that do all the time-consuming, routine calculations for you!

Customize your spreadsheet. Use your spreadsheet to set up a simple budgetary model that exactly reflects your establishment's budget plan. Once it's set up, all you have to do is change a few numbers each time you update the spreadsheet. Stick to the relevant. On other hand, you may get carried away by the range of opportunity offered for refining your budget—in which case, explore the possibilities! The scope for cost trimming can be quite a revelation!

Graphs and charts at the click of a button. When presenting budgets and forecasts to other people, using a visual approach is often more effective. Use your spreadsheet to display your information graphically.

Multi-unit operations. Larger enterprises may be better off with software aimed specifically at the beverage industry. Investigate the following suppliers:

QuickPlan
www.atlantic-pub.com
800-814-1132

Synergy International
www.synergy-intl.com
800-522-6210

Caterware
www.caterware.com
800-853-1017

Cost-Volume-Profit (CVP) Analysis—The Key to Budgetary Success

One of the simplest ways of performing budget analysis is the cost-volume-profit method. Sometimes referred to as "break-even," this is fundamental budgetary analysis. Budget analysts need to do more than just review the links between costs, sales, volumes and profits; they should constantly be on the lookout for alternative ways of reducing costs and boosting profits. Ask yourself the following questions, and use simple graphs to illustrate your points:

Profit goals. How many drinks does this establishment need to serve in order meet budgeted profit targets?

Cost increases. When variable and fixed costs increase, how many extra drinks will we have to serve in order to maintain budgeted profit targets?

Opening hours/quiet periods. Is it worth considering expanding opening hours? Would it be profitable? Or should the outlet remain open during predictably quiet "drinking" times?

Balance and perspective. Get it right. Too rigid an application of CVP findings can be counterproductive. You can't risk losing guest goodwill and employee support. Too heavy-handed an approach can cause your profits to plummet!

CVP software. Check out **CVP Optimizer**, available from

- ZD Net – **www.zdnet.com**

- 32 Bit – **www.32bit.com**

- Virtual Software – **www.virtualsoftware.com**

Monitoring Your Budget Plan

An operational budget plan is no good if you don't use it. Sound complicated? It doesn't have to be. Simply focus on three main areas for maximum benefit: income, expenses and profit.

Income. Income falling below projected levels? Do you feel that you're busier than ever but sales volumes aren't increasing? Select from a handful of alternative strategies without delay. For example, are you overstaffed, overstocked, selling the right drinks, pitching markup too low? The bottom line is if sales volumes are lower than originally projected, management must immediately take measures to increase income.

Expenses. Just as it isn't always easy to predict future sales volumes accurately, it isn't easy to estimate future expenses either. Income varies, and so does expense. One way to avoid too many nasty shocks is to use a "yardstick" method to determine expense "standards." Simply compare budgeted expense performance with actual performance, over several volume levels. Apply this yardstick method to stock, labor and general expenditure.

Profit. Income – Expense = Profit. Or more specifically: Budgeted income – Budgeted expense = Budgeted profit. Budgeted profit must be realized if your operation is going to survive. The solution is to protect (at all costs) your operational income by constantly investigating alternatives in all areas of the operation.

Chapter 31

Cash Control, Costing and Margins

The Basic Mathematics of Profitability

A typical beverage operation generates a constant stream of data and information, endless columns of figures, and daily records. But you'd be surprised how few managers actually do anything with these figures, let alone fully grasp their implications. So how can you tell if you're operating profitably? The answer is you can't, unless, of course, you understand some basic mathematics. For a start, you'll need to know how to perform a few simple calculations, such as working out an item's cost percentage. You don't need to be a mathematician to figure the following straightforward formulas:

Cost per ounce. This is the basic unit cost of a drink. For example, to calculate the cost per ounce of a liter bottle, divide the wholesale cost of the bottle by 33.8 ounces, or in the case of a 750 ml bottle, by 25.4 ounces. The figure you arrive at is the cost per ounce.

Cost per portion. To be able to price a certain drink, you must first calculate the base cost of the serving. Use the cost per ounce to work out the cost per portion. For example, if the cost per ounce is $0.60 and the recipe requires 1.5 ounces, then the portion cost is $0.90.

Cost percentage. Master this formula; you cannot function without it! To calculate the cost percentage of an item, divide the product's cost (or portion's cost) by its sale price and then multiply by 100. This simple calculation gives you the cost percentage. **Profitability hangs on this key calculation.** This calculation is the most frequently used formula in the beverage industry. It indicates the profit margin of any drink and represents the difference between the cost of the item and the price for which it is sold. If cost percentage increases, profit margins decrease.

Measuring Bottle Yield

You know the theory: To obtain the cost per ounce, you must divide the cost of the bottle by the number of ounces in the bottle. Fine, so far. But sometimes, in practice, the final sales volumes and profits can seem disappointing. You're confused because you have done everything by the book, and now, somehow, the figures don't quite add up. Get wise.

Consider evaporation and spillage. When calculating a bottle's cost per ounce, the secret is to deduct an ounce or two up front, before dividing, to allow for evaporation or spillage. Although this will slightly increase the cost per ounce, it will also give you a more realistic starting point.

Calculation errors. Slight variations can easily creep into a calculation involving both liters and ounces. For example, assume a highball contains 1½ ounces of spirit (or 45 ml): using ounces, a liter bottle yields 22.54 measures, whereas, using milliliters, the bottle gives 22.22 measures. Round down in the interests of reality.

Maximize potential yield. You know that a bottle of liquor yields so many measures at a certain cost. However, you also know that sloppy pouring methods can wipe out potential profits. The best way to overcome this problem is to automate portion serving as much as possible. You've paid for the liquor and want maximum returns.

Buy big. High-turnover liquor, wines and spirits should always be purchased in larger bottles for better yield per measure.

Drink Pricing for Optimum Profits

Sensitive pricing can make or break your operation. Pricing decisions should never, ever, be made arbitrarily. It is crucial to achieve that fine balance between pricing for optimum profits and making customers feel that they're getting value for money. Of course, you want to sell the drinks at their optimum sales volume, but if you tip the balance by raising the sales price too high, the sales volume will actually drop. So will the profits.

Research target audience. Investigate your potential market. Check out the opposition, even if this means visiting every liquor outlet in your locality. Get a feel for how much guests are prepared to pay for certain types of drinks.

Compete. A realistic view of market positioning is essential. Aim to match, beat or pitch for exclusivity (known as a "highball decision," in the beverage industry). All three methods can work. What won't work is a "muddling along" approach. Make a decision, set your goals, and price accordingly.

Type of operation. Customers' image and perception of your establishment play a major role in establishing a pricing structure. Guests have fixed expectations about costs. For example, they expect to pay above-average prices at a smart nightclub or "adult" establishment. They expect neighborhood bars, on the other hand, to be cheaper. Devise a pricing strategy that meets customer expectations.

Portion costs. You may have done your research and drawn up the perfect plan to wipe out the opposition, but if you haven't "bought in" at competitive prices, you're not going to win. Keep portion costs to a minimum by buying low.

Take a Fresh Look at How You Apply Your Pricing Strategy

Having carefully considered all aspects of your pricing strategy, including cost, availability, competition and target audience, it is essential to make your pricing plan as user-friendly and easy to operate as possible. Simplify.

Price lists. A complicated price list with too many options and variables leads to employee confusion and incorrect charging. Even if those errors result in higher gross sales, customers will soon complain and you will lose business.

Devise main price categories. Group products according to their wholesale costs. Use standard increments, like 50 cents, to separate price categories.

Keep drink prices based on quarters. Prices ending in quarters—$0.25, $0.50 and $0.75—are easier for bartenders to mentally add up.

List product prices with their corresponding specific portion size. For example, alongside each item in the liquor inventory, list the appropriate portion size for that drink.

POS. Make bartenders' lives a lot easier. Invest in an automated system, where a few keystrokes are all that's required to find any drink or item on the price list. For more information about POS systems, contact:

> Action Systems
> **www.actionsystems.com**
> 800-356-6037
>
> Vital Link
> **www.vitallink.com**
> 877-770-7795
>
> Canfield POS
> **www.possales.com**
> 502-456-2299

Markups—Where to Pitch Them

There are no standard markup guidelines in the beverage industry. Getting it right is very important. Profitability, cost control, and so much more hang upon those difficult markup decisions. Here are a few guidelines to point you in the right direction:

Broad guidelines. You need to start somewhere. The following markup suggestions may help:

- Cocktails—3½–4 times cost

- Other liquor—4–5 times cost

- Beer—2½–3 times cost

- Wine by the glass—3–4 times cost

- Carafe wine—2½–3 times cost

- Dessert wines—2–2½ times cost

Based on the above markup guidelines, the total beverage cost is approximately 28 percent.

Three main pricing methods. There are, however, three general approaches to markups in the beverage industry. A basic understanding of these options will guide you in the right direction:

- **Traditional markup.** A combination of intuition and local competition. Don't rely on intuition alone.

- **Cost plus markup.** Here, price is determined by adding a markup to the cost of the item. Easy to apply, this method is popular in the beverage industry.

- **Item cost percentage markup.** Similar to cost plus markup, but linked to profit targets.

Type of establishment. Markup is often driven by the type of establishment. For example, luxury hotels, restaurants and nightclubs can command heftier markups. Bars and taverns, on the other hand, have to compete more fiercely with similar outlets in the locality.

Bar Cash-Control Procedures

Cash flow, in the bar trade, means just that: cash. It is a cash-dominated environment, and that cash needs to be carefully controlled. It is the beverage manager's responsibility to make sure that all cash receipts end up where they should be—in the cash register. Establish strict cash-handling procedures. It's the only way to survive in the industry, make a profit, and keep costs under control.

On-hand cash. Record the "house bank" total at the beginning and end of every shift. Make the opening bartender responsible for counting it. Keep the on-hand cash in a separate, secure drawer behind the bar. Never let the closing bartender total his or her own end-of-shift bank.

Random spot-checks. Introduce impromptu cash counts—by the manager. Keep bar staff on their toes!

Count cash when you are least likely to be disturbed. Be aware of the possibility of distractions and never leave cash unattended, even for just a few seconds.

Opening bank. Make sure staff have enough cash in each denomination, thus removing the need to leave the register unattended during business hours.

Security. Keep opening banks in bags in the office safe until required by the bartender. Staff must always verify and sign for the amount. Closing banks should follow the same strict procedures.

Tighten Up Daily Cash Procedures

Fact: Improved daily control of cash leads to lower costs and increased profits. Monitor cash at every stage throughout the operation—daily. One weak link is enough to wipe out the entire business. The sequence of activities will vary according to the size and type of beverage outlet. Certain procedures, however, are common to all establishments:

Routine. It may sound dull, but sticking to repetitive procedures is the best way to make sure that no link in the daily cash cycle is overlooked.

Complete count of reserve cash. Do this daily. Include cash from the opening bank, plus on-hand cash. It's a good idea to count on-hand cash after the bank deposit has been completed. This gives you tighter control because the sales cash already will have been counted.

Assign register drawers to specific shifts. Separate drawers protect the honest employee and disclose the dishonest. Include the adding machine printout with the opening bank.

Remove all large bills at intervals during each shift. Place them in the safe.

Take a "Z" reading of the cash register at the end of each shift. Remove both the drawer and the "Z" report from the bar. Take them to the office.

Reconcile all cash in a secure environment. This is essential.

Bevinco Auditing Services. Investigate this powerful cash-control tool. A software package aimed at the beverage industry, it offers independent, precise monitoring of bar inventory. Contact Bevinco, 250 Consumers Road, Suite 1103,

Toronto, Ontario, Canada, M2J 4V6, **www.bevinco.com**.

Audit Net. Free beverage audit resources are available on the Audit Net Web site at **www.audit.net**.

Take the Hassle out of Cash Reconciliation

Save time and money by introducing simple step-by-step cash-reconciliation procedures. The process should be the same whether you're handling cash from a point-of-sale system or a cash register. The following ten-point guideline will help. It summarizes the information (no more, no less) that you need to record for the purposes of cash reconciliation:

1. Count and record all the cash in the cash drawer. Enter each denomination in a separate column of the cash drawer reconciliation form. Also, enter a grand total for all coins.

2. Enter the total amount of credit card sales.

3. Enter the total amount of check sales.

4. Record non-beverage merchandise sales in a separate column.

5. Enter all cash paid out for miscellaneous purchases in another column.

6. Next, enter the subtotals for cash, credit cards, checks, other sales and "paid outs."

7. Create the "opening bank" for the next shift. Record the total, and place the opening bank in the safe.

8. Subtract the amount of the opening bank from the subtotal to arrive at the total "accountable funds" for the shift.

9. Enter this figure in the final column of the cash drawer reconciliation form.

10. Last, record the gross sales figure for the register's "Z" report. Positive figures mean that the total is "over"; negative, that it is "under" or short. This figure is the final figure that you need to enter on the reconciliation form.

Gross Profits—The Lowdown

There is no better indicator of a business's success than its gross profit figure. By definition, gross profit is the cash difference between an item or portion cost and its sales price. All attempts to reduce costs should focus on this gross profit figure. Learn how to figure out some important calculations related to gross profits.

Gross profit. To calculate a drink's gross profit, simply subtract its portion cost from its sale price.

Gross profit margin. This figure represents the percentage amount of profit made by the sale. Divide the amount of profit by the sales price and then multiply by 100. The result is the gross profit margin.

Sales percentage profits. To calculate the selling price (based on the required gross profit margin), divide the portion cost by the gross profit margin percentage "reciprocal"; that is, the figure you get from subtracting the target gross margin from 100.

Cost multiplier. This calculation is often used in the beverage industry to figure out the target selling price for a drink based on its portion cost. Divide the cost percentage you require by 100 and then multiply the result by the portion cost of the product.

Mixed-drink prime ingredient costing. A calculation used to determine the target sales price for a mixed drink that has only one main ingredient, such as gin and tonic or Scotch on the rocks. All you have to do is divide the drink's portion cost by the target cost percentage.

Common Cash-Control Problems—Troubleshooting

You notice that the pouring costs (PC) are escalating, but you can't figure out why. Check out the following possibilities and take measures to recover the situation:

Have liquor costs risen, but your prices remained the same? Cover costs immediately. You need to up the drink prices to match. But don't price yourself out of the market.

Not sure whether to include tax in your pricing? Confused over how to handle the small cash denominations generated by tax charges? Having to hand over small change on each purchase can really annoy customers and bartenders alike. Set your prices at a round level and include the tax in the price.

Sales volume decreasing? First take a look at the competition. You may not have been keeping tabs on competitors' prices or promotions. Remember, their liquor costs are similar to yours.

Does the slump in business coincide with taking on new bar staff? Check whether they are pouring drinks correctly and following drink recipe guides. Review daily figures to see if the PC is higher on shifts when a particular staff member is on duty.

Are sales down despite an increase in the number of bottles requisitioned from stock? Be wary. Perhaps members of staff are either drinking on the job or thieving.

Problems outside of business hours? Inventory discrepancies? First suspect dishonest activities. Narrow down which personnel might have been on the premises while the establishment was closed. Investigate further.

It still doesn't add up? Are employees giving away drinks to friends? Are bartenders over-pouring (in which case, change from free-pouring to more controlled pouring methods)? Go back to basics and double-check shipment totals against invoices.

Yves Roubaud is vice president and executive chef of **Shaw's Crab House**, **Mity Nice Grill** *and* **Vong's Thai Kitchen** *in Chicago. A major part of his job is keeping an eye on costs.*

One way to control food cost and improvement on food cost is to know the food cost of each menu item. That cost should be known before it is added to the menu. Keep in mind food cost versus gross profit margin. For example, a steak has a high food cost but a great gross profit margin. Your menu mix should reflect this knowledge.

As a rule, appetizers should be at a medium food cost. Soup, salad and dessert are at a low food cost and the main course should be close to the ideal food cost. Specials should be at a lower food cost than the menu item. We can price a special higher than a regular menu item to make it really feel like something special.

Let's see now how can we approach all that. One way is to break down the menu by categories; for example: appetizers, soup, salad, sandwich, pasta, seafood, meat and dessert. Knowing the food cost of each item and now by each category, we can decide what we want to sell. This can be achieved by telling the waitstaff what to sell.

We can determine the percentages of customers who purchase each item. (For example: 70 percent may buy an appetizer, 45 percent soup, 25 percent salad, 25 percent sandwich, 15 percent pasta, 30 percent seafood, 30 percent meat, and 35 percent dessert). In theory, the sum of all the main courses purchased should always equal 100 percent, but the appetizers, soups, salads and dessert can exceed 100 percent.

A reasonable goal is to sell one appetizer plus a soup or salad and a dessert to the greatest number of customer. This will have a positive effect on food cost because of the lower food cost attached to these two categories. Take a daily inventory of your cooler to control production and waste. Keep a low inventory. To know the food cost of each menu item and the percentage of sale mix will help you control the food cost.

Chapter 32

Beverage Purchasing Strategies That Work

Customize a Buying Strategy That Reduces Costs

Do you have a purchasing strategy? If not, you need one—now! It's never too late. A good buying plan is one of the quickest (and easiest) ways to reduce costs and make sure that your establishment gets the most for its money. Remember, the best place to control costs is in the purchasing department. The plan doesn't have to be complicated—just well thought out and straightforward to implement. A few bulleted points will do. Keep your plan simple and stick to it.

Use a simple five-prong purchasing strategy. You want to buy:

1. The right product.

2. The right quality.

3. At the right price.

4. At the right time.

5. From the right source.

Think of purchasing as a cycle, not a one-time activity. Purchasing is not just a matter of phoning or e-mailing another order. You don't want to run out, nor do you want to overstock.

Purchasing is not a separate activity. What, how and when you buy must always (yes, always!) reflect the overall goals of your establishment. Trends change—so must you, the purchaser.

Commit your purchasing strategy in writing. Write your plan down on paper, save it on your computer, or any place where it is easily accessible. You never know when other members of staff will need to deputize.

Step back. Get an overview. Ask yourself whether you're buying on the basis of long-term fixed prices or current market prices. You should be doing both.

Tighten Up Your Purchasing Procedures

Although it's not always the easiest thing to do when you're busy, the introduction of even a few basic "tightening up" procedures can make the purchasing manager's life a whole lot easier—and reduce costs!

Use your written purchasing strategy as a step-by-step guide. It saves time and money in the long run. Even if you are 100 percent familiar with your establishment's current purchasing procedures, it's all too easy to overlook a crucial link in the procedure and end up wasting time backtracking or duplicating effort.

Reassess your timing techniques. Timing is crucial. Tune in to the drinks' market price fluctuations. The wine industry in particular is prone to seasonal fluctuations. Also consider the bulk buying of soft drinks in anticipation of the summer season.

Review your purchasing schedule regularly. Consumption of liquor, wines and beverages fluctuates, from month to month and year to year. A buying pattern that worked well last year may be be way off the mark today. Consider whether it is better to buy daily, weekly or, in the case of certain drinks, monthly.

Take a fresh look at the layout of your purchase order. Is it accurately laid out? Are your instructions easy to follow? Remove any ambiguity—and remove the unnecessary hassle of processing returns.

Check out your vendors. Do they have a good track record for quality and reliability? Are they easy to deal with when things go wrong? Update your vendor contact list regularly, and always remain alert to possible new suppliers. Keep existing vendors on their toes!

Buy Quality

The quality of the merchandise purchased sets the tone and standards for the whole establishment. Don't leave quality to chance. Mistakes can be expensive. Word spreads fast and you want a good reputation!

Be upfront about quality. Make a conscious decision to purchase quality merchandise at the stage when the goals of the business are being established.

The products you are buying must be suitable for their intended use. Studies have proven that the more suitable a product, the higher its quality. Make sure that the quality of any product measures up to the needs of your establishment.

Quality must apply throughout the establishment. When it comes to quality, don't concentrate on alcohol beverages alone. Of course the types of wines, spirits, beers and liqueurs you sell are all crucially important, but don't forget the nonalcoholic beverages, such as quality coffee and soft drinks. Consumers in this sector of the market are a discerning and vociferous bunch! Something as simple as a poor cup of coffee can drive a customer away, never to return.

Don't compromise on quality. Don't be distracted by poor-quality offers or bulk buys that you think, on the spur of the moment, might just "do." They won't. You'll end up regretting the purchase.

Evaluate each product's quality in relation to cost. The most expensive product is not necessarily the best product for your enterprise. When making purchasing decisions, there is no need to sacrifice quality.

Look at quality from a guest's perspective. What level of quality do your guests expect? Meet their requirements.

Review your vendors for quality. Do you suffer from wastage due to poor-quality products? Assess the quality level of potential vendors by first asking for samples. Document quality specifications to vendors. It is important to avoid misunderstandings.

A Good Purchasing Security System Can Save You Big Bucks

Build security into your purchasing procedures. The choice of security system, however, depends a lot upon the size of your operation. If you are the "head cook and bottle washer" of a small establishment, security is a much simpler issue. If, however, you are part of a larger enterprise where a number of personnel are involved in purchasing, then security becomes a major concern. If this is your lot, give the following issues serious consideration:

Set up a reliable purchasing-control system. Whether your chosen system is manually operated or computerized, it must be free from loopholes. There are several good-value computerized packages available on the market today that are specifically designed for the liquor and beverage industry. Most of these packages offer a range of built-in security features. Get more information at:

Atlantic Publishing
www.atlantic-pub.com
800-814-1132

Cash Trrap
www.trrap.com
515-957-8478

Food-Trak
www.foodtrak.com
800-553-2438

Beware of bogus documentation. Make sure that routine purchasing procedures are accurately documented from start to finish. Attention to detail in this area will help alert you to breaches of security. Be constantly on the lookout for calculation "errors," deliberate duplication, "incorrect" invoices, and bogus credit requests. These are all common ploys used by unscrupulous purchasers and vendors.

Beware of the possibility of kickbacks. Some buyers have been known to "work" with suppliers in return for benefits such as money or gifts. Unfortunately, it happens all too often. Such "practiced" buyers and sellers are often masters of disguise, so don't be green, be keen!

Beware of purchaser theft. This can take several forms. Purchasers may order merchandise for their own personal use or they may buy wholesale with the intention of "selling on." A carefully designed purchasing system will take care of most of these problems.

Keep Purchasing Procedures Simple

Whatever the size of your operation, certain repetitive purchasing procedures are unavoidable. At the very minimum, a buyer has to complete a purchasing requisition, a purchase order, a shipping instruction, a receiving report, and carry out some form of quality control. Purchasing procedures, however, exist for a good reason. Save time, effort and money by simplifying them.

Change your attitude. Instead of viewing purchasing procedures as an irritation, think of them as a support system. Accurate documentation in this area has rescued many a business from the jaws of liquidation.

Concentrate on basics. Buyers should always have adequate purchasing procedures in place. The key, however, is to avoid overkill. If a certain procedure in the buying cycle is irrelevant to your establishment, get rid of it. A written requisition, for example, may not be necessary if you regularly "call off" stock ordered on a contract basis. Adapt and be flexible.

Save time. Establish a pared-down requisition procedure that identifies ongoing requirements and automatically triggers the purchasing cycle.

The purchase order. No skimping here! The purchase order is a legal contract between purchaser and vendor. Even in small organizations, the purchase order needs to be put in writing. Get it right. It can save time, hassle and money in the long run. A computer-generated purchase order considerably reduces human error.

The shipping instruction. Keep it simple. This piece of documentation is merely a confirmation of instructions from the buyer to the seller. Whether handwritten or computerized, the shipping instruction needs only to contain simple information. It should include the purchase order number for the shipment, and it, too, should be numbered for recordkeeping purposes.

The receiving report. Again, simplify. Although an important document in the purchasing cycle, it only needs to contain basic information: the quantity and condition of the merchandise, whether the merchandise tallies with the original purchase order, a record of stock shortages, the recipient's signature, and the date of receipt.

Define Your Purchasing Duties

It is all too easy to get bogged down in the day-to-day activities of purchasing. Remind yourself of your areas of responsibility. It helps you to focus on doing a good job.

Don't lose sight of your overall goal. Your responsibility, as a purchasing manager, is to maximize value so that your establishment gets the most for its money. No more, no less.

The cycle of duties. Always bear in mind that a purchaser's areas of responsibility cover an entire cycle of activities: identifying the needs of the establishment, planning, sourcing merchandise, ordering, receiving, storing, and issuing.

Control. Effective management and control of the purchasing cycle, with a constant eye on costs, is your number-one duty.

Dealing with vendors. The purchasing department (even if you are a one-person band) is responsible for all external dealings with vendors. The purchaser should be able to handle all vendor-related queries.

Avoid taking your purchasing problems onto the "shop floor." Front-of-the-house personnel will not appreciate interruptions while they are trying to please customers. Apart from emergencies, keep all purchasing queries for later.

High standards. It is the purchaser's duty to make sure that all merchandise purchased is fit for its purpose and of a consistently high quality. High standards = good value.

Streamline Your Receiving Procedures

This area of purchasing offers a great scope for cost reductions. Unfortunately, it is often neglected. Do so at your peril! Many well-devised purchasing plans fall at this last hurdle. Don't marginalize this important procedure.

Check merchandise thoroughly. Even when you are in a hurry, it is vital to check all received merchandise carefully. It may be your only (and last) chance to identify problems. Most vendors have a time limit written into their contracts for notifying them of discrepancies and shortages.

Adopt a "checklist" approach. The person receiving the merchandise needs to do the following:

- Verify the supplier.

- Check quality.

- Check quantity.

- Check price (if applicable).

- Note any discrepancies on the receiving note.

- Sign and date, only when satisfied with the above.

Follow up any queries. Contact the vendor (preferably in writing), outlining any shortages, discrepancies or other problems, immediately. Most problems are quickly resolved. But stating your dissatisfaction, in writing, is a wise move. Sometimes queries become wrangles and you can end up with a long, drawn-out dispute on your hands. It's good to have something in writing!

Tie up paperwork. Tedious, but important! The person who receives the goods or a designated member of staff needs to mark all invoices with some form of "Received" stamp, noting the date of receipt and who received the merchandise.

Introduce a random audit of your receiving process. Identify any problem areas before they get out of hand! A basic audit should compare quantity and quality of merchandise delivered with the original purchase order. Carry out a volume or unit count of liquor, wines and beverages. Also, double-check that cases contain the number of bottles stated on the "outer." Finally, check that all documentation has been accurately processed.

Define Your Purchase Specifications—Define Your Standards

As a purchasing manager, it is important to set standards. Decide up front exactly what types of drinks you need to purchase and the conditions under which you will place an order. These are your purchase specifications.

Consult fellow members of staff. Their input is important. Of course you want them on your side, but oftentimes, it is they who know best what will sell (and what won't!).

Purchase specifications must reflect the image of your establishment. Consider your target audience, the standards it demands, and the price it is prepared to pay.

Keep a written copy. It represents your establishment's overall purchasing standards and rules. It doesn't have to be a lengthy document; a few bulleted points will do.

Purchase specifications should focus on the following areas: quality, quantity, consistency, reliability of vendors, and availability of merchandise.

Document your purchase specifications to vendors. Vendors need to be reminded of the standards you expect from them. Specs are also useful in the event of a dispute.

Backup your purchase specification document with an additional product information list. Tabulate the information in chart format. Include information such as brand, country of origin, alcohol content (where applicable) and, in the case of wines, year and vintage. Use it to jog your memory when writing out purchase orders or placing orders by phone. This type of handy list can also help you spot "substitutes" when you receive the goods!

Decide up front exactly what types of drinks you need to purchase and the conditions under which you will place an order.

Reduce Purchasing Costs

The purchasing department is the linchpin when it comes to reducing costs. It is much easier to control costs in this area than anywhere else in the operation. The bottom line is that astute buying techniques offer the best opportunity for a business to increase its overall profits.

Monitor market trends. An upsurge in popularity of a certain beverage can lead to increased competition amongst vendors. Play them off against each other occasionally. Negotiate. You have nothing to lose!

Welcome new ideas. Purchasers should always be on the lookout for new ideas and new ways of reducing costs. Don't close your door to sales representatives; they may genuinely have something of interest to your establishment. Consider their promotional discounts.

Opportunity buys. Don't rule them out. Take a look at items that may soon be discontinued or overstocked merchandise where a supplier has simply miscalculated demand. You could make big savings.

Cooperative purchasing. Consider "pool" purchasing with other enterprises. It can give you added purchasing power.

Change purchase unit size. Buy drinks in larger volumes. This can trim costs considerably, particularly in the case of liquor purchases where sell-by dates tend to be more generous.

Legal and Ethical Issues—Avoid Expensive Mistakes

Whether you like it or not, there's no getting away from the fact that almost every aspect of purchasing has certain legal or ethical implications. Daunting? It shouldn't be. All you need is a very basic grasp of those areas of contract and commercial law that affect your company. A little understanding of the consequences of your actions as a buyer will go a long way. It will help you protect your company's interests.

Acquire a few basics. Read a beginner's guide on the subject of contract law or search the Internet for information.

Know your limitations. A basic grasp of the risks will enable you to recognize problems that require specialized legal advice or intervention. If in doubt, consult the experts. You have done what is required of you: you have identified the problem.

Contracts. Ask a legal professional to draft all written company contracts. No amount of legal "reading around" will equip you with the knowledge to draw up a bona fide contract. Bear in mind, however, that contracts don't have to be written.

Familiarize yourself with all your suppliers' contracts. Content can differ considerably.

Liquor, wine and beverage descriptions. A veritable legal minefield—if you get it wrong. Every detail of the drinks list must be 100 percent accurate. If selling substitutes, state so clearly. Keep your guests informed.

Create a network of trust with your vendors. This is particularly important in the liquor and beverages industry where, unfortunately, unethical practices are commonplace.

Conform to ISM standards. Every company purchaser should abide by the ethical credo of the "Institute for Supply Management." It advocates: "Loyalty to this company; Justice to those with whom you deal; Faith in your profession." For more information, visit **www.ism.ws** or call 800-888-6276.

A master chef who trained in Paris, **Monique Hooker** *has worked at fine restaurants in New York and owned Monique's Café in downtown Chicago. Now the consulting chef for Organic Valley, the nation's largest organic food cooperative, Hooker has always focused on eliminating waste and inefficiency.*

One way to cut waste is to double up on ingredients whenever possible. If I made lobster bisque one day, the next day I would use the sauce with grilled fish. You can also save a lot of time by designating the preparation properly and using your staff efficiently. We had a worksheet for every person in the kitchen for each day.

It is not cost efficient to prepare the same material over and over. If you have someone slicing mushrooms for salad, for example, they can also be using the same mushrooms for sauce and soups. The same goes for carrots. We always kept two bins in the refrigerator: one for soup trimmings and the other for stock trimmings. Nothing was ever to be wasted. In fact, I used to check the garbage cans to make sure my staff was not throwing away anything usable. I even based their pay raises on what I found.

Use a simple five-prong purchasing strategy. You want to buy the right product, of the right quality, at the right price, at the right time, and from the right source

Chapter 33

Beverage Inventory Control

General Inventory Procedures

Minor overall changes can result in major cost reductions. Take a fresh look at your existing inventory system. In every establishment, there is general room for improvement. For minimum effort, you can get maximum value out of your stock.

Timing. Move all drinks to a designated storage area as soon as they arrive. Don't let stock hang around. Drinks (and wine especially) need to be stored in an ambient environment, or their quality can deteriorate rapidly—and so can your profits! Also, unattended drinks, languishing in receiving areas, present a great temptation. Liquor is high on any thief's hit list.

Faulty goods. When receiving merchandise, look out for cracked and chipped bottles, mislabeled boxes, outdated or cloudy beer, correct type and vintage of wine, raised corks, leaking and weeping bottles, damaged labels, and wrong-size bottles. Contact the supplier immediately about any discrepancies.

Storage area. Your storage area must be fit for its purpose. Poor storage conditions can result in poor quality, breakage and escalating costs.

Security. Basic, but obvious. A good security system removes temptation and reduces the risk of external break-ins.

Rotate stock. First in, first out. This is important and avoids wastage, overstocking, and running out. Pay special attention to beers: their shelf-life is limited. Most beverages have no longer than a month before the sell-by date.

Control. Large or small, every beverage outlet needs some form of control procedure. Track your products from the moment they arrive at your premises to when they are sold. While this doesn't have to be complicated, the key to any good control system is to make sure that all the liquors, wines and beverages are located in the right place at the right time and are being rotated properly.

Make the Most of Your Storage Areas

Where and how you store your liquor, wines and beverages can make a big difference in turnover and profits. Once you have taken delivery, treat your inventory with respect—it has the potential to make or break your business.

Location. Define storage areas. Are you using the most convenient areas for storage? Centrally located storerooms and walk-in coolers make ideal storage areas. Easy access saves time and money.

Other storage areas. "Storage" means more than an area for dumping received goods. Storage locations include shelves, workstations, reach-in refrigerators and behind the bar. Keep all of these areas accessible and clutter-free. It speeds up your operation and reduces breakage.

High-value wines. Consider separate cellaring for prestige wines, somewhere away from the busy "shop floor" environment. As turnover of such wines is slower, accessibility is not top priority. More important is security and perfect storage conditions (even vibrations can affect the quality of good wines!).

Extra security. All drinks should be stored in a secure area. Organize the layout of storage areas to offer maximum security for liquor and high-value wines. Only personnel who need keys should have them.

Quantity. Drinks can be stored in bulk in the main storage area. Drinks in general storage areas, such as behind the bar, are better stored in the units or quantities in which they are sold.

Environment. Know your product and store it accordingly. Maintain proper temperatures, humidity and ventilation. Wine is particularly sensitive to environmental influences. It can easily absorb odors from nearby food storage areas. Poor storage practices can quickly reduce the quality of stored inventory—and nothing affects profits like quality!

Track Inventory—Track Costs

In order to control inventory, you need to know exactly what stock you have/had and where it is or when you sold it (known in the trade as "cradle-to-grave" accounting). To operate a cost-effective tracking procedure, it is crucial that you document all liquor, wines and beverages as they progress through the inventory cycle. Choose whatever tracking method works best for your establishment, but don't think you can do without some form of system. You can't. On a positive note, however, developing such a system is one of the best ways of keeping a tight rein on expenditures. Follow this six-step guideline and you shouldn't go wrong! There are several cheap, off-the-shelf forms that you can use to help you with your recordkeeping.

Step 1: Purchase order. The purchase order is the first form in the cycle. It provides a detailed record of every item purchased.

Step 2: Perpetual inventory. This second form tracks the movement of liquor, wines and beverages from the storeroom to various locations within the establishment. It also tracks each product's turnover rate. The perpetual inventory is also used for accounting purposes.

Step 3: Requisition form. This records the actual transfer of inventory from the storeroom to a specific location within the operation. This form is also used to record breakage.

Step 4: Bar par form. This records the quantity of each brand of liquor, wine or beverage currently stocked behind the bar.

Step 5: Depletion allowance form. This form is used to track the amount of spillage and wastage and to record any complimentary drinks.

Step 6: Physical inventory form. Used primarily when completing end-of-period accounts, it records the result of physical stock audits.

Monthly and Annual Inventory Control

Daily inventory control is the first, essential step towards keeping costs in check. In fact, no business can function without daily records. But look ahead; to maximize control of overall costs, establish sound monthly and annual inventory procedures. Drain every dime out of your liquor, wine and beverage inventory—long-term!

Monthly inventory. Month-end figures are crucial for determining the financial success of your operation. Devise a simple monthly inventory sheet and use it, without fail.

Physical count. Carry out a monthly physical bottle count. Check totals against the perpetual inventory figures.

The "Cyclops." This handheld scanner reads the Universal Pricing Code (UPC). It can really speed up the monthly stock check! For information about bar-code scanners, see the following sites:

- Symbol: **www.symbol.com**

- Barcode Man: **www.barcodeman.com**

Weighing scale. Use a precision liquor-weighing scale. These devices are extremely fast and easy to use. They can calculate to within 1/40 of a fluid ounce.

Annual inventory. Use annual inventory figures to review overall costs. For example, now is the time to consider price increases or to discontinue lines that are no longer cost-effective.

Resolve queries. Merely recording monthly and annual inventory figures is not enough. Resolve any discrepancies immediately. It all adds up!

Inventory Levels Affect Cash Flow

The aim is to maintain that fine balance between running out and holding too much stock. Get it wrong, and you'll find that your working capital isn't working for you! Remember, the larger your inventory, the more difficult it is to control.

Keep inventory at a minimum level, but not so low that you risk running out. Recommended inventory for high-turnover brands is approximately one to two weeks' worth of stock.

Jump in with special promotions. If you think you've miscalculated and overstocked, shift the inventory sooner rather than later, while it still has high value.

Get to know the drinking patterns of your regular patrons. This information helps you calculate the bar pars or minimum inventory levels for each bar and the main stockroom.

The perpetual inventory is a valuable tool. Keeping tabs on the flow of liquor, wines and beverages through your operation is probably the best way of knowing where to pitch inventory levels. Monitor stock daily.

Weekly deliveries. In the drinks industry, this is the norm. Work your inventory levels around these weekly deliveries and avoid the cardinal sin of running out.

Manage Your Stock Wisely and Maximize Profits

Your challenge, in a nutshell, is to order liquor, wine and other beverages in the right size and quantity and at the right time and price.

Timing of inventory deliveries. Schedule well liquor, beer and house wine deliveries for the same day each week, ideally a couple days after you place the order.

Well liquor quantities. Order items with a short turnover rate, such as well liquor, in bulk. Well liquor moves fast, offering you a great opportunity to boost cash flow. Take advantage of case discounts. Also, consider larger 1.75-liter bottles instead of the usual 1-liter bottles if you think your turnover warrants it. There are big savings to be made in this area. Use larger bottles for special promotions.

Beer is different. In order to sell beer at its freshest, arrange for deliveries on a weekly basis, or daily, if your establishment has the capacity to cope with the extra workload. Little and often is better when it comes to maximizing on beer profits.

Wine. Order house wine weekly, other wine bottles by the case once a month.

Only buy special vintage wines once or twice a year. Take a specialist's advice before stocking up on expensive wines. They can cost you dearly.

Liquor and liqueurs. The following is a useful guideline: If it takes less than five weeks to turn a product, order by the case. If it takes longer than five weeks to sell a particular brand of spirits, order by the bottle.

Reduce Inventory Pilferage

Don't leave stock security to chance. Any slackness in this area can seriously dent profits. Your central storeroom may well be as secure as a vault, but this isn't good enough. Tight security is essential in all locations where inventory is stored—from reception to behind the bar. Design a security system that ensures that all liquor, wines and beverages stay in their correct location throughout the operation. The following security techniques will help reduce pilferage:

Storeroom keys. Change locks and combinations regularly. Insist that all keys remain on the premises at all times.

Roll-down screens and lockable cabinets. Keep high-value inventory inaccessible to cleaning staff and other employees when the bar is closed.

Limit access. Only key members of staff, such as management, receiving and storage personnel, should be allowed to enter the storeroom. It is also a good idea to limit the issuing of inventory to specific, set times.

Lockable refrigerators and walk-in coolers. All storage areas should be completely lockable. Alternatively, have at least one lockable shelf for the highest-value inventory.

Bar stock security. Danger zone! Keep the quantity of liquor and beverages stored behind the bar to a workable minimum.

Investigate state-of-the-art locking devices. They may prove a sound long-term investment. Systems that involve combinations, codes, PINs and swipe cards are becoming increasingly popular.

Reduce Costs—Streamline Issuing Procedures

Revise your existing issuing procedures. You'll be surprised at how much cost trimming you can achieve in this area. Issuing procedures are particularly vulnerable to employee theft and wastage. Establish a simple issuing procedure that focuses on reducing costs. Keep the following basic records:

End of shift. Bartenders need to record the name of each liquor, wine and beverage emptied during their shifts. They should also note the number of empty bottles and the size of the bottles. Make bartenders responsible for this activity.

Manager authorization. Managers should check empty bottles against the beverage requisition form at the end of each shift. It is much easier and more cost-effective for resolving any problems immediately than letting minor queries develop into major problems at a later date.

Issuing replacement stock. Either the manager or the bartender is the best person to return empty bottles and the completed requisition form to the storeroom. The person replacing the empties should check all of the information on the requisition and issue replacements, bottle for bottle.

Breakage. It is important to account for breakage each time the requisition form is completed. Not only does it give you tighter control over cash flow, it also helps identify potential (and costly) problem areas—sooner rather than later.

Daily cost-keeping. Calculate, on a daily basis, the total cost of inventory issued. This should be viewed as a separate management or administrative function. It provides an essential "cross-check."

Computerized issuing. A manual issuing procedure works well in many small establishments, but if you have the resources, opt for a computerized system. It will quickly repay your investment. For information about computerized solutions, contact:

> ICE
> **www.horizons.bc.ca/ice/index.html**
> 604-589-8130
>
> Scannabar
> **www.liquorinventory.com**
> 800-666-0736

AccuBar is an excellent example of a computerized inventory system. Customers report a 50–80 percent time savings when using the AccuBar system. It's easy to learn: most users are up and running within 30 minutes. The patented technology eliminates the need to estimate levels; simply tap the fluid level on the bottle outline. Once you tap the bottle outline, data entry is complete. There is no further human intervention. Since no data entry or third party is involved, reports are generated immediately. It also provides a running perpetual inventory. Transfers between locations and returns of defective items are also covered. AccuBar also helps gauge which items aren't selling, allowing you to consider stocking something else that might bring a better return. AccuBar also recommends what needs to be ordered from each supplier based on current perpetual, par and reorder point. The order is totally customizable. When a shipment

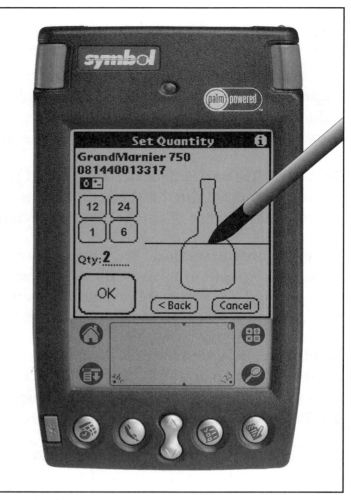

The AccuBar system, available at www.accubar.com, or call 800-806-3922 for more information.

arrives, simply scan the items, and any discrepancy from what was ordered is caught immediately. AccuBar can also track food, glassware, china, and other essentials.

Inventory Valuation Made Easy

Daunted by the pros and cons of the various accounting procedures used in today's liquor, wine and beverage industry? No need. Choose the approach that best meets the requirements of your establishment. Keep it simple. The following methods are tried and tested. They are also known for their ability to control cash flow and to reduce overall costs.

First in, first out (FIFO). This means that items in storage are valued at the level of the most-recently purchased items. FIFO helps maximize profits by extending inventory value, particularly when inflation is high. A word of warning, though: Make sure that all profits are accurately recorded and that all drinks are rotated on a strictly first-in, first-out basis.

Last in, first out (LIFO). Here, the most recent items are recorded as the first ones used. This method is useful when prices are rising, fast. Rotate stock on a FIFO basis, but make sure that the value of the inventory reflects the oldest purchase prices. If your product valuation is keenly affected by inflation, use LIFO!

Actual method. With the actual method, the inventory is valued at actual cost. It's a bit time consuming, unless you have a computerized system—even then, the actual method is probably not the best choice for reducing costs.

Last price method. Similar to FIFO, this is one of the most common accounting procedures used in the beverage industry today. It involves using the last purchase price to extend inventory value.

Computerized packages. Whatever your choice of method, a good off-the-shelf package for calculating inventory values is a must.

Bar Inventory

Waste, spillage, employee theft, oversights and inefficiency are most likely to occur in the working environment of a busy bar. Improved management of bar inventory can make a big impact on profits. Even one bottle of liquor represents a substantial profit—or loss. Introduce a few changes behind the bar. Small adjustments can make a big difference!

Security-mark bottles. Security-mark every bottle of liquor destined for the bar when it is received into the storeroom. This identifying mark, stamp or nonremovable label (placed on the bottom or side of the bottle) proves that the bottle belongs to your operation. If you are using a computer-controlled inventory system, consider using a bar-coded label for better inventory control.

Unauthorized sales. Empty bottles returned without a mark indicate that bar staff may possibly be serving liquor from unauthorized bottles. It is not unknown for employees to bring in their own bottles in the hope of making a fast buck!

Control cards. All inventory requisitioned by the bar must be recorded in the perpetual inventory, usually by computer. A backup card system can act as an invaluable "double-check." Don't make it complicated. All you need is a date and signature against the item.

Bin cards. Bin cards give you extra control over high-value items. Fix small index cards (known in the trade as bin cards) to the shelves where such items are located. Keep a careful eye on the running totals.

Backup liquor. Even on a typical busy night, one bottle of premium liquor and two to six bottles of well liquor is sufficient backup.

Accurate records. Distinguish clearly between unopened and opened bottles when valuing inventory. Opened bottles should be measured to the nearest tenth of a bottle, using dipsticks or by weight.

Chapter 34

Portion Control Behind the Bar

Portion Standardization—Putting It into Practice

Behind a busy bar, it just isn't realistic to expect a bartender to stop and consult a lengthy list of standard portion requirements every time a customer places an order! Yet, standardization of all liquor, wine and beverage portions is critical. Here are a few shortcuts:

Know your establishment's regular clientele. Devise a simple chart of the most popular drinks requested on a regular basis. A few clear, bulleted instructions are all you'll need most of the time. This list will probably cover around 90 percent of orders. It should provide a quick point of reference for busy bartenders. In the interests of credibility, keep it out of customer sight.

The full guidelines. To cover all other eventualities, keep a detailed guideline to portion standardization easily accessible behind the bar. Make sure that the information is simple to follow and regularly updated.

Educate employees. Portion errors caused by ignorance can ruin your operation, fast! You can also lose out when bartenders are tired, bored or under pressure. They're easy to spot: they will often take shortcuts, such as lining up glasses and pouring straight across the top without pausing. Eliminate this type of activity.

Keep an eye on "mixer" portions. Strict portion standardization should apply equally to the nonalcoholic content of all "mixed" drinks. Bartenders need to be reminded of the fact that all portions add up—alcoholic and nonalcoholic alike.

Consistency. A vital factor in achieving portion standardization. Make sure that all drinks are poured in a consistent fashion. This helps ensure accurate portion control as well as consistency in quality.

Precision Portioning Boosts Profits

So much hinges on portion control! If portion size fluctuates, so will profit margins. For example, if a bartender over-pours the high value of a drink by as little as half an ounce on a regular basis, the cost of that drink can escalate by as much as 6–10 percent. Multiply this wastage over a period of time and the results can be devastating. It is, therefore, essential to implement an effective strategy for portion control, or profits will suffer. The following is a summary of the main pros and cons of methods used for portion control in the drinks industry.

Free-pouring. The bartender has to rely on a spout attached to the bottle to control the rate of flow. Although the free-pouring method is fast and easy, it has obvious shortcomings when it comes to cost control.

Handheld portioning. This involves pouring the liquor into a shot glass or "jigger"—a popular method that is reasonably reliable and cost effective.

Bottle-attached controls. Better than free-pouring and handheld measuring, these devices can deliver with impressive accuracy.

Liquor-control systems (LCS). The use of technologically advanced portion-control systems is becoming increasingly commonplace in today's drinks industry. LCSs are particularly effective at controlling liquor costs. They can also virtually eliminate employee theft. LCSs are marketed on the basis of a typical return on investment within 12 months. The following suppliers offer LCSs:

Berg Company
www.berg-controls.com
608-221-4281

AzBar
www.azbaramerica.com
214-361-2422

Bristol BM
www.bristolnf.com/liquor.htm
709-722-6669

Easybar Beverage Management Systems
www.easybar.com
503-624-6744

Easybar Beverage Managment Systems have multiple solutions for beverage portion control. The Easybar CLCSII is a fully computerized beverage dispensing system that controls beverage pour sizes, improves bartender speed, and ensures perfectly portioned drinks and cocktails. This system also prevents product loss by eliminating over-pouring, spillage, breakage and theft. It accounts for all beverages dispensed through the system and boosts receipts by lowering costs and increasing accountability.

Also available is the Easypour Controlled Spout System. This offers control for drinks that are dispensed directly from a bottle. The controlled pour spouts allows only preset portions to be dispensed and will not allow drinks to be dispensed without being recorded.

Easybar's Cocktail Station creates cocktails at the touch of a button. The cocktail tower can dispense up to 48 liquors plus any combination of 10 juices or sodas. It mixes cocktails of up to five ingredients, and ingredients dispense simultaneously to cut pour time. All ingredients dispense in accurate portions every time.

Control Portions and Meet Customer Expectations

Inadequate portion control can lead to unforeseen customer care problems—customer dissatisfaction is only one of them! Incorrect portioning can also have costly legal implications. Consider the following:

Portion inconsistency is a major source of customer complaint. If drink portions are strictly controlled, guests will be served the same drink every time, no matter which bartender pours it. The customer is satisfied.

Get ratios right. Customers will complain (and quite rightly so) if drinks are mixed in the wrong proportions. Standard recipes must comply with fixed portions for each ingredient. Mistakes can cost you more than the price of an extra portion; they can cost you a regular customer.

Dram Shop Acts. Many states have passed legislation imposing third-party liability on liquor servers and licensees who cannot control the effects of customer intoxication. Proprietors can be held responsible (under certain circumstances) for the actions of customers who consume excessive amounts of alcohol. Incorrect portioning is frequently to blame. In the worst cases, this can result in bankruptcy for the bar owner. For more resources, visit **www.tf.org/tf /alcohol/ariv/dram4.html**.

Beware of serving doubles. A double is more than twice as potent as a single. This is because the ratio of spirit to mixer is inverted. Doubles are good for profit, but serve them with caution.

Monitor Portions Effectively

It is the obligation of every beverage manager to meet the rigorous standards for portion control as defined by the drinks industry. Once standards have been established, however, they need to be monitored continuously. Herein lies the challenge for the busy bar manager:

Be realistic. Strike a balance between the time and effort required to develop a portion-monitoring system and its effectiveness in practice.

Be specific at the purchasing stage. State size, weight and count (and any other details that are specifically related to portion control) in sufficient detail to guide suppliers and receiving personnel.

Standard recipes. Always stick to the correct formulas for the proportions of all drinks. Do not improvise.

Enforce the serving of standard portions behind the bar. Use pouring methods that are effectively self-monitoring.

Introduce monitoring tools. These need to be the types of devices that will actually help, rather than hinder, busy bartenders. Automated beverage dispensers are a good idea.

Monitor the cost of portions as well as the size. Work out the cost of preparing (as well as the cost of the ingredients) for one drink. It is all too easy to assume that if the size is right, so is the cost. The results could be interesting! Review this aspect of portion control on a regular basis. It is a lucrative area for reducing costs.

Improve Portion Control in the Restaurant

How drinks are served at the table can have a major impact upon an establishment's overall costs and profits. Portion control is a far more complex issue in a restaurant environment. Here, the serving of drinks is only one aspect of the whole dining experience. Other factors have to be considered, such as the relationship between server and diner.

The customer is always right. Guest satisfaction should lead the way to portion control. This approach might at first seem contradictory, but it will ultimately prove a more effective way in which to control drink portions.

Don't under-pour. Again, it may seem somewhat contradictory, but short measures invariably lead to customer dissatisfaction and the demand for over-compensation.

Drink menus. Make sure that menus on both the bar and tables specify the exact contents of each drink. This information applies not only to the ingredients but also to the alcohol/nonalcohol ounce content. Customers like to know exactly what they're drinking—and in what volume.

Wine and spirit glasses. Attractive drinking glasses considerably enhance diner enjoyment and result in the impulse ordering of additional portions.

Standardize drink portions—unobtrusively! Servers must be trained to fill glasses to just the right level—no more, no less. They should also, at the same time, make the procedure appear effortless.

Mixed drinks. Drinks waiters in the restaurant need to apply the same rigid portion controls as bar staff. It is easy to over-pour in a dining environment.

Wine portions. Serve wine in both a "regular" and a "large" wineglass. If the customer doesn't stipulate a preference, you are not breaking the law by defaulting to "large," merely boosting profits.

Reduce Waste, Reduce Portion Costs

A certain amount of wastage is inevitable in any drinks outlet. The key, however, is to keep it to a minimum. Introduce a few practical measures that can really make a difference.

Inter-bar transfer. Discourage this activity as much as possible. Only move bottles around the establishment if it is absolutely necessary. Ideally, stock should be moved only twice: from reception to storeroom and from storeroom to bar.

Cleanliness. Make sure that all draft beer lines are scrupulously clean and functioning at optimum capacity. If in doubt, ask the brewery that supplied you the beer to carry out regular maintenance checks.

Don't skimp on the "pulling through" of draft beers. This applies to the first portion of beer from a new barrel. It is crucial to "waste" a complete portion in order to maintain quality standards. To do otherwise is false economy.

Complimentary drinks. Remind bar staff to record complimentary drinks at all times. Even one unrecorded portion per shift can have a long-term impact on profits.

Bar layout. Careful planning is required to allow bartenders maximum freedom of movement. Cramped serving conditions can result in excessive spillage and wasted portions. You will find a sample bar layout on the following page.

Spoilage. Don't overlook the portions of "add on" ingredients, such as ice cream, that are stored in open containers behind the bar. Only keep sufficient stock to fill the orders for one shift. Leftovers cannot be reused.

Mixed Drinks—Get the Proportions Right

Correct portioning is a vital aspect, not only of achieving customer satisfaction, but also of maintaining profitability and reducing costs behind the bar. Guests will notice immediately if drinks lack "balance."

Fixed portions. Establish serving portions for each main type of mixed drink served in your establishment. Stick to these predetermined portions at all times.

Portioning guidelines. Bartenders must be given clear instructions regarding the exact composition of each mixed drink. This applies to all types of drink, from highballs to liqueur coffees.

Optics. The best way to ensure consistency in mixed drinks with multiple liquors is to use an optic dispensing system. If that is not possible, make sure consistent portion methods discussed previously in this book are used.

"Baby" bottles are another easy way to correctly portion mixed drinks.

Don't ignore the trimmings. Add-ons, such as ice, lemon slices and cream, also need to be served in correct-size portions.

Computerized recipe calculators. Install off-the-shelf or online recipe management software that calculates the correct proportions for standard mixed drinks. A great time-saver, it will also reduce error margins significantly. Check out the following suppliers:

- Ace Bartender: **www.acebartender.com**

- Bar Bug: **www.barbug.com**

- Bar Fliers: **www.barfliers.com**

Serve Drinks in the Correct Glassware

Using the correct glassware is one of the best ways of improving portion control. Serve drinks in the appropriate glass, and you'll soon notice the difference! It is also a simple yet effective way of reducing costs and boosting profits.

Range of glassware. Invest in a range of the most common-sized glassware, such as six- to eight-ounce rock glasses, nine- to ten-ounce highball, eleven- to fourteen-ounce bucket glasses and six- to fourteen-ounce snifters. These high-usage glasses will help to ensure that drinks are served in the correct portions.

Individuality. Don't be afraid to choose glassware that reflects the style of your establishment. For example, if you sell mainly draft beer, you will need to stock up on traditional pint and half-pint glasses—good for the image but also essential for portion control.

Present premium cocktails in expensive-looking glassware. Boost sales in this high-profit sector of the drinks market. Sophisticated cocktail glasses will practically market the drinks for you.

Marked glasses. Don't shy away from stocking up on glasses marked with the required standard liquor levels. Customers, in general, prefer their drinks served in these types of glasses. They know they are not being "short measured." You also benefit from more accurate portion control.

Pouring Beers and Ales in the Correct Portions

Portion control of beers and ales can present quite a challenge compared with serving almost any other beverage. Beer, brewed and fermented from cereal grains, and ale, a similar product but with a higher hop content, are complex drinks that demand extra-special care and attention.

Don't overstock. Beers and ales are highly perishable. Quality will quickly deteriorate, especially in the case of draft beer. Even canned and bottled beers can have "pull dates" or sell-by dates as short as a couple of weeks.

Rotate stock. Stock rotation is extremely important with beers and ales. Monitor all dates on draft, bottled and canned beers, both in the storeroom and behind the bar.

Quality. Apart from monitoring consistent freshness, make sure that beer is served cold, at approximately 40°F. Customers will soon complain if the temperature is wrong.

Draw or pour beer properly. The skilled bartender must acquire the correct technique for pouring beer, whether draft or from a bottle or can. Regular spillage down the side of the glass can reduce profits dramatically.

Beer "head." Control the size of the "head" you put on each glass by holding the glass at a slight angle at the beginning of the draw. Too sharp of an angle will result in excess foam and portion wastage.

Alcoholic Beverages and the Law—Strict Portion Control

All establishments, including bars, taverns, restaurants, banquet venues and nightclubs—any outlet that sells beverages containing ethyl alcohol—must comply with strict government alcohol regulations. Federal inspectors demand total compliance.

Stock and serve standard portions only. Portion control means more than just cost control. It has serious legal implications.

Know the rules. You have no option but to familiarize yourself with government legislation regarding the selling and serving of alcoholic drinks. Pay special attention to the "Dram Shop Laws." These acts stipulate that the alcohol server is liable for the actions of intoxicated guests. Understand your obligations.

Alert bar staff. Train employees to serve alcoholic beverages in the correct portions. They should also be able to spot the early signs of customer intoxication. If in doubt, bartenders should refuse to serve anyone who is visibly intoxicated. Management should always support their decisions.

Clear labeling. The federal government has fixed standards for identifying all types of distilled spirits, wines and malt beverages. Stick to these standards. Make sure that all alcoholic products sold in your establishment are clearly labeled with the correct alcohol content and point of origin.

Chapter 35

Beverage Theft

Insider Theft

This is an alarming fact: Most types of beverage operations lose a crippling percentage of profits through insider theft. The vast majority of employees in the beverage industry are honest and hardworking; it is the small minority of staff that can ruin your business through dishonesty. Insider theft can often escalate if there are weaknesses in the following general areas of the operation:

Lack of supervision. Theft from behind the bar, storeroom or storage areas is a major problem. Curb losses by increasing supervision, either in person or by means of strategically positioned security cameras.

Proprietor attitude. Don't make matters worse by treating all employees with suspicion. Get the honest staff on your side.

Weak management. Unfortunately, some beverage managers compound the issue of insider theft by turning a "blind eye" and simply increasing prices to cover "shrinkage." Owners need to question unwarranted price increases.

Pouring costs (PC). A common danger area. These costs need to be carefully monitored, especially in relation to bartender productivity.

Inventory records. This is one of the easiest areas for dishonest employees to "fiddle the books." Tighten up your recordkeeping. Never leave inventory control to one person. Double-check.

End-of-shift cash count. Another prime target area for insider theft. Never let a bartender reconcile the cash in the register at the end of his or her shift.

Bartender Theft—Top Ten Common Ploys

Controlling theft behind the majority of bars is no mean task; eliminating it altogether is virtually impossible. Temptation is a fine thing, and unfortunately the opportunity for bartender theft is overwhelming. However, in the interests of long-term survival, you have no choice but to tackle the problem head on. Be wary of the following top-ten common ploys:

1. **Open theft.** A bartender pours a drink, doesn't ring the cash register and puts
   the cash in a "holding" place, such as the tip jar.

2. **Overcharging.** Bartender pockets the difference. A variation is to charge regular prices but ring up "Happy Hour" prices and, again, pocket the difference.

3. **Ringing "00" on the cash register.** The bartender simply steals the value of the drink.

4. **Over-pouring.** Bartender hopes to get a heavy tip.

5. **Under-pouring.** Bartender keeps a mental note of the number of half measures poured throughout the evening and then thieves the equivalent value in drinks, gives them away, or drinks them himself.

6. **Rounds of drinks.** Bartender rings up for a "round" rather than separate items. It makes it easier to inflate the overall price of a round of drinks, particularly if guests are unfamiliar with individual prices.

7. **Shortchanging.** Common variations include counting aloud while handing the customer less money, distracting the customer by sliding the change along the bar, and giving change for lower-denomination bills while keeping the difference.

8. **"Soft" inventory.** Bartender neglects to charge for the mixer component of
a drink.

9. **Substitution—bringing in own liquor.** This is often done with vodka because it is odorless and looks like water. Dilution is another similar ploy.

10. **Padding the tab.** The bartender pencils in an inflated total and later erases it, replacing it with the correct total. Warning: Ban pencils from behind the bar!

Common Employee Theft Techniques

This is an alarming fact: Most types of beverage operations lose a crippling percentage of profits through insider theft. The vast majority of employees are honest and hardworking; it is the small minority of staff that can ruin your business through dishonesty.

The more experienced the dishonest employee, the better equipped he or she is to manipulate the system. Thieving members of staff are quick to detect exactly how much an owner really understands about the business. In the beverage industry, take nothing for granted. Alert yourself to the following possibilities.

Tip jar. Positioning cash jars too close to the cash register is asking for trouble. It's far too easy for bartenders to slip stolen cash from the register into the jar, a temporary hiding place. Also, in some establishments the tip jar is used to get change for the register. Bad move. Thieves can easily exchange tip cash for larger denominations from the cash drawer during this type of transaction.

Time cards. Time-clock fraud is quite a common occurrence. Time is money, so it's a good idea to get the manager on duty to sign employees' time cards at the end of each shift.

No sale. Nip this one in the bud. Watch out for bartenders who sell a drink and then ring up "no sale." The easiest way to restrict this practice is to have a security feature added to the "no sale" button. Another suggestion is to insist that bartenders ring in the sale before serving the drink.

Bartender brings in counterfeit money. Fraudsters tend to reserve such bills specifically for passing trade and tourists.

Reusing closed tabs. The bartender appears to ring up the drink price but, in fact, only halfway enters the tab into the register. He or she then hits "0" to give the impression of ringing it in.

Cash register tape. The bartender brings in his or her own cash register tape, prepared on a leased cash register that is identical to the one in the workplace. Total takings can be "adjusted" according to the greed of the thief. Warning: Don't let bartenders "Z" tapes from their own shifts!

Over-ringing. When the customer isn't looking, the thief over-rings an amount on the tab and then re-rings the tab for less than the amount charged.

"Paid outs." The bartender claims that the money was refunded for various reasons, such as faulty cigarette machines.

Charge cards. Old, manual, slide-style machines are particularly vulnerable. The thief may place a "block" between the top copy and the remaining copies and later alter the total.

Jigger substitution. The bartender brings in his own shot glass that looks identical to the official jigger but is actually smaller. Several short measures over a shift add up.

Changing shifts. It is easy for the thief to make and serve several drinks and collect payment during a busy "hand-over" period.

Deliberate mistakes. Drinks are then returned and resold or given to a friend.

Breaking empty bottles and pretending they were full. Full bottles are then requisitioned to replace the "broken" empty bottles.

Substituting water in the drip tray. The bartender pretends he or she had to waste a pint to clear the lines and then pockets the difference.

Introduce Theft-Reduction Procedures That Are Easy to Enforce

Theft-reduction policies and procedures are no good unless they are strictly enforced. Employees must be made clearly aware of the dire consequences of flouting house rules. There can be no gray areas. New members of staff should be asked to sign a confirmation that they have read the rules and fully understand the implications.

Prohibit bartenders from totaling the cash at the end of their shifts. This policy also protects honest bar staff.

Prohibit bartenders from both on- and off-duty drinking. Off-duty drinking leads to fellow bar staff over-pouring, giving away free drinks, or undercharging.

Prohibit bartenders from taking part in physical inventory counts. Ideally this should be a management-only function.

Bartenders should not be involved in ordering, receiving or issuing inventory. Again, this should be a management-only function.

Security. Enforce security procedures for all liquor, wine, beer, spirits and any other high-value inventory. Also, only key personnel should have access to the storeroom.

Require bartenders to record post-shift bar par readings. This refers to the number of bottles behind the bar at any given time. Bartenders should take a bar par reading at the end of the night shift.

Prohibit bartenders from recording more than one transaction per drink ticket. If bartenders are allowed to use a "running" ticket, they can easily neglect to record all the drinks they have actually sold.

Enforce voiding procedures. Bartenders should request managerial approval before continuing with a void.

Test a bartender's honesty. Sneaky, but effective! Slip an extra $10 or $20 bill into the opening bank. Ask bartenders to verify the amount of money in the register's opening bank and see whether they inform you of the planted "over."

Minimize Inventory Theft

This is no mean task in the beverage industry! But you can take damage-limitation measures. Strict control of inventory procedures throughout the operation can have a major impact upon reducing costs through unnecessary "wastage." Implement the following tried and proven procedures.

Bartenders should not take part in physical inventory procedures. This gives dishonest employees the perfect opportunity to alter the records to offset previous theft. Taking the bar's physical inventory should be a management function.

Bartenders should not take part in purchasing, ordering, receiving or issuing liquor. These, also, should be managerial functions.

Secure inventory. Lock all liquor, wine, beer and high-value inventory in a secure storeroom or storage area. Limit access to key personnel.

Banquet or "function" bartenders should not be allowed behind the main bar. Otherwise, it would be easy for banquet bartenders to move liquor to the bar and then steal it later on.

Control inventory in transit from store to bar. The scope is immense here for the dishonest bartender. It has even been known for full bottles of liquor to find their way into outside trash cans, to be recovered later by the thief.

Computerized inventory control. Manual inventory recordkeeping is wide open to abuse. The best way of reducing costs incurred through inventory theft is to install a computerized perpetual inventory system. Investigate computerized solutions, including:

> Scannabar
> **www.liquorinventory.com**
> 800-666-0736
>
> Berg Company
> **www.berg-controls.com**
> 608-221-4281

Chapter 36

Drink Selection

Develop a Successful Beer Program

Beer is a major seller in most bars, clubs and liquor outlets; it accounts for a hefty percentage of sales. Draft beer is particularly popular. It can prove a lucrative area of any beverage operation, if you get it right. It is estimated that wastage, spillage, excess foam, over-pouring, poor quality, theft, giveaways, and other draft beer-related problems can drain your operation of an amazing 20 percent of inventory. Never underestimate the scope for cost reductions in this area!

Promotions. Beer is a perishable product. As draft beer expires quickly, always consider discounting draft beer before bottled beer.

Computer-controlled draft beer technology.
A good control system is essential. The best type of control is a flow meter attached to each tap. If your usage is over two kegs per week, then you could justify the installation of an electronic device that counts fractions of an ounce. Take a look at the Berg Tap 1 Control System

(**www.berg-controls.com**) and AzBar's product offerings (**www.azbaramerica. com**).

EasyBar Beverage Management Systems (**www.easybar.com**) offers a portion dispenser for draught beer. The system has three programmable pour sizes to ensure the perfect glass, pint or pitcher. The bartender simply pushes a button and the glass or pitcher is filled. This system keeps track of every portion dispensed and is compatible with most point-of-sale systems. Controls can be added to existing draught beer or provided along with a complete beer dispensing system.

Foam head. Control the size of the head and really make an impact on cost reductions. A good head of foam is essential, but it is up to you to control the depth of the foam. For example, in a 16-ounce glass a ½-inch head of foam yields around 136 glasses of draft per keg, whereas a 1-inch head yields up to 152 glasses per keg. Add up the difference! Train all bartenders to achieve one-inch heads of foam.

Stop selling beer in pitchers. Pitchers sell at a lower profit margin than beer by the glass. Although pitchers are a better deal for customers, they do little for your profitability. You're far better off selling four glasses of draft than one pitcher of beer.

Make the Right Choice of Wines

Choice of wine is a very individual matter. There are no rights or wrongs. It is important, however, to pander to customer preferences. Whether you run a bar, restaurant, club or specialized wine bar, you must purchase wine according to the demands of your clientele. If you get it right, profits will soar. But if you choose wines that aren't a hit with your customers, you end up pouring your profits, as well as the unsold wine, down the drain.

Keep up to date with which wines are moving well. Read trade journals and publications, such as the *California Wine Growers Institute*, to learn more about current trends or consult the

California Association of Wine Grape Growers: 555 University Avenue, Suite 250, Sacramento, CA 95825; **www.cawg.org**.

Review the wine list. Be ruthless—if a wine is slow-moving, remove it from the list.

Get ahead of the crowd. Introduce wines from up-and-coming wine regions. Suggestions include: New Zealand Riesling, Gewürztraminer and Sauvignon Blanc for whites, and South African Pinot Noir or Merlot for reds.

Storage. Wine is a vulnerable product. One of the most effective ways of reducing costs and avoiding waste is to store wine in the correct environment (temperature, light and ventilation are particularly important). See **www.storing-wine.com** for handy tips on storing wine.

Opened bottles. Establish par levels for each wine stocked behind the bar. Only open as many bottles as you need for one shift. All wines, particularly whites and cheaper house reds, become oxidized and deteriorate quickly once opened. A useful tip is not to pull the cork completely out of the bottle. If a cork is only partly pulled, the wine remains sealed, preventing oxygen from entering the bottle.

Cost controls on empty bottles. Count empty wine bottles at the end of each shift. This practice makes sure that bartenders aren't over-pouring. For example: You use six 1.5 liter bottles of wine during a shift; your standard portion for wine is 5 ounces; sales for 60 to 61 glasses should show up on the register tape.

Discount premium wines. Discounting premium wines results in a higher potential for profits. It also gives bartenders the opportunity to up-sell customers from standard house wines. This plan works well with "special buys" and wholesaler promotions.

Innovate. If wine is a big seller in your establishment, you may want to invest in a Wine Bar. OZ Winebars Wine Service Equipment (**www.ozwinebars .com**) adds speed, excitement and reliability to wine-by-the-glass programs at all levels of operation. Appropriately distributed prep times and ample on-hand backstock capacity reduces order filling

cycles by more than half of that needed for hunt/uncork/free-pour/recork and replace cycles. Electronic Tap Rail options, inventory, and complete POS interface are available. OZ Winebars are the only spec-grade commercial Winebars produced worldwide bearing the assurances of full CSA/UL and NSF Certifications.

Image. Remember that when people perceive a higher value for an item, they are willing to pay more for it. You can create a very high-class image for your wine with a functional storage cabinet. Vinotemp Wine Cellars (**www.vinotemp .com**) offers a premier selection of wine cellars and wine cellar accessory equipment: storage systems, cooler systems, wine racks, wine storage cabinets, humidors, liquor cooler cabinets, wine cellar design, and wine storage.

Nonalcoholic Beverages—An Area of Opportunity

This sector of the beverage industry, known in the trade as NABs, needs to be taken very seriously if you want to cash in on current drinking trends. More customers today (often affluent, young, career-oriented clientele with plenty of disposable income) are choosing to drink NABs. Health issues, stricter DWI laws, and maybe even image are influencing their decisions to turn to NABs. The fact remains: this trend can mean big bucks. Tap into the possibilities:

Promotions. Which NABs are consistently popular in your establishment? Buy bulk and sell on promotion. Publicize offers that your customers just cannot resist. Use a large chalkboard or place "in-your-face" table tents on tables and at the bar.

Specialize. Don't bother with expensive market research. Consult your regular customers. Ask them what they'd like to see on the menu. Decide on a few in-house specialties. Profits will increase noticeably, as margins for NABs are generally higher than for alcoholic beverages.

Bottled water. This is no passing fad. Both in the dining room and at the bar, people are choosing to alternate alcoholic drinks with bottled water. Shelf dates tend to be generous (particularly for still, noncarbonated waters), so cash in: buy in bulk for big savings.

Added value. Serve NABs in sophisticated, unusual glasses that scream "quality"! Customers will happily pay that little bit extra for a "wow" experience.

Don't price too low. A word of warning: To make the most of this burgeoning area of the drinks market, keep your prices in line with your establishment's other alcoholic beverages. If NABs are priced too low, bartenders will be reluctant to promote them, and customers will think they're nothing special.

Cocktails—Reduce Costs While Increasing Customer Satisfaction

Cocktails are good for profits, and cocktail hour can be serious, big business. The customer feel-good factor is crucial. This can be achieved at no extra cost. Imagination is free.

Well brands. Reduce costs by sticking to well brands for cocktails. Don't pour away your profits by using premium brands in cocktail recipes.

Signature drinks. Above all, a signature drink must look special. Choose unusual colors. Use different garnishes, such as asparagus, pepperonis, jumbo shrimp, crab claw or scallions. Stand out from the crowd.

"Stirred, not shaken." Don't shake mixed drinks that contain carbonated ingredients, particularly if those components are clear liquids. The bubbles will go flat, and the liquids will become cloudy. Stir instead.

Presentation. Dare to be different. How about serving Chambord on the side for a Meltdown Raspberry Margarita? Let customers pour the liqueur portion themselves. As the liqueur blends into the drink, it will release wonderful aromatic raspberry flavors. It will also look visually stunning. Guests will think "value."

Champagne. Many recipes use champagne as a base ingredient. Once opened, a bottle of champagne or sparkling wine becomes a liability because the bubbles are short-lived. Buy a bottle sealer specifically designed to cope with this problem. Ensure that bartenders know how to use it. You can't afford champagne wastage.

Ice. Choose a cocktail station that has a deeper-than-average ice bin (up to 15 inches maximum capacity). Put a divider through the middle of the bin and use it for storing both crushed and cubed ice. When the bar is busy, hanging around waiting for ice supplies costs money.

Speed. Reposition liquor, wine and soda guns directly above the cocktail station. The soda gun should be placed on the left-hand side of the station, so that the bartender's right hand is free to hold a liquor bottle at the same time. A bartender using both hands is working at top speed and maximum efficiency.

Trim Liquor Costs

Liquor prices don't vary a great deal from one wholesaler to another. Packaging and size also tend to be fairly consistent. So what can you do about reducing liquor costs in your operation? The answer is quite a lot! It's a misconception in the liquor trade that your options are limited when it comes to selling liquor. Consider the following opportunities:

Bulk buys. Purchase staple liquors, such as whiskey, gin, vodka, brandy, rum and other popular spirits (e.g., fruit brandies) in bulk. They have a long shelf life and you know you can sell them within a reasonable period of time. Just remember when purchasing these items in bulk, you need to ensure adequate storage and that your cash will be tied up in this inventory until depleted.

Trends. Stay ahead of consumption trends. Respond quickly. For example, the current trend in the United States is toward "light" spirits such as 80- and 86-proof whiskies instead of 100-proof (50 percent alcohol) bonded whiskies. Wholesalers, too, are keen to promote these alternatives.

Distilled spirits. Their shelf life is exceptionally long. Buy distilled whenever possible, and minimize wastage.

Well liquors. Which well liquors you choose can really make a difference in reducing costs. But don't buy at any price and compromise on quality. Your reputation is at stake. Customers often judge an establishment by the quality of its well liquor.

Call liquors. Increase margins on call liquors (brand names). Guests who ask for Gordon's gin or Jack Daniel's whiskey, for example, are loyal to the brand and will probably not question the price.

Choose Drink Mixes Carefully—Make an Impact on Cost Reductions

Just because mixes aren't a drink's main ingredients, one shouldn't ignore their impact on your operation's profitability. There is considerable scope for trimming costs in this area. Despite being sold in small portions, drink mixes have a high overall sales volume; it is also predictable and consistent. Review the range of drink mixes used in your establishment. It all helps to reduce costs.

Fresh orange juice. It is worth investing in a good commercial juicer for orange juice. A handy tip is to rinse oranges under hot water before placing them in the juicer—the juice yield will be higher.

Sunkist offers a line of high-quality commercial juice products. The Sunkist Commercial Juicer operates at 1,725 rpm, making it extremely easy for an operator to extract 10–12 gallons of juice per hour using precut citrus. It has a unique strainer that oscillates 3,450 times per minute to help separate the juice from the pulp. Its quiet yet heavy-duty motor is housed in gleaming chrome-plated steel and looks great with any décor. The Sunkist Commercial Juicer comes with three different-size extracting bulbs (one each for lemon/lime, orange, and grapefruit). Removable parts can go in a commercial dishwasher for quick and easy sanitizing.

Purchase Sunkist Foodservice Equipment from your dealer or order direct by calling the company toll free at 800 383-7141. More information can be found on the Sunkist Web site: www.sunkistfs.com/equipment.

For garnishes, the Sunkist Sectionizer will save you many hours in kitchen/bar prep time. It makes quick work of slicing, halving and wedging a wide variety of fruits and vegetables. In addition to sectionizing citrus fruit, it can core and wedge apples and pears. It will also slice firm tomatoes and mushrooms for sandwiches and pizzas, or wedge them for salads. The Sectionizer can slice and/or wedge hardboiled eggs, kiwi fruit, small to medium potatoes, strawberries; just about any firm (not hard) fruit or vegetable without pits that will fit through the blade cup. It is as simple to use as pulling a handle, and is much safer than cutting fruits and vegetables with a knife. The Sunkist Sectionizer has seven interchangeable blade cups to choose from, making it one of the most versatile manual food cutters on the market. Blade cups and plungers are commercial dishwasher safe.

From-scratch drink mixes. Preparing a whole range of drink mixes from scratch is too time consuming and all too often results in inconsistent quality. You're better off buying ready-made mixes. Test samples of mixes before making a decision. Prepared mixes can vary considerably in taste and quality. There are a variety of drink mixes available. Check out **www.zingzang.com** for a complete line of mixers.

Cheat. Have one drink mix that you prepare from scratch, say sweetened lemon juice. Promote its excellence. Customers will assume that because you make lemon juice from scratch, the same applies to all your other drink mixes.

Cut garnish costs. Your choice of garnishes to accompany drink mixes can, quite literally, eat into your profits. Bartenders are notorious for nibbling olives, cherries, pineapple wedges, chocolate shavings, peppermint sticks, pretzels, etc. Store garnishes in airtight containers in a cooler, away from temptation. Also, establish par levels for fruit garnishes and only prepare enough for one shift.

Unusual juices. Use single-portion 6-ounce cans for less frequently served juices. Trade higher cost for time saving, convenience and for reduced wastage.

Choosing the Right Suppliers for Your Beverage Requirements

A lot depends on your location. Some states have an almost monopolistic control over alcohol distribution; other states operate by licensing wholesalers. You need to familiarize yourself with county and local laws. They vary considerably from state to state. Where do you start?

Source a supplier. Take a look at your local beverage trade publications or

Yellow Pages for a list of suppliers and wholesalers. The chances are you'll need to deal with several suppliers in order to get the full range of beverages required by your establishment.

Service. As well as competitive prices, also look for exceptional service from your suppliers. For example, do they offer "emergency" deliveries at no extra cost to their regular customers? The time it takes to get extra stock means an extra expense for you.

Visit warehouses. Before deciding, visit a few different warehouses to see how they operate. More important, do they handle their stock with care? Bear in mind that returning faulty or poor merchandise can be time consuming and expensive. Also, customer dissatisfaction is hard to quantify.

Beware of hidden charges for minimum orders. Choose only a supplier that does not penalize you for minimum orders.

Pool buying. If pool buying is legal in your state, choose a supplier that will give you the biggest savings. Negotiate, but don't compromise. Get a written quotation first.

Boost Profits by Choosing the Right Drink Recipes

The recipes you choose to feature on your drinks menu must do more than satisfy customer requirements. Plan carefully; a lot of thought needs to go also into keeping costs down, while at the same time maintaining a fine reputation for quality and imagination. This is no mean task, but the following simple suggestions may help:

Communicate your recipe preparation techniques. Add a brief description about your unique preparation techniques underneath each recipe on the drinks menu. Tempt your customers to try "something different." The secret lies in your method of communication, rather than in the actual recipes themselves.

Dare to be different: recipes on napkins. Get some recipes that you want to promote printed on napkins. It's different, and it's a good marketing tool. It also channels customers into ordering the recipes that you want them to buy. Choose the "special" recipes on the basis of higher profit margins, but promote them as "added value" recipes.

Mobile mini-bar. As well as serving recipe drinks from the main bar, introduce a mini-bar on wheels. Get a bartender to wheel it around, selling "taster recipes" at promotional prices. The spontaneity of this approach is excellent for generating extra income.

Highballs. Although highballs can be served in a variety of different-sized glasses, the ideal size for maximum efficiency and controlling costs is a 9-ounce glass. It accommodates the exact proportions for a standard highball recipe. The glass looks full to capacity; the customer is happy. Also, you know that the portions of ingredients are correct.

Identify Loss Leaders and Turn Them into Profit

You know exactly what stock you need to shift, but how do you do it? The way in which you choose to promote slow movers, stock where shelf dates are looming, or "mistake" purchases can mean the difference between profit and loss. Treat promotions as more than a damage-limitation exercise; you can actually make money out of loss leaders.

Image. Promote your chosen drink (or recipe) as something "hot," "clever" and "smart." Simple flattery never fails; it is one the best promotional tools available. Word your advert to imply that this drink is "ahead of the crowd"!

Oversized glassware. You want to shift volume—and you want to shift it fast. Serve promotions in specialty, oversized glassware. Play on the fun element of presentation. For example, if you're trying to promote a certain beer, serve it in chunky 16-ounce beer mugs. Invent a novel name for the glass, such as "Hefty Handful"!

Glowing neon serving trays—a real talking point, and younger clientele love them. For maximum effect, keep the bar lighting low. Contact Glo-Tray at 203-226-3090 for further information. Or, light your drinks with Floralyte LED Lighting (**www.chillinprod-ucts.com**). The emphasis will be on presentation rather than the loss-leader drinks you're trying to shift.

Timing and exclusivity. Timing is the key to exclusivity. Only offer specials at a certain time of day and on certain days. A good move is to avoid "Happy Hour" altogether. Customers think of this period as cheap and cheerful, but nothing special. Instead, choose to promote your loss leaders at a time when the bar is buzzing, perhaps on a Friday or Saturday evening.

Choose Well Liquors Wisely—Mistakes Can Bankrupt Your Business

Well liquors are probably the most important products in any successful beverage operation. Approximately 50 percent of a typical bar's liquor depletion comes from well liquor. Therefore, how you select, handle and sell these liquors is crucial to the long-term sustainability of your operation. Bear in mind the following:

Avoid supplier "come-ons." Suppliers are always keen to off-load excess stocks of well liquor. Only succumb if you think that you can easily sell the extra volume at a significant profit.

Quality. Consistency and quality of well liquors varies considerably. Two factors are really important when choosing which well liquors to sell: quality and cost. Select well liquors that exactly match the quality expectations of your clientele. If your customers are picky, you cannot skimp on quality. It would cost you too dearly.

Sequence. The traditional liquor sequence (bourbon, whiskey, gin, vodka, rum, tequila), where dark liquors are separated from light liquors, isn't the most cost-effective method of sequencing your well liquor. Try the more modern approach. Alternate light and dark liquors; for example: gin, bourbon, vodka, Scotch, etc. It reduces costly wastage. Bartenders are less likely to mistake one well liquor for another.

Well liquor grade. Match the grade of well liquor to your type of establishment. No need for costly overkill. For example, exclusive clubs may have no choice but to sell predominantly premium brands. Less image-conscious outlets can reduce costs by selling semi-premium or pouring brands.

Chapter 37

Bar Staff Recruitment, Management and Training

Good Staff Is a Business's Greatest Asset—Hire the Best

Any beverage outlet is highly dependent upon the quality of its staff. Employees need to be multi-talented: honest, hardworking, reliable, prepared to work unsociable hours, friendly, polite, and oozing hospitality—a tall order! Be realistic. Rapid expansion within the hospitality sector in recent years has created a flood of new bartender jobs. This means that job seekers are picky about where they work; but so must you, the recruiter, be picky about whom you employ. Avoid the following pitfalls:

Employee rights. Strict federal and state regulations govern employment procedures. Get an attorney to check out your terms of contract and hiring procedures. A vindictive employee (or ex-employee) could cost you dearly.

Recruitment advertisement. There are laws that govern what can and cannot be stated in a recruitment advertisement. Above all, avoid violating discrimination laws regarding sex, age, nationality, and minority groups.

Staff selection. Cut out the cost of advertising in newspapers, etc. One of the best ways to attract new staff is to ask existing bartenders you trust if they know of anyone looking for a job. Their suggestions are likely to be productive.

Incentives. Offer reliable staff an incentive for "recruiting" the right person—say, for example, if they recruit someone who successfully manages to complete his or her first three months on the job.

Shop the competition. Check out the opposition. Watch their bartenders in action. If you like what you see, don't be afraid to offer an incentive to come and work for you. It's human nature to do a good job if you've been "head-hunted."

Ongoing recruitment. Staff turnover in the beverage industry is notoriously high. Save time and money by maintaining an open job application file. Remain alert to recruitment possibilities. Oftentimes, potential employees who approach you are already familiar with your establishment and its clientele. More than likely they will fit in well.

Tips for Reducing Labor Costs

The key to controlling labor costs is to retain a stable, reliable and happy workforce. In today's beverage industry, it's becoming increasingly difficult to recruit and retain a good staff. The cost involved in replacing employees is considerable. This creates a vicious circle. Management needs to allocate sufficient funds for creating desirable working conditions. It must also offer attractive pay packages while at the same time strive to reduce overall operational costs. Focus on the following crucial issues:

Help new employees learn the job. Whatever it takes (advice, training, supervision), make sure that new members of staff are operating at maximum capacity as quickly as possible. So much money is wasted if new recruits don't know what they're supposed to be doing.

Offer a benefits package that is better than the competition. Regard this as a long-term investment. It will reduce staff turnover, thus reducing overall costs. "Extras" don't have to be costly. Consider, for example, additional in-house training or extra vacation time.

Treat all staff as human beings. Recognize and praise their efforts whenever you can. It costs you nothing. What it does is help you to avoid the expense of recruiting and retraining new members of staff.

Tips. Reward exceptional performance with a larger share of the tips. Extra cash in hand is one of the best motivators. A happy employee will remain loyal to your establishment.

How You Train New Employees Can Have a Major Impact on Your Business

No area of management offers greater scope for increased employee productivity and healthy profits than effective training. Forget the assumption that training is expensive; it need not be. Sending your staff away on formal training courses can indeed prove costly, but the best form of training—the training that will really make a difference—can be carried out in-house, at no extra cost. Good first impressions on new employees can really make a difference.

Start training immediately. When a new employee walks through the door, don't keep him or her hanging around. However busy you are, nothing can be more important than making the new recruit feel welcome and enthusiastic about joining the team.

Allocate the function of training to an experienced and trusted member of staff. This works! The trainer feels honored and the trainee feels he or she has someone to turn to with queries, without "bothering" management.

Timing. Choose quiet times to go through the specific routines and requirements of the job. Also, make sure that you have the time to give each new employee an overview of the operation. Productivity improves if employees feel they are more than a cog in a wheel.

The main purpose of cost control is to provide information to management about daily operations. Cost controls are about knowing where you are going. Furthermore, most waste and inefficiencies cannot be seen; they need to be understood through the numbers.

Orientation program. All employees should be given a specific job description, plus information about all the issues that affect their performance. Examples of the latter include information on periodic or annual performance reviews, emergency procedures, disciplinary and grievance procedures, personal conduct issues, work schedule expectations, and availability of additional training.

Training references. If you aren't sure how to go about training, invest in *The Encyclopedia of Restaurant Training*. This manual is an out-of-the box employee training program for all food service positions, including bar and beverage. From orientating the new employee to maintaining performance standards to detailed training outlines and checklists for all positions, this book will show you how to train your employees in all positions in the shortest amount of time. One of the best features of this book is that the companion CD-ROM contains the training outline for all positions in MS Word, so you can easily customize the text. There are numerous training forms, checklists and handouts. There are job descriptions for all positions including General Manager, Kitchen Manager, Server, Dishwasher, Line Cook, Prep Cook, Busperson, Host/Hostess, and Bartender. To order or for more information, visit **www.atlantic-pub.com** or call 1-800-814-1132 (Item # ERT-02 $79,95).

Front-of-the-House Management Tips

Hands-on front-of-the-house management is central to the success of your enterprise. Never underestimate the impact that a skilled floor manager can have on the profitability of your establishment. Sweeping changes aren't necessary; what does make a difference is attention to detail. Have you thought of the following?

Smile. Greet regular customers by name and ask them meaningful questions that make them feel treated as individuals. If one of your regulars is in the hospital, send "Get Well" greetings from the establishment.

Entrance. Make sure the entrance to your establishment is clean and welcoming. Position an interesting feature, such as a sculpture or painting, near the door. It makes a good talking point and sets you apart from the competition.

New customers. Try to meet new customers each shift. Add their names to your customer mailing list. Exchange business cards.

Exceed expectations. Be prepared to help out when it's busy. Take cocktail orders or even help behind the bar with bottle opening, barrel changing, or glass washing.

Impress customers. Ask customers how they'd like their drinks mixed and served. Some have strong preferences for a particular type of glassware. Others are fussy about the balance of dry and sweet ingredients. Demonstrate concern for individual tastes—it's guaranteed to impress!

Lasting impressions. As customers leave, open the door for them. Thank them for coming. Leave them with a favorable impression that makes them want to return.

Pre-shift meeting. A few minutes spent with the bar staff setting goals for the shift is time well spent. Enlist the support of your team. Keep them briefed. Always welcome two-way communication.

Role model. How you react to customers will set a standard for your employees. Lead by example. Customers' impressions of your bar are directly affected by the service they receive from your employees.

Ongoing Training Is One of the Most Effective Ways of Retaining Staff

It is common courtesy to offer your employees ongoing training. It is also crucial to the profitability of your operation. You want to keep good staff and avoid the unnecessary expense of constant recruitment and retraining. Managers who demonstrate a positive attitude about ongoing training are more likely to retain a loyal team of motivated employees.

Plan. Take the time to plan training sessions. Make sure that they are relevant—not just paying lip service to the general notion of training. Time spent planning training sessions is time well spent.

Set times for training. Allocate a set time for ongoing training sessions. Most employees want to do a good job and will look forward to taking part in these fixed, mutually beneficial sessions.

Keep it simple. Ongoing training programs don't have to be complicated. In fact, the simpler, the better. A basic training session could include the following:

1. Trainer chooses either: a) an area of the operation that needs attention; for example, "How to avoid lines of customers building up at the bar," or

b) invites an open discussion about how routine daily procedures could be improved.

2. The trainer must be observed listening to suggestions and acting upon them.

3. The trainers also should use the session as an opportunity to identify individual employee training requirements. A relaxed atmosphere that invites open dialog is essential.

4. After the session, the trainer must address points raised, plus any individual employee training needs. This must be accomplished in as informal and positive manner as possible.

Winning Personal Serving Techniques—Set High Standards

Don't assume that all employees are natural communicators who can instinctively generate an ambiance of generous hospitality. Some can; the majority, however, require clear guidelines. Indeed, most employees prefer to know exactly what's expected of them. As well as insisting that servers greet customers with a pleasant smile, you can suggest several other techniques that can make a big difference. Try the following:

Individual greetings. Servers need to introduce themselves by name, at some point during the greeting. But, to make a really good impression, insist that their first words are not the standard: "Hi, my name is _____. How can I help you?" This type of greeting is far too commonplace. Ask staff to think first, then adopt a more individual approach. Suggest they slip their name into the conversation, towards the end of the greeting. It works!

Personal interest. If a bartender recognizes a "regular," he or she should always address that person by name and engage him or her in conversation about things that are of real interest to that guest.

Let serving staff take the initiative. Give your serving staff a free hand to enhance customer service. After all, they're in a strong position to identify potential problems or areas in which service can be improved. Support their decisions, as far as you can.

Keep personal problems under wraps. An unhappy employee may be tempted to bemoan their lot to a willing listener. Servers should be instructed to hide their problems behind a smile until their shift is over.

Comfort factor. Fine hospitality involves more than leaning on the bar chatting with customers. Guest comfort matters. Small actions, such as removing dirty glasses, cleaning ashtrays, and wiping tables at regular intervals, can significantly enhance customer satisfaction. It encourages guests to linger and spend more money in your establishment.

Balance. Servers need to be told how to strike a balance between attentiveness and neglect. They should be taught when to approach customers to see whether they're ready for the next round of drinks.

Limit damage when ejecting a drunken or abusive patron. Avoid making a scene. Try to calm the aggressor by making a positive gesture. Volunteer to call for a cab. Pour the customer a free cup of coffee or a soft drink—in a quieter area of the establishment. Keep the patron's pride intact.

Practical Tips for Training Bartenders

In practice, training bartenders often can be a haphazard affair: too much advice, too little, or worse: all theory and nothing that is of any practical use to them once they're standing behind the bar with a line of impatient customers waiting to be served. Before you let a new employee loose on your precious customers, make sure that he or she really understands and is competent in the following five main areas:

1. **Cash procedures.** Ensure that all bartenders fully understand and stick to establishment procedures for all money transactions. They must be completely competent at operating the cash register. There is no room for ambiguity of training in this area.

2. **Dispense liquor efficiently.** Train bartenders to use equipment, and familiarize them with how each drink should be prepared.

3. **Bar inventory.** Show them how to record stock, enter details on the perpetual inventory, requisition replacement stock and deal with empties, and where to locate each beverage behind the bar.

4. **Speed.** Make it quite clear that, under normal circumstances, bartenders are expected to pour drinks quickly and in a fixed amount of time. Define times that are appropriate to your establishment.

5. **Cleanliness.** Spell it out. Bartenders must abide by house standards.

Employee Mismanagement Can Bankrupt Your Business

Poor management results in low staff morale, absenteeism, and an increased incidence of internal theft. And that's just for starters! It can also put you out of business, fast. Learn to anticipate potential management problems. Tackle minor issues before they get out of control. Watch out, especially for the following warning signals:

Favoritism. Does the manager appear to be acting unfairly or irrationally towards certain members of staff? Maybe the manager is letting other employees get away with poor time keeping or offering them free drinks, for instance. Inconsistent behavior on the part of management is guaranteed to adversely affect productivity.

Public verbal reprimands. Never tolerate verbal reprimands by management in front of customers or fellow employees. Disciplinary issues should be dealt with in private, at the end of the shift.

Lack of guidance. The business will suffer at the hands of incompetent staff. General morale will also plummet. Hands-on guidance and constructive supervision are essential ingredients of any successful management strategy.

Lack of respect. Managers who show a lack of respect for fellow employees create a negative atmosphere that is detrimental to the smooth running of the establishment. Managers should also categorically avoid making sexual advances towards members of personnel or making derogatory or embarrassing comments about any member of staff.

Lack of support. It is the duty of a manager to acknowledge and praise good performance. He or she is also obliged to resolve any work-related disagreements. Turning a blind eye just won't do.

Bartender Recruitment and Selection Tips

The cost of hiring the wrong bartender can actually cripple your business. Unfortunately, however, even if you put a great deal of thought and preparation into your recruitment plan, it can still go horribly wrong. In practice, selection is really a process of elimination. Rarely is it a case of "Yes, I just know I've chosen the right person!" View recruitment as something of a damage-limitation exercise.

Avoid hasty decisions. Don't rush into replacing a bartender if an existing member of staff leaves suddenly. Recruit in haste; repent at leisure!

Avoid using generic job application forms. Think about what makes your establishment "tick." What types of employees are best at realizing its success? Define candidate requirements accordingly. See Chapter 39 for a restaurant-specific application.

Test applicants' specific knowledge of the beverage industry. For example, can they identify a wide range of spirits? How much do they know about the origins and main characteristics of different wines? Do they know what the minimum drinking age is and what constitutes acceptable forms of identification? In Chapter 39 you will also find an Alcohol Awareness Test. Use this as a screening tool for applicants.

Practical test. Talking to candidates will only get you so far. Take them into the bar and ask them to perform a simple dexterity test, such as pouring a glass of draft beer. Don't expect miracles, but it will give you some indication of their suitability.

Consult existing members of staff. Try to engineer a situation where, at some point during the interview, fellow bartenders can take a sneak preview. It is vitally important that the interviewee fits in with the rest of the team.

Attitude. Ask questions that are likely to expose a candidate's true work ethic. How many hours a week do they need to work (as opposed to want to work)? Also, how much money do they actually need to earn? These types of questions are excellent indicators of future commitment.

Keep Staff Happy—Keep Labor Costs Down

It costs nothing to treat employees with respect and consideration. Treat them as professionals, and they will reward you with loyalty and a sense of commitment. This means, of course, that you won't have to worry so much about the time-consuming and alarmingly expensive business of recruiting and training new staff. Remind yourself, daily, of the following opportunities to maintain a positive and amicable working environment:

Don't raise false hopes. When you offer someone work as a bartender, don't oversell the job or idealize the establishment. This will result only in disillusionment when reality sets in.

Consistent behavior. Working in the beverage industry can often prove stressful for management and bar staff alike. Management, however, must be seen to behave consistently. In particular, make sure that all employees abide by the establishment's policies and set procedures. No one should be allowed to "cut corners." Favoritism leads to overwhelming resentment.

Avoid social involvement. Associating with fellow employees outside working hours ruins your credibility as a manager.

Money talks. The easier you make it for employees to earn more money, the happier they will be and the less likely to move on to another job. Distribute tips as generously as possible. Pay over the odds for extra time worked. It will save you money in the long run and also reduce the temptation for internal theft.

Chapter 38

Other Opportunities to Control Costs in the Beverage Industry

---

The Working Environment—Cunning Cost-Reducing Tips

Take a fresh look at all aspects of your working environment. It's so easy to overlook the obvious when you're preoccupied with the day-to-day details of running a busy beverage operation. There is always room for improvement, in every establishment. The opportunity for reducing costs will surprise you.

Control heating and air-conditioning. Put timers and locks on all thermostats. Make sure that staff cannot override the settings.

Safeguard the CO_2 gas system. Avoid costly accidents (and excess spillage). Equip your gas pressure regulator with a pressure-relief device that is fitted with a release valve. Excess pressure builds up quickly if the equipment is not properly controlled. This can lead to barrels exploding and serious accidents.

Reduce the likelihood of workers' compensation claims. Slip-fall accidents are one of the leading causes of injury in the workplace. Introduce preventive measures, such as rubber mats behind the bar to avoid slipping. Check out **www.griprock.com** for safety mats. Grip Rock and Super G floor mats by Matrix Engineering are durable, long lasting and lightweight.

Also look into safety gadgets for bartenders who have to slice fruit and garnishes, back supports for staff who have to move heavy kegs of beer, etc.

Alarm buttons. Anticipate fights breaking out. Install concealed alarm triggers behind the bar. Have backup management on hand to intervene and recover the situation before any damage is done.

Security guard. Employ a security guard. This is not a major expense. Indeed, a reliable guard is a sound investment. By monitoring people wandering in and out of your establishment, as well as spotting insider theft at all levels, he or she can make a major contribution to keeping costs down.

Extra Cost-Reducing Serving Tips

Service need not suffer. Customer satisfaction remains high. A few well-disguised shortcuts will reduce costs and may, at the same time, improve overall efficiency. Consider the following small changes to your drink serving routines:

Acrylic glassware. Suitability depends on the type of establishment, but you'd be surprised at the number of establishments where acrylic glassware is perfectly acceptable. In fact, it is often preferable at outdoor outlets such as sports venues. It doesn't break and it's cheaper. Also, customers are not as tempted to steal "disposable" glasses.

Premix Bloody Marys. It's too time consuming to make your own. Consistency can be an issue if different bartenders don't stick to the recipe. Buy Bloody Marys premixed. The quality is every bit as good.

Garnishes. In a time warp? Go for cheaper fruit that's in season. Or, review bulk-buying less expensive yet more eye-catching decorative flags, etc.

Frozen drinks. Reduce the amount of liquor in frozen drinks. The law doesn't specify that the liquor content be 1 ounce or 1¼ ounces. The choice is yours.

Mixers. Use off-brand mixers, such as lime juice and grenadine.

Draft beers. Spillage is extremely high for draft beers. Introduce ounce-counting technology; make it a priority.

Extra Cost-Reducing Staffing Tips

It may, at first, seem hard to save on staffing costs, but in the interests of long-term survival, you have no choice. Only the owner or manager sees the overall picture and can make these decisions. After all, your employees want to be in a job this time next year!

Unpaid breaks. Employment law requires that employers must give their employees a 30-minute break after a continuous 4-hour shift. But what is not so commonly known is that employers are not obliged to pay for this break.

Smoking. Smoking breaks definitely should be unpaid. They add up over the course of a shift. What's more, non-smoking employees harbor resentment for this break privilege, particularly if it's paid.

Daily labor costs. Review labor costs daily and for each shift. Send employees home early if business is quiet.

Staff leasing. Consider the benefits of leasing your employees from a staff leasing company. It offers you flexibility and significant savings on your annual workers' compensation premium and unemployment compensation rate. Staff leasing companies will also do your payroll and carry out most human resources functions for you. Employees also benefit with realistic medical insurance, for instance. Everyone wins.

Dispensing Draft Beer—Cost-Reducing Tips

No beverage offers greater potential for wastage and spillage than draft beer. The opportunities to cut costs in this area are, therefore, considerable. Consider the following facts: Draft beer pours at 2 ounces per second. Cost varies between approximately 2.5 cents and 8 cents per ounce, depending upon brand and beverage outlet. Therefore, using a 10-ounce glass, a spillage or over-pour of 10 percent will occur in just half a second or less. Multiply this in terms of lost income. Worrying? These suggestions will help you recover the situation:

Practical evaluation. First, get some facts. Measure how much draft beer is served in your glasses and pitchers. Count how many kegs you purchase weekly. Calculate how much beer you actually sell during the same period. The difference will surprise you.

Install a flow meter. It measures the exact amount of beer served in each glass, mug or pitcher. It also records the amount of beer poured at each draft tap during each shift. Visit **www.berg-controls.com**.

Use the flow meter report at the end of each shift. Identify problems immediately. Reduce your pour costs and maximize your profits simultaneously.

Install an empty beer keg detector. These detectors will automatically shut down the line when a keg is empty, keeping beer in the line while a new keg is hooked up, thus preventing excess loss of draft beer.

Shop the Opposition

Call it market research. Shopping the opposition is one of the cheapest and best ways of working out a marketing strategy for your operation. However, successful "shopping" involves more than copying your competitors' ideas. You need to be realistic. Take an objective look at your own operation. Ask yourself where exactly you should position yourself in relation to your direct competition. How do customers perceive your respective businesses? Identify your market position.

Enter a competitor's establishment and sit at the bar. Listen to the regulars, particularly those "bar hoppers" who like to think they're an authority on every bar in the neighborhood. They'll give you all the information you need—and more!

Shop on a regular basis. After all, you do want a representative sample, and you need to keep up to date. Remember, the beverage industry can be very fickle; bars go in and out of favor all the time.

Don't be sneaky. When you get a chance, introduce yourself as the manager from down the road. Compliment their establishment. Be positive. The "Mr. Nice Guy" approach works better long-term. You also may attract some new customers to your establishment—or even find their good bartenders knocking on your door for a job!

Key information. When shopping the competition, look out for the following:

- **Stock.** What quality liquor do they carry in the well: pouring, call or premium? Do they carry anything you don't? What beer labels do they offer? What is their house wine?

- **Pricing.** From highballs to beer to wine—you need to know.

- **Marketing.** What sorts of promotions are they running? Do they sell a popular product that you don't?

- **Ambiance.** Note the background music, the seating arrangements, and the lighting. Do they offer entertainment? If so, what type?

- **Staff.** Do they appear better trained and motivated?

- **Glassware and portions**. How do they dispense alcohol: automatic or free-pour? How big are their wine portions? Do they use beer pitchers? If so, what size?

Banquet Beverages—Tips for Reducing Costs but Not Quality

The main type of alcoholic beverage sold at banquets is bottled wine, and there's a lot you can do to maximize profits in this area, without lowering standards. The usual format involves a fixed number of bottles placed on each table. The host/customer then pays for the total number of bottles opened by the end of the banquet. Here are a few suggestions for reducing costs:

Improve stock control. Stick to a "fixed number of bottles" agreement. Some hosts prefer to offer payment per glass, but this method is best avoided, if possible. The "total bottles" approach gives both you and the customer better control of the situation.

Reduce staffing costs. Encourage the guests to pour their own wine at the table. It appears more generous toward the guests. It also saves on staffing costs.

Champagne toasts. If a champagne toast is called for, and the host has no strong views on the matter, serve a quality sparkling wine instead. Despite being a cheaper product, the scope for heftier markups is there for the taking. Also, the perceived quality of a top-of-the-range sparkling wine is far superior to mediocre champagne. Some of the best sparkling whites today are being produced by subsidiaries of champagne producers.

Cash bar. Most banquets operate a cash bar, where patrons can purchase additional drinks. To prevent theft, have a separate cashier station that handles money and distributes tickets for drinks. Make sure that the cashier is not close to the bar, to prevent collusion between employees.

Market Your New Bar—Profit-Boosting Tips

Don't feel you've got to throw big bucks into marketing your new bar. It can be achieved on a shoestring. Careful planning and a dash of inspiration are all that's required. Also, after the initial promotion, it's important to keep up the good work. Seize every opportunity to market your establishment. View marketing as an essential part of your ongoing business strategy.

Image. Concentrate on projecting a distinct image for your bar. Choose a simple eye-catching logo. Perhaps design the logo yourself. Use a home computer to print out your menus and table tent promotions, with the logo emblazoned at the head.

Promote yourself as proprietor. Make people want to drink at your bar. Involve yourself in your neighborhood community. Support local charities. Join the local chamber of commerce.

Pre-opening publicity. Organize a pre-opening get-together. Invite all those people you think can add to the long-term success of your operation: suppliers, competitors, local business persons, civic leaders, etc. It is so important that they are the first to enjoy what your establishment has to offer.

Teaser campaign. About six weeks before you open, introduce billboards, banners or bumper stickers with a hint at something exciting about to happen. For example, "JUMPIN' JACKS IS COMING...SOON!"

Press release. Write your own press release, or get someone clever with words to write it for you. Send it to the local newspaper. Call the newspaper's publicity department as the official opening date approaches and remind them that you're about to open this exciting new venture. It's worth being pushy just to get all this free publicity.

Professional Web site. An attractive Web site is an excellent promotional tool. Consult the professionals. Try The House of Blues: **www.houseofblues.com**, or Hooters: **www.hooters.com**. Both can point you in the right direction. Also, how about using your Web site to boost sales by merchandising your in-house products? Use your Web site to give directions, build a mailing list, and post employee schedules.

Signage. Get noticed. Neon signage is guaranteed to do the job. Contact your suppliers; they may be prepared to help out in exchange for you promoting their products.

Tips for Streamlining Your Bar Par Procedures

An accurate and well-maintained bar par is at the heart of any successful beverage operation. Discrepancies or sloppy management in this area and your business is doomed. Consider the following suggestions:

"Sheet-to-shelf." Arrange bottles behind the bar in the same order as they appear on the liquor requisition form and the monthly inventory form. This approach is both time and cost effective.

Triplicate bar par record sheets. Record bar par totals on a triplicate record set. Keep one copy behind the bar, one in the beverage storeroom, and one in the manager's storeroom. This is not overkill. It makes it much easier to resolve disputes and discrepancies at a later date.

One shift at a time. Ideally, keep sufficient full bottles behind the bar to last you for one shift. If, in practice, this isn't feasible, make sure that no more than one day's worth of stock is stored behind the bar.

Weekly pouring cost inventory. Check your pouring costs (PCs) weekly. It helps reduce costs by maintaining tight bar par controls. Simply total the cost value of your requisitions for the week and then divide this figure by total liquor sales for the week. The difference should be no greater than 1.5 percent of normal monthly PCs.

Counting empty bottles. Ask bartenders to place all their empties on top of the bar at the end of each shift. It's the quickest and easiest way to see if bar and requisition totals tally.

Encourage Bartenders to Do More Than Serve

You've trained your bar staff; they know what drinks to serve and how to serve them. They even know quite a lot about the product. Why not put this knowledge to good use? Encourage your bartenders to do more than answer customer queries about products and serve them. Train employees to adopt a "suggest sale" approach. It will boost profits instantly.

Offer incentives. Reward staff that actively sell your products with whatever you know they would appreciate—perhaps better shifts or a small raise.

New products. Suggest that bartenders promote new products with lead-in questions, such as: "Would you be interested in trying our special house wine/recipe/draft beer?"

Get bar staff to up-sell liquor. If a customer orders a highball, try to channel him or her in the direction of a premium brand label. For example, if the customer requests a gin and tonic, the bartender could reply, "Would that be Gordon's, sir/madam?"

Product knowledge. Encourage bartenders to use their product knowledge. Customers enjoy discussing the merits of the drink that they have just ordered. A little reinforcement that they've made a wise decision goes a long way towards generating repeat sales.

Surprise Your Customers with New Ideas on a Regular Basis

The element of surprise can work wonders. Customers like to know that you're always keen to welcome them through your doors. But, above all, they appreciate your attention to detail and the fact that you want to please. Novelty is always good for profitability. Subtlety, however, is the key. Keep "surprises" simple, and don't let them intrude upon the general ambiance of your establishment.

Inspiration. Always be on the lookout for new ideas that will keep you on top of current trends and promotions. Attend trade shows where they have useful seminars on a wide range of topics related to the beverage industry. For example, the National Licensed Beverage Association holds annual conventions in about twenty states; for further information, contact the NLBA at 800-441-9894.

VIP cards. Convert one-off customers to regulars. VIP membership cards aren't expensive to produce in bulk. Invest in the magnetic strip version. Apart from bringing in extra revenue, they can provide you with the information to set up a mailing system—a real win-win situation.

Jukebox. Tried and tested, the jukebox appeals to a wide range of clientele. It also brings in the crowds. A word of warning, though: avoid the "package" type of jukebox, where the machine comes prestacked with music supplied by a vendor. Make your own selection. Fill it with discs that you know your customers will enjoy.

Posters. You can easily change your bar décor with posters. Beer and alcohol companies frequently distribute posters, so rotate on a continual basis. Other posters will help you sell new and different drinks. Check out Atlantic Publishing's alcohol service poster series. Decorative and instructional, these posters will be popular with both your employees and customers. Containing essential information, drink photos, recipes and more, they will help increase sales and grab attention. The series consists of seven posters; all are laminated to reduce wear and tear and measure 11" x 17". Visit **www.atlantic-pub.com** or call 1-800-814-1132 (Item # ASP-PS, $59.95).

Darts. If you have the space, consider introducing a new-technology version of the old favorite pub game: the dartboard. Coin-operated dart systems are becoming increasingly popular nowadays. Introduce a darts tournament on a slack night.

Pool table. Install a pool table

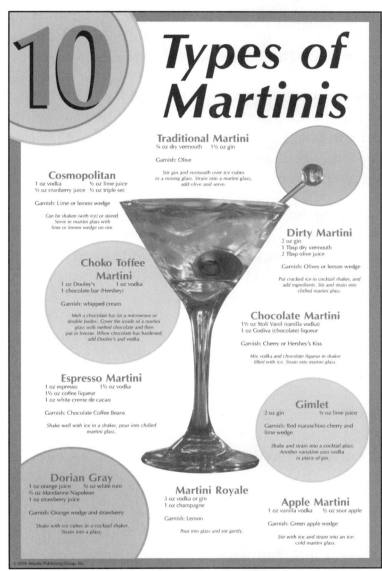

Above is the "10 types of Martinis" poster, complete with recipes. This poster is one of a seven-part series from Atlantic Publishing. Other posters include 12 Classic Cocktails with Recipes, 12 Popular Cocktails with Recipes, Types of Beer, Categories of Liquor, Drink Garnishes, and Common Bar Abbreviations. Posters are $9.95 each or $59.95 for the set. A wine posters series is also available.

in a back-room bar. As with darts, pool never goes out of fashion. Better still, it is likely to draw a faithful crowd who will become regular drinkers at your establishment. After the initial investment, pool tables are easy to maintain and don't need regular updating.

Coin-operated entertainment. Introduce a couple of profit-based coin-operated machines. It costs you nothing. All suppliers require is a share of the profit. Not bad, considering you don't have to shell out on installation or maintenance costs.

Floater liquors and glass giveaways. Introduce specialty drinks with novelty giveaway glasses (if you can strike a good deal). For example, have a frozen drink promotion, where you add a half shot as a float of liquor on top of the drink, for a small extra charge of, say, $1.50.

Bar snack "nibblers." Create a few simple and inexpensive snack dishes to complement whatever drinks are on promotion. Arrange them in small bowls on the bar; for example: German "wurst" with Beck's Dark beer, or olives with a simple Italian "Vino Da Tavola." Tip: Keep the bowls small—customers won't want to appear greedy in company!

Vending machines with a difference. Focus on your customer requirements. Is there any extra product they would appreciate apart from the usual vending machine offerings? Consider additional lines of toiletries, antacids, aspirins, breath mints—whatever you think would appeal. Try harder to please your regular patrons.

Staff uniforms. Alternate the color of their shirts on a regular basis. Customers will notice. Or use giveaway promotional T-shirts to promote whatever drinks you're trying to sell!

New items. Have a "new item" section on the menu that changes every week, without fail. Build up such an impressive repertoire of "new" ideas that eventually you'll be able to "recycle" the "new" ideas without anyone noticing!

Streamline Bar Layout

A well-designed and compact bar will directly affect bartender productivity. If the layout of the workstation is carefully planned, bartenders will be able to function to maximum capacity, saving time and money that could be better deployed in other areas of your establishment. Here are a few suggestions to make the bartender's life a lot easier:

SAMPLE BAR LAYOUT

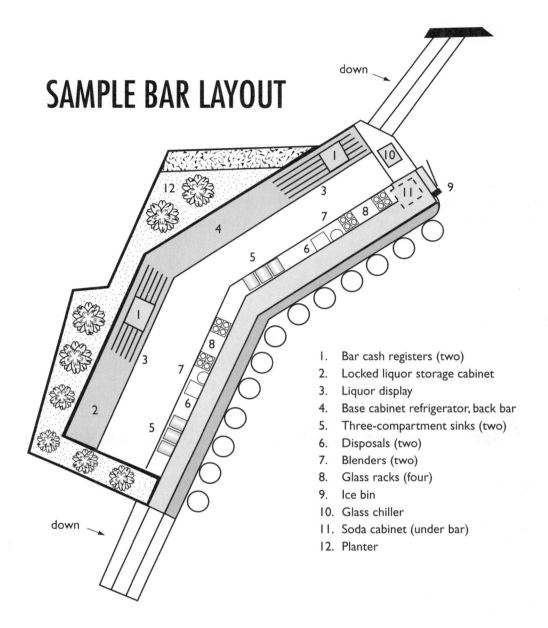

1. Bar cash registers (two)
2. Locked liquor storage cabinet
3. Liquor display
4. Base cabinet refrigerator, back bar
5. Three-compartment sinks (two)
6. Disposals (two)
7. Blenders (two)
8. Glass racks (four)
9. Ice bin
10. Glass chiller
11. Soda cabinet (under bar)
12. Planter

Position of ingredients. Every ingredient required to fulfill a drinks order should be located within a 6-foot radius of the bartender's position in front of the workstation. This 6-foot radius represents a step and an arm's reach.

Effective use of space. Equipment should be positioned so that the bartender is able to complete the drinks order with the least number of actions. Wasted movements mean wasted time and profits.

Well liquor. Place well liquors in a "speed rack" mounted to the front of the workstation. Easy access is essential.

Premium liquors and liqueurs. Position these high-margin drinks where they are clearly visible and enticing to customers, but, at the same time, away from the immediate serving area of the busy bartender. A good location is on the back bar at approximately 42 inches above bar level.

Shelving. Display-case shelves should be wide enough to accommodate bottles two-deep. Design shelves that are between 12- and 16-inches deep. This will make the most of the available storage space behind the bar.

Minimize "cross-handed" actions. As most employees are right-handed, position glasses to the left of the bar. Right-handed bartenders will instinctively reach for the bottle with their right hand and the glass with their left.

Glassware. Glassware should be stored to the left of the workstation, with the most frequently used glasses within easy bartender reach.

Lighting. Adequate lighting is essential for accurate drink making. A good idea is to fix fluorescent strip lighting just beneath the bar top.

Sales Are Slumping, Trade Is Dwindling—What Do You Do Next?

You can't quite put your finger on it. You've investigated all the obvious possibilities—bar pars, perpetual inventory, stockroom, security, labor costs, purchasing levels, stock rotation, wastage, thieving, etc., but you're still none the wiser? Oftentimes, the answer lies in that almost-intangible element of "quality, superior service." Take a another look at the following aspects of your operation and ask yourself the following questions. Be honest. Small changes can make a big difference.

Product knowledge. Do you genuinely know everything about every product that you sell in your establishment? If you don't, what hope can you have for front-of-the-house servers?

Attention and recognition. Are your bartenders in a rut? Do they serve customers with the appearance of being on "auto pilot"? Do they attach greater importance to making the drink than tending to the customer? Easily done in a busy bar, but customers who are treated like numbers will take their trade elsewhere.

Up-selling. Are all your bartenders fully trained to up-sell routinely, not just for promotional drinks? "Suggestive selling" should be second nature to all servers and management alike—at all times.

Make the most of new customers. Do bartenders spend too much time talking either to each other or to a handful of regulars and simply ignore the "untapped" potential of new guests?

Environment. Are your employees exhibiting sloppy habits in front of customers? For example, do they eat, smoke or chat noisily amongst themselves in front of guests?

Encourage patrons to linger longer. Turn negative into positive. A simple move that works well is to make sure that staff ask customers the right questions. For example, instead of "Would you like the bill?" direct employees to ask, "May I get you another round of (whatever the customers happen to be drinking)?"

Headset communication. In a busy bar or club, consider issuing serving staff radio headsets. They can be great time savers for both staff and customers. Also, the equipment will not seem obtrusive in a large, noisy environment.

Negative image. Are the restrooms clean? If they are unhygienic, customers can boycott your establishment for that reason alone. Also, are intoxicated customers or potential fights anticipated and dealt with as quickly as possible? No one feels comfortable drinking in an unpleasant environment.

Provide Internet access. Install an Internet terminal in a quiet area of your bar. Keep it separate from the main floor but close enough to the bar so that customers will be tempted to combine business with pleasure. If your establishment already has the infrastructure for Internet access, the cost of an additional terminal or two will be negligible. For further information, contact KIS at 303-466-5471; **www.kis-kiosk.com**.

ATM. Install an ATM. Encourage customers to linger in your establishment. You don't want them to leave early simply because they're short on cash. Also, keep customers happy; avoid the types of machines that charge a nominal transaction fee.

Top Ten Tips for Increasing Tips

Take a proactive approach to the business of tips. After all, it's in the establishment's best interest to encourage customers to tip servers more generously. Unfortunately, most managers are too busy controlling tips and trying to prevent thieving to consider tipping an area of great opportunity. Think again. Here are ten ways in which employees can increase their income. Staff will thank you for it—and so will your accountant!

1. **Cash in on ambiance.** Serve drinks in as relaxing and comfortable an environment as possible. Persuade your servers that it's in their best interest to pander openly to customers. A relaxed customer is a generous customer.

2. **Greet customers by name.** It makes guests feel important, particularly if they are accompanied by a group of potential new customers. Guests who feel special will repay your establishment by tipping generously. Everybody's happy!

3. **Anticipation.** Train servers to anticipate customers' needs. Customers shouldn't have to hang around waiting to order that next round of drinks.

4. **Celebrations.** Offer regulars, or even new customers, a free drink if you find out that it's their birthday. It's a good move for encouraging loyalty.

5. **Make change in a combination of denominations.** For example, if the required change is $5, never hand over a $5 bill. Break the change down into four
one-dollar bills and four quarters. It can really make a difference in the size of the tip.

6. **Hand over change in a certain order.** First, hand over the coins and then place the bills on top. The customer is likely to remove the last bill placed in his hand or on the table and use it as a tip instead of the coins.

7. **Take tips as they're offered.** For example, a customer may place a tip on the table as soon as the server delivers the first round of drinks. If the tip is not removed immediately, with a gracious "thank you," the next round may well go un-tipped.

8. **Attentiveness.** Open a packet of cigarettes for a customer or even offer to light the first cigarette.

9. **Overpayment.** If a customer overpays by mistake, the server should point out the overpayment immediately. Honesty is always the best policy, and your establishment will reap the long-term dividends.

10. **Lost property.** If a customer leaves any personal item of value behind in the bar, do everything you can to reunite the customer with his or her mislaid property as quickly as possible. Simply putting the item aside for

safekeeping isn't good enough. You want to show you care. A hefty tip is the likely outcome.

Additional Bar Equipment That Will Help Reduce Costs

As well as the many computerized total control packages specifically designed to control costs in the beverage industry, there are a number of other useful tools available. The following are well worth considering:

Automated liquor dispensers. Equipment such as the Raymaster Pro 100, can measure, count and report on up to 100 different brands of liquor.

Cost-analysis spreadsheets. "The Calculators," for example, is a package in spreadsheet format that can speed up cost analysis in your bar. It runs under Microsoft Excel and can tackle tasks such as potential profit and loss and return-on-investment calculations.

Gun systems. A number of manufacturers offer "gun systems." They feature handheld guns that can handle up to 48 different brands and 16 premixed cocktails. With these systems, the bartender need never touch a bottle! For additional information, refer to **www.easybar.com** or **www.wunderbar.com**.

Vita-Mix blenders. These machines make great-tasting frozen drinks—fast. The bartender can preset the time that the blender runs, so a consistent drink is produced every time. Visit **www.vita-mix.com** for more details.

Portion-control pour spouts. Available in several shot sizes, they control liquor portion size. A sensible compromise between "free pour" and "shot glass" for bars where customers expect free-pouring. The market leader is Posi-Pour (see **www .atlantic-pub.com**).

No beverage offers greater potential for wastage and spillage than draft beer. The opportunities to cut costs in this area are, therefore, considerable.

Chapter 39

Essential Cost-Cutting and Time-Saving Forms

Food Service Employment Application 473

Employee Performance Evaluation Form 475

Customer Comment Form 476

Restaurant Shopper's Report 477

Dining Room Safety Inspection Form 486

Perpetual Inventory Form 487

Sign-Out Sheet 488

Daily Preparation Form 489

Minimum Amount Needed Form 490

Daily Yields Form 491

Cashier's Report Form 492

Ticket Issuance Form 493

Cook's Form 494

Ticket Itemization Form 495

Want Sheet 496

Standard Recipe Card A 497

Standard Recipe Card B 498

Standard Recipe Card C 499

Cooking Yield Chart 500

Ingredient Substitutions 501

Standard Portion Sizes 503

Meat Count Form 504

Thaw Pull Chart 505

Prep Chart 506

Prep Sheet 507

Spoilage Report 508

Food Mishap Report 509

Attainable Food Cost 510
Food Cost Calculator 511
Product Request Log.. 512
Event Food Production & Portion Control Form ... 513
Daily Production Report....................................... 514
Bid Sheet... 515
Dishroom Equipment Layout 516
Detailed Layout of Kitchen Equipment................. 517
Bar Terminology 518
Beverage-Specific Garnishes 519
Beverage Recipes Card.. 520
Wine Terminology 521
Alcohol Awareness.. 522
Alcohol Awareness Test 524
Alcohol Awareness Test Answer Key 526
Service Refusal Form 528
Liquor Requisition 529
Beverage Perpetual Inventory............................. 530
Bottled Beer Count Form..................................... 531
Bartender's Report.. 532
Liquor Inventory Form... 533
Liquor Order Form 534
Liquor/Wine Inventory Form 535
Beverage Consumption Report............................. 536
Pour Cost Chart 537
Commonly Used Costing Formulas 538
Sales Forecast Work Sheet.................................. 539
Operational Budget Form 540
Performance to Budget Summary 541
Break-Even Cost Analysis.................................... 542
Materials Cost Projection Form........................... 543
Operational Supplies Cost Projection Form.......... 544
Cashier's Report II.. 545
Cashier's Log.. 546
Change Funds 547
Cash Turn-In Report 548
Check Log... 549
Guest Check Record 550
Payroll Budget Estimate 551
Employee Turnover Rate & Cost Chart 552

Food Service Employment Application

Notice to Applicant: We are an Equal Opportunity Employer and do not discriminate on the basis of applicant's race, color, religion, sex, national origin, citizenship, age, physical or mental disability or any other characteristic.

PERSONAL INFORMATION (please print)

Name: _____ Social Security Number: _____

Address: _____

_____

_____

City: _____ State: _____ Zip: _____

Phone Number: _____

POSITION INFORMATION

Position applied for (check all that apply):

❑ Executive Chef   ❑ Expediter   ❑ Assistant Manager
❑ Host/Hostess   ❑ Baker   ❑ Kitchen Manager
❑ Banquet Manager   ❑ Prep Cook   ❑ Bartender
❑ Pantry Cook   ❑ Beverage Manager   ❑ Server
❑ Busperson   ❑ Cashier   ❑ Cocktail Server
❑ Cook   ❑ Counter Person   ❑ Dining Room Manager

❑ Other _____

Have you ever worked for this organization: ❑ Yes ❑ No

If yes, date(s): _____

Prior position: _____

Reason(s) for leaving: _____

_____

_____

EDUCATION (List from present to past)

School/Institution	Major or Area of Study	Degree or Number of Years

OTHER INFORMATION

Name of friends and/or relatives employed by this organization:_____

_____

Position(s) held: _____

_____

If you are eligible, are you interested in health insurance? ❏ Yes ❏ No

AWARDS/ACHIEVEMENTS

_____

_____

_____

_____

REFERENCES *(Please list at least three people who are not related to you)*

Name	Occupation	Phone Number

EMERGENCY CONTACT *In the event of an emergency, who should we contact?*

Name: _____ Relationship to applicant: _____

Address: _____

City:_____ State: _____ Zip: _____

Phone Number:_____

ACKNOWLEDGMENT *(please read carefully)*

I hereby certify that the information contained in this application form and in any attachments (hereafter made a part of this application) is true and correct to the best of my knowledge and agree to have any of the statements checked by the organization unless I have indicated to the contrary. I authorize the references listed above to provide the company any and all information concerning my previous employment and any pertinent information that they may have. Further, I release all parties and persons from any and all liability for any damages that may result from furnishing such information to the company as well as from the use or disclosure of such information by the organization or any of its agents, employees or representatives. I understand that any misrepresentation, falsification or material omission of information on this application may result in my failure to receive an offer or, if I am hired, in my dismissal from employment.

Applicant's Signature _____ **Date** _____

Employee Performance Evaluation Form

Name: _____ Position: _____

Interviewer: _____ Date: _____

Last Evaluation Date: _____ Current Salary: _____

For each of the following categories, grade the employee's performance on a sliding scale of 1 to 10 (see scale below). The overall grade is the average of all scores plus the interviewer's comments.

1-2 poor   3-4 below average   5 average   6-7 above average   8-9 very good   10 exceptional

1. **KNOWLEDGE OF JOB** procedures, paperwork, skill, function   1 2 3 4 5 6 7 8 9 10
   Comments: _____
   _____

2. **QUALITY** up to specification, accuracy, consistency   1 2 3 4 5 6 7 8 9 10
   Comments: _____
   _____

3. **ATTITUDE** towards work, management, other employees, customers   1 2 3 4 5 6 7 8 9 10
   Comments: _____
   _____

4. **LEADERSHIP** ability to give direction   1 2 3 4 5 6 7 8 9 10
   Comments: _____
   _____

5. **RELIABILITY** dependable, on time, follows through on assignments   1 2 3 4 5 6 7 8 9 10
   Comments: _____
   _____

6. **PRODUCTIVITY** volume, utilization of time   1 2 3 4 5 6 7 8 9 10
   Comments: _____
   _____

7. **APPEARANCE** uniform, neat   1 2 3 4 5 6 7 8 9 10
   Comments: _____
   _____

8. **SERVICE** alert, fast   1 2 3 4 5 6 7 8 9 10
   Comments: _____
   _____

OVERALL RATING: _____ / 80

SALARY ADJUSTED: ❑ YES ❑ NO   **NEW SALARY:** _____

Signature of reviewer: _____

Customer Comment Form

Prepared By: _____ Position: _____

Day: Sunday Monday Tuesday Wednesday Thursday Friday Saturday

Date: _____ Shift: _____ Manager: _____

SERVICE	FOOD	FACILITY
Comments heard:	Comments heard:	Comments heard:
Guest's name (if known):	Guest's name (if known):	Guest's name (if known):
Overall, comments were: ❑ positive ❑ negative ❑ neutral	Overall, comments were: ❑ positive ❑ negative ❑ neutral	Overall, comments were: ❑ positive ❑ negative ❑ neutral

Restaurant Shopper's Report

RESERVATION PROCESS

The telephone call to make the reservation was answered within three rings.   ❏ Yes   ❏ No

The employee answering the phone was pleasant, identified himself/herself and the restaurant.   ❏ Yes   ❏ No

The employee taking the reservation was courteous, repeated your reservation information and thanked you.   ❏ Yes   ❏ No

The employee taking the reservation was knowledgeable, helpful and able to answer any questions (e.g., directions to restaurant).   ❏ Yes   ❏ No

Additional Notes: _____

_____

_____

_____

_____

RESTAURANT EXTERIOR

The restaurant's sign was easily seen from a distance, easy to read, and in good condition.   ❏ Yes   ❏ No

The restaurant's parking lot and grounds were free of debris and well-maintained.   ❏ Yes   ❏ No

The area around the dining room was landscaped and well-lit.   ❏ Yes   ❏ No

The restaurant had adequate parking.   ❏ Yes   ❏ No

Additional Notes: _____

_____

_____

_____

_____

ARRIVAL & SEATING

You were greeted quickly upon entering.   ❏ Yes   ❏ No

The host/hostess was appropriately dressed, smiling and pleasant.   ❏ Yes   ❏ No

The host/hostess asked your smoking preference.   ❏ Yes   ❏ No

You were seated within a reasonable time.   ❏ Yes   ❏ No

The lounge was offered as an alternative if you had to wait for your table.	❏ Yes	❏ No
The booths and tables were not crowded and easily accessible.	❏ Yes	❏ No
The table or booth was comfortable and appropriate for your party.	❏ Yes	❏ No
The host/hostess distributed menus for each guest and they were easily within reach.	❏ Yes	❏ No
The host/hostess informed you of specials.	❏ Yes	❏ No
The host/hostess told you the server's name.	❏ Yes	❏ No
The host/hostess had a pleasant demeanor and treated you graciously.	❏ Yes	❏ No

Additional Notes: _____

_____

_____

_____

_____

MENU

The menu was in good, clean condition.	❏ Yes	❏ No
The menu matched the restaurant's theme.	❏ Yes	❏ No
The menu size was physically easy to handle.	❏ Yes	❏ No
Available specials were listed prominently or separately.	❏ Yes	❏ No
The menu was well-organized, with selections grouped in an easy-to-read and easy-to-find manner.	❏ Yes	❏ No
The type on the menu was easy to read.	❏ Yes	❏ No
The number of selections was appropriate.	❏ Yes	❏ No
Appetizing descriptions were provided for menu items.	❏ Yes	❏ No
The menu had complete descriptions of side orders included or offered for each item.	❏ Yes	❏ No
The menu offered additional information as a marketing tool.	❏ Yes	❏ No
Vegetarian portions were offered.	❏ Yes	❏ No
Children's portions were offered.	❏ Yes	❏ No

Senior citizens' portions were offered. ❏ Yes ❏ No

Additional Notes: _____

_____

_____

_____

WAITSTAFF

The waiter's or waitress's uniform was clean and attractive.	❏ Yes	❏ No
The waiter's or waitress's hands and fingernails were clean.	❏ Yes	❏ No
The waiter or waitress approached your table within three minutes after being seated.	❏ Yes	❏ No
The waiter or waitress greeted you pleasantly and introduced himself or herself.	❏ Yes	❏ No
The waiter or waitress smiled, was cordial, and created a genial atmosphere.	❏ Yes	❏ No
The waiter or waitress was familiar with the menu and able to answer questions.	❏ Yes	❏ No
The waiter or waitress used suggestive selling techniques, such as offering appetizers, in a friendly and non-offensive manner.	❏ Yes	❏ No
The waiter or waitress served beverage items promptly and from the left.	❏ Yes	❏ No
The waiter or waitress served food items in a timely manner and from the left.	❏ Yes	❏ No
The timing between courses was well-spaced.	❏ Yes	❏ No
The waiter or waitress knew each guest's selections and served them correctly.	❏ Yes	❏ No
The waiter or waitress returned to the table to check on satisfaction and provide additional service after the main course arrived.	❏ Yes	❏ No
It was not necessary to summon the waiter or waitress during the meal.	❏ Yes	❏ No
The waiter or waitress was attentive to guests' needs during the meal.	❏ Yes	❏ No
The waiter or waitress seemed to enjoy their job.	❏ Yes	❏ No
Overall, the waiter or waitress did a good job.	❏ Yes	❏ No

Additional Notes: _____

_____

_____

BUS STAFF

The busperson provided water quickly after being seated.	❑ Yes	❑ No
The busperson made sure water glasses were refilled promptly.	❑ Yes	❑ No
The busperson was responsive to any service requests.	❑ Yes	❑ No
The busperson removed dirty dishes quickly, so they were not left sitting on the table after being emptied.	❑ Yes	❑ No
The busperson removed dirty dishes from the right.	❑ Yes	❑ No
The busperson removed dirty ashtrays properly and replaced them quickly.	❑ Yes	❑ No
The busperson was polite and courteous.	❑ Yes	❑ No
The busperson was presentable, clean and well-groomed.	❑ Yes	❑ No
The busperson's uniform was clean and attractive.	❑ Yes	❑ No
The busperson did a good job, and service was not disruptive.	❑ Yes	❑ No

Additional Notes: _____

_____

_____

_____

_____

FOOD

Food matched its menu description.	❑ Yes	❑ No
All items ordered were available.	❑ Yes	❑ No

Appetizer

Please list appetizer(s) ordered: _____

_____

_____

Please rate overall appetizer quality:	❑ Excellent	❑ Good	❑ Fair	❑ Poor
Appetizing appearance		❑ Yes	❑ No	
Proper temperature (hot items hot, cold items cold)		❑ Yes	❑ No	
Tasted good		❑ Yes	❑ No	

Soup

Please list soup(s) ordered: _____

_____

Please rate overall soup quality:	❏ Excellent	❏ Good	❏ Fair	❏ Poor
Appetizing appearance			❏ Yes	❏ No
Proper temperature (hot items hot, cold items cold)			❏ Yes	❏ No
Tasted good			❏ Yes	❏ No

Bread

Please list type of bread(s) ordered: _____

_____

Please rate overall bread quality:	❏ Excellent	❏ Good	❏ Fair	❏ Poor
Appetizing appearance			❏ Yes	❏ No
Proper temperature (hot items hot, cold items cold)			❏ Yes	❏ No
Tasted good			❏ Yes	❏ No

Salad

Please list type of salad(s) ordered: _____

_____

Please rate overall salad quality:	❏ Excellent	❏ Good	❏ Fair	❏ Poor
Appetizing appearance			❏ Yes	❏ No
Proper temperature (hot items hot, cold items cold)			❏ Yes	❏ No
Tasted good			❏ Yes	❏ No
Dressing choices adequate			❏ Yes	❏ No
Dressing amount correct			❏ Yes	❏ No

Entrée

Please list entrée(s) ordered: _____

_____

_____

_____

Please rate overall entrée quality:	❏ Excellent	❏ Good	❏ Fair	❏ Poor
Appetizing appearance			❏ Yes	❏ No
Proper temperature (hot items hot, cold items cold)			❏ Yes	❏ No
Tasted good			❏ Yes	❏ No
Portions appropriate			❏ Yes	❏ No

Side Orders

Please list side order(s) ordered: _____

_____

Please rate overall side orders quality: ❏ Excellent	❏ Good	❏ Fair	❏ Poor

Appetizing appearance   ❏ Yes ❏ No

Proper temperature (hot items hot, cold items cold)   ❏ Yes ❏ No

Tasted good   ❏ Yes ❏ No

Portions appropriate   ❏ Yes ❏ No

Dessert

Please list dessert(s) ordered: _____

_____

Please rate overall dessert quality: ❏ Excellent ❏ Good ❏ Fair ❏ Poor

Appetizing appearance   ❏ Yes ❏ No

Proper temperature (hot items hot, cold items cold)   ❏ Yes ❏ No

Tasted good   ❏ Yes ❏ No

Portions appropriate   ❏ Yes ❏ No

Additional Notes: _____

_____

_____

DINING AMBIANCE

Noise level in dining room is not too loud.	❏ Yes	❏ No
Music pleasant, not too loud and not distracting.	❏ Yes	❏ No
Lighting in dining room is not too bright or dim.	❏ Yes	❏ No
Table decorations are clean and attractive.	❏ Yes	❏ No
Table decorations are unobtrusive and do not block diners' view of each other.	❏ Yes	❏ No
The restaurant presented a unified theme in décor, music, employee uniforms and overall atmosphere.	❏ Yes	❏ No
Décor, furnishings and plants are in good physical condition and tastefully exhibited.	❏ Yes	❏ No

Additional Notes: _____

_____

FACILITY CLEANLINESS

The entrance, lounge, bar and dining room were clean.	❑ Yes	❑ No
The dining table is clean, in good condition, and has no food residue, crumbs or stains.	❑ Yes	❑ No
Chairs and booths are clean, stain-free and stable.	❑ Yes	❑ No
Glasses are clean and do not have water spots.	❑ Yes	❑ No
Flatware is clean and does not have water spots.	❑ Yes	❑ No
Dishes are clean and do not have water spots.	❑ Yes	❑ No
Napkins are clean, not stained, and folded nicely.	❑ Yes	❑ No
The ceiling is clean and in good condition.	❑ Yes	❑ No
Lighting fixtures are working and clean.	❑ Yes	❑ No
The walls and floors are clean and well-maintained.	❑ Yes	❑ No

Additional Notes: _____

_____

_____

_____

_____

RESTROOMS

Men's and women's restrooms clearly marked and in an easy-to-find location.	❑ Yes	❑ No
The restroom door is clean and well-maintained.	❑ Yes	❑ No
Overall, the restroom is clean and doesn't have any objectionable odors.	❑ Yes	❑ No
The restroom lighting is in good working order and sufficiently bright.	❑ Yes	❑ No
The restroom is adequately stocked with toiletries, soap and disposable paper towels (or a hot-air hand dryer).	❑ Yes	❑ No
The restroom sink areas and fixtures are clean.	❑ Yes	❑ No
The restroom mirrors are clean.	❑ Yes	❑ No

The restroom walls, floors and windows are clean and well-maintained.   ❑ Yes   ❑ No

An infant changing area is available, clean and in good condition.   ❑ Yes   ❑ No

Additional Notes: _____

_____

_____

_____

_____

DEPARTURE

The check was presented in an appropriate and timely manner.   ❑ Yes   ❑ No

The check was placed in a discreet location.   ❑ Yes   ❑ No

The check is itemized, readable and easy to understand.   ❑ Yes   ❑ No

The check is totalled correctly and reflects the items ordered.   ❑ Yes   ❑ No

The waiter or waitress informs you that he or she will return for
payment at your convenience.   ❑ Yes   ❑ No

The waiter or waitress properly tabulated and processed credit card payment.   ❑ Yes   ❑ No

The waiter or waitress brought your correct change directly from the cashier.   ❑ Yes   ❑ No

The waiter or waitress thanked you upon receiving payment.   ❑ Yes   ❑ No

The waiter or waitress thanked you for coming and said "It was a pleasure
to server you" and "Please come again."   ❑ Yes   ❑ No

Exits were well-lit and departure from dining room was free of obstacles.   ❑ Yes   ❑ No

Additional Notes: _____

_____

_____

_____

_____

OVERALL RATINGS

Overall service quality was:
❑ Excellent   ❑ Good   ❑ Fair   ❑ Poor

Overall food quality was:
❏ Excellent   ❏ Good   ❏ Fair   ❏ Poor

Overall dining experience was:
❏ Excellent   ❏ Good   ❏ Fair   ❏ Poor

Please note any areas of service that could be improved:

_____
_____
_____
_____
_____
_____
_____
_____
_____
_____

Please note any areas of service that were exceptional or above ordinary:

_____
_____
_____
_____
_____
_____
_____
_____
_____
_____

Additional Notes:

_____
_____
_____
_____
_____

Dining Room Safety Inspection Form

Completed By: _____ Date _____

EMERGENCY PROCEDURES

Is there a functional emergency lighting system?   ❑ Yes ❑ No

Are all employees instructed in emergency procedures?   ❑ Yes ❑ No

Are the emergency numbers clearly posted for fire, police, hospital and ambulance? ❑ Yes ❑ No

Are any employees trained in first aid procedures such as CPR or Heimlich Maneuver? ❑ Yes ❑ No

Comments or Corrective Actions Needed: _____

_____

_____

ELECTRICAL

Are all electrical switches and outlets covered?   ❑ Yes ❑ No

Are there any extension cords in use?   ❑ Yes ❑ No

Are all exposed electrical cords untangled, properly insulated and in good condition? ❑ Yes ❑ No

Comments or Corrective Actions Needed: _____

_____

_____

EQUIPMENT

Is all equipment clean, well-maintained and in good working order?   ❑ Yes ❑ No

Do hot beverage machines, such as coffee urns, have scald warnings posted?   ❑ Yes ❑ No

Before using any piece of equipment, are all employees properly trained?   ❑ Yes ❑ No

Comments or Corrective Actions Needed: _____

_____

_____

FLOORING, STAIRWAYS & EXITS

Are floor mats in use, especially near wet or greasy areas?   ❑ Yes ❑ No

For high-traffic areas, are rugs and runners utilized?   ❑ Yes ❑ No

Is there adequate lighting in areas with steps or staircases?   ❑ Yes ❑ No

Are steps equipped with handrails and slip guards?   ❑ Yes ❑ No

Do all exits have properly lit exit signs?   ❑ Yes ❑ No

Are all exits free from obstructions?   ❑ Yes ❑ No

Do all exit doors have panic bars?   ❑ Yes ❑ No

Do all exit doors open easily?   ❑ Yes ❑ No

Comments or Corrective Actions Needed: _____

_____

Perpetual Inventory Form

ITEM	1 2	3 4 5	6 7 8	9 10 11	12 13 14 15 16	17 18 19	20 21 22 23 24 25 26	27 28 29 30 31	1
+ · =									
+ · =									
+ · =									
+ · =									
+ · =									
+ · =									
+ · =									
+ · =									
+ · =									

Sign-Out Sheet

ITEM	DATE	AMOUNT/WT.	EMPLOYEE

Daily Preparation Form

ITEM	MINIMUM AMOUNT	AMOUNT DEF./ORD.	BEGINNING AMOUNT	AMOUNT PREPPED	STARTING TOTAL

Minimum Amount Needed Form

ITEM	MON	TUES	WED	THURS	FRI	SAT	SUN

Daily Yields Form

ITEM	STARTING WEIGHT (OZ.)	# OF PORTIONS	TOTAL PORTION WEIGHT (OZ.)	YIELD %	PREP/ COOK

Cashier's Report Form

Prepared By: _____

Date: _____ **Day:** _____ **Shift:** _____

		BAR REGISTER		SERVICE REGISTER		TOTAL
		Day	Night	Day	Night	All Shifts
1	**BANK DEPOSIT** Part I					
2	Currency					
3	Silver					
4	Checks					
5	**SUB TOTAL**					
6	**CREDIT CARDS:**					
7	MasterCard/Visa					
8	American Express					
9	Diner's Club					
10	Other					
11	**OTHER RECEIPTS:**					
12	**TOTAL BANK DEPOSIT**					
13	**CASH SUMMARY** Part II					
14	Sales per Register					
15	Sales Tax per Register					
16	**ADJUSTMENTS:**					
17	Over/Under Rings					
18	Other: Complimentaries					
19	Other					
20	**TOTAL ADJUSTMENTS**					
21	Sales to Be Accounted For					
22	Sales Tax to Be Acctd. For					
23	Accounts Collected					
24	Other Receipts:					
25						
26						
27	**TIPS CHARGED:**					
28	MasterCard/Visa					
29	American Express					
30	Diner's Club					
31	Other					
32	House Accounts-Tips					
33	**TOTAL RECEIPTS**					
34	**DEDUCT: PAID OUTS**					
35	Tips Paid Out					
36	House Charges					
37	Total Deductions					
38	**NET CASH RECEIPTS**					
39	**BANK DEPOSIT** (Line 12)					
40	**OVER or SHORT**					

Ticket Issuance Form

WAITPERSON	INITIALS	TOTAL #	# THRU	RETURN # VERIFIED

Cook's Form

ITEM	START	ADDITIONS	STARTING BALANCE	BALANCE ENDING	# SOLD

Ticket Itemization Form

ITEM	USE A ✓ MARK TO DESIGNATE ONE SOLD	TOTALS

Want Sheet

ITEM	EMPLOYEE	APPROVED	ORDERED ON	RECEIVED

Standard Recipe Card A

Recipe No.:   Name:

Portion Size: Yields:

Cost Per Portion:

INGREDIENTS   Weight/Measure   Cost

DIRECTIONS:

SERVICE:

Standard Recipe Card B

ITEM:

FORECASTED YIELD: PORTION SIZE:

INGREDIENTS:	ACTUAL:		PREPARED YIELD:	
	Weight	Measure	Weight	Measure

DIRECTIONS:

ORDERING/NOTES:

Standard Recipe Card C

RECIPE NAME: _____

RECIPE NUMBER: _____ QUANTITY: _____

INGREDIENTS: PREPARATION:

_____   _____

_____   _____

_____   _____

_____   _____

_____   _____

_____   _____

_____   _____

_____   _____

_____   _____

RECIPE NAME: _____

RECIPE NUMBER: _____ QUANTITY: _____

INGREDIENTS: PREPARATION:

_____   _____

_____   _____

_____   _____

_____   _____

_____   _____

_____   _____

_____   _____

_____   _____

_____   _____

Cooking Yield Chart

ITEM: _____

PREPARED BY: _____ DATE: _____

ITEM DESCRIPTION:

PREPARATION PROCEDURES:

GROSS WEIGHT OR VOLUME: _____

COOKING OR PREPARATION LOSS: _____

YIELD AFTER COOKING: _____

ALLOWANCE FOR SERVICE LOSS: _____

TRIMMING, SLICING AND TASTING: _____

NET YIELD: _____

Ingredient Substitutions

Ingredient	Recipe Substitutions
1 tsp allspice	$\frac{1}{2}$ tsp cinnamon + $\frac{1}{2}$ tsp ground cloves
1 tsp baking powder	$\frac{1}{4}$ tsp baking soda + $\frac{1}{2}$ tsp cream of tartar + $\frac{1}{4}$ tsp cornstarch, or $\frac{1}{3}$ tsp baking soda + $\frac{1}{2}$ tsp cream of tartar
1 cup bread crumbs	$\frac{2}{3}$ cup all-purpose flour
1 cup butter	1 cup margarine, or 1 cup shortening + $\frac{1}{2}$ tsp salt, or $\frac{7}{8}$ cup cooking oil + $\frac{1}{2}$ tsp salt
1 cup buttermilk	1 Tbsp vinegar or lemon juice + enough milk (or plain yogurt) to make 1 cup; let stand 5 minutes
1 cup catsup	1 cup tomato sauce + $\frac{1}{2}$ cup sugar + 2 Tbsp vinegar
1 oz chocolate, unsweetened	3 Tbsp unsweetened cocoa + 1 Tbsp oil
$\frac{1}{4}$ cup cocoa	1 ounce (square) chocolate (decrease fat called for in recipe by $\frac{1}{2}$ Tbsp)
1 cup cornmeal (self-rising)	$\frac{7}{8}$ cup plain cornmeal + $1\frac{1}{2}$ Tbsp baking powder + $\frac{1}{2}$ tsp salt
1 Tbsp cornstarch	2 Tbsp all-purpose flour, or 2 Tbsp granulated tapioca
1 cup corn syrup	$\frac{3}{4}$ cup sugar + $\frac{1}{4}$ cup water or 1 cup honey
1 cup cream, half and half	$\frac{7}{8}$ cup milk + $1\frac{1}{2}$ Tbsp melted butter
1 cup cream, heavy	$\frac{3}{4}$ cup milk + $2\frac{1}{2}$ Tbsp fat
$\frac{1}{2}$ tsp cream of tartar	$1\frac{1}{2}$ tsp lemon juice or vinegar
1 large egg, whole	4 Tbsp beaten egg, or 2 yolks + 1 Tbsp water
1 egg yolk	2 Tbsp sifted, dry egg yolk powder + 2 tsp water, or $1\frac{1}{3}$ Tbsp thawed frozen egg yolk
1 cup flour, all-purpose	1 cup + 2 Tbsp cake flour, or $\frac{1}{2}$ cup all-purpose flour + $\frac{1}{2}$ cup whole-wheat flour, or 1 cup rolled oats, $\frac{1}{2}$ cup all-purpose flour + $\frac{1}{2}$ cup bran, or $\frac{5}{8}$ cup potato flour, or $\frac{7}{8}$ cup cornmeal, or $1\frac{1}{4}$ cups rye flour
1 Tbsp flour, all-purpose (as thickener)	$\frac{1}{2}$ Tbsp cornstarch, potato starch or arrowroot, or 2 tsp quick-cooking tapioca
1 cup flour, self-rising	1 cup all-purpose flour + $1\frac{1}{4}$ tsp baking powder + $\frac{1}{4}$ tsp salt
Flour, whole wheat (any amount)	Substitute whole wheat flour for $\frac{1}{4}$ to $\frac{1}{2}$ of the white flour called for

Ingredient	Recipe Substitutions
1 medium clove garlic	$1/8$ tsp garlic powder or instant minced garlic, or $1/2$ to 1 tsp garlic salt (reduce amount of salt called for in recipe)
3-ounce package gelatin, flavored	1 Tbsp plain gelatin and 2 cups fruit juice
1 Tbsp ginger, fresh, minced	$1/4$ tsp ground ginger
1 Tbsp herbs, fresh	1 tsp whole dried, or $1/4$ tsp ground
1 cup honey	$1^1/4$ cups granulated sugar + $1/4$ cup liquid
1 Tbsp horseradish, fresh, grated	2 Tbsp prepared horseradish
1 tsp lemon juice	$1/2$ tsp vinegar
2 cups maple syrup	2 cups sugar and 1 cup water, bring to clear boil; take off heat; add $1/2$ tsp maple flavoring
1 cup milk, skim	$1/3$ cup instant nonfat dry milk + water to make 1 cup, or $1/2$ cup evaporated skim milk + $1/2$ cup water
1 cup milk, whole	2 tsp melted butter + enough skim milk to make 1 cup, or $1/2$ cup evaporated milk + $1/2$ cup water, or 1 cup soy milk, or $1/3$ cup nonfat dry milk + water to make 1 cup + 1 Tbsp fat
1 can milk, sweetened condensed	Heat the following ingredients until sugar and butter are dissolved: $1/3$ cup and 2 Tbsp evaporated milk + 1 cup sugar + 3 Tbsp butter or margarine
1 small onion	1 tsp onion powder, or 1 Tbsp instant minced onion
1 tsp pumpkin pie spice	$1/2$ tsp cinnamon, $1/4$ tsp ginger, $1/8$ tsp allspice, and $1/8$ tsp nutmeg
1 cup sour cream	1 cup yogurt or $1/3$ cup butter + $3/4$ cup buttermilk
4 Tbsp soy sauce	3 Tbsp Worcestershire sauce + 1 Tbsp water
1 cup sugar, granulated	1 cup packed brown sugar, or $1^3/4$ cups powdered sugar (do not substitute in baking), or $1^1/2$ cups corn syrup (reduce liquid in recipe by $1/2$ cup), or 1 cup honey (reduce liquid in recipe by $1/4$ to $1/3$ cup)
1 cup tomato juice	$1/2$ cup tomato sauce + $1/2$ cup water + 1 dash salt
1 cup tomato puree	$1/2$ cup tomato paste + $1/2$ cup water
1 Tbsp yeast, dry active	1 package ($1/4$ oz) active dry yeast, or 1 cake compressed yeast
1 cup yogurt, plain	1 cup buttermilk, or 1 cup sour milk

Standard Portion Sizes

VEGETABLES

Beans-Green or Wax
Buttered .... 3 oz
Creamed .... 3$\frac{1}{2}$ oz

Beans-Lima
Buttered .... 3 oz
Succotash .... 3$\frac{1}{2}$ oz

Beets
Buttered .... 3 oz
Harvard .... 3 oz

Broccoli
Au Gratin .... 3$\frac{1}{2}$ oz
Buttered .... 3 oz

Cabbage
Buttered .... 3 oz

Carrots
Buttered .... 3$\frac{1}{2}$ oz
With Peas .... 3$\frac{1}{2}$ oz

Cauliflower
Au Gratin .... 3 oz
Buttered .... 3 oz

Corn
Buttered .... 2$\frac{1}{2}$ oz
Creamed .... 3 oz
Escalloped ...... 3$\frac{1}{2}$ oz

Onions
Creamed .... 3$\frac{1}{2}$ oz
Fried .... 3 oz

Parsnips
Baked .... 3 oz
Buttered .... 3 oz

Peas
Buttered .... 3 oz
Creamed .... 3 oz

Potatoes
Au Gratin .... 5 oz
Boiled .... 4$\frac{1}{2}$ oz
French Fried .... 2 oz
Mashed .... 4$\frac{1}{2}$ oz

Tomatoes
Stewed .... 4 oz

FRUITS/OTHERS

Fruits
Apple Sauce .... 3 oz
Baked
   Apple Rings ...... 4 oz
Rhubarb Sauce ... 3 oz

Meat Substitutes
Baked Beans ...... 6 oz
Chili .... 6 oz
Macaroni &
   Cheese .... 6 oz
Spanish Rice .... 8 oz

FISH & POULTRY

Fish
Fillets (raw) .... 5 oz
Haddock (baked) . 4 oz
Salmon Loaf .... 4 oz
Scallops .... 5 oz

Poultry
Chicken a
   la King .... 5 oz
Creamed Chicken &
   Sweetbreads .... 6 oz
Roast Turkey .... 3 oz
Turkey
   Sandwich .... 3 oz

MEATS

Beef
Braised .... 5 oz
Corned .... 4 oz
Ground .... 5 oz
Liver .... 3 oz
Pot Roast .... 4 oz
Prime Rib .... 4 oz
Stew .... 6 oz

Lamb
Roast .... 3 oz
Shoulder Chop ... 4 oz
Stew .... 7 oz

Pork
Baked Ham .... 3 oz
Chops .... 4 oz
Fresh Ham .... 3 oz
Roast Loin .... 3 oz

Veal
Heart .... 3$\frac{1}{2}$ oz
Roast .... 3 oz

Meat Count Form

DATE: _____ **SUN M T W TH F SAT** (circle one) **MANAGER:** _____

OPENING COUNTS

Item	Beginning Count	+ / - Purchases	Total Start

CLOSING COUNTS

Ending Counts	Total End	Use	Actual Use	Variance + / -

Thaw Pull Chart

Be sure to thaw food correctly in one of the following ways:

UNDER COLD RUNNING WATER

IN THE REFRIGERATOR

DURING THE COOKING PROCESS

IN THE MICROWAVE

All thaw items should be pulled far enough in advance so they are THAWED COMPLETELY at the time of use. All thaw items must be labeled, dated and rotated.

ITEM	THAW TIME	SHELF LIFE	ON HAND	PULL	NOTES

Prep Chart

ITEM	SHELF	MON			TUES			WED			THURS			FRI			SAT			SUN		
		1	P	Y	1	P	Y	1	P	Y	1	P	Y	1	P	Y	1	P	Y	1	P	Y

Prep Sheet

DATE: _____ **SUN   M   T   W   TH   F   SAT** (circle one)   **EMPLOYEE:** _____

ITEM	LIFE	ON HAND	PREP	YIELD	NOTES

Spoilage Report

DATE:	EMPLOYEE:
ITEM:	**REASON FOR SPOILAGE:**
PRICE:	

DATE:	EMPLOYEE:
ITEM:	**REASON FOR SPOILAGE:**
PRICE:	

DATE:	EMPLOYEE:
ITEM:	**REASON FOR SPOILAGE:**
PRICE:	

Food Mishap Report

ITEM:	EMPLOYEE:
DATE:	MISHAP:
DAY:	
SHIFT:	

ITEM:	EMPLOYEE:
DATE:	MISHAP:
DAY:	
SHIFT:	

ITEM:	EMPLOYEE:
DATE:	MISHAP:
DAY:	
SHIFT:	

ITEM:	EMPLOYEE:
DATE:	MISHAP:
DAY:	
SHIFT:	

Attainable Food Cost

DATE PREPARED: _____ PREPARED BY: _____ TIME PERIOD: _____

ITEM	# SOLD	PORTION COST	TOTAL COST	MENU PRICE	TOTAL SALES	ATTAINABLE FOOD COST

Food Cost Calculator

MENU ITEM: _____ DATE PREPARED: _____ PREPARED BY: _____

INGREDIENT	QUANTITY	UNIT	UNIT COST	EXTENSION

Total Recipe Cost $ _____
Per Serving Cost $ _____

CALCULATE NUMBER OF SERVINGS

Enter Recipe Yield (in ounces) _____

Ounces Per Serving _____

Figure Servings Per Recipe _____

CALCULATE MENU PRICE

Cost Per Serving _____
MENU ITEM CALCULATION
Portion Cost of Recipe _____
Additional Side Item _____
Additional Side Item _____
TOTAL PLATE COST _____

Number of Servings _____
Target Food Cost   30%
Target Menu Price _____
Current Menu Price _____
Current Food Cost _____

Product Request Log

DATE	ITEM	REQUESTED BY

Event Food Production & Portion Control Form

Name of Event: _____ **Date of Event:** _____

Prepared By: _____ **Day of Week of Event:** _____

Guaranteed Guest Count: _____ **Amount to Prepare Count:** _____ **Confirmed Count:** _____

○ **Full-Service** ○ **Buffet** ○ **Other** _____ **Food Service Time:** _____

Menu Item	Quantity Prepared	Portion Size	Possible Number	Weight of Amount Left	Portions of Amount Left	Amount Used

Daily Production Report

DATE: _____ DEPARTMENT: _____ SHIFT: _____

MENU ITEM	AMT. ORDERED	AMT. PRODUCED	# SOLD	% OF SALES	LEFTOVERS

Bid Sheet

Category: _____

Date Bid: _____ Bids Reviewed By: _____

Vendors: A. _____ Bid Received By: ○ phone ○ fax ○ mail

Vendors: B. _____ Bid Received By: ○ phone ○ fax ○ mail

Vendors: C. _____ Bid Received By: ○ phone ○ fax ○ mail

ITEM	Quantity	VENDOR A		VENDOR B		VENDOR C	
		Unit	Total	Unit	Total	Unit	Total

Dishroom Equipment Layout

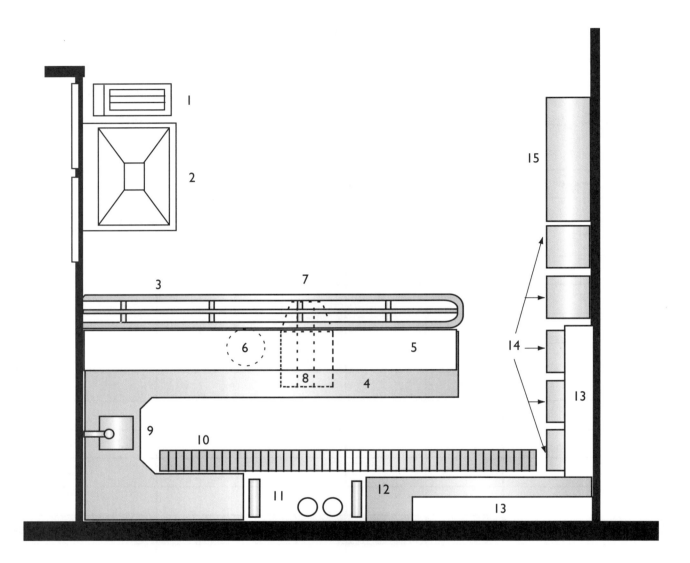

1. Silver burnisher	6. Disposal (3 h.p. hammermill type) and scrap chute	10. Dish-rack conveyor
2. Linen hamper	7. Silverware chute	11. Dish machine
3. Tray rail	8. Silverware soak tank	12. Clean-dish table
4. Soiled-dish table	9. Prerinse sink with flexible spray arm	13. Overshelves (two)
5. Glass rack overshelf		14. Dish-rack dollies (five)
		15. Storage cabinet

Detailed Layout of Kitchen Equipment

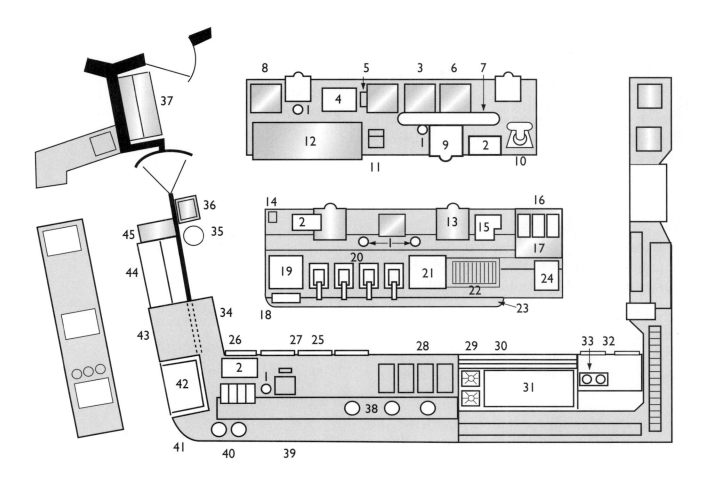

1. Knife wells (five)
2. Composition cutting boards (three)
3. Stainless-steel combination pot and pan washing table with three-compartment sink and meat and vegetable drawers (two)
4. Disposal (3 h.p. hammermill type)
5. Recirculating centrifugal pump
6. Flexible spray rinse arm
7. Overhead pot rack
8. Single-compartment sink
9. Stainless-steel salad preparation work table with undershelf
10. 12-quart mixer on mobile stand
11. Portion scale
12. Reach-in refrigerator
13. Stainless-steel meat and vegetable preparation worktable with angle-compartment sink, drawers (two), overshelf and undershelf

14. Can opener
15. Slicer
16. Closed-top range
17. Exhaust canopy
18. Wooden cutting board
19. Microwave oven
20. Deep fat fryers (four)
21. Griddle
22. Open-top broiler
23. Base cabinet refrigerator with overshelf
24. Steamer
25. Base cabinet refrigerator
26. Cold food wells (eight)
27. Sandwich grill
28. Hot food wells (four) and undercounter dish storage
29. Open-top burners (two)

30. Wooden cutting board
31. Griddle
32. Base cabinet refrigerator
33. Waffle grill
34. Pass-through window
35. Trash can
36. Wash basin
37. Ice machine
38. Heat lamps (two)
39. Waitstaff pickup counter
40. Soup wells (two)
41. Soup bowl lowerators
42. Reach-in refrigerator, sliding-door type
43. Customer takeout back counter
44. Fountain
45. Milkshake machine

Bar Terminology

Aperitif   A drink taken before a meal designed to stimulate the taste buds and appetite. It can be a liqueur, wine or cocktail. Sherry is an example of a popular aperitif.

Back   The companion drink, or a second cocktail, served in a second glass. "Bloody Mary with beer back" would be served in two glasses: one with the Bloody Mary and the other with the beer. Also referred to as a chaser.

Bitters   A very concentrated flavoring made from roots, barks, herbs and berries; used in an Old Fashioned cocktail.

Call Liquor   Any liquor other than well liquor. The term refers to "calling" the liquor brand by name, such as "Captain Morgan® and Coke®" rather than "rum and Coke."

Cordial   A liquor (or liqueur) made by mixing or redistilling neutral spirits. Fruits, flowers, herbs, seeds, roots, plants or juices are used and a sweetening is added. Most cordials are sweet, colorful and highly concentrated. Many are made from secret recipes and processes.

Creme   A cordial, such as Creme de Menthe, with a very high sugar content. Its cream-like consistency gives it its prefix.

Dash   One-sixth of a teaspoon.

Dry   "Dry" typically means "not sweet." A dry Manhattan means use dry vermouth instead of sweet vermouth. A dry martini refers to the use of dry vermouth.

Double   Combining two drinks in one large glass. Double drinks may be stronger as there is less room for the mixer.

Flag   An orange slice and a cherry garnish held together by a fruit pick.

Frappes   Several liqueurs combined and poured over shaved or crushed ice.

Highball   A liquor served with ice, soda, plain water, ginger ale or other carbonated liquids.

Jigger   A jigger, or shot, is a small drinking glass-shaped container used to measure liquor.

Liqueur   A sweet alcoholic beverage made from an infusion of flavoring ingredients and a spirit.

Liquor   A distilled, alcoholic beverage made from a fermented mash of various ingredients.

Mist   Crushed ice rather than cubed.

Neat   Liquor that is drank undiluted by ice, water or mixers.

On The Rocks   A beverage served over ice without adding water or other mixers.

Proof   The measure of the strength of the alcohol. One (degree) proof equals one-half of one percent of alcohol. For example, 100 proof equals 50% alcohol.

Straight Up   Cocktails that are served without ice.

Top Shelf   Expensive, high-quality brands such as Courvoisier®.

Twist   A lemon peel garnish. The peel is twisted over the drink, run around the rim and dropped in the drink.

Virgin   A cocktail without alcohol.

Well   The standard "house" brand of liquors. Also the area where the drinks are made.

Beverage-Specific Garnishes

GARNISH GUIDELINES

- For alcoholic beverages, one straw for every drink with ice.

- Kiddie Cocktails – an orange flag or two cherries.

- Three cocktail onions per sword – in drink.

- Two olives per sword – in drink.

- Cherries – no sword.

- Twist – lemon peel used to flavor rim of glass, then dropped in drink.

DRINK GARNISHES

Manhattans: cherry

Gibson: cocktail onions

Martini: olives or a twist (ask customer's preference)

Collins and Sours: orange speared with a cherry

Tonic Drinks: lime wedge

Rob Roy: cherry

Old Fashioned: cherry

Drinks with Bloody Mary Mix: lime wedge or wheel and celery or pickle

Coffee Drinks: whipped cream, cherry

All Coolers: lime wheel or wedge

Pineapple Juice Drinks: pineapple wedge speared with a cherry

Orange Juice Drinks: orange speared with a cherry

Margaritas/Daiquiri: lime wheel or wedge

Beverage Recipes Card

DRINK NAME	
Ingredients:	Photo of Beverage
Mixing Procedure:	
Type of Glass:	Garnish:

Wine Terminology

Acidity Refers to the wine's degree of sharpness or tartness to the taste. Acidity is an essential element that applies to the citric, malic, tartaric and lactic acids in wine.

Aftertaste Aftertaste is the the taste that lingers in the back of your mouth. Also known as "finish."

Astringency The quality that creates the dry, puckering sensation in the mouth, typically a result of the tannin content. Moderate astringency is considered desirable in most red table wines.

Austere Tannin or acid can make a wine hard or uninteresting.

Body A wine's density and viscosity with reference to the impression of fullness or weight on the palate, such as light-bodied, medium-bodied, full-bodied.

Bouquet The part of a wine's fragrance which originates from fermentation and aging; as distinguished from aroma.

Breathing Leaving wine at room temperature for approximately 30 minutes upon opening to let the air mix with the wine to enhance flavor and aromas.

Brut Very dry champagne.

Cellar Storage place for wine, typically temperature-controlled.

Complex A variety and range of aromas and bouquets and multiple layers of flavor.

Dry The absence of sweetness. A wine in which most of the original grape sugar has been converted into alcohol.

Fermentation The process of transforming sugar into alcohol (the juice of grapes into wine).

Fortified Increasing the alcohol content of wine by adding brandy. Fortified wines, such as Sherry and port, are about 50% stronger than table wines.

Sediment Material that settles to the bottom of a wine, common in old vintage red wines. The bottle should be stored upright before serving, so particles settle to the bottom.

Soft Low in acid and/or tannin; wines with a pleasant finish.

Sommelier A wine steward or expert who offers guidance on choosing wine and serves wine.

Sound A wine with overall pleasing qualities: pleasant to look at, good-smelling and tasting.

Split A 6-ounce bottle of wine.

Tannin The organic compounds more often found in red wines than white. Tannins influence the flavor and taste on the palate.

Varietal Wine For a wine to be labeled a varietal, it must contain at least 75% of the named grape variety.

Vintage Wine If a vintage date is used on a label (1980), it means that at least 95% of the wine must be from grapes grown in that year.

Alcohol Awareness

BLOOD ALCOHOL LEVELS

Alcohol is is a mood-altering drug. It may appear to be a stimulant, but it is actually a depressant, limiting bodily functions. As it is absorbed into the bloodstream, behavioral changes can occur. As the the liver oxidizes the alcohol and removes it from the body, the person's behavior returns to normal. This is often called "sobering up."

Only the passage of time rids the body of the effects of alcohol. Unfortunately, remedies such as black coffee, cold showers and exercise are not effective.

When you consume more alcohol than your liver can oxidize, the amount of alcohol in your blood increases. Blood Alcohol Concentration (BAC) is the amount of alcohol in the bloodstream. It is measured in percentages. For instance, having a BAC of 0.10 percent means that a person has 1 part alcohol per 1,000 parts blood in the body. BAC is the legal standard frequently used to indicate when a person is "driving under the influence" (DUI) or "driving while intoxicated" (DWI). BAC can be measured by breath, blood or urine tests.

Visible changes occur as a person's BAC increases. Their behavior changes visibly. Responsible servers are aware of the the progressive affects of alcohol and alert to the signs of over-indulgence. Although any one particular behavior may not indicate intoxication, a combination of several behaviors is a definite warning signal.

INTOXICATION VS. IMPAIRMENT

Impairment and intoxication are not the same thing. Impairment starts at the first drink. Impairment is the point where a person's intake of alcohol affects their ability to perform appropriately. Judgement, coordination and reaction time may be affected. Intoxication is a **legal** term defining the level of alcohol in the blood where impairment is so severe that criminal actions may be taken for driving or other activities. The level of legal intoxication is .08 in most states. Several states have additional definitions for people under age 21 (.00-.02). Some states also have mandatory jail time for drinking and driving while intoxicated.

CHECKING IDS

Serving alcohol to a minor can have very serious consequences. In fact, it is advisable to check the ID of any patron under who appears to be under 30, unless you are certain of a guest's age. In some cases, you could even be held accountable for serving someone with a fake ID. So be careful.

- Look for state seals or holograms.

- Look for any alterations, such as a cut around year of birth, or typesets that don't match.

- Make sure it's not someone else's ID. Carefully examine the picture/description to make sure it matches the person using it.

- Look for groups that 'pool' cash to an older person in the party.

In most states an acceptable ID is:
- A valid state driver's license, or a valid state identification for non-drivers.

- A valid passport.

- A valid United States Uniformed Service Identification (your employer should provide you with an example).

All IDs should have a picture, signature, birth date

and description. Expired IDs are not acceptable.

GUIDELINES TO DETERMINE THE SYMPTOMS OF INTOXICATION

Service Guidelines
- Before serving a guest, determine his or her condition.

- If you think a customer is already intoxicated, offer snacks and get them a menu quickly.

- Keep track of drinks served. The service order is a ready reference of how many drinks each person consumed.

- Watch for changes in the customer's behavior. Don't hesitate to decline further service, if you think the customer is becoming intoxicated.

- Don't serve. If you have any doubts about a customer's condition, refuse service.

Intoxication Indicators
- Ordering more than one drink at a time.

- Buying drinks for others.

- Concentration problems, losing train of thought (especially when ordering).

- Drinking very fast.

- Careless with money on the bar, or can't pick up change.

- Complaining about drink strength, preparation or prices.

- Overly friendly with customers or employees.

- Loud behavior: talking or laughing and annoying other patrons or making too many comments about others in the establishment.

- Brooding, remaining very quiet, detached from others, continually drinking.

- Mood swings: happy to sad, or vice versa.

- Use of foul language.

- Lighting the wrong end of a cigarette.

DEALING WITH INTOXICATED PATRONS
If you notice someone appears to be intoxicated:
- Do not offer alcohol. Refill water, nonalcoholic beverages and bread. Offer dessert.

- Alert your supervisor immediately. He or she may arrange for a safe ride home for the guest or refuse service.

Employer Responsibilities
- Employers should record incidences of refusal of sales in your manager's log. It serves as a legal record of your responsible alcohol practices in the event of a liability claim.

- Signs should be posted within guests' view with policies on alcohol consumption and responsible hospitality.

- All employees are trained in alcohol awareness and attendance has been documented.

Alcohol Awareness Test

1. Drinking and driving is the number-two killer of Americans between the ages of 17–24, second only to cancer.
   - a. True
   - b. False

2. Statistically, in the United States, one person is killed in drunk driving accidents every:
   - a. 24 hours
   - b. 72 hours
   - c. 90 minutes
   - d. 22 minutes

3. A bartender sells a pitcher of beer with four glasses to a customer who is over 21 years of age. The customer takes the beer and glasses to a table. Later, police officers determine two of the four at the table are only 18. The bartender is not at fault.
   - a. True
   - b. False

4. The legal drinking age in your area is:
   - a. 18
   - b 20
   - c. 21

5. If a customer appears to be over the legal drinking age, you do not have to request an ID in order to serve them an alcoholic beverage.
   - a. True
   - b. False

6. Due to their bodies' fat distribution and a decreased amount of alcohol-metabolizing enzymes, women may respond more quickly to alcohol:
   - a. True
   - b. False

7. Intoxication is a legal term that establishes a certain level of alcohol in the blood as the point of impairment severe enough that criminal sanctions may be enforced for driving and other actions. You can be impaired without being intoxicated.
   - a. True
   - b. False

8. To counter the effects of alcohol, people should drink coffee or take a cold shower to "sober up."
   - a. True
   - b. False

9. Which of the following are acceptable IDs to determine the age of a guest who is requesting an alcoholic beverage:
   - a. A valid state driver's license, a valid state identification with a photograph and date of birth for those who don't drive, a valid passport, a valid United States Uniformed Service Identification.
   - b. A valid state driver's license, a birth certificate and credit card with the same name listed in combination, a school ID from a valid university with a birth date listed next to the picture, a valid passport.
   - c. A valid state driver's license, a school ID from a valid university with a birth date listed next to the picture, a valid passport, a valid United States Uniformed Service Identification.

10. One drink is the equivalent of a 12-oz. glass of beer, a 5-oz. pour of wine or a mixed drink with about 1 oz. of alcohol. Approximately how long does it take the liver to eliminate the alcohol in one drink from the body?
    - a. 15 minutes
    - b. 30 minutes
    - c. One hour
    - d. Two hours

11. Blood Alcohol Concentration charts are the only way of determining the amount of alcohol circulating in a person's bloodstream.
    - a. True
    - b. False

12. Everyone metabolizes alcohol at the same rate.
    - a. True
    - b. False

13. Beer and wine have less alcohol than tequila.
    - a. True
    - b. False

14. Offering low- or nonalcoholic beverages, appetizers, bread and water are good ways of promoting responsible alcohol consumption.
    - a. True
    - b. False

15. Which of the following behaviors are possible signs that a customer may be intoxicated? (Check all that apply.)

  ❑ He or she is overly friendly and annoying other customers.

  ❑ Eyes are glassy, the pupils are somewhat dilated, unfocused, sleepy-looking.

  ❑ Trying to light a cigarette but is unable to do so upon the first try.

  ❑ Purse is open and items are falling out but doesn't notice.

  ❑ Spilling drinks.

  ❑ Speech is slurred.

  ❑ Loses his train of thought while trying to communicate order to you.

  ❑ Sways and staggers a little and appears to lose balance only for a quick moment.

16. Once you have determined that a customer entering the establishment is intoxicated, what is the proper course of action?

  a. The customer should be served no more than one drink. Since he or she drank more elsewhere, if you serve them only one drink, you will not be liable and won't make him or her angry.

  b. The customer should be asked to leave.

  c. The customer should not be served any additional alcoholic beverages, and arrangements should be made so the customer is not driving.

17. Restaurant patrons' dining experience can be enhanced by enjoying wine and alcohol with their meal in a responsible manner.

  a. True
  b. False

18. As a special promotion for a certain brands of alcohol, it is legal to have "super cheap and super double shooter nights" if you count the number of "super cheap and super double shooters" each customer consumes.

  a. True
  b. False

19. The best way to inform someone that they have had their quota of drinks is by:

  a. Communicating with him or her in a friendly, caring and non-threatening manner and alerting a manager if necessary.

  b. Pretending not to hear his or her requests

for additional drinks.

  c. Asking the patron to leave.

20. Food and water may slow the onset of alcohol into the bloodstream, so it's important that water and appetizers are offered, and bread is served right away. As long as a customer is eating, you can serve him or her as much alcohol as he or she would like.

  a. True
  b. False

21. If you serve alcohol to someone who is intoxicated, you may be personally liable for any damages that incur from their drunken behavior and may have to pay monetary damages.

  a. True
  b. False

22. Statistically, how many Americans do NOT drink alcohol?

  a. One in ten
  b. One in twenty
  c. One in three

23. Serving alcohol in a responsible manner protects you, your friends, your family and your employer's or your business.

  a. True
  b. False

24. Intoxication is the point where one's intake of alcohol affects their ability to perform appropriately.

  a. True
  b. False

25. Blood Alcohol Concentration, or BAC, measures the number of grams of alcohol in 100 milliliters of blood. The level of legal intoxication is .20 in most states.

  a. True
  b. False

Alcohol Awareness Test Answer Key

1. Drinking and driving is the number-two killer of Americans between the ages of 17–24, second only to cancer.
   a. True
   b. **False–it is the number one killer.**

2. Statistically, in the United States, one person is killed in drunk driving accidents every:
   a. 24 hours
   b. 72 hours
   c. 90 minutes
   d. **22 minutes**

3. A bartender sells a pitcher of beer with four glasses to a customer who is over 21 years of age. The customer takes the beer and glasses to a table. Later, police officers determine two of the four at the table are only 18. The bartender is not at fault.
   a. True
   b. **False**

4. The legal drinking age in your area is:
   a. 18
   b. 20
   c. **21–in most states**

5. If a customer appears to be over the legal drinking age, you do not have to request an ID in order to serve them an alcoholic beverage.
   a. True
   b. **False**

6. Due to their bodies' fat distribution and a decreased amount of alcohol-metabolizing enzymes, women may respond more quickly to alcohol:
   a. **True**
   b. False

7. Intoxication is a legal term that establishes a certain level of alcohol in the blood as the point of impairment severe enough that criminal sanctions may be enforced for driving and other actions. You can be impaired without being intoxicated.
   a. **True**
   b. False

8. To counter the effects of alcohol, people should drink coffee or take a cold shower to "sober up."
   a. True
   b. **False–Only removal of alcohol from the body via the liver sobers people**

9. Which of the following are acceptable IDs to determine the age of a guest who is requesting an alcoholic beverage:
   a. **A valid state driver's license, a valid state identification with a photograph and date of birth for those who don't drive, a valid passport, a valid United States Uniformed Service Identification.**
   b. A valid state driver's license, a birth certificate and credit card with the same name listed in combination, a school ID from a valid university with a birth date listed next to the picture, a valid passport.
   c. A valid state driver's license, a school ID from a valid university with a birth date listed next to the picture, a valid passport, a valid United States Uniformed Service Identification.

10. One drink is the equivalent of a 12-oz. glass of beer, a 5-oz. pour of wine or a mixed drink with about 1 oz. of alcohol. Approximately how long does it take the liver to eliminate the alcohol in one drink from the body?
    a. 15 minutes
    b. 30 minutes
    c. **One hour**
    d. Two hours

11. Blood Alcohol Concentration charts are the only way of determining the amount of alcohol circulating in a person's bloodstream.
    a. True
    b. **False**

12. Everyone metabolizes alcohol at the same rate.
    a. True
    b. **False**

13. Beer and wine have less alcohol than tequila.
    a. True
    b. **False**

14. Offering low- or nonalcoholic beverages, appetizers, bread and water are good ways of promoting responsible alcohol consumption.
    a. **True**
    b. False

15. Which of the following behaviors are possible signs that a customer may be intoxicated? (Check all that apply.)
    - ☑ **He or she is overly friendly and annoying other customers.**
    - ☑ **Eyes are glassy, the pupils are somewhat dilated, unfocused, sleepy-looking.**
    - ☑ **Trying to light a cigarette but is unable to do so upon the first try.**
    - ☑ **Purse is open and items are falling out but doesn't notice.**
    - ☑ **Spilling drinks.**
    - ☑ **Speech is slurred.**
    - ☑ **Loses his train of thought while trying to communicate order to you.**
    - ☑ **Sways and staggers a little and appears to lose balance only for a quick moment.**

16. Once you have determined that a customer entering the establishment is intoxicated, what is the proper course of action?
    a. The customer should be served no more than one drink. Since he or she drank more elsewhere, if you serve them only one drink, you will not be liable and won't make him or her angry.
    b. The customer should be asked to leave.
    c. **The customer should not be served any additional alcoholic beverages, and arrangements should be made so the customer is not driving.**

17. Restaurant patrons' dining experience can be enhanced by enjoying wine and alcohol with their meal in a responsible manner.
    a. **True**
    b. False

18. As a special promotion for a certain brands of alcohol, it is legal to have "super cheap and super double shooter nights" if you count the number of "super cheap and super double shooters" each customer consumes.
    a. True
    b. **False**

19. The best way to inform someone that they have had their quota of drinks is by:
    a. **Communicating with him or her in a friendly, caring and non-threatening manner and alerting a manager if necessary.**
    b. Pretending not to hear his or her requests for additional drinks.
    c. Asking the patron to leave.

20. Food and water may slow the onset of alcohol into the bloodstream, so it's important that water and appetizers are offered, and bread is served right away. As long as a customer is eating, you can serve him or her as much alcohol as he or she would like.
    a. True
    b. **False**

21. If you serve alcohol to someone who is intoxicated, you may be personally liable for any damages that incur from their drunken behavior and may have to pay monetary damages.
    a. **True**
    b. False

22. Statistically, how many Americans do NOT drink alcohol?
    a. One in ten
    b. One in twenty
    c. **One in three**

23. Serving alcohol in a responsible manner protects you, your friends, your family and your employer's or your business.
    a. **True**
    b. False

24. Intoxication is the point where one's intake of alcohol affects their ability to perform appropriately.
    a. True
    b. **False—that is the definition of impairment.**

25. Blood Alcohol Concentration, or BAC, measures the number of grams of alcohol in 100 milliliters of blood. The level of legal intoxication is .20 in most states.
    a. True
    b. **False—the level of legal intoxication is between .08 and .10 in most states.**

Service Refusal Form

If, at any time, you feel a patron is intoxicated and should not be served any more alcohol, notify your supervisor immediately. Then fill out the form below to the best of your ability.

Date: _____

Name of Employee Refusing Service: _____

Please write a short description of why you felt the individual should not have been served alcohol or when the decision was made to discontinue further service. _____

_____

_____

_____

_____

_____

_____

Did the patron exhibit signs of intoxication, such as the following? Check all that apply.

- ❑ Slurred speech
- ❑ Difficulty lighting a cigarette
- ❑ Arguing with or annoying other guests
- ❑ Tearfulness
- ❑ Drowsiness
- ❑ Difficulty focusing eyes
- ❑ Memory loss
- ❑ Spilling drinks
- ❑ Falling or stumbling
- ❑ Difficulty picking up change

Please provide specific information about the customer.

Customer's Name (if known): _____

Sex: ○ M ○ F Height: _____ Weight: _____

Hair: _____ Eyes: _____ Age: _____

Approximately how long was the customer on the premises? _____

Please list, if known, the time the customer entered, left and was denied service:

Arrival _____ a.m./p.m.
Departure _____ a.m./p.m.
Time Service Denied _____ a.m./p.m.

How many drinks did the customer have on the premises? ○ 1-2 ○ 3-4 ○ 5-6 ○ 7-10 ○ _____

What was the customer drinking? _____

_____

How much money did the patron spend? _____

_____

What was the customer's reaction to being refused service? _____

_____

_____

_____

_____

Was a cab called for the customer? ○ Yes ○ No

Was an alternate method of transportation offered?
○ Yes (please list) _____ ○ No

Were the police called? ○ Yes ○ No

Did anyone witness the refusal of service?
○ Yes ○ No If so, please list their names.

_____

_____

_____

_____

_____

_____

Liquor Requisition

DATE: _____ SERVICE AREA: _____ SHIFT: _____

ITEM	# EMPTIES	BOTTLE SIZE	BAR	MANAGEMENT

Beverage Perpetual Inventory

Product: _____   Distributor: _____

Size: _____   Case Cost: $_____   Bottle Cost: $ _____

Date	Requisitioned Inventory/Size	Purchases/Size	On-Hand Inventory/Size	Manager's Initials

Bottled Beer Count Form

Date: _____ Employee: _____

Brand	Begin Inventory	Bar Req.	Adjust. Inventory	End Inventory	Depletion	Sales Price	Est. Sales
	+	=	-	=	x	$	$
	+	=	-	=	x	$	$
	+	=	-	=	x	$	$
	+	=	-	=	x	$	$
	+	=	-	=	x	$	$
	+	=	-	=	x	$	$
	+	=	-	=	x	$	$
	+	=	-	=	x	$	$
	+	=	-	=	x	$	$
	+	=	-	=	x	$	$
	+	=	-	=	x	$	$
	+	=	-	=	x	$	$
	+	=	-	=	x	$	$
	+	=	-	=	x	$	$
	+	=	-	=	x	$	$
	+	=	-	=	x	$	$
	+	=	-	=	x	$	$
	+	=	-	=	x	$	$
	+	=	-	=	x	$	$
					Total Estimated Sales		$
					(subtract) Complimentary Sales @ Retail		$
					(subtract) Waste & Spillage @ Retai		$
					(EQUALS) Adjusted Estimated Sales		$
					(subtract) Cash Register Sales		$
					EXTENSION TOTAL		$

Bartender's Report

BARTENDER _____   **BARTENDER** _____

MANAGER _____   **MANAGER** _____

BOOKKEEPER _____   **BOOKKEEPER** _____

CASH IN

$100.00 _____	$1.00 _____
$50.00 _____	$0.50 _____
$20.00 _____	$0.25 _____
$10.00 _____	$0.10 _____
$5.00 _____	$0.05 _____
$1.00 _____	$0.01 _____
TOTAL	TOTAL

CASH OUT

$100.00 _____	$1.00 _____
$50.00 _____	$0.50 _____
$20.00 _____	$0.25 _____
$10.00 _____	$0.10 _____
$5.00 _____	$0.05 _____
$1.00 _____	$0.01 _____
TOTAL	TOTAL

CHARGES

1. _____
2. _____
3. _____
4. _____
5. _____
6. _____

TOTAL

SALES SUMMARY

LIQUOR SALES	_____
FOOD SALES	_____
WINE SALES	_____
MISC. SALES	_____
TOTAL	_____
SALES TAX	_____
VOID SALES	_____

Note: Itemize checks separately on back.
Enter figure in sale and sales breakdown.

ITEM	LIQUOR	WINE
Housed	_____	_____
Manager	_____	_____
Comp	_____	_____

EMPLOYEE _____

Total # _____ #__# _____ Initial ____
Return _____ Verify _____

EMPLOYEE _____

Total # _____ #__# _____ Initial ____
Return _____ Verify _____

EMPLOYEE _____

Total # _____ #__# _____ Initial ____
Return _____ Verify _____

Liquor Inventory Form

Date: _____   **Total Liquor:** _____

Inventory By: _____   **Total Beer:** _____

Extension By: _____   **Total Wine:** _____

Examined By: _____

Product	Size	Open Bottles	Full Bottles	Storeroom	Total	Cost	Extension

Liquor Order Form

Item	Build to Amount	Date							

Liquor/Wine Inventory Form

Item	Size	Quantity				Total	Cost	Extension

Beverage Consumption Report

Date: _____   Event: _____

Beverage Type	Beginning Amount	Additions	Total Avail.	End Amount	Total Usage	Unit Cost	Total Cost
BEER							
1.							
2.							
3.							
4.							
LIQUOR							
1.							
2.							
3.							
4.							
5.							
6.							
WINE							
1.							
2.							
3.							
OTHER							
1.							
2.							
3.							
						TOTAL PRODUCT COST	

Total Product Cost: _____   Cost Per Guest: _____   # Guests Served: _____

Pour Cost Chart

Drink: _____ **Priced By:** _____ **Date:** _____

UNIT	ITEM	PRICE/OZ	TOTAL
		Subtotal	
		Loss	
		TOTAL	

Commonly Used Costing Formulas

Standard Accounting

Liabilities (+) Owner's equity = Assets

Current assets (÷) Current liabilities = Current ratio

Current assets (-) Current liabilities = Working capital

Total liabilities (÷) Total assets = Debt-to-assets ratio

Profit (÷) Sales = Return on sales (ROS)

Sales (÷) Working capital = Working capital ratio

Total sales (÷) Average amount of accounts receivable = Accounts receivable turnover

Profit (÷) Total invested = Return on investment (ROI)

Profit (÷) Average owner's equity = Return on owner's equity

Profit (÷) Average total assets = Return on assets

Income & Expenses

Income (-) Expense = Profit
Part (÷) Whole = Percent
Expense (÷) Income = Expense %
Profit (÷) Income = Profit %
Actual (÷) Budget = % of budget

Managing Food & Beverage

Cost in product category (÷) Total cost in all categories = Proportion of total product cost

Cost of product (÷) Desired product cost % = Selling price

100 (÷) Desired product cost % = Pricing factor

Pricing factor (x) Product cost = Selling price

Product cost (+) Contribution margin desired = Selling price

EP weight (÷) AP weight = Product yield %

AP price per pound (÷) Product yield % = Cost per servable pound

Sales Volume

Total sales (÷) # of guests served = Average sales per guest

Labor Costs

Cost of labor (÷) Sales = Labor cost %

Sales (÷) Labor hours used = Sales per labor hour

Guest served (÷) Cost of labor = Guests served per labor dollar

Cost of labor (÷) Guests served = Dollars expended per guest served

Guest served (÷) Labor hours used = Guests served per labor hour

Food & Beverage Costs

Total # of specific menu items sold (÷) Total # of all menu items sold = Percent selecting

# of expected guests (x) % selecting = Predicted # sold

Yield desired (÷) Current yield = Conversion factor

Product loss (÷) AP weight = Waste %

1.00 (-) Waste % = Yield %

EP required (÷) Yield % = AP required

AP required (x) Yield % = EP required

Item amount (x) Item value = Inventory value

Beginning inventory (+) Purchases = Goods avail. for sale
Goods available for sale (-) Ending inventory
(-) Employee meals =
Cost of food consumed

Cost of food consumed (÷) Sales = Food cost %

Cost of beverages consumed (÷) Beverages sales = Beverage cost %

Item dollar sales (÷) Total sales = Item's % of total sales

Sales Forecast Work Sheet

RESTAURANT NAME: _____ SEATING CAPACITY: _____

PREPARED BY: _____ DATE: _____

BREAKFAST

ESTIMATED DAILY SALES REVENUE

_____ Seats (x) _____ Customer turnover = _____

(-) $1/3$ Vacant seat factor = _____

(x) $ _____ Average menu price = _____

BREAKFAST DAILY SALES $_____

30-DAY SALES ESTIMATE

30 days serving (x) $_____ Daily sales = $_____

LUNCH

ESTIMATED DAILY SALES REVENUE

_____ Seats (x) _____ Customer turnover = _____

(-) $1/3$ Vacant seat factor = _____

(x) $ _____ Average menu price = _____

LUNCH DAILY SALES $_____

30-DAY SALES ESTIMATE

30 days serving (x) $_____ Daily sales = $_____

DINNER

ESTIMATED DAILY SALES REVENUE

_____ Seats (x) _____ Customer turnover = _____

(-) $1/3$ Vacant seat factor = _____

(x) $ _____ Average menu price = _____

DINNER DAILY SALES $_____

30-DAY SALES ESTIMATE

30 days serving (x) $_____ Daily sales = $_____

MONTHLY & ANNUAL SALES

ESTIMATED BEVERAGE SALES (30 DAYS)

Liquor $ _____ _____ %

Wine $ _____ _____ %

TOTAL $ _____ _____ %

ESTIMATED FOOD SALES (30 DAYS)

Breakfast $ _____ _____ %

Lunch $ _____ _____ %

Dinner $ _____ _____ %

TOTAL $ _____ _____ %

TOTAL FOOD & BEVERAGE SALES

$_____ Total beverage sales (+)

$_____ Total food sales =

$ _____

30-DAY SALES PROJECTION

$_____ 30-Day sales projection (x) 12 =

$ _____

PROJECTED ANNUAL REVENUE

Operational Budget Form

Item	Budgeted	%	Actual	%
SALES				
Food				
Liquor				
TOTAL SALES				
MATERIALS				
Food Costs				
Liquor Costs				
Wine Costs				
TOTAL COSTS				
GROSS PROFIT				
LABOR				
Manager Salary				
Employee				
Overtime				
TOTAL LABOR COSTS				
Controller Oper. Costs				
China & Utensils				
Glassware				
Kitchen Supplies				
Dining Room Supplies				
Uniforms				
Laundry/Linen				
Services				
Trash Pick-Up				
Laundry Cleaning				
Protection				
Freight				
Accounting				
Maintenance				
Payroll				

Performance to Budget Summary

PERIOD: _____ DATE: _____

PREPARED BY: _____

Item Description	Budget	Actual	% of Budget
Meals Served			
Income			
Food Expense			
Labor Expense			
Other Expenses (List below)			
Total Expenses			
PROFIT			

Break-Even Cost Analysis

Cost	Type	Fixed	Variable	Total

Materials Cost Projection Form

FOOD
Beginning Inventory
Purchases
Comp/Manager
Ending Inventory
Cost
Sales
TOTAL FOOD-COST PERCENTAGE

WINE
Beginning Inventory
Purchases
Comp/Manager
Ending Inventory
Cost
Sales
TOTAL WINE-COST PERCENTAGE

LIQUOR
Beginning Inventory
Purchases
Comp/Manager
Ending Inventory
Cost
Sales
TOTAL LIQUOR-COST PERCENTAGE

Operational Supplies Cost Projection Form

CATEGORY	#
Beginning Inventory	
Purchases	
Ending Inventory	
Cost	
Sales	
TOTAL COST PERCENTAGE	
CATEGORY	#
Beginning Inventory	
Purchases	
Ending Inventory	
Cost	
Sales	
TOTAL COST PERCENTAGE	
CATEGORY	#
Beginning Inventory	
Purchases	
Ending Inventory	
Cost	
Sales	
TOTAL COST PERCENTAGE	
CATEGORY	#
Beginning Inventory	
Purchases	
Ending Inventory	
Cost	
Sales	
TOTAL COST PERCENTAGE	

Cashier's Report II

DATE: _____ DAY: _____ SHIFT: _____

CASHIER: _____ PREPARED BY: _____

Total Cash/Check Guest Checks

Total Charged Guest Checks

TOTAL RECEIPTS _____

    Total Cash Guest Checks _____

    Total Cash Turned In _____

DIFFERENCE (note + or -) _____

REASON FOR DIFFERENCE : _____

_____

_____

_____

REGISTER READING (Taken by Manager Only)

    End Reading _____

    Beginning Reading _____

DIFFERENCE (note + or -) _____

    REGISTER READING _____

    TOTAL RECEIPTS _____

DIFFERENCE (note + or -) _____

REASON FOR DIFFERENCE : _____

_____

_____

Cashier's Log

Day	Date	Location	Shift	Amount Received	Cashier's Name	Initials

Change Funds

DATE: _____   PREPARED BY: _____

BILLS

Large Bills $ _____
$20.00 Bills $ _____
$10.00 Bills $ _____
$5.00 Bills $ _____
$1.00 Bills $ _____
TOTAL BILLS $ _____

CHANGE

Half-Dollars $ _____
Quarters $ _____
Dimes $ _____
Nickels $ _____
Pennies $ _____
TOTAL CHANGE $ _____

OTHER

Register Banks $ _____
_____ $ _____
_____ $ _____
_____ $ _____
TOTAL OTHER $ _____

CHECKS (list by name)

_____ $ _____
_____ $ _____
_____ $ _____
_____ $ _____
_____ $ _____
_____ $ _____
_____ $ _____
_____ $ _____
_____ $ _____
_____ $ _____
_____ $ _____
_____ $ _____
_____ $ _____
_____ $ _____
_____ $ _____
_____ $ _____
_____ $ _____
_____ $ _____
_____ $ _____
_____ $ _____
_____ $ _____
_____ $ _____
TOTAL CHECKS $ _____

TOTAL CASH ON HAND:

_____
Signature of Manager

Cash Turn-In Report

CASHIER NAME: _____

SHIFT: _____

DATE: _____

BILLS: $100		
$50		
$20		
$10		
$5		
$1		
COINS: $.50		
$.25		
$.10		
$.05		
$.01		
CHECKS & VOUCHERS:		
Total Amount Enclosed:		
- Due Back		
= Deport		
- Deposit (from cash sheet)		
DIFFERENCE (over/short)		

Check Log

Check #	Amount	Date	Written To	Invoice #	Deposit	Acct. Balance

Guest Check Record

Date	Table	Server	# of Guests	Check #

Payroll Budget Estimate

DATE PREPARED: _____ WEEK OF: _____

PREPARED BY: _____

HOURLY EMPLOYEES

EMPLOYEE NAME	POSITION	PAY RATE	HOURS	OVERTIME	TOTAL EARNED
				TOTAL	

Allowance for Social Security, Medicare, Federal & State Unemployment Taxes:

Total Hourly Wages _____ x Rate _____ = _____

EMPLOYEE MEALS & TOTALS

Estimated Number of Meals _____ Cost _____ **Total Cost of Meals** _____

TOTAL (Wages & Meals) _____

Estimated Sales for Week _____

Estimated Payroll Cost Percentage for Week _____

Payroll Cost Percentage Goal _____

Employee Turnover Rate & Cost Chart

| PREPARED BY: _____ |
| DATE: _____ |

EMPLOYEE TURNOVER RATE

Number of Completed W-2s _____

(-)

Current Number of Employees _____

(=)

Number of Past Employees _____

Number of Past Employees _____

(÷)

Average Number of Employees Employed _____

(x 100)

Employee Turnover Rate Percentage _____ %

COST OF EMPLOYEE TURNOVER

Number of Past Employees _____

(x)

Cost to Hire Each Employee $_____

(=)

Cost of Employee Turnover $_____

Glossary of Terms

A

AP WEIGHT As-purchased weight.

ACCOUNTANT A person skilled in keeping and adjusting financial records.

ACCOUNTS PAYABLE Money owed for purchases.

ACCOUNTS RECEIVABLE Money owed to you by your customers.

ACTUAL-PRICING METHOD All costs plus the desired profits are included to determine a menu selling price.

ADVERTISING Purchase of space, time or printed matter for the purpose of increasing sales.

AFFIRMATIVE ACTION Steps to eliminate the present effects of past discrimination.

AGE DISCRIMINATION IN EMPLOYMENT ACT OF 1967 Protects individuals over 40 years old.

AMBIANCE Sounds, sights, smells and attitude of an operation.

AMERICANS WITH DISABILITIES ACT (ADA) Prohibits discrimination against disabled persons.

ANNUAL Happening once in 12 months.

APPLICATION FORM A form that, when filled out by a potential employee, gives information on education, prior work record and skills.

AS PURCHASED (AP) Item as purchased or received from the supplier.

AS SERVED (AS) Weight, size or condition of a product as served or sold after processing or cooking.

ASSETS Anything of value; all property of a person, company or estate that can be used to pay debts.

B

BALANCE The amount that represents the difference between debit and credit sides of an account.

BALANCE SHEET Written statement that shows the financial condition of a person or business. Exhibits assets, liabilities or debts and owner's equity.

BEGINNING INVENTORY The quantity and value of beverage and food products or operational supplies in stock at the beginning of an accounting period.

BENEFITS Indirect payments given to employees. These may include paid vacation time, pension, health and life insurance, education plans and/or rebates on company products.

BID SHEET A sheet that is used in comparing item prices from different vendors.

BLOCK SCHEDULING Workers begin and end work at the same time on a specified shift.

BOTTOM-UP BUDGET Secondary employees prepare a budget and then send it to upper management for additions and approval.

BREADING The process of placing an item in flour, egg wash (egg and milk), and then bread crumbs before frying or baking.

BREAK-EVEN ANALYSIS A computative method used to find the sales amount needed for a food service operation to break even.

BREAK-EVEN POINT The association between the amount of business and the resulting sales income, expenditures and profits or losses; when income and costs are equal.

BUDGET A plan for a specific period that estimates activity and income and determines expenses and other adjustments of funds; planning the company's expenditures of money, time, etc.

BURNOUT Depletion of physical and mental capabilities usually caused by setting and attempting unrealistic goals.

BUSINESS PLAN Defines the business image, clarifies goals, calculates markets and competition, and determines costs and capital needs.

BUTCHER AND YIELD TESTS Testing of products to determine usable amounts after preparation.

BY-PRODUCT Item or items that are made in the course of producing or preparing other items.

C

CALCULATE Compute or estimate an amount.

CALENDAR YEAR Consisting of 365 days. The period that begins on January 1 and ends on December 31.

CALL BRAND The brand (of a type of liquor) asked for by customers.

CALL DRINK A drink made with brand-name liquor.

CAPACITY The volume limit.

CAPITAL Financial assets.

CASH BUDGET The amount of money received, the amount of money disbursed, and the resulting cash position.

CASH FLOW Profit plus depreciation

allowances.

CELSIUS A unit used to measure temperature in the metric system, divided into 100 equal parts called degrees.

CLASSES Groupings of jobs based on a set of rules for each grouping. Classes usually contain similar jobs.

CLASSIFICATION (OR GRADING) METHOD Categorizing jobs into groups.

COMMISSION An individual's pay based on the amount of sales personally derived.

COMPENSABLE FACTOR A fundamental, compensable element of a job, such as skills, effort, responsibility, and working conditions.

COMPENSATION Something given in return for a service or a value.

COMPOUND Composed of more than one part.

COMPUTERIZED By means of a computer or computers.

CONTROL To have charge of.

COOK/CHILL SYSTEM Cooking food item to "almost done" state, packaging it (above pasteurization temperature), and chilling it rapidly.

CO-OP BUYING A group of similar

operations working together to secure pricing through mass purchasing at quantity discount prices.

COST The amount paid to acquire or produce an item.

COST LEADERSHIP Being the low-cost leader in an industry.

COST OF SALES Food and beverage cost for menu items in relation to the sales attained by these items during a specific period.

COST PER PORTION The cost of one serving calculated by total recipe cost divided by the number of portions.

COST PER SERVABLE POUND The cost calculated by multiplying the purchase price by the cost factor.

COST-BENEFIT ANALYSIS Determining the cost, in monetary terms, of producing a unit within a program.

COST-PLUS Paying vendor's cost plus a percentage.

COUNT The number of units or items.

CPA (CERTIFIED PUBLIC ACCOUNTANT) An accountant who has fulfilled certain requirements and abides to rules and regulations prescribed by the American Institute of Certified Public Accountants.

CURRENT LIABILITY A debt or obligation that will become due within a year.

CURRENT RATIO Current assets divided by current liabilities.

CVP The relationship between cost, volume and profit.

D

DAILY PRODUCTION REPORT A list of items and quantities produced during a specific shift or day.

DEBIT Showing something owed or due.

DEDUCTION A value that may be subtracted from taxable income.

DEFAULT Failure to pay when due.

DELEGATION Distribution of authority and responsibility downward in the chain of command.

DEPOSIT To put in a place, especially a bank, for safekeeping.

DEPRECIATION Lessening or lowering in value.

DESIGNATE Point out; indicate definitely.

DIRECT COSTS (FOOD) The costs associated with direct purchases.

DIRECT LABOR Labor used directly in the preparation of a food item.

DISCIPLINE A correction or action towards a subordinate when a rule or procedure has been violated.

DIVIDEND An owner's share of the surplus when a company shows a profit at the end of a period.

E

EP WEIGHT Edible portion weight. The usable portion after processing.

EDIBLE PORTIONS (EP) The actual yield available for processing a food item.

ELECTRONIC SPREADSHEET Computerized worksheet with vertical and horizontal columns that are easily manipulated.

EMBEZZLEMENT Taking of property by someone to whose care it has been entrusted.

EMPLOYEE COMPENSATION Any form of pay or reward an employee gets from his or her employment.

EMPLOYEE ORIENTATION Introduction of basic company background information to new employees.

ENDING INVENTORY The quantity and value of items on hand at the end of a period.

ENTRÉE The main dish of a meal.

EQUIPMENT Machines or major tools necessary to complete a given task.

EQUIVALENT Equal in value or power.

ESTIMATE Judgment or guess determining the size, value, etc., of an item.

EVALUATE To find the value or amount of.

EXPENDITURE Amount spent.

EXPIRATION The date on which a food or beverage product ceases to be usable.

EXTENSION To equate out, lengthen or widen.

F

FACTOR One of two or more quantities, multiplied.

FINANCES Funds, money or revenue; financial condition.

FINANCIAL STATEMENTS Used in a business operation to inform management of its exact financial position.

FISCAL YEAR The time between one yearly settlement of financial accounts and another.

FIXED BUDGET Budget figures based on a definite level of activity.

FIXED EMPLOYEES Employees who are necessary no matter the volume of business.

FLEX PLAN A plan giving employees choices regarding benefits.

FLEXIBLE BUDGET Projected revenue and expenditures based on production.

FOOD COST The cost of food items purchased for resale.

FOOD COST PERCENTAGE Cost of food divided by sales from that food.

FORMULA A recipe or equation.

FRANCHISE A franchise grants the right to use a name, methods and product in return for franchise fees.

FREEZER BURN Loss of moisture in frozen food, evidenced by a dry, discolored surface.

G

GARNISH To decorate.

GENERAL LEDGER (GL) A ledger containing all financial statement accounts.

GOURMET A lover of fine foods and drinks.

GRADUATED Arranged in regular steps, stages or degrees.

GRATUITY/TIP A gift or money given in return for a service.

GRIEVANCE A complaint against the employer that may include factors involving wages, hours or conditions of employment.

GROSS The overall total.

GROSS MARGIN Sales minus the cost of food.

H

HOST/HOSTESS The person who receives guests.

HOUSE BRAND The brand of liquor normally served by a given bar.

HVAC Heating, ventilation and air-conditioning.

I

INGREDIENT One part of a mixture.

INSURANCE Trading the possibility of a loss for the certainty of reimbursement. Paid by premiums.

INTEGRATED BEVERAGE CONTROL SYSTEM An automatic beverage dispensing system integrated with a computer or point-of-sale register.

INTEREST Money paid for the use of borrowed money.

INTERNAL CONTROL The methods and measures within a business to safeguard assets, check the accuracy and reliability of accounting data, and promote operational efficiency.

INVENTORY A list of items with their estimated value and the quantity of each.

INVENTORY CONTROL System used for maintaining inventories.

INVENTORY TURNOVER The amount of times inventory turns over during a specific period.

INVERT Turn upside down.

INVOICE Shows prices and amounts of goods sent to a purchaser.

ITEMIZE To list by item.

J

JIGGER Used to serve a predetermined volume of a beverage.

JOB DESCRIPTION A description of tasks and duties required of a job.

L

LIABILITY Being under obligation or debt.

LIQUIDITY RATIOS Ratios that show the ability to meet short-term obligations.

LIQUOR COST Amount paid for liquor after discounts.

LIQUOR COST PERCENTAGE The portion cost divided by the selling price.

M

MANUAL Done by hand.

MARGIN The difference between the cost and the selling price.

MARKET Groups with similar characteristics, wants, needs, buying power and willingness to spend for dining or drinking out.

MARKETING Means by which an outlet is exposed to the public.

MARKETING STRATEGY Overall plan of action that enables the outlet to reach an objective.

MARKUP Amount by which a higher price is set.

MEDIA Various types of advertising, such as television, radio and newspapers.

MEDICARE A federal health insurance program for people 65 or older and certain disabled people.

MENU A list of dishes served at a meal.

MENU MIX Menu popularity calculation.

MENU PRICE The amount that will be charged for an item.

N

NET The remaining amount after deducting all expenses.

NET PROFIT Profit after all product costs, operating expenses and promotional expenses have been deducted from net sales.

O

OPERATING BUDGET Detailed revenue and expense plan for a determined period.

ORGANIZATIONAL CHART Shows the relationships of jobs to each other with lines of authority, responsibility and communication.

OUTPUT The end product.

OUTSOURCING Calling upon other companies to help supply your products.

OVERTIME Time exceeding regular hours.

P

P&L SHEET A profit and loss statement.

PAR STOCK Stock levels established by management for individual inventory items in varying locations.

PARKINSON'S LAW Workers adjust pace to the work available.

PAYROLL A list of employees and amounts to pay them, as well as records pertaining to these payments.

PENSION PLANS Plans that provide a fixed sum when employees reach a predetermined retirement age or when they no longer work due to disability.

PERPETUAL INVENTORY Accounting for inventory changes. Beginning and ending inventory figures are changed along with any sales or purchases.

PHYSICAL INVENTORY A count of all items on hand.

POINT-OF-SALE (POS) SYSTEM A sales transaction register and processor.

PORTION One serving.

PORTION CONTROL Ensures that the correct amount is being served each time.

PORTION COST The cost of one serving.

PRIME COST The cost of a product after calculating and adding in labor.

PRO FORMA Statement prepared on the basis of anticipated results.

PROCEDURE The method of doing a task.

PRODUCT SPECIFICATION A listing of quality and service requirements necessary for each product to be purchased from a vendor.

PRODUCTION SCHEDULE The items and quantities that must be produced for a specific meal, day, etc.

PROFIT Gain.

PROPORTION The relationship between one thing and another with regard to size, number or amount.

PURCHASE SPECIFICATIONS Standard requirements established for procuring items from suppliers.

PURVEYOR One who supplies provisions or food.

Q

QUALITY CONTROL Assuring the execution of tasks and responsibilities according to established standards.

QUANTITY The amount; how much.

QUICK RATIO Current assets less inventory value divided by current liabilities.

R

RATIO The ratio between two quantities is the number of times one contains the other.

RECEIPT A written statement that something has been received.

RECEIVING REPORT A report that

indicates the value and quantity of items received.

RECIPE Directions used for preparing a menu item.

RECIPE COST The total cost of all ingredients in a recipe.

RECIPE YIELD The weight, count or volume of food that a recipe will produce.

REPORT An account of facts used to give or get information.

REQUISITION To apply for something needed.

REVENUE Income.

S

SALARY A regular payment for services rendered.

SALES MIX The number of sales of individual menu items.

SALES REVENUE Money from the sale of certain items.

SEAT TURNOVER The number of times a seat is occupied during a meal period. Calculate by dividing the number of guests seated by the number of available seats.

SHRINKAGE The amount of food lost due to cooking, dehydration or theft.

SHRINKAGE (INVENTORY) The difference between what is on hand and what should be on hand.

SPECIFICATION A detailed statement of the particulars of an item.

SPILLAGE The alcohol lost during the drink-making process.

SPOILAGE Loss due to poor food handling.

STAGGERED SCHEDULING Scheduling employees to start and stop at different times according to the work pattern.

STANDARDIZED RECIPE Directions describing the way an establishment prepares a particular dish.

STANDING ORDER An order for delivery that is automatic.

STOCK OPTION The right to purchase a stated number of shares in a company at today's price at a future time.

STOCKHOLDER The owner of stocks or shares in a company.

SUMMARIZE Briefly express, stating the main points.

SYSTEM Components working together in the most efficient way.

T

TARGET FOOD COST The amount a company hopes to spend for a particular menu item.

TOP-DOWN BUDGET A budget prepared by upper management and "passed on" to operating units.

TRAINING Teaching new employees the basic skills needed to perform their jobs.

TRIM The part or quantity of a product removed during preparation.

U

UNIT Refers to the number or amount in a package.

UNIT COST The purchase price divided by the applicable unit.

USABLE PORTION The part of a fabricated product that has value.

V

VARIABLE COST The production cost that changes in direct proportion to sales volume.

VARIATION The extent to which a thing changes, or the change itself.

VENDOR The person or company who sells.

VERSATILE Easily changing or turning from one action to another.

VOLUME Calculated as length times width times height.

VOUCHER Evidence of payment in written form, such as a receipt.

W

WAGES The amount paid or received for work.

WEIGHT The measurement of mass or heaviness of an item.

WELL DRINK A drink not made with name-brand liquor.

WITHHOLDING TAX The deduction from a person's paycheck for the purpose of paying income taxes.

WORKING CAPITAL The difference between current assets and current liabilities.

X

X MODE Allows reports to be produced on the POS register without resetting totals.

Y

YIELD The total created or the amount remaining after fabrication. The usable portion of a product.

YIELD PERCENTAGE/YIELD FACTOR The ratio of the usable amount to the amount purchased.

Z

Z MODE Produces final reports and clears information from a POS register.

ZERO-BASED BUDGET A budget prepared without previous budget figures.

State Restaurant Associations

A

ALABAMA

**Alabama Restaurant and
Foodservice Association**
P.O. Box 230207
Montgomery, AL 36123-0207
334-244-1320
FAX: 334-271-4621

Physical Address:
2000 Interstate Park Dr., Suite 402
Montgomery, AL 36109

ALASKA

**Alaska Cabaret, Hotel and
Restaurant Association**
341 East 56th Avenue
Anchorage, AK 99518
901-563-8133
FAX: 907-563-8640

ARIZONA

Arizona Restaurant Association
2701 N 16th Street, Suite 221
Phoenix, AZ 85006
602-234-0701
FAX: 602-266-6043

ARKANSAS

Arkansas Hospitality Association
603 Pulaski Street
P.O. Box 3866
Little Rock, AR 72203-3866
501-376-2323
FAX: 501-376-6517

C

CALIFORNIA

**California Restaurant
Association**

3435 Wilshire Blvd., Suite 2230
Los Angeles, CA 90010
213-384-1200 • 800-794-4272
FAX: 213-384-1623

**California Restaurant Association,
Government Affairs**
980 9th Street, Suite 1480
Sacramento, CA 95814
916-447-5793 • 800-765-4842 (in CA)
FAX: 916-447-6182

Golden Gate Restaurant Association
415-781-5348

**State Restaurant Association of
California (CALSRA)**
P.O. Box 418446
Sacramento, CA 95841
888-994-2257
FAX: 888-993-2922

**Western Restaurant Association
(CALSRA)**
P.O. Box 418446
Sacramento, CA 95841
888-994-2257 • 888-994-2257
FAX: 888-993-2922

**American Restaurant Association
(CALSRA)**
P.O. Box 418446
Sacramento, CA 95841
888-994-2257
FAX: 888-993-2922

COLORADO

Colorado Restaurant Association
899 Logan Street, Suite 300
Denver, CO 80203
303-830-2972
FAX: 303-830-2973

CONNECTICUT

Connecticut Restaurant Association
731 Hebron Avenue
Glastonbury, CT 06033
203-633-5484
FAX: 203-657-8241

D

DELAWARE

Delaware Restaurant Association
P.O. Box 7838
Newark, DE 19714-7838
302-366-8565
FAX: 302-738-8865

Physical Address:
Five Embry Court
Drummond North
Newark, DE 19711

DISTRICT OF COLUMBIA

**Restaurant Association of
Metropolitan Washington, Inc.**
7926 Jones Branch Dr., Suite 530
McLean, VA 22102-3303
703-356-1315
FAX: 703-893-4926

F

FLORIDA

Florida Restaurant Association
200 West College Avenue

Tallahassee, FL 32301
904-224-2250
FAX: 904-222-9213

Physical Address
4930 Umarilla
Boise, ID 83709

G

GEORGIA

Georgia Hospitality and Travel Association
600 W Peachtree St., Suite 1500
Atlanta, GA 30308
404-873-4482
FAX: 404-874-5742

H

HAWAII

Hawaii Restaurant Association
1188 Bishop Street, Suite 1507
Honolulu, HI 96813
808-536-9105
FAX: 808-534-0117

I

IDAHO

Idaho Hospitality & Travel Association, Inc.
P.O. Box 7587
Boise, ID 83707
208-362-2637 • 800-959-2637 (in ID)
FAX: 208-362-0855

ILLINOIS

Illinois Restaurant Association
350 W Ontario
Chicago, IL 60610
312-787-4000
FAX: 312-787-4792

INDIANA

Restaurant and Hospitality Association of Indiana
115 W Washington St., Suite 11655
Indianapolis, IN 46204
317-673-4211
FAX: 317-673-4210

IOWA

Iowa Hospitality Association
606 Merle Hay Tower
Des Moines, IA 50310
515-276-1454
FAX: 515-276-3660

K

KANSAS

Kansas Restaurant and Hospitality Association
359 S Hydraulic
Wichita, KS 67211
316-267-8383
FAX: 316-267-8400

KENTUCKY

Kentucky Restaurant Association
422 Executive Park
Louisville, KY 40207
502-896-0464
FAX: 502-896-0465

L

LOUISIANA

Louisiana Restaurant Association
2700 N Arnoult
Metairie, LA 70002
504-454-2277
FAX: 504-454-2299

M

MAINE

Maine Restaurant Association
Five Wade Street
P.O. Box 5060
Augusta, ME 04330-0552
207-623-2178
FAX: 207-623-8377

MARYLAND

Restaurant Association of Maryland, Inc.
7113 Ambassador Road
Baltimore, MD 21244
410-298-0011
FAX: 410-298-0299
www.marylandrestaurants.com

MASSACHUSETTS

Massachusetts Restaurant Association
95-A Turnpike Road
Westborough, MA 01581-9775
508-366-4144 • 800-852-3042 (in MA)
FAX: 508-366-4614

Massachusetts Restaurant Association, Government Affairs
141 Tremont Street, 6th Floor
Boston, MA 02111
617-426-1081
FAX: 617-426-8564

MICHIGAN

Michigan Restaurant Association
225 W Washtenaw Street
Lansing, MI 48933
800-968-9668

MINNESOTA

Minnesota Restaurant Association
871 Jefferson Avenue
Street Paul, MN 55102
612-222-7401
FAX: 612-222-7347

MISSISSIPPI

Mississippi Restaurant Association
P.O. Box 16395
Jackson, MS 39236
601-982-4281
FAX: 601-982-0062

MISSOURI

Missouri Restaurant Association
P.O. Box 10277
Kansas City, MO 64171
816-753-5222
FAX: 816-753-6993

Physical Address:
4049 Pennsylvania Ave., Suite 201
Kansas City, MO 64111

MONTANA

Montana Restaurant Association
1537 Avenue D, Suite 320
Billings, MT 59102
406-256-1105
FAX: 406-256-0785

Physical Address:
3495 W Broadway
Missoula, MT 59802

N

NEBRASKA

Nebraska Restaurant Association
5625 O St. Building, Suite 7
Lincoln, NE 68510
402-483-2630
FAX: 402-483-2746

NEVADA

Nevada Restaurant Association
4820 Alpine Place, Suite B202
Las Vegas, NV 89107
702-878-2313
FAX: 702-878-5009

NEW HAMPSHIRE

New Hampshire Lodging and Restaurant Association
4 Park Street, Suite 413
P.O. Box 1175
Concord, NH 03301

603-228-9585
FAX: 603-226-1829

NEW JERSEY

New Jersey Restaurant Association
One Executive Drive, Suite 100
Somerset, NJ 08873
908-302-1800
FAX: 908-302-1804

NEW MEXICO

New Mexico Restaurant Association
7800 Marble NE, Suite 4
Albuquerque, NM 87110
505-268-2474
FAX: 505-268-5848

NEW YORK

New York State Restaurant Association
505 Eighth Avenue, 7th Floor
New York, NY 10018
212-714-1330
FAX: 212-643-2962

New York State Restaurant Association
455 New Karner Road
Albany, NY 12205
800-452-5212
FAX: 518-452-4497

NORTH CAROLINA

North Carolina Restaurant Association
P.O. Box 6528
Raleigh, NC 27628
919-782-5022
FAX: 919-782-7251

Physical Address:
3105 Charles B. Root Wynd
Raleigh, NC 27612

NORTH DAKOTA

**North Dakota State
Hospitality Association**
P.O. Box 428
Bismarck, ND 58502
701-223-3313
FAX: 701-223-0215

Physical Address:
919 S. 7th Street, Suite 601
Bismarck, ND 58504

O

OHIO

Ohio Restaurant Association
1525 Bethel Road, Suite 301
Columbus, OH 43215
614-442-3535 • 800-282-9049
FAX: 614-442-3550

OKLAHOMA

Oklahoma Restaurant Association
3800 N Portland
Oklahoma City, OK 73112
405-942-8181
FAX: 405-942-0541

OREGON

Oregon Restaurant Association
8565 SW Salish Lane, Suite 120
Wilsonville, OR 97070
503-682-4422
FAX: 503-682-4455

P

PENNSYLVANIA

Pennsylvania Restaurant Association
100 State Street
Harrisburg, PA 17101-1024
717-232-4433 • 800-346-7767
FAX: 717-236-1202

R

RHODE ISLAND

Rhode Island Hospitality Association
P.O. Box 6208
Providence, RI 02940
401-732-4881
FAX: 401-732-4883

Physical Address:
1206 Jefferson Blvd.
Warwick, RI 02886

S

SOUTH CAROLINA

**South Carolina Restaurant
Association**
Barringer Building, Suite 505
1338 Main Street
Columbia, SC 29201
803-765-9000
FAX: 803-252-7136

SOUTH DAKOTA

South Dakota Restaurant Association
P.O. Box 638
Pierre, SD 57501
605-224-5050
FAX: 605-224-2059

Physical Address:
320 E Capitol
Pierre, SD 57501

T

TENNESSEE

Tennessee Restaurant Association
P.O. Box 681207
Franklin, TN 37068-1207
615-790-2703
FAX: 615-790-2768

Physical Address:
1224-A Lakeview Drive
Franklin, TN 37064

TEXAS

Texas Restaurant Association
P.O. Box 1429
Austin, TX 78767
512-472-3666
FAX: 512-472-2777

Physical Address
1400 Lavaca
Austin, TX 78701

U

UTAH

Utah Restaurant Association
1555 E Stratford Street, #100
Salt Lake City, UT 84115
801-487-4821
FAX: 801-467-5170

V

VERMONT

Vermont Lodging and Restaurant Association
Route 100 N R1, #1522
Waterbury, VT 05676
802-244-1344
FAX: 802-244-1342

VIRGINIA

Virginia Hospitality and Travel Association-Restaurant Division
2101 Libbie Avenue
Richmond, VA 23230
804-288-3065
FAX: 804-285-3093

W

WASHINGTON

Restaurant Association of the State of Washington, Inc.
2405 Evergreen Park Drive SW, Suite A2
Olympia, WA 98502
360-956-7279

WEST VIRGINIA

West Virginia Hospitality and Travel Association
P.O. Box 2391
Charleston, WV 25328
304-342-6511
FAX: 304-345-1538

Physical Address:
20003 Quarrier Street
Charleston, WV 25311

WISCONSIN

Wisconsin Restaurant Association
2801 Fish Hatchery Road
Madison, WI 53713
608-270-9950 • 800-589-3211
FAX: 608-270-9960
www.wirestaurant.org

WYOMING

Wyoming Lodging & Restaurant Association
P.O. Box 1003
Cheyenne, WY 82003-1003
307-634-8816
FAX: 307-632-0249

Physical Address:
211 W 19th, Suite 201
Cheyenne, WY 82001

OUTSIDE OF UNITED STATES

CANADA

Canadian Restaurant & Foodservices Association
316 Bloor Street W
Toronto, Ontario Canada
M5S 1W5
416-923-1450
FAX: 416-923-1450

Ontario Restaurant Association
121 Richmond Street W
Suite 1201
Toronto, Ontario Canada M6S 2P2
416-359-0533
FAX: 416-359-0531

U.S. VIRGIN ISLANDS

Virgin Islands Restaurant & Bar Association
c/o Virgin Rhythms Public Relations
P.O. Box 12048
St. Thomas, VI 00801
809-777-6161
FAX: 809-777-6036

PUERTO RICO

Puerto Rico Hotel and Tourism Association
954 Ponce de Leon Avenue
Suite 703
San Juan, PR 00907-3605
805-725-2901

Journals & Trade Publications

B

Bar & Beverage Business Magazine
Mercury Publications
1839 Inkster Blvd.
Winnipeg, Manitoba R2X 1R3

Bartender Magazine
Foley Publishing Corporation
P.O. Box 158
Liberty Corner, NJ 07938-0158

Beer, Wine & Spirits Beverage Retailer
Oxford Publishing
307 W Jackson Avenue
Oxford, MS 38655

Beverage & Food Dynamics
Adams Business Media
1180 Avenue of the Americas
11th Floor
New York, NY 10036-8401

Beverage Bulletin
6310 San Vicente Blvd., Suite 530
Los Angeles, CA 90048

Beverage World Periscope
Keller International Publishing Corporation
150 Great Neck Road
Great Neck, NY 11021

C

Center of the Plate
American Culinary Foundation
10 San Bartola Drive
St. Augustine, FL 32086-5766

Cheers
Adams Business Media
50 Washington Street, 10th Floor
Norwalk, CT 06854

Chef
Talcott Communication Corp.
20 N Wacker Drive, #1865
Chicago, IL 60606-2905

Coffee & Cuisine
1218 3rd Avenue, #1315
Seattle, WA 98101-3021

Consultant
Foodservice Consultants Society
International
304 W Liberty, Suite 201
Louisville, KY 40202-3011

Cooking For Profit
CP Publishing
P.O. Box 267
Fond du Lac, WI 54936-0267

Correction Foodservice
International Publishing Company of
America
665 La Villa Drive
Miami, FL 33166-6095

**Council on Hotel, Restaurant
& Institutional Education
Communique**
Council on Hotel, Restaurant &
Institutional Education
3205 Skipwith Road
Richmond, VA 23294-3006

Culinary Trends
Culinary Trends Publications
6285 Spring Street, 107
Long Beach, CA 90808-4000

E

El Restaurante Mexicano
Maiden Name Press
P.O. Box 2249
Oak Park, IL 60303-2249

F

Fancy Foods & Culinary Products
Talcott Communication Corporation
20 N Wacker Drive, #1865
Chicago, IL 60606-2905

FEDA News & Views
Foodservice Equipment Distributors
Association
223 W Jackson Blvd., #620
Chicago, IL 60606-6911

Food & Beverage News
886 W Bay Drive, #E6
Largo, FL 33770-3017

Food Arts Magazine
M Shanken Communications
387 Park Avenue S, 8th Floor
New York, NY 10016-8872

Food Businesses: Snack Shops, Speciality Food Restaurants & Other Ideas
Prosperity & Profits Unlimited
P.O. Box 416
Denver, CO 80201-0416

Food Channel
Noble & Associates
515 N State Street, 29th Floor
Chicago, IL 60610-4325

Food Distribution Research Society News
Silesia Companies
P.O. Box 441110
Fort Washington, MD 20749-1110

Food Distributors International
201 Park Washington Court
Falls Church, VA 22046-4519

Food Management
Donohue/Meehan Publishing
The Penton Media Building
1300 E 9th Street
Cleveland, OH 44114-1503

Food Service Equipment and Supplies Specialist
Cahners Business Information
2000 Clearwater Drive
Oak Brook, IL 60523

FoodService and Hospitality
23 Lesmill Road, Suite 101
Toronto, Ontario M3B 3P6

Foodservice Equipment and Supplies
Cahners Business Information

1350 East Touhy Avenue
Des Plaines, IL 60018

FoodTalk
Pike & Fischer
1010 Wayne Avenue, Suite 1400
Silver Springs, MD 20910

Fresh Cup Magazine
P.O. Box 14827
Portland, OR 97293-0827

Frozen Food Executive
National Frozen Food Association
4755 Linglestown Road, Suite 300
Harrisburg, PA 17112-8526

H

Healthcare Foodservice
International Publishing Company of America
665 La Villa Drive
Miami, FL 33166-6095

Hotel, Restaurant, Institutional Buyers Guide
Urner Barry Publications
P.O. Box 389
Toms River, NJ 08754-0389

I

International Association of Food Industry Suppliers

1451 Dolly Madison Boulevard
McLean, VA 22101

J

Journal of Food Protection
International Association for Food
Protection
6200 Aurora Avenue, Suite 200W
Des Moines, IA 50322-2863

Journal of Restaurant and
Foodservice Marketing
Haworth Press
21 E Broad Street
West Hazelton, PA 18201-3809

M

Midwest Foodservice News
Pinnacle Publishing
2736 Sawbury Blvd.
Columbus, OH 43235

N

National Association of
Concessionaries
35 E Wacker Drive, Suite 1816
Chicago, IL 60601-2270

National Culinary Review
American Culinary Federation
10 San Bartola Drive
St. Augustine, FL 32086-5766

National Dipper
US Exposition Corp.
1841 Hicks Road, #C
Rolling Meadows, IL 60008-1215

Nation's Restaurant News
Lebhar Friedman
425 Park Avenue
New York, NY 10022-3506

Nightclub & Bar Magazine
Oxford Publishing
307 W Jackson Avenue
Oxford, MS 38655

O

On Campus Hospitality
Executive Business Media
825 Old Country Road
P.O. Box 1500
Westbury, NY 11590

Onboard Services
International Publishing Company of
America
665 La Villa Drive
Miami, FL 33166-6095

OnSite
Nation's Restaurant News
3922 Coconut Palm Drive
Tampa, FL 33619-8321

P

Pizza Today
ProTech Publishing & Communications
P.O. Box 1347
New Albany, IN 47151-1347

Prepared Foods
Cahners Business Information 2000
Clearwater Drive
Oak Brook, IL 60523

R

Restaurant Business
Bill Communications
353 Park Avenue S
New York, NY 10010-1706

Restaurant Digest
Panagos Publishing
3930 Knowles Avenue, #305
Kensington, MD 20895-2428

Restaurant Hospitality
Penton Media
The Penton Media Building
1300 East 9th Street
Cleveland, OH 44114-1503

Restaurant Management Today
Atcom
1541 Morris Avenue
Bronx, NY 10457-8702

Restaurant Marketing
Oxford Publishing
307 W Jackson Avenue
Oxford, MS 38655

Restaurant Wine
Wine Profits
P.O. Box 222
Napa, CA 94559-0222

Restaurants & Institutions
Cahners Business Information
1350 East Touhy Avenue
Des Plaines, IL 60018

Restaurants USA
National Restaurant Association
1200 17th Street NW
Washington, D.C. 20036-3006

Restaurants, Resorts & Hotels
Publishing Group
P.O. Box 318
Trumbull, CT 06611-0318

S

Showcase Magazine
National Association for the Specialty
Food Trade
120 Wall Street, 27th Floor
New York, NY 10005-40001

Southern Beverage Journal
14337 SW 119th Avenue
Miami, FL 33186-6006

W

Wine on Line Food and Wine Review
Enterprise Publishing
138 N 16th Street
Blair, NE 68008

Y

Yankee Food Service
Griffin Publishing Company
616 Main Street
Dennis, MA 02638

Index

A

absenteeism 215

accounting 538

accounts payable 51, 322

actual-cost pricing 307

actual food-cost percentage 292

actual method 415

advertising 25

air-conditioning 112

alcohol-free 76

alcohol awareness 522

alcohol awareness test 524, 526

ambiance 66

American Culinary Federation 178

appearances 183

aprons 129

aromas 72

assets 43

attitudes 212

B

background checks 184

balance sheet 43

barstaff 445

bartenders 431, 446, 462, 532

bar cash-control 389

beer 411, 433, 457, 524, 526, 531

beginning inventory 289

beverage 530, 538

beverage consumption 536

beverage inventory control 54

bids 515

billboards 174

bin cards 416

bottle yield 386

brands 313

break-even point 41

breakage 149, 413

breakfast 539

budget 83, 382, 540, 551

budgeting 377

buildings 237

bulk 313

bulk mail 109

business plan 25

carpet 70

cashier 140, 350

cashier report 352

cash flow 98

cash reconciliation 391

chairs 69

champagne 437, 459

change 547

chart of accounts 31

check average 102

check log 549

chefs 299

classified ads 173

cleaning equipment 250

coffee 283

comment form 476

communication 200

compensation 100

competition 103

competitive pricing 48

complaints 77

condiments 284

contribution margin 41

C

candles 72

convection ovens 341

convenience foods 275

cooking 500

cooking equipment 251

cooking procedure 341

cooperative purchasing 321

cost control 95

cost-volume-profit (CVP) analysis 383

costs 161

costs survey 260

cost control 29

cost projection 543

cost ratios 38, 289

coupon 139

cross-contamination 331

cross-promotion 83

cross-training 199

current ratio 44

customers 57, 77, 225

customer surveys 103

D

dairy products 331

darts 463

data 202

debt 102

deep chilling 332

deep frying 342

deliveries 314

Department of Labor 170

depreciation 25

dessert 80

dining room 486

dinner 539

disabled worker 192

disciplinary action 217

dishroom 516

dishwashing 340

Dram Shop Acts 420

drinks 281, 437

drink pricing 387

drug screening 184

dry storage 330

E

eggs 334

electronic ordering systems 367

employee 475, 552

employee benefits 170

employee supervision 209

ending inventory 290

environment 408

equipment 127, 130, 299, 340, 517

ergonomics 69, 239

expenses 538

expiration dates 328

F

factor pricing 306

family leave 171

feedback surveys 59

FIFO 330, 415

fixed budget 378

flexibility 227

flexible budget 378

food-cost percentage 38, 260, 291

food-cost percentage pricing 305

food-cost tracking 297

food cost 511

forecasting 377

formulas 538

free-pouring 418

freezers 152

frozen storage 332

fruit 503

fryer 117

furniture 69, 134

G

garnish 300

glassware 122, 145, 150, 423, 459, 466

gratuities 170

grease 121

griddle 116

gross-profit pricing 307

gross margin 42

guest tickets 350

H

HACCP 316

health insurance 101, 171

highballs 442

I

ice 438

ice machine 132, 253

impairment 522

incentives 462

income 538

income statement 41

independent contractors 176

ingredients 300, 465, 497, 501

inspections 138

insurance 25, 100

internal controls 49

interview 180

intoxication 523

intuitive pricing 48

inventory 40, 51, 281, 314, 316, 322, 411, 432, 530, 533

inventory controls 337

invoice 328

issuing 35, 335

J

janitorial services 129

jargon 204

job description 168, 203

juice 76

jukebox 463

K

kickbacks 398

kitchen 114, 134, 245, 338, 517

kitchen layout 147

kitchen waste 283

L

labor 52, 102, 337

labor cost 309, 538

laundry 128

leadership 200, 210

liabilities 43

liability expenses 134

lighting 67, 466

linen 127

links 86

liquidity ratios 44

liquor 438, 462, 529

liquor-control systems 418

lunch 79, 539

menu sales analysis 309

motivation 160

music 68

N

napkin rings 128

National Restaurant Association 31,
111, 169, 173, 218, 320, 358, 368

net margin 42

nonalcoholic beverages 436

M

maintenance 127

management 445

marinades 334

market-driven prices 47

marketing 83

markup 47

meal food cost 303

menu 34, 59, 77, 90, 276, 280, 284,
339, 511

menu design 108

menu pricing 301

O

office expenses 107

on-break schedules 53

on-call scheduling 53, 224

operating margin 42

operational budget 96

ordering 51, 318

orientation 204

outsourcing 107, 176

oven 116

overstaffing 226

overtime 225

P

painting 133

part-time employees 107, 225

payroll 26, 108, 187, 371

performance standards 201

perpetual inventory form 264, 487

personnel 25

personnel management 200

phone 109

phone log 110

pitchers 434

plants 68

point-of-sale systems 32

pool table 463

portioning 36, 345

portions 419, 497, 503

portion control 283, 417

portion size 300

postage 109

postcards 109

POS systems 34, 353, 368

potential food-cost percentage 292

pouring costs 427

premiums 100

prep 35, 507

preparation instructions 300

prep equipment 250

presentation 349

pricing 47, 273

pricing beverages 53

prime-cost pricing 308

printing 108

production 337, 514

productivity 229

productivity standards 201

profits 160, 538

profit planning 29, 35

psychological pricing 48

purchasing 35, 51, 318, 319

purchasing-control system 398

Q

quality standards 201

Quickbooks® 31

quickplan 383

R

raw meat 331

receiving 35, 325

recipe 284, 337, 441 497, 501, 511

reconciliation 261

recruitment 445

references 185

referrals 172

refreezing 334

refrigerated storage 331

refrigerator 120

rent 25, 99

repair 127

reservations 477

restrooms 72

revenue 539

S

safety 357, 486

salaries 26

sales 285, 538

sales history 304

sales history form 98

sauces 334

scales 346, 410

scheduling 52, 221

seat turnover 41

security 137

service 35, 159, 337

service refusal 528

shelves 331, 466

silverware 150

smoking 457

spatulas 127, 346

specialty items 79

spices 334

spillage 386

spirits 438

spoilage 149, 333, 334, 508

staff 338

standardized recipes 273, 281, 298

standard food cost 292

standard portion 275

statement of cash flows 45

steam cooking 117

storage 35, 51, 322, 330

structure component charts 259

suppliers 315

supplies 25, 544

T

tablecloths 128

Tasty Profits 31

tax deductions 189

tea 76

technology 234, 370

temperatures 68, 114, 330, 341

thaw 505

theft 138, 398, 427

thermometer 343

thermostat 68

timers 111

tips 447

trade schools 175, 205

training 199, 445

trial-and-error pricing 48

turnover 219, 552

U

understaffing 225

uniforms 129

Uniform System of Accounts for
Restaurants 31

usable trim 275

utensils 127

utilities 26

V

vacations 171

W

wages 164, 168

waitstaff 58

walk-ins 152

waste 275, 422

waste management 121

water 344, 437

weighted food-cost percentage 293

well liquor 411

wine 411, 434, 521

workflow 243, 339

working capital 44

Y

yield 275, 282, 300

yield costs 275

yield percentage 102, 347

yield tests 348

Z

zero-based budget 378

DID YOU BORROW THIS COPY?

Have you been borrowing a copy of *The Food Service Manager's Guide to Creative Cost Cutting* from a friend, colleague or library? Wouldn't you like your own copy for quick and easy reference? To order, photocopy the form below and send to:

Atlantic Publishing Company
1210 SW 23rd Place • Ocala, FL 34474-7014

YES! Send me_____copy(ies) of *The Food Service Manager's Guide to Creative Cost Cutting* (Item # CCC-01) for $79.95 + $5.00 for USPS shipping and handling.

Atlantic Publishing Company
1210 SW 23rd Place
Ocala, FL 34474-7014

Add $5.00 for USPS shipping and handling. For Florida residents PLEASE add the appropriate sales tax for your county.

Please Print

_____
Name

_____
Organization Name

_____
Address

_____
City, State, Zip

Order toll-free
800-814-1132
FAX 352-622-5836

❑ My check or money order is enclosed. *Please make checks payable to Atlantic Publishing Company.*

❑ My purchase order is attached. *PO #_____*

www.atlantic-pub.com • e-mail: sales@atlantic-pub.com

DID YOU BORROW THIS COPY?

Have you been borrowing a copy of *The Food Service Manager's Guide to Creative Cost Cutting* from a friend, colleague or library? Wouldn't you like your own copy for quick and easy reference? To order, photocopy the form below and send to:

Atlantic Publishing Company
1210 SW 23rd Place • Ocala, FL 34474-7014

DID YOU BORROW THIS COPY?

Have you been borrowing a copy of *The Food Service Manager's Guide to Creative Cost Cutting* from a friend, colleague or library? Wouldn't you like your own copy for quick and easy reference? To order, photocopy the form below and send to:

Atlantic Publishing Company
1210 SW 23rd Place • Ocala, FL 34474-7014

YES! Send me____copy(ies) of *The Food Service Manager's Guide to Creative Cost Cutting* (Item # CCC-01) for $79.95 + $5.00 for USPS shipping and handling.

Atlantic Publishing Company
1210 SW 23rd Place
Ocala, FL 34474-7014

Add $5.00 for USPS shipping and handling. For Florida residents PLEASE add the appropriate sales tax for your county.

Order toll-free
800-814-1132
FAX 352-622-5836

Please Print

_____
Name

_____
Organization Name

_____
Address

_____
City, State, Zip

❏ My check or money order is enclosed. *Please make checks payable to Atlantic Publishing Company.*

❏ My purchase order is attached. *PO #_____*

www.atlantic-pub.com • e-mail: sales@atlantic-pub.com

Other great books available from Atlantic Publishing:

15 BOOKS AVAILABLE!

This 15-book series from the editors of the *Food Service Professional Magazine* are the best and most-comprehensive books for serious food service operators available today. These step-by-step guides on specific management subjects are easy to read, easy to understand, and will take the mystery out of the subject. The information is "boiled down" to the essence. They are filled to the brim with up-to-date and pertinent information. These books cover all the bases, providing clear explanations and helpful, specific information. All titles in the series include the phone numbers and Web sites of all companies discussed.

1-800-541-1336 Call toll-free 24 hours a day, 7 days a week. Or fax completed form to: **1-352-622-5836.**
Order Online! Just go to **www.atlantic-pub.com** for fast, easy, secure ordering.

SOFTWARE GUIDE

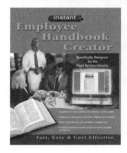

SAVE 40%
EMPLOYEE HANDBOOK CREATOR GUIDE
Finally, a cost-effective solution for developing your own employee handbook. Simply review the 100-plus policies already written for you and insert your own information when prompted. Complete with table of contents, introduction, and a form for each employee to sign. Use with Windows or any word processor.

Item # EHB-CS ~~$99.95~~ **Sale $59.95**

Qty.	Order Code	Book Title	Price	Total
	Item # EHB-CS	Employee Handbook Creator Guide	$59.95	
	Item # FS1-01	Restaurant Site Location	$19.95	
	Item # FS2-01	Buying & Selling a Restaurant Business	$19.95	
	Item # FS3-01	Restaurant Marketing & Advertising	$19.95	
	Item # FS4-01	Restaurant Promotion & Publicity	$19.95	
	Item # FS5-01	Controlling Operating Costs	$19.95	
	Item # FS6-01	Controlling Food Costs	$19.95	
	Item # FS7-01	Controlling Labor Costs	$19.95	
	Item # FS8-01	Controlling Liquor Wine & Beverage Costs	$19.95	
	Item # FS9-01	Building Restaurant Profits	$19.95	
	Item # FS10-01	Waiter & Waitress Training	$19.95	
	Item # FS11-01	Bar & Beverage Operation	$19.95	
	Item # FS12-01	Successful Catering	$19.95	
	Item # FS13-01	Food Service Menus	$19.95	
	Item # FS14-01	Restaurant Design	$19.95	
	Item # FS15-01	Increasing Restaurant Sales	$19.95	
	Item # FSALL-01	**Entire 15-Book Series**	**$199.95**	

Best Deal! **SAVE 33%**
15 GUIDE TO SERIES books for $199.95

Subtotal	
Shipping & Handling	
Florida 6% Sales Tax	
TOTAL	

SHIP TO:

Name_____ Phone(____)_____

Company Name_____

Mailing Address _____

City _____ State _____ Zip _____

FAX (____)_____ E-mail _____

❏ My check or money order is enclosed ❏ Please send my order COD ❏ My authorized purchase order is attached

❏ Please charge my: ❏ MasterCard ❏ VISA ❏ American Express ❏ Discover

Card # ☐☐☐☐-☐☐☐☐-☐☐☐☐-☐☐☐☐ Expires ☐☐-☐☐

Please make checks payable to: **Atlantic Publishing Company** • 1210 SW 23rd Place • Ocala, FL 34474-7014
USPS Shipping/Handling: add $5.00 first item, $2.50 each additional or $15.00 for the whole set. Florida residents PLEASE add the appropriate county sales tax.

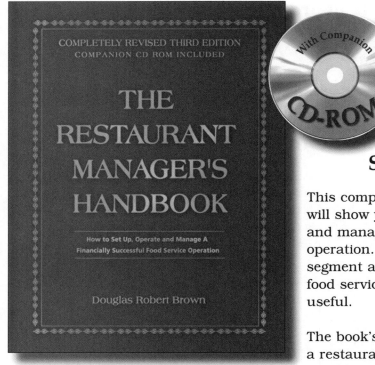

The Restaurant Manager's Handbook: How to Set Up, Operate and Manage a Financially Successful Food Service Operation

This comprehensive and massive 600-page book will show you step by step how to set up, operate and manage a financially successful food service operation. Operators in the non-commercial segment as well as caterers, and anyone in the food service industry, will find this volume very useful.

The book's 19 chapters cover the entire process of a restaurant start-up and ongoing management in an easy-to-understand way, pointing out methods to increase your chances of success and showing how to avoid the many common mistakes. The companion CD-ROM contains all the forms demonstrated in the book for easy use in a PDF format.

Item # RMH-02 $79.95
600 Pages Hardbound
ISBN 0-910627-09-6
Publication Date: 2003

While providing detailed instruction and examples, the author leads you through finding a location that will bring success, learn how to write a winning business plan, how to buy and sell a restaurant, franchising, basic cost-control systems, profitable menu planning, sample restaurant floor plans and diagrams, successful kitchen management, equipment layout and planning, food safety and HACCP, successful beverage management, learn how to set up computer systems to save time and money, learn how to hire and keep a qualified professional staff, IRS tip-reporting requirements, managing and training employees, generate high-profile public relations and publicity, learn low-cost internal marketing ideas, low- and no-cost ways to satisfy customers and build sales, learn how to keep bringing customers back, accounting and bookkeeping procedures, auditing, budgeting and profit planning, as well as thousands of great tips and useful guidelines.

The extensive resource guide details over 7,000 suppliers to the industry; this directory could be a separate book on its own. This *Restaurant Manager's Handbook* covers everything for which many companies pay consultants thousands of dollars.

There are literally hundreds of innovative ways demonstrated to streamline your restaurant business. Learn new ways to make the kitchen, bars, dining room and front office run smoother and increase performance. Shut down waste, reduce costs and increase profits. In addition, operators will appreciate this valuable resource and reference in their daily activities and as a source of ready-to-use forms, Web sites, operating and cost-cutting ideas and mathematical formulas that can be easily applied to their operations. Highly recommended!

To order call toll-free 800-814-1132 or visit www.atlantic-pub.com

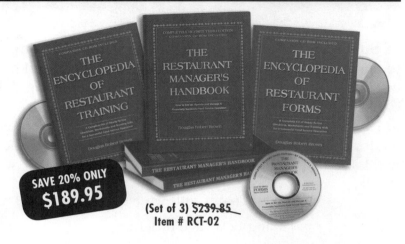

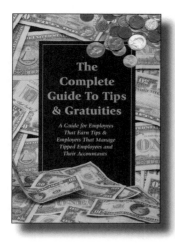

The Complete Guide to Tips & Gratuities: A Guide for Employees Who Earn Tips & Employers Who Manage Tipped Employees and Their Accountants

There are millions of workers in the United States that rely on tips for most of their income, and there are well over two million businesses where the employers rely on tipped employees. According to recent statistics from the U.S. Department of Labor, food and beverage service-related workers held 6.5 million jobs in 2000 alone. The U.S. Department of Labor estimated in a 2001 study that tips and gratuities accounted for well over $5 billion per year being left on plates and tip trays, financed on credit cards and handed directly into happy, open palms.

For the first time, this new book deals with all aspects of tips and gratuities. For the employee or self-employed, learn how to earn more tips and how to properly account for and pay taxes on them. For the employer, learn how to manage and properly account for the taxes on tipped employees. For the bookkeeper and accountant, get the latest on tax and withholding laws. Apart from all the great and practical advice in the book, it has to be remembered that tips have to be earned; thus, there are literally hundreds of little tricks, hints and suggestions to help tipped employees, well, make more tips!

Item # CGT-02 $19.95
144 Pages • ISBN 0910627-38-X

The Waiter & Waitress and Waitstaff Training Handbook: A Complete Guide to the Proper Steps in Service for Food & Beverage Employees

This training handbook was designed for use by all food service serving staff members and all types of service including French, American, English, Russian, Family-Style and Banquet. It covers every aspect of restaurant customer service for the positions of host, waiter or waitress, head waiter, captain and bus person. Step-by-step instructions on hosting, seating guests, taking/filling orders, loading/unloading trays, table side service, setting an elegant table, folding napkins, promoting specials and side orders, handling problems, difficult customers, managing tips, handling the check and money, and more.

Plus, learn advanced serving techniques such as flambé and carving meats, fish, and fruits. It also features a chapter devoted exclusively to food safety and sanitation. Food service managers will find this an excellent foundation for your organization's training program.

Item # WWT-TH $29.95
288 pages • ISBN 091062747-9

This Title Also Available in Spanish
Item # WWT-SP • $29.95
288 pages • ISBN 0910627-48-7

How to Open a Financially Successful Bed & Breakfast or Small Hotel

This comprehensive handbook will clearly demonstrate how to set up, operate and manage a financially successful bed and breakfast or small hotel. Whatever your reason for wanting to open a bed and breakfast, keep in mind that it takes more than dreams and rooms to achieve success; it is a business that must show a profit. This book will separate the romantic notions of owning a B&B from the business end. Owning a B&B is a lifestyle more than a job, and potential owners need to be absolutely sure it's the right lifestyle for them.

There are hundreds of innovative ways demonstrated to streamline your business. Learn new ways to make the kitchen, dining room and front office run smoother. Shut down waste, reduce costs and increase profits. In addition, operators will appreciate this valuable resource and reference in their daily activities and as a source of ready-to-use forms, Web sites, operating and cost-cutting ideas and mathematical formulas that can be applied to their operations.

The companion CD-ROM contains all the forms in the book as well as a sample business plan you can adapt for your own use.

Item # SBB-02 $39.95
288 Pages • ISBN 0910627-30-4

How to Open a Financially Successful Coffee, Espresso & Tea Shop

The explosive growth of coffee shops across the country has been phenomenal. Here is the manual you need to cash in on this highly profitable segment of the food service industry. This new book is a comprehensive study of the business side of the specialty coffee and beverage shop.

This superb manual should be studied by anyone investigating the opportunities of opening a cafe, tea shop or coffee kiosk. This complete manual will arm you with everything you need including: worksheets and checklists for planning, opening and running day-to-day operations; sample menus; coffee drink recipes; inventory lists; plans and layouts; and dozens of other valuable, time-saving tools of the trade that no coffee entrepreneur should be without.

Item # CET-02 $39.95
288 Pages • ISBN 0910627-31-2

The companion CD-ROM contains all the forms in the book as well as a sample business plan you can adapt for your own use.

To order call toll-free 800-814-1132 or visit www.atlantic-pub.com

HACCP & Sanitation in Restaurants and Food Service Operations: A Practical Guide Based on the FDA Food Code

According to the FDA, it is estimated that up to 76 million people get a food-borne illness each year. Since people don't go to the doctor for mild symptoms, the actual number of illnesses can't be known, but 5,000 people a year die from food-borne illness in the United States, and many others suffer long-term effects.

Most all of this sickness and death could have been prevented with the proper procedures that are taught in this comprehensive book. If these numbers don't upset you, realize that a food-borne outbreak in your establishment can put you out of business, and if the business survives, it will certainly be severely damaged; this, of course, after the lawsuits are resolved. If you do not have proper sanitation methods and a HACCP program in place, you need them today.

This book is based on the USDA Food Code, and will teach the food service manager and employees every aspect of food safety, HACCP and sanitation, from purchasing and receiving food to properly washing the dishes. They will learn:

- Time and temperature abuses

- Cross-contamination

- Personal hygiene practices

- Biological, chemical and physical hazards

- Proper cleaning and sanitizing

- Waste and pest management

- Basic principles of HACCP (Hazard Analysis of Critical Control Points)

- Explain what safe food is and how to provide it

- Bacteria, viruses, fungi and parasites

- Various food-borne illnesses

- Safe food-handling techniques

- Purchasing, receiving and food storage

- Food preparation and serving

- Sanitary equipment and facilities

- Cleaning and sanitizing of equipment and facilities

- Accident prevention and crisis management

- Food safety and sanitation laws

HACCP & SANITATION
in restaurants and food service operations

A Practical Guide
Based on the
USDA Food Code
With Companion CD-ROM

With Companion CD-ROM

Item # HSR-02 $79.95
600 Pages Hardbound
ISBN 0910627-35-5

To order call toll-free
800-814-1132 or visit
www.atlantic-pub.com

The companion CD-ROM contains all the forms and posters needed to establish your HACCP and food-safety program.

ALCOHOL AWARENESS POSTERS

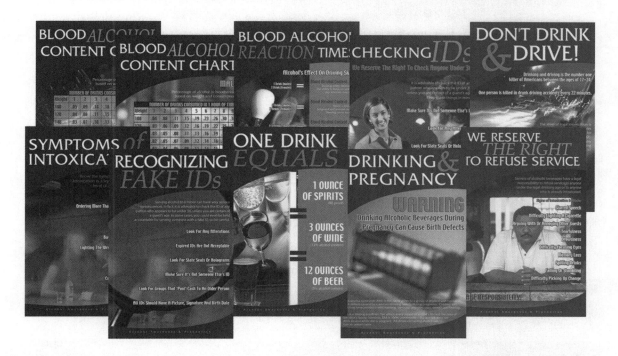

Alcohol awareness is an important issue. This new FULL-COLOR poster series covers ten fundamental topics and should be posted in any establishment that serves alcohol. Posters are laminated to reduce wear and tear and measure 11" x 17".

Series of 10 Posters Item # AAP-PS • $89.95

Right to Refuse Service
Item # RTR-PS • $9.95

One Drink Equals
Item # ODE-PS • $9.95

Spotting a Fake ID
Item # FID-PS • $9.95

Symptoms of Intoxication
Item # SIO-PS • $9.95

We Check IDs
Item # CID-PS • $9.95

Drinking & Pregnancy
Item # D&P-PS • $9.95

Blood Alcohol Content Chart—
Female Item # BACF-PS • $9.95

Blood Alcohol Content Chart—Male
Item # BACM-PS • $9.95

Don't Drink & Drive
Item # DDD-PS • $9.95

Alcohol Slows Reaction Times
Item # ASR-PS • $9.95

ALCOHOL SERVICE POSTERS

Decorative and instructional, these FULL-COLOR posters will be popular with both your employees and customers. Containing essential information, drink photos, recipes and more, they will help increase sales and grab attention. Posters are laminated to reduce wear and tear and measure 11" x 17".

**Series of 7 Posters
Item #ASP-PS • $59.95**

**12 Classic Cocktails with Recipes
Item #CC-PS • $9.95**

**12 Popular Cocktails with Recipes
Item #PC-PS • $9.95**

**Types of Beer
Item #TOB-PS • $9.95**

**Categories of Liquor
Item #COL-PS • $9.95**

**10 Types of Martinis
Item #TOM-PS • $9.95**

**Drink Garnishes
Item #DG-PS • $9.95**

**Common Bar Abbreviations
Item #GBA-PS • $9.95**

WINE SERVICE POSTERS

These five FULL-COLOR posters cover all the wine basics—from service to pronunciation. Essential information for anyone serving, pouring or selling wine, yet attractive enough to display in your dining room. Posters are laminated to reduce wear and tear and measure 11" x 17".

**Series of 5 Posters
Item # WPS-PS • $39.95**

**Wine Pronunciation Guide
Item # WPG-PS • $9.95**

**Proper Wine Service
Item # PWS-PS • $9.95**

**Red Wine
Item # RWP-PS • $9.95**

**White Wine
Item # WWP-PS • $9.95**

**Sparkling Wine & Champagne
Item # SWC-PS • $9.95**

To order call toll-free 800-814-1132 or visit www.atlantic-pub.com